Fodor's
BUENOS
AIRES

WELCOME TO BUENOS AIRES

Glamorous and gritty, Buenos Aires is two cities in one. What makes Argentina's capital so fascinating is its dual heritage—part European, part Latin American. Plaza de Mayo resembles a grand square in Madrid, and the ornate Teatro Colón would not be out of place in Vienna. But you'll know you're in South America by the leather shoes for sale on cobbled streets and impromptu parades of triumphant soccer fans. Limited-production wines, juicy steaks, and ice cream in countless flavors are among the old-world imports the city has perfected.

TOP REASONS TO GO

★ **Food:** Modern Andean cuisine, tantalizing tapas, and some of the world's best beef.

★ **Tango:** On packed dance floors or at ritzy shows, people move to the 2/4 beat.

★ **Shopping:** Palermo for hipsters, Recoleta for the jet set, San Telmo for bohemians.

★ **Nightlife:** Artsy cafés, romantic wine bars, pounding clubs, or packed rock concerts.

★ **History:**Eva Perón and Che Guevara are among the city's unforgettable figures

★ **Modern Art:** Paintings at the museums, colorful murals on walls throughout town.

Fodor's BUENOS AIRES

Publisher: Amanda D'Acierno, *Senior Vice President*

Editorial: Arabella Bowen, *Editor in Chief*; Linda Cabasin, *Editorial Director*

Design: Fabrizio La Rocca, *Vice President, Creative Director*; Tina Malaney, *Associate Art Director*; Chie Ushio, *Senior Designer*; Ann McBride, *Production Designer*

Photography: Melanie Marin, *Associate Director of Photography*; Jessica Parkhill and Jennifer Romains, *Researchers*

Maps: Rebecca Baer, *Senior Map Editor*; Mark Stroud (Moon Street Cartography), David Lindroth, *Cartographers*

Production: Linda Schmidt, *Managing Editor*; Evangelos Vasilakis, *Associate Managing Editor*; Angela L. McLean, *Senior Production Manager*

Sales: Jacqueline Lebow, *Sales Director*

Marketing & Publicity: Heather Dalton, *Marketing Director*; Katherine Punia, *Senior Publicist*

Business & Operations: Susan Livingston, *Vice President, Strategic Business Planning*; Sue Daulton, *Vice President, Operations*

Fodors.com: Megan Bell, *Executive Director, Revenue & Business Development*; Yasmin Marinaro, *Senior Director, Marketing & Partnerships*

Copyright © 2015 by Fodor's Travel, a division of Random House LLC

Writers: Allan Kelin, Karina Martinez-Carter, Sorrel Moseley-Williams, Victoria Patience, Dan Perlman

Editors: Mark Sullivan, Sue MacCallum-Whitcomb

Production Editor: Jennifer DePrima

4th Edition

ISBN 978-0-8041-4284-7

ISSN 1941-0182

SPECIAL SALES

This book is available at special discounts for bulk purchases for sales promotions or premiums. For more information, e-mail specialmarkets@randomhouse.com

PRINTED IN THE UNITED STATES OF AMERICA

10 9 8 7 6 5 4 3 2 1

CONTENTS

Fodor's Features

CONTENTS

ABOUT THIS GUIDE

Fodor's Recommendations

Everything in this guide is worth doing—we don't cover what isn't—but exceptional sights, hotels, and restaurants are recognized with additional accolades. **Fodor's** Choice★ indicates our top recommendations; and **Best Bets** call attention to notable hotels and restaurants in various categories. Care to nominate a new place? Visit Fodors.com/contact-us.

Trip Costs

We list prices wherever possible to help you budget well. Hotel and restaurant price categories from **$** to **$$$$** are noted alongside each recommendation. For hotels, we include the lowest cost of a standard double room in high season. For restaurants, we cite the average price of a main course at dinner or, if dinner isn't served, at lunch. For attractions, we always list adult admission fees; discounts are usually available for children, students, and senior citizens.

Hotels

Our local writers vet every hotel to recommend the best overnights in each price category, from budget to expensive. Unless otherwise specified, you can expect private bath, phone, and TV in your room. For expanded hotel reviews, facilities, and deals visit Fodors.com.

Top Picks	Hotels & Restaurants
★ **Fodor's** Choice	🏨 Hotel
	↵ Number of rooms
Listings	⫿○⫿ Meal plans
✉ Address	✕ Restaurant
✉ Branch address	🕾 Reservations
☎ Telephone	👔 Dress code
🖷 Fax	⊟ No credit cards
⊕ Website	$ Price
✉ E-mail	
🎫 Admission fee	**Other**
⊙ Open/closed times	⇨ See also
Ⓜ Subway	☞ Take note
⊹ Directions or Map coordinates	🏌 Golf facilities

Restaurants

Unless we state otherwise, restaurants are open for lunch and dinner daily. We mention dress code only when there's a specific requirement and reservations only when they're essential or not accepted. To make restaurant reservations, visit Fodors.com.

Credit Cards

The hotels and restaurants in this guide typically accept credit cards. If not, we'll say so.

EUGENE FODOR:

Hungarian-born Eugene Fodor (1905–91) began his travel career as an interpreter on a French cruise ship. The experience inspired him to write *On the Continent* (1936), the first guidebook to receive annual updates and discuss a country's way of life as well as its sights. Fodor later joined the U.S. Army and worked for the OSS in World War II. After the war, he kept up his intelligence work while expanding his guidebook series. During the Cold War, many guides were written by fellow agents who understood the value of insider information. Today's guides continue Fodor's legacy by providing travelers with timely coverage, insider tips, and cultural context.

EXPERIENCE BUENOS AIRES

BUENOS AIRES TODAY

The insistent 2/4 beat of a tango, the banging bass drum at a protest march, the screams of fútbol fans when a player scores a game-winning goal: tune in to the soundtrack of Buenos Aires and your pulse is sure to quicken. *Porteños* (as residents of Buenos Aires are known) take their passions very seriously—you'll notice this when you see them sampling a sizzling cut of beef at their favorite neighborhood steakhouse or listening to live music at a basement club—and those passions can be contagious.

Blending Old and New

Cobbled streets, wrought-iron billboards, and quaint cafés that seem untouched since 1940 are all part of Buenos Aires' trademark time-warp look. But though porteños are nostalgic, even they've had enough of exquisite stone facades crumbling (sometimes plummeting) through lack of maintenance. Suddenly scaffolding is everywhere, as old buildings are revamped and savvy developers transform century-old mansions and warehouses into hotels—some boutique, others behemoth.

Even though the Argentine economy has been on shaky ground over the past several years, new buildings have continued to push heavenward. Notable new structures include architect Sir Norman Foster's first Latin American project, a residential building called El Aleph in swanky Puerto Madero. Local-boy-gone-global César Pelli has completed a modest (by his high-flying standards) skyscraper nearby.

Controversy shrouds some of the makeovers: the city government was accused of selling the historic cobblestones they replaced with asphalt, and the restoration of the Teatro Colón went way over schedule and budget. Still, like other aging local beauties, many of Buenos Aires' historical buildings are looking younger by the minute.

Eating and Drinking

Foodie culture has hit Argentina in a big way. Celebrity chefs are busy evangelizing enthralled TV audiences, and former table-wine drinkers now vigorously debate grape varieties and name-drop boutique vineyards. Their beer-drinking peers are turning from the ubiquitous bottles of Quilmes lager to local craft beers. A growing number of food blogs and food tours alert both locals and visitors to the dishes of the day, often found behind the unmarked entrances of *puertas*

WHAT'S NEW

The hottest accessory on the city streets is a bicycle. Some 80 miles of new bicycle paths, a free bike-sharing program, and a traffic-reduction plan targeting downtown streets are slowly convincing locals that two wheels might be better than four. Boutique bike shops and bike tours are part of the burgeoning trend, and the monthly Critical Mass rides draw hundreds of non-motorized *porteños*. Local drivers still aren't totally on board, however: their driving habits and aggressive manner often make cycling in the city feel more like an extreme sport.

Argentineans have always been patriotic, but flags are flying higher and brighter than usual in the aftermath of the bicentennary of the May Revolution in 2010. Celebrations culminated in five days

cerradas, the city's famous "closed door" restaurants.

The food scene is rife with contradiction, however. Argentina is one of the world's largest producers of organic produce, but nearly all of it gets exported. A small slow-food and farm-to-table movement is fighting back at the farmers' markets scattered around Buenos Aires and the rest of the country. Saddest of all, the exponential growth of genetically modified soy farming is pushing Argentina's famed grass-fed cattle from the Pampas and into feedlots—these days only very high-end restaurants can guarantee you are enjoying a totally grass-fed steak.

Taking to the Streets

Forget writing to your political representatives when you've got a gripe with the system—in Buenos Aires you take to the streets. Strikes, marches, rallies, and *piquetes* (road blocks) have long been fixtures of daily life. Plaza and Avenida de Mayo fill regularly with drum-and-banner-toting crowds. Sometimes they're protesting or petitioning to change laws; other times they are celebrating victories both political and sporting.

One of these events has become famous around the world. The Asociación Madres de Plaza de Mayo (Mothers' Association of the Plaza de Mayo), the brave women who organized the first protests against the military junta, continue the weekly marches around Plaza de Mayo that they started 40 years ago in search of their missing children.

Going Global

Argentina is a long, long way from a lot of places. The weak peso makes it hard for porteños to travel abroad—instead, the world comes to Buenos Aires. Locals say that they can't get over the number of out-of-towners there are today. (Thankfully, the numbers are still small enough to keep sightseeing from being a competitive sport.)

And more and more of the visitors are staying: Buenos Aires has growing Asian and Latin American communities, the number of exchange students at city universities has soared, and there's a thriving English-language expat scene complete with how-to blogs and magazines. And the urban landscape is changing, too: the ultimate nod to globalization came when Starbucks opened its first branches in Buenos Aires. But some things never change: the city's time-honored cafés are as popular as ever.

of parades and musical performances attended by 6 million people on the massive Avenida 9 de Julio, which was closed to traffic for the occasion. The festivities are set to return in 2016, the 200th anniversary of the country's independence.

Being out has never been this in. Argentina is the first country in Latin America—and only the ninth in the world—to fully legalize same-sex marriage, sealing Buenos Aires' claim on the title of Latin America's gay capital. The Marcha del Orgullo Gay (Gay Pride March) is a big draw every November. It doesn't attract the millions of Rio de Janeiro or São Paulo, but the 250,000 participants it attracted in 2015 still place it among the largest in the world.

WHAT'S WHERE

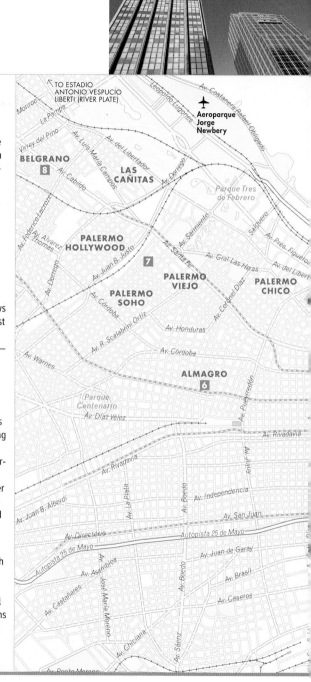

1 Centro. Locals use "Centro" or "El Centro" as umbrella terms for several busy downtown districts. The heart of the city is filled with bars, cafés, and bookstores—not to mention crowds. The area around Plaza and Avenida de Mayo is the hub of political life and home to some of the city's oldest buildings.

2 Puerto Madero. Gleaming skyscrapers, an elegant boardwalk, and the Museo Fortabat are among the draws in Puerto Madero, the poshest part of town. Its high-rise residential and office towers—many designed by big-name architects—are flanked by a sprawling nature reserve.

3 San Telmo. Antiques shops and hip clothing stores compete for store space along San Telmo's dreamy cobbled streets—ideal for lazy wandering and relaxing at bars or cafés. Highbrow art is another attraction, and its two world-class museums are dedicated to contemporary works.

4 La Boca. Gritty La Boca was the city's first port, which explains a name that means "The Mouth." Visitors come for a snapshot of the colorful Caminito area, and soccer fans fill the Boca Juniors stadium. A magnet for art lovers, the

1

0   1/2 mile

0   1/2 kilometer

Fundación Proa sits on the waterfront in La Boca.

5 Recoleta. The elite live, dine, and shop along Recoleta's gorgeous Paris-inspired streets. They're also often buried in the sumptuous mausoleums of its cemetery. Art galleries and museums—including the Museo Nacional de Bellas Artes—are also draws.

6 Almagro. Peruvian restaurants, fringe theater, and a lively tango scene distinguish Almagro. The area is home to the sprawling Abasto shopping mall and the hip arts venue Centro Cultural Konex.

7 Palermo. Large Palermo has many subdistricts. If it's cool, chances are it's in Palermo Viejo: bars, restaurants, boutiques, galleries, and hotels line the streets surrounding Plaza Serrano. The hipster action spills over into Palermo Hollywood. There are two excellent museums (the MALBA and Museo Evita) in Palermo Chico, the barrio's northern end.

8 Belgrano. Posh apartment buildings and interesting boutiques fill the landscape of residential Belgrano.

BUENOS AIRES PLANNER

What To Buy

The array of open-air *ferias* (markets) in Buenos Aires testifies to the fact that locals enjoy stall-crawling as much as visitors do. Argentina holds its craftspeople, both traditional and contemporary, in high esteem. The selections include crafts, art, antiques, curios, clothing, and jewelry; stalls are often attended by the artists themselves, who are happy to explain to you how something was made. Bargaining isn't the norm, although you may get a small discount for buying lots of items.

Visitor Info

Turismo Buenos Aires. The website of the city tourist board, Turismo Buenos Aires, is packed with useful information and suggested itineraries. English-speaking staffers can be found at information booths at the airports and seven other locations around the city. The handiest locations are near Plaza San Martín (⊠ *Florida at Marcelo T. de Alvear*), Plaza de Mayo (⊠ *Florida 50*), and the Recoleta Cemetery (⊠ *Quintana 596*). They're open weekdays 10–5 and weekends 9–6. ⊕ *www.turismo. buenosaires.gob.ar.*

Getting Around

Intriguing architecture, an easy-to-navigate grid layout (a few diagonal transverses aside), and ample window-shopping make Buenos Aires a wonderful place to explore on foot. SUBE, a rechargeable swipe card, can be used on the subway, buses, and commuter trains.

Public Transit. Service on the *subte* (subway) is quick, but trains are often packed and strikes are common. Four of the six underground lines (A, B, D, and E) fan out west from downtown; north–south lines C and H connect them. Single-ride tickets cost 5 pesos. Monday through Saturday, the subte opens at 5 am and shuts down between 10:30 and 11 pm, depending on the line. On Sunday, trains run between 8 am and 10–10:30 pm.

Colectivos (city buses) connect the city center with its barrios and the greater Buenos Aires area. If you pay by SUBE card, fares within the city cost 2.50 to 2.70 pesos, but are double that if you pay cash (on-board ticket machines accept coins only). Bus stops are roughly every other block, but you may have to hunt for the small, metal route-number signs: they could be stuck on a shelter, lamppost, or even a tree. Stop at a news kiosk and buy the *Guía T,* a route guide.

Taxis. Black-and-yellow taxis fill the streets and take you anywhere in town and short distances into greater Buenos Aires. Fares start at 11.80 pesos, with 1.10 pesos for each click of the meter. You can hail taxis on the street or ask hotel and restaurant staffers to call for them.

Safety

Although Buenos Aires is safer than most Latin American capitals, petty crime is a concern. Pickpocketing and mugging are common, so avoid wearing flashy jewelry, be discreet with money and cameras, and be mindful of bags and wallets. Phone for taxis after dark.

Protest marches are a part of life in Buenos Aires: most are peaceful, but some end in confrontations with the police. They often take place in the Plaza de Mayo or along Avenida de Mayo.

Where to Stay

Booming visitor numbers in Buenos Aires and the rest of Argentina have sparked dozens of new accommodation options. There's plenty of variety, whether you're looking for the reliability of a tried-and-tested international chain, the hipness of a boutique property, or the charm of a family-run B&B.

Hotels. There are plenty of names you'll recognize when you consider where to stay in Buenos Aires, from Four Seasons and InterContinental to Hilton and Sheraton. Some of the most common chains are more familiar to South American and European travelers, but they have the same high level of service. If you're looking for more modern accommodations, you'll find them in more recently developed areas like Puerto Madera. But perhaps a better choice would be the grandes dames that show off the charm of a bygone era while treating you to all the most modern amenities.

Bed-and-Breakfasts. If you're looking for local flavor, consider a smaller hotel or bed-and-breakfast. Some are simple family-run affairs, others are boutique properties; many are housed in recycled old buildings that pack plenty of charm. Friendly, personalized service is another major appeal. Although many now use the term B&B, *posada* is the more traditional term. Most hotels in Argentina include breakfast in their rates, so they could be considered B&Bs even if they don't actively advertise themselves as such.

Apartments. Self-catering options are plentiful in Argentina and increasingly popular with visitors. The savings are especially significant if you're traveling as a family or group. In Buenos Aires and other big cities you can rent furnished apartments (and sometimes houses) daily, although weekly and monthly rates are usually cheaper. Some properties are in new buildings with pools, gyms, and 24-hour concierges; others are in atmospheric, but less luxurious older buildings.

Estancias. For a taste of how Argentina's landed elite live, book a few nights on an *estancia* (ranch). Most estancia accommodation is in grandiose, European-inspired, century-old country mansions. Rates include activities such as horseback riding and four generous meals daily, usually shared with your hosts and other guests. Estancias vary greatly: some are still working cattle or sheep farms, but many have switched entirely to tourism. At traditional establishments you'll be hosted by the owners, and stay in rooms that once belonged to family members. Accommodations are usually tastefully furnished, but rarely luxurious.

When to Go

Remember that when it's summer in the United States, it's winter in Argentina, and vice versa. Winters (July–September) are chilly. Summer's muggy heat (December–March) can be taxing at midday but makes for warm nights. During these months Argentines crowd resorts along the Atlantic and in Uruguay.

Spring (September–December) and autumn (April–June), with their mild temperatures are ideal for urban trekking. It's usually warm enough for just a light jacket, and it's right before or after the peak seasons. The best time for trips to Iguazú Falls is August–October, when temperatures are lower and the falls are fuller.

Buenos Aires Temperatures

BUENOS AIRES
TOP ATTRACTIONS

Museo Nacional de Bellas Artes

(A) Originally the city's waterworks, this russet-color, columned building in Recoleta is your one-stop shop for Argentine painting and sculpture, although renovation work means much of the collection is temporarily out of bounds. A surprisingly comprehensive collection of lesser works by European and North American masters, spanning the 13th century to the present, is an added boon.

Plaza de Mayo

(B) Since the city was founded, civic and political life has centered on this large, palm-shaded square in El Centro. The favored stage of protesters and politicians alike, this was where Evita told a rally of thousands not to cry for her. Since the 1976–83 dictatorship, a group of mothers (now nongovernmental organizations called Madres and Abuelas de Plaza de Mayo) have been protesting their children's disappearances here each week.

The presidential palace, a cathedral, the central bank, a colonial town hall, and the senate all flank the square.

Cementerio de la Recoleta

(C) The city's illustrious departed rest in mausoleums as sumptuous as their mansions. Heavily adorned with marble facades and dramatic statues, these second homes are arrayed along shaded avenues, forming an eerie but beautiful city of the dead. Residents include the must-see Evita, national heroes, sporting greats, writers, and several wandering ghosts—or so local legend goes.

Museo de Arte Latinoamericano de Buenos Aires

(D) Buenos Aires' first truly world-class museum is a luminous temple to the gods of 20th-century Latin American art. A vigorous acquisitions program means you see the latest talents as well as Frida Kahlo, Diego Rivera, and Fernando Botero. The architecture, rooftop views

over surrounding Palermo, and gift shop are excuses in themselves to stop by.

Parque Tres de Febrero (Los Bosques de Palermo)

(E) Porteños desperate for some green relief love this 400-acre Palermo park, which includes wooded areas, a rose garden, lakes, a planetarium, and a small art museum. Bask in the sun with a picnic and/or a book, or make like sporty locals and go for a run around its trails.

Calle Museo Caminito

(F) An entire postcard industry has been built on the Technicolor corrugated-iron constructions on this street in La Boca. A purpose-built tourist attraction, Caminito is unashamedly tacky and brash, but is still an exuberant must-see (and must-snap) on your first visit to Buenos Aires.

Plaza Dorrego

(G) Sunday sees this quiet San Telmo square transformed into the Feria de San Pedro Telmo, Buenos Aires' biggest antiques market. Junk, memorabilia, and, occasionally, genuine antiques are all part of the cult of nostalgia celebrated here in the shadow of century-old townhouses. A beer or coffee at a traditional bar is an essential part of the experience.

Museo Evita

(H) Forget Madonna: for the true scoop on Argentina's most iconic citizen, come to this well-curated museum. Evita's life, works, and wardrobe are celebrated through insightful displays and original video footage, all housed in a gorgeous turn-of-the-20th-century mansion she requisitioned as a home for single mothers.

BUENOS AIRES' OLDEST AND NEWEST

Most buildings from the colonial era and the early days of the republic have long since been built over, but San Telmo still offers glimpses of bygone Buenos Aires. Adjacent Puerto Madero is the fastest-changing part of town, home to some of Latin America's most expensive real estate.

Time Travel in San Telmo

Start in **Plaza Dorrego**, the city's second-oldest square and the heart of San Telmo, and head north up Defensa. Late 19th-century town houses line the street—most now contain antiques shops or clothing boutiques. Detour left onto Estados Unidos to explore the **Mercado de San Telmo**, a produce market dating from 1897 (antiques now outnumber the apples on sale). Continue north up Defensa to No. 755, **El Zanjón de los Granados**, a restored 18th-century house (guided visits include the tunnels under it). Turn right into Pasaje San Lorenzo, a cobbled alley. At No. 380 stands **Casa Mínima**, the city's thinnest building—about 8 feet wide—which once belonged to a freed slave.

Backtrack down Defensa and left onto Pasaje Giuffra, another quiet lane, then right onto Balcarce, lined with more old houses. Follow Estados Unidos east and over busy Paseo Colón. The huge neoclassical building is now the University of Buenos Aires' **School of Engineering**, but was the headquarters of Evita's social-aid foundation.

Watery Wonders

Cross Avenida Huergo onto Puerto Madero—Estados Unidos changes its name to Rosario Vera Peñaloza and becomes a wide boulevard with a leafy pedestrian median. Facing the end of the street is an ornate white fountain, **Fuente Las Nereidas,** sculpted by Argentinean Lola Mora in 1902. It was commissioned for Plaza de Mayo, but the nude nymphs were considered too scandalous to stand so close to the cathedral.

Wander north along the Costanera Sur: to your left are Puerto Madero's skyscrapers; to your right is a stretch of water separating Puerto Madero proper from the **Reserva Ecológica.** (The ecological reserve's entrance is through the trees behind Fuente Las Nereidas—a detour here will add gorgeous greenery and lots of extra mileage to your walk.) Be sure to try a *vaciopán* (steak sandwich) sold by the food carts along the Costanera.

Urban renewal

Turn left onto Martha Lynch, which curves past the **Parque de las Mujeres Argentinas,** a small park, and ends at one of Puerto Madero's former docks, now home to Buenos Aires' newest buildings (and newest construction sites). The original redbrick warehouses over the water now house restaurants and offices.

Just ahead is Santiago Calatrava's sculptural pedestrian bridge, **Puente de la Mujer.** Continue up the side of the docks along Pierina Dealessi: the compact steel-and-concrete structure at the end of Dique 4 contains the **Colección Fortabat** art museum, which also has a stylish café.

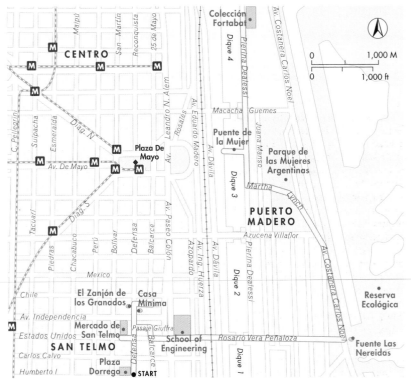

Where to Start:	Intersection of Defensa and Humberto I, Plaza Dorrego
Time/Length:	3 hours; just under 5 km (3 miles)
Where to Stop:	Colección Fortabat, intersection Pierina Dealessi and Mariquita Sánchez de Thompson
Best Time to Go:	After 11 am, Monday to Saturday
Worst Time to Go:	Sunday: the antiques market in Plaza Dorrego makes it impossible to move.
Highlights:	Plaza Dorrego, El Zanjón de Granados, Puente de la Mujer, Colección Fortabat

RECOLETA TO PALERMO: ART IN THE PARKS

Locals see busy Avenidas Figueroa Alcorta and Libertador as functional routes connecting downtown with the northern suburbs. But the parallel avenues also join Recoleta's major sights to Palermo's, and woven between them are beautiful green spaces. Use the avenues to get your bearings, but do your actual walking through the squares and parks.

Iconic Recoleta

From the **Cementerio de Recoleta** and **Centro Cultural Recoleta,** wind your way through Plaza Francia's market stalls (weekends) or past the couples lounging on the grass midweek and over Avenidas Pueyrredón and Libertador to the **Museo Nacional de Bellas Artes,** with the world's biggest Argentine art collection. The colonnaded building behind it, over Avenida Figueroa Alcorta, is the University of Buenos Aires' School of Law—continue past it into Plaza Naciones Unidas and the giant metal flower sculpture **Floralis Genérica.**

Art and Barrio Parque

Cross back over Avenida Figueroa Alcorta and weave through Plaza Uruguay and Plaza República de Chile. The white stone mansion on the other side of Libertador is the **Museo Nacional de Arte Decorativo.** Continue along Rufino de Elizalde, a curving cobbled street that's part of the Barrio Parque mini-neighborhood. Writer and socialite Victoria Ocampo commissioned the house at No. 2831 as an homage to Le Corbusier. The architect, Alejandro Bustillo, also designed the French neo-classical building opposite it at No. 2830, now the Belgian embassy.

Other mansions line the rest of the street and adjoin Alejandro M. de Aguado, which leads you back to Avenida Figueroa Alcorta. The block-long brown building opposite is the **Palacio Alcorta,** built by an Italian, Mario Palanti, for an American automobile company, Chrysler, but now bearing a French name, the Museo Renault. Consecrated modern Latin American masters are on display next door at the **Museo de Arte Latinoamericano de Buenos Aires,** and up-and-coming ones are at the **Daniel Maman** gallery at Libertador 2475, two blocks away down San Martín de Tours.

Los Bosques de Palermo

Steel yourself for two blocks along busy Avenida Libertador, then cross back into green space at Cavia: a diagonal route through Plaza Alemania takes you to the entrance of the **Jardín Japonés**—stop off to see the bonsai and carp. Then wander on through the **Parque Tres de Febrero** roughly following Avenidas Berro and Iraola to Infanta Isabel. Skirting the lake's south side takes you to the **Paseo del Rosedal,** a large rose garden. Stroll southeast through Plaza Holanda, parallel to Libertador. The white-marble column at the intersection with Sarmiento honors four Argentine regions (note the bronze allegories in the pool at the base) but is known as the **Monumento de los Españoles.** Turn right onto quiet República de la India, which flanks the **Buenos Aires Zoo**—you can glimpse century-old pavilions and some animals through the railings—or turn right when you hit Avenida Las Heras to the entrance on Plaza Francia.

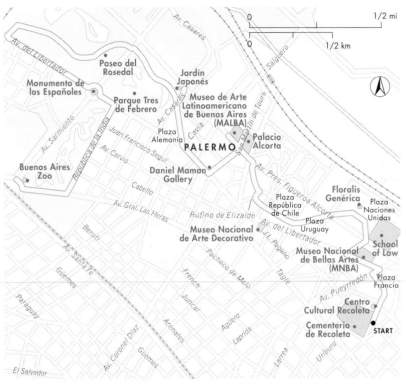

Where to Start:	Outside Cementerio de Recoleta at Junín 1760 in Recoleta
Time/Length:	3–5 hours (about 6 km/4 miles), depending on how many museums you visit
Where to Stop:	Entrance to Buenos Aires Zoo, intersection of Avenidas General Las Heras and Sarmiento, Plaza Francia
Best Time to Go:	Early morning if you're interested only in the parks, early afternoon to take in museums, too
Worst Time to Go:	When it's rainy or baking hot
Highlights:	MNBA and MALBA, Jardín Japonés, Paseo El Rosedal. In November, the mass of lilac-blue blossoms on the jacaranda trees.

BUENOS AIRES WITH KIDS

Family is a big part of local life. Porteños definitely believe kids should be seen and heard, and local children keep pretty much the same schedule as their parents. Don't be surprised to see local kids out until the wee hours.

It's completely normal for kids to sit through adult dinners, and restaurants (and other diners) are fine with them dozing at the table. Children's menus aren't common in Buenos Aires: local kids usually eat the same as adults, in smaller portions.

When it comes to rewarding—or bribing—their kids, porteño parents are unanimous: *helado* (ice cream) is the way to go. There are shops on nearly every block, but classy chains Freddo, Un'Altra Volta, and Persicco do the creamiest scoops.

There's not much of a language barrier when it comes to entertainment geared toward younger members of the family. You don't need Spanish-language skills to enjoy *circo* (circus), *títeres* (puppets), and *rock para chicos* (kiddie rock). Listing for these and other events are in the local newspapers.

Best Museums

Kids can go to the bank, shop at a supermarket, and play at adult jobs in the **Museo de los Niños** (Children's Museum) in Almagro. Although the museum is entirely in Spanish, activities like crawling through a large-scale plumbing system and operating a crane on a building site have universal appeal.

The motto of Recoleta's **Museo Participativo de las Ciencias** (Participative Science Museum) says it all—"*Prohibido No Tocar,*" or "Not Touching Is Forbidden." The colorful interactive displays—which explain how music, light, and electricity work—are hands-on enough for most kids to enjoy them despite the Spanish-only explanations. Better yet, it's on the first floor of the Centro Cultural Recoleta, so you can squeeze in some adult cultural time, too.

The gloriously retro building of the **Planetario Galileo Galilei** is alien-looking enough to attract your kids' attention. So does the state-of-the-art night-sky projection room, with seats that vibrate during meteorite collisions. Cotton candy and popcorn machines near the asteroid collection outside make for more earthly postmuseum treats.

The Great Outdoors

The best place for unbridled running and jumping is Palermo's **Parque Tres de Febrero.** There are acres and acres of well-maintained greenery, and you can rent bicycles of all sizes (including ones with child seats), in-line skates, and pedal boats. There are also hamburger stands, balloon sellers, and clowns.

The gross factor is high at the **Jardín Japonés,** where your kids can pet the slimy koi carp swimming in ornamental ponds (and you might manage to sneak some sushi). Even more back-to-nature is the unkempt **Reserva Ecológica**—*guided* moonlight walks are an extra thrill.

The **Zoo de Buenos Aires** is home to pumas, tapirs, llamas, *aguará guazús* (a kind of wolf), and *yacarés* (caymans). And these are just some of the South American animals here that your kids might never have seen.

FREE
(OR ALMOST FREE)

With so many world-class galleries and museums, Buenos Aires can put a dent in your wallet. But the good news is that even the city's top spots for art have days when you can visit for little or nothing. And some of the favorite pastimes, including wandering around the Cementerio de la Recoleta or finding a bargain in the flea market at San Telmo, are always gratis.

Art and Archtecture

It costs absolutely nothing to visit what is arguably the best collection of Argentine art in the world: Recoleta's **Museo Nacional de Bellas Artes** is free all week. Entrance to most other state-run museums is less than a dollar or two.

Take in art both old and new on Tuesday, when you can gaze for free at the antique furnishings of the **Museo Nacional de Arte Decorativo** and the contemporary works at the **Museo de Arte Moderno,** also free on Thursday. Wednesday, go for handicrafts and 19th-century painting at the **Museo de Artes Plásticas Eduardo Sívori**; it's in the middle of the Parque Tres de Febrero.

Check out colonial art downtown in Retiro free of charge on Tuesday and Thursday at the **Museo de Arte Hispano-americano Isaac Fernández Blanco.** The one serious artistic saving you can make is at Palermo's **Museo de Arte Latinoamericano de Buenos Aires,** which reduces its 50-peso entry fee to 25 pesos on Wednesday—expect to compete for floor space, though.

History Lesson

It costs thousands to spend an afterlife in the **Cementerio de la Recoleta,** but nothing to spend a morning or afternoon there. San Telmo is the best barrio for a free local history lesson: churches and traditional houses (many now antiques shops) are some of the historic buildings open to the public.

Seeing the City

You can pay as little—or as much—as you want on the popular **Buenos Aires Local Tours** (⊕ *www.buenosaireslocaltours. com*), which use city buses to keep its overhead low. You will want to tip the enthusiastic young guides at the end, however. Tours take place on Monday, Wednesday, and Saturday, usually in the morning. To take part, register online as early as possible.

Enthusiastic local volunteers are your guides on the free city tours run by **Cicerones de Buenos Aires** (⊕ *www.cicerones.org. ar*). You can see the city on two wheels for free by checking out one of bicycles that are part of a city program called **EcoBici** (⊕ *www.ecobici.buenosaires.gob.ar*). Take your passport and a photocopy of it to any bike station to register. (Locations are listed online). Check your bike and helmet back into any other station within an hour.

Cheap Entertainment

During January and February there are free outdoor concerts and festivals in parks around the city. Wednesday is reduced-price day at every cinema in town; many also do discount tickets Monday through Thursday and for the first screening of each day.

Instead of forking out hundreds at a fancy "for export" tango show, head to a low-key *milonga*. The cover charge is usually only around 50 pesos, drinks are cheap, and the dancing is excellent. Tangoing street performers also abound on Calle Florida, in plazas Dorrego and Serrano, and around the Caminito.

ARGENTINA'S WINES

Wine is officially Argentina's national drink, and no wonder. As the world's seventh-largest consumer of the drink and fifth-largest producer, Argentina has become an international wine powerhouse. While most of the country's wine production is centered in Mendoza, 600 miles west of Buenos Aires in the foothills of the Andes, the capital's *vinotecas* (wine shops) and wine bars provide plenty of opportunity to sample the fruits of the vintners' labors.

The shelves and menus at these establishments feature domestic wines almost exclusively—the exchange rate makes imported wine prohibitively expensive for Argentine consumers. Fortunately for wine-loving travelers to the country, this means that excellent Argentine wines are available at bargain prices. Knowing a little about the country's wines can help you make informed buying decisions.

A Little History

Grapes have been cultivated in western Argentina since the mid-16th century, when clerics established vineyards to produce communion wine. The near-perfect growing conditions of the eastern flanks of the Andes and the know-how of successive waves of European immigrants meant that production flourished. However, consumption of Mendoza's wine remained local for years, as the area was geographically isolated until the late 19th century, when a railroad connected Mendoza to Buenos Aires. Wine from Mendoza was finally traded throughout the country.

For the next 100 years vintners produced mainly simple wines in accordance with local tastes and budgets. Following the success story of neighboring Chile, they began to look to the export market in the 1990s. An influx of investment from

France, Spain, Italy, and the United States significantly improved growing and production practices, resulting in top-quality wines that caught on locally as well as abroad. Now there are more than 1,500 wineries in Argentina, and the country's wines are widely exported.

Growing Conditions

Argentina's wine band extends along the western border of the country, comprising 10 regions, from Salta in the north to the Rio Negro in Patagonia, at the country's southern end. The vineyards are clustered in irrigated plots in areas that would otherwise be desert. Most vines are planted at high elevations, between 2,000 and 3,000 feet above sea level. The climate here can be temperamental, so producers must be prepared for downpours, hailstorms, and scorching, dehydrating winds.

The most significant wine regions are Mendoza and San Juan, located in the middle of the country, which together account for about 90% of the country's wine production. Mendoza and San Juan are dry, temperate regions, with fewer than eight inches of rain per year, and temperatures that range from around 33°F in the winter to 94°F in the summer.

Wines to Try

Dozens of imported grape varieties—from popular chardonnay to obscure bonarda—are planted in Argentina. A large percentage of vineyard area is still planted with domestic grapes varieties like criolla and cereza, which yield basic table wines and grape juice. But international varieties are quickly replacing these historic grapes. Some of the most important types include the following:

Malbec: Still a minor blending variety in France's Bordeaux wines, malbec has become Argentina's signature varietal,

and is said to find its best expression here. Malbecs are deep-colored, full-bodied wines, concentrated with plum and raspberry flavors.

Cabernet Sauvignon: Argentine cabernets are full-bodied, with high acid and tannin, typically expressing bold black cherry and herbal notes. They're perfect with grilled steaks.

Red Blends: The red blends here may be mixtures of classic Bordeaux varieties—mainly merlot, cabernet sauvignon, and malbec—but they express the fruit-forward results typical of New World wines. Other red blends include nontraditional pairings like Italy's sangiovese with syrah.

Chardonnay: This international varietal can vary widely in its expression depending upon where it is grown. Some Argentine bottlings express citrus and honey flavors, while others are packed with tropical fruit. Most chardonnays are oaked, so expect toasty, buttery notes as well.

Torrontés: Argentina's favorite white wine—considered an indigenous grape—has prominent aromatics of flowers and herbs in a full-bodied, dry wine. Often tangy and lively, torrontés makes an excellent aperitif.

Wine Tasting Primer

Ordering and tasting wine—whether at a vinoteca, winery, or restaurant—is easy once you master a few simple steps.

Look: Hold your glass by the stem, raise it to the light, and take a close look at the wine in the glass. Note the wine's hue, color depth, and clarity. For white wine, is it greenish, yellow, or gold? For red wine, is it purplish, ruby, or garnet? For depth, is the wine's color pale, medium, or deep? Is the liquid clear or cloudy? (This is easiest to tell if you can move the glass in front of a white background).

Sniff: Swirl the wine gently in the glass to intensify the scents, then sniff over the rim of the glass. What do you smell? Try to identify aromas like fruits (citrus, green fruit, black fruits), flowers (blossoms, honey), spices (sweet, pungent, herbal), vegetables (fresh or cooked), minerals (earth or wet stones), dairy (butter, cream), oak (toast, vanilla), or animal (leathery) notes. Are there any unpleasant notes, like mildew or wet dog? That might indicate that the wine is "off."

Sip: Take a first sip and swish the wine around your mouth for a few seconds to "prime" your palate, then swallow or spit it into a discard bucket. Then take another sip and begin to evaluate the wine. In the mouth, you experience sweetness on the tip of the tongue, acidity on the sides of the tongue, and tannins (an astringent, mouth-drying sensation) on the gums. Is the sipping experience pleasant, or is one of the wine's elements out of balance? Also consider the body—does the wine feel light in the mouth, or is there a sensation of richness? Are the flavors you taste consistent with the aromas you smelled? If you like the wine, try to pinpoint what you like about it, and vice versa if you don't like it. Most of all, take time to savor the wine as you're sipping it—the tasting experience may seem a little scientific, but the end goal is your enjoyment.

THE SPORTING LIFE

Get Your Kicks

Tens of thousands of ecstatic fans jump up and down in unison, roaring modified cumbia classics to the beat of carnival drums; crazed supporters sway atop 10-foot fences between the stands and the field as they drape the barbed wire with their team's flags; showers of confetti and sulfurous smoke from colorful flares fill the air. The occasion? Just another day's *fútbol* (soccer) match in Argentina.

Matches are held year-round and are seriously exciting—and sometimes dangerous. You're safest in the *platea* (preferred seating area), which cost 150 to 450 pesos depending on location and the importance of the match, rather than in the chaotic 80-peso *popular* (standing room) section. Be careful what you wear—fans carry their colors with pride, and not just on flags and team shirts. Expect to see painted faces, hundreds of tattoos, and even women's underwear with the colors of the best-known teams: Boca Juniors (blue and gold) and their archrivals River Plate (red and white), as well as Independiente (red), Racing (light blue and white), and San Lorenzo (red and blue).

You can buy tickets at long lines at the stadiums up to four days before matches or online through **Tangol** (☎ *11/4312–7276* ⊕ *www.tangol.com*). Though pricey, the company's packages include well-located seats, transportation both ways, and a soccer-loving guide. Expect to pay more to see the most popular teams.

Estadio Boca Juniors. Walls exploding with huge, vibrant murals of insurgent workers, famous inhabitants of La Boca, and fútbol greats splashed in blue and gold let you know that the Estadio Boca Juniors is at hand. The stadium that's also known as La Bombonera (meaning "candy box,"

supposedly because the fans' singing reverberates as it would inside a candy tin) is the home of Argentina's most popular club. The extensive stadium tour is worth the extra money. Lighthearted guides take you all over the stands as well as to press boxes, locker rooms, underground tunnels, and the emerald grass of the field itself. ✉ *Brandsen 805, at Del Valle Iberlucea, La Boca* ☎ *11/4309–4700 for stadium* ⊕ *www.museoboquense.com* ✉ *80 pesos* ☉ *Daily 11–5.*

Horse Around

Combine the horsey inclinations of Argentina's landed elite with the country's general sporting prowess, and what do you get? The world's best polo players. The game may be as posh as it gets, but local sports fans take pride in the stunning athletic showmanship.

Campo Argentino de Polo (*Argentine Polo Field*). Major polo tournaments take place at the Campo Argentino de Polo, run by the Asociación Argentina de Polo (Argentine Polo Association). Admission to autumn (March to May) and spring (September to December) matches is free. The much-heralded Campeonato Argentino Abierto (Argentine Open Championship) takes place in November; admission to the whole championship starts at about 500 pesos. You can buy tickets online in advance or at the polo field on the day of the event. ✉ *Av. del Libertador 4300, at Dorrego, Palermo* ☎ *11/4777–6444* ⊕ *www.aapolo.com.*

A PASSIONATE HISTORY by Victoria Patience

If there's one thing Argentinians have learned from their history, it's that there's not a lot you can count on. Fierce—often violent—political, economic, and social instability have been the only constants in the story of a people who seem never to be able to escape that famous Chinese curse, "May you live in interesting times."

Although most accounts of Argentine history begin 500 years ago with the arrival of the conquistadors, humans have been living in what is now Argentina for around 13,000 years. They created the oldest recorded art in South America—a cave of handprints in Santa Cruz, Patagonia (c. 7500 BC)—and eventually became part of the Inca Empire.

Spanish and Portuguese sailors came in the early 16th century, including Ferdinand Magellan. The Spanish were forced out 300 years later by locals hungry for independence. Though autonomous on paper, in practice the early republic depended heavily on trade with Europe. Conflict and civil war wracked the United

Provinces of the South as the region struggled to define its political identity and the economic model it would follow.

Spanish and Italian immigrants arrived in the 20th century, changing Argentina's population profile forever. Unstable politics characterized the rest of the century, which saw the rise and fall of Juan Perón and a series of increasingly bloody military dictatorships. More than 30 years of uninterrupted democracy have passed since the last junta fell, an achievement Argentines value hugely.

(left) Ferdinand Magellan (c. 1480–1521)
(right) Stamp featuring Eva Duarte
de Perón (1919–1952)

Magellan sails down
Argentinian coast

Juan de Garay
founds Buenos Aires

PRE-1500s INCA INVASION   1500   1600

(top left) Cave paintings, Cueva de las Manos, Santa Cruz; (top right) Indigenous inhabitants of Río de la Plata area pictured by Hendrick Ottsen; (bottom) Relief detail, San Ignacio Miní Mission, Misiones Province.

PRE-CONQUEST/INCA

PRE-1500

Argentina's original inhabitants were a diverse group of indigenous peoples. Their surroundings defined their lifestyles: nomadic hunter-gatherers lived in Patagonia and the Pampas, while the inhabitants of the northeast and northwest were largely farming communities. The first foreign power to invade the region was the Inca Empire, in the 15th century. Its roads and tribute systems extended over the entire northwest, reaching as far south as some parts of modern-day Mendoza.

BIRTH OF THE COLONY

1500–1809

European explorers first began to arrive at the River Plate area in the early 1500s, and in 1520 Ferdinand Magellan sailed right down the coast of what is now Argentina and on into the Pacific. Buenos Aires was founded twice: Pedro de Mendoza's 1536 attempt led to starving colonists turning to cannibalism before running for Asunción; Juan de Garay's attempt in 1580 was successful. Conquistadors of Spanish origin came from what are now Peru, Chile, and Paraguay and founded other cities. The whole area was part of the Viceroyalty of Peru until

1776, when the Spanish king Carlos III decreed present-day Argentina, Uruguay, Paraguay, and most of Bolivia to be the Viceroyalty of the Río de la Plata. Buenos Aires became the main port and the only legal exit point for silver from Potosí. Smuggling grew as fast as the city itself. In 1806–07 English forces tried twice to invade Argentina. Militia from Buenos Aires fought them off with no help from Spain, inciting ideas of independence among *criollos* (Argentinian-born Spaniards, who had fewer rights than those born in Europe).

(left) Julio Roca
(right) Monument to
General San Martín;

BIRTH OF THE NATION: INDEPENDENCE AND THE CONSTITUTION

1810—1860s

Early-19th-century proto-Argentinians were getting itchy for independence after the American Revolution. On May 25, 1810, Buenos Aires' leading citizens ousted the last Spanish viceroy. A series of elected juntas and triumvirates followed while military heroes José de San Martín and Manuel Belgrano won battles that allowed the Provincias Unidas de América del Sur to declare independence in Tucumán on July 9, 1816. San Martín went on to liberate Chile and Peru.

Political infighting marked the republic's first 40 years. The conflict centered on control of the port. Inhabitants of Buenos Aires wanted a centralist state run from the city, a position known as *unitario*, but landowners and leaders in the provinces wanted a federal state with greater Latin American integration. The federal side won when Juan Manuel de Rosas came to power: he made peace with indigenous leaders and gave rights to marginal social sectors like gauchos, although his increasingly iron-fisted rule later killed or outlawed the opposition. The centralist constitution established on his downfall returned power to the land-owning elite.

RISE OF THE MODERN STATE

1860—1942

Argentina staggered back and forth between political extremes on its rocky road to modern statehood. Relatively liberal leaders alternated with corrupt warlord types. The most infamous of these was Julio Roca, whose military campaigns massacred most of Argentina's remaining indigenous populations in order to seize the land needed to expand the cattle ranching and wheat farming. Roca also sold off services and resources to the English and started the immigration drive that brought millions of Europeans to Argentina between 1870 and 1930.

(top left) Juan Perón and his wife Eva Duarte attend a party in 1951; (top right) Juan Perón addressing the congress, Buenos Aires, May 6, 1949; (bottom) Perón in discussion c. 1950

1942–1973

THE RISE AND FALL OF PERONISM

A 1943 coup ended a decade of privatization that had caused the gap between rich and poor to grow exponentially. One of the soldiers involved was a little-known general named Juan Domingo Perón. He rose through the ranks of the government as quickly as he had through those of the army. Uneasy about Perón's growing popularity, other members of the military government imprisoned him, provoking a wave of uprisings that led to his release and swept him to the presidency as head of the newly formed labor party in 1946.

Mid-campaign, he quietly married the young B-movie actress he'd been living with, Eva Duarte, soon to be known universally as "Evita." Their idiosyncratic, his'n'hers politics hinged on a massive personality cult. Together, they rallied the masses with their cries for social justice, political sovereignty, economic independence, and Latin American unity. Then, while he was busy improving worker's rights and trying to industrialize Argentina, she set about press-ganging Argentina's landed elite into funding her social aid program. Their tireless efforts to close the gap between rich

and poor earned them the slavish devotion of Argentina's working classes and the passionate hatred of the rich. But everything began to go wrong when Evita died of uterine cancer in 1952. By 1955, the Marshall Plan in Europe reduced Argentina's export advantage, and the dwindling economy was grounds for Perón being ousted by another military coup. For the next 18 years, both he and his party were illegal in Argentina—mentioning his name or even whistling the Peronist anthem could land you in prison.

IN FOCUS A PASSIONATE HISTORY

(top left) Leopoldo Galtieri led the last military dictatorship in Argentina. (top right) Argentina military junta during the Falkland's War; (bottom right) Argentine prisoners of war—Port Stanley;

1973–1983

DICTATORSHIP, STATE TERRORISM & THE FALKLANDS

The two civilian presidencies that followed both ended in fresh military coups until Perón was allowed to return in 1973. Despite falling out with left-wing student and guerrilla groups who had campaigned for him in his absence, he still won another election by a landslide. However, one problematic year later, he died in office. His farcical successor was the vice-president, an ex-cabaret dancer known as Isabelita, who was also Perón's third wife. Her chaotic leadership was brought to an end in 1976 by yet another military

coup widely supported by civil society. The succession of juntas that ruled the country called their bloody dictatorship a "process of national reorganization"; these days it's referred to as state-led terrorism.

Much of the world seemingly ignored the actions of Argentina's government during its six-year reign of terror. Throughout the country, students, activists, and any other undesirable element were kidnapped and tortured in clandestine detention centers. Many victims' children were stolen and given up for adoption by pro-military families after their parents' bodies had

been dumped in the Rio de la Plata. More than 30,000 people "disappeared" and thousands more went into exile. Government ministries were handed over to private businessmen. Massive corruption took external debt from $7 million to $66 million. In 1982, desperate for something to distract people with, the junta started war with Britain over the Islas Malvinas, or Falkland Islands. The disastrous campaign lasted just four months and, together with increasing pressure from local and international human rights activists, led to the downfall of the dictatorship.

TIMELINE   Menem elected|
president
|Falklands War

State of emergency declared|

Cristina Kirchner re-elected
Bicentenary|
Economic revival|

INFLATION REACHES 3,000%   1990   ECONOMY IN TATTERS   2000   2010

(top) President Carlos Menem mobbed by
the public; (top right) a revitalized economy
brings new construction. (bottom) Argentine
riot police drag away a demonstrator near
the Casa Rosada in Buenos Aires.

RETURN OF DEMOCRACY
1982–1999

Celebrations marked
the return to democ-
racy. The main players
in the dictatorship
went on trial, but received
relatively small sentences
and were eventually par-
doned. Inflation reached a
terrifying 3,000% in 1988 and
only stabilized when Carlos
Menem became president
the following year. Menem
pegged the peso to the dollar, privatized services and
resources, and even changed
the constitution to extend
his mandate. But despite an
initial illusion of economic
well-being, by the time
Menem left office in 1999
poverty had skyrocketed, and
the economy was in tatters.

CRISIS & THE K YEARS
2000–PRESENT

The longer-term results
of Menem's policies
came in December
2001, when the
government tried to
prevent a rush on
funds by freezing all private
savings accounts. Thousands
of people took to the streets
in protest; on December 20,
the violent police response
transformed the demonstrations into riots. President
Fernando de la Rúa declared
a state of emergency, then
resigned, and was followed
by four temporary presidents
in almost as many days.
When things finally settled,
the peso had devalued
drastically, many people
had lost their savings, and
the future looked dark.

However, under the
center-leftist government of
Argentina's following president, Néstor Kirchner, the
economy slowly reactivated.
Kirchner reopened trials of
high-ranking military of-
ficials and championed local
industry. In a rather bizarre
turn of political events,
he was succeeded by his
wife, Cristina Fernández.
Her fiery speeches have
inspired both devotion and
derision, but her social and
economic policies ensured
her landslide re-election.
Times may be better than a
few years ago, but Argen-
tines have lived through
so many political ups and
downs that they never take
anything for granted.

MADE IN ARGENTINA

There's no doubt that Argentinians are an inventive lot. And we're not talking about their skill in arguing their way out of parking tickets: several things you might not be able to imagine life without started out in Argentina.

Una *birome* (ballpoint pen)

BALLPOINT PEN

Although László Jósef Bíró was born in Hungary and first patented the ballpoint pen in Paris, it wasn't until he launched his company in Argentina in 1943 that his invention began to attract attention. As such, Argentines claim the world's most useful writing instrument as their own.

BLOOD TRANSFUSION

Before ER there was Luis Agote, an Argentine doctor who, in 1914, was one of the first to perform a blood transfusion using stored blood (rather than doing a patient-to-patient transfusion). The innovation that made the process possible was adding sodium citrate, an anticoagulant, to the blood.

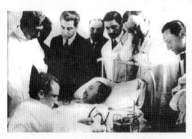

Luis Agote was one of the first to perform a nondirect blood transfusion, in Buenos Aires on November 9, 1914.

FINGERPRINTING

In 1891, Juan Vucetich, a Croatian-born officer of the Buenos Aires police force, came up with a system of classifying fingerprints. He went on to make the first-ever criminal arrest based on fingerprint evidence. Although his method has since been refined, it is still used throughout Latin America.

Huellas digitales (fingerprints)

■ Other useful Argentine claims to fame include the first working helicopter (1916); the first one-piece floor mop (1953); and the first one-use-only hypodermic syringe (1989).

EXPLORING
BUENOS AIRES

By Victoria
Patience

For 500 years, Buenos Aires has been in the throes of a powerful identity crisis. The unlikely lovechild of a troubled marriage between Europe and Latin America, Argentina's capital has never wholly aligned itself with either of the cultures that spawned it. Each wave of immigration has brought new flavors to the mix, and the resulting fusion— or creative confusion—is attracting more visitors to this city than any other in South America.

There's no denying Buenos Aires' architectural appeal: the graceful stone facades of its 19th-century townhouses and civic constructions speak of Paris or Madrid, so just wandering the streets is a memorable experience. The shopping is world-class, too, whether you covet contemporary couture or quality handcrafts; and the electric nightlife further heightens B.A.'s cosmopolitan ambience. Many of the city's classic cultural institutions have been renovated, and bleeding-edge spaces are keeping hipsters happy. Traditional dance floors, moreover, have come back to life thanks to a booming tango—and tango tourism—revival. Meanwhile, marriage and equal rights for same-sex partnerships plus a thriving scene have made the city a prime gay destination.

But grit offsets the glamour. Crumbling balconies, uneven sidewalks, and fresh layers of photo-worthy graffiti are reminders of your real coordinates. The devalued peso means that Buenos Aires keeps getting cheaper for anyone with hard currency, despite rising prices—though growing numbers of homeless people and ever-expanding shanty towns within the city limits speak of tough times to come for on-the-edge residents. In the face of so much change, however, some things do remain the same. Food, family, and fútbol are still the holy trinity for most *porteños* (as the locals are called), and they still approach life with as much dramatic intensity as ever.

CENTRO AND PUERTO MADERO

Sightseeing
★★★★
Dining
★
Lodging
★★
Shopping
★★★
Nightlife
★

Porteños love to brag that Buenos Aires has the world's widest avenue (Avenida 9 de Julio), its best steak, and its most beautiful women. The place to decide whether they're right is the city's heart; known simply as "El Centro," it contains the oldest and newest districts as well as many other superlatives. Cross Santiago the sleek and curvaceous Puente de la Mujer (Bridge of the Woman) and you're in the upscale waterfront neighborhood of Puerto Madero.

CENTRO

The historic heart of Buenos Aires, El Centro is still the focus of contemporary civic and commercial life. Plaza de Mayo is the original main square, and civic buildings both past and present are clustered between it and Plaza Congreso. Many of Argentina's most historic events—including revolutions, demonstrations, and terrorist attacks—took place on this square. Bullet-marked facades, sidewalks embedded with plaques, and memorials where buildings once stood are reminders of all this history, and the protesters who fill the streets regularly are history in the making.

More upbeat gatherings—picture open-air concerts, soccer victory celebrations, post-election reveling—take place around the Obelisco, a scaled-down Washington Monument lookalike that honors the founding of Buenos Aires. Inescapably phallic, it's the butt of local jokes about male insecurity in this oh-so-macho city. It's even dressed in a giant red condom each year on AIDS Awareness Day.

The city's most highbrow cultural events are hosted a few blocks away in the spectacular Teatro Colón, and the highest-grossing theatrical productions line Avenida Corrientes. The center of Argentina's biggest scandals is Tribunales, the judicial district around Plaza Lavalle.

Commercial action, meanwhile, revolves around brash Calle Fi
its high-street stores and fast-food joints keep the area's army of or
workers in cool suits and hot lunches.

Building buffs get their biggest kicks in this part of town, too. Architectural wonders of yesteryear—French-inspired domes and towers with
Iberian accents—line grand avenues, as do dreamy art deco theaters
and monumental Peronist constructions.

PLANNING YOUR TIME

Crowds and traffic can make touring draining: try to do a few short
visits rather than one long marathon. Half a day in the Centro is enough
to take in the sights, though you could spend a lot more time caught
up in the shops and boutiques. Office workers on lunch breaks make
the Centro even more hectic than usual between noon and 2. If you're
planning on hard-core shopping, come on a weekend. The area is quiet
at night, and a little dangerous in its desolation.

TOP ATTRACTIONS

Casa Rosada. The eclectic Casa de Gobierno, better known as the Casa
Rosada or Pink House, is at Plaza de Mayo's eastern end, with its back
to the river. The building houses the government's executive branch—
the president works here but lives elsewhere—and was built in the late
19th century over the foundations of an earlier customhouse and for-
tress. Swedish, Italian, and French architects have since modified the
structure, which accounts for the odd mix of styles. Its curious hue dates
from the presidency of Domingo Sarmiento, who ordered it painted
pink as a symbol of unification between two warring political factions,
the *federales* (whose color was red) and the *unitarios* (represented by
white). Local legend has it that the original paint was made by mixing
whitewash with bull's blood.

The balcony facing Plaza de Mayo is a presidential podium. From this
lofty stage Evita rallied the *descamisados* (the "shirtless"—meaning
the working class), Maradona sang along with soccer fans after winning one World Cup and coming second in another, and Madonna
belted out her film rendition of "Don't Cry for Me Argentina." Check
for a small banner hoisted alongside the nation's flag, indicating "the
president is in."

On weekends, hour-long guided tours leave every 10 minutes, taking
in some of the presidential offices and the newly opened Galería de los
Patriotas Argentinos del Bicentenario (Bicentennial Gallery of Patriots),
a pictorial who's who of Argentina's national heroes. The country's
heroines have a room of their own here, the Salón Mujeres Argentinas,
which is often used for presidential press conferences. An impassioned
Evita presides over black-and-white photographs of Argentina's other
great dames. ⊠ *Balcarce 50, Plaza de Mayo* ☎ *11/4344-3714* ⊕ *www.
presidencia.gov.ar/visitas-guiadas* 🎫 *Free* ☉ *Weekends 10–6* Ⓜ *A to
Plaza de Mayo; D to Catedral; E to Bolívar.*

La Manzana de Las Luces *(The Block of Illuminaton).* More history is
packed into this single block of buildings southwest of Plaza de Mayo
than in scores of other city blocks put together. Its name, which literally
means "the Block of Lights," is a metaphorical nod to the "illuminated"

[Map of Buenos Aires Microcentro with the following labels:]

Plaza Vte. López
Museo de Arte Hispanoamericano Isaac Fernández Blanco
Arenales
Malpú
Edificio Kavanagh
ERMO
Av. Santa Fe
SAN MARTÍN
Plaza San Martín
RETIRO
RECOLETA
M.T. de Alvear
Plaza Libertad
Galería Ruth Benzacar
Plaza R. Peña
Paraguay
Carlos Pellegrini
Suipacha
Esmeralda
Maipú
Av. Córdoba
Av. Libertador
Av. Eduardo
Av. Córdoba
Plaza Lavalle
Teatro Colón
Florida
Galerías Pacífico/ Centro Cultural Borges
CALLAO
Viamonte
TRIBUNALES
CENTRO
Tucumán
Calle Florida
← TO ALMAGRO
Lavalle
LAVALLE
LEANDRO N. ALEM
San Martín
Av. Leandro N. Alem
Bouchard
La Giralda
C PELLEGRINI
FLORIDA
Av. Corrientes
Obelisco
9 DE JULIO
Palacio Elortondo-Alvear
Reconquista
25 de Mayo
Av. Rosales
Junín
Ayacucho
Riobamba
Av. Callao
Rodríguez Peña
Sarmiento
DIAG NORTE
Av. 9 de Julio
Saenz Peña
Galería Güemes
Museo del Bicentenario
Tte. General Juan Domingo Perón
Uruguay
Talcahuano
Libertad
Cerrito
Bank Boston
Catedral Metropolitana
Bartolomé Mitre
Paraná
Montevideo
SAENZ PEÑA
CATEDRAL PERÚ
Plaza de Mayo
Parque Colón
CONGRESO
Rivadavia
Rivadavia
Av. de Mayo
LIMA
Rivadavia
Museo Histórico Nacional del Cabildo
Casa Rosada
Palacio del Congreso
Plaza del Congreso
Hipólito Yrigoyen
AV DE MAYO
BOLÍVAR
PLAZA DE MAYO
Chan Chan
Adolfo Alsina
La Morada
La Manzana de las Luces
Plaza de las Luces
Carlos Pellegrini
Suipacha
Esmeralda
Combate de Los Pozos
Av. Entre Ríos
Luis Sáenz Peña
Virrey Cevallos
Solís
San José
Santiago del Estero
Salta
Lima
Bernardo de Hiqoven
Perú
Bolívar
Defensa
Balcarce
Av. Paseo Colón
Sarandí
San José
Moreno
Museo de la Ciudad
Plaza A.P. Justo
TO SAN TELMO & LA BOCA
Av. L. N. Roca
Tacuari
Piedras
Chacabuco
Museo Etnográfico Juan B. Ambrosetti
Av. Belgrano

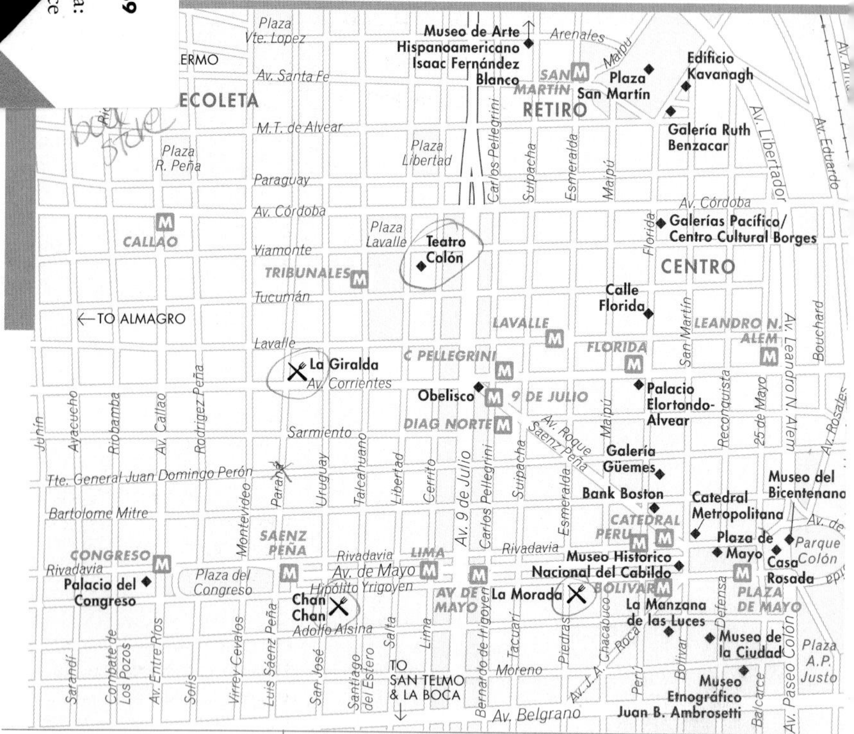

TOP EXPERIENCES

Reflecting: on Argentina's indigenous history at the Museo Etnográfico Juan B. Ambrosetti.

Witnessing: demonstrations in Plaza de Mayo, where Evita waved to crowds.

Listening: to opera singers in the glittering Teatro Colón or to the equally talented songbirds in the Reserva Ecológica.

Wandering: along Juana Manuela Gorriti and Pierina Dealessi to see Puerto Madero's "recycled" warehouses; Avenida de Mayo for 19th-century style; or Calle Florida for hustle, bustle, and souvenirs.

THE TERRITORY

The Microcentro runs between avenidas L. N. Alem and 9 de Julio and north of Avenida de Mayo. There are two axes: Avenida Corrientes (east–west) and pedestrian-only shopping street Florida (north–south). Florida's northern end leads into Plaza San Martín in Retiro. South of the Microcentro lies Plaza de Mayo. From here Avenida de Mayo runs 12 blocks west to Plaza del Congreso. Puerto Madero borders the Centro to the east. The main thoroughfares, Avenida Alicia M. de Justo and Olga Cossentini, run parallel to the river.

SAFETY AND PRECAUTIONS

Be especially alert for "stain scammers" downtown: they squirt foul-smelling liquid on you surreptitiously, then "helpfully" offer to clean it off (as they pick your pocket). Use ATMs only during bank hours (weekdays 10–3); thieves target them after hours.

Centro and Puerto Madero

KEY

✕ Quick bites

Ⓜ Subte stops

QUICK BITES

Chan Chan. Peruvian dishes at bargain prices have made a name for Chan Chan. The deep-fried corn kernels are almost a meal in themselves. ⊠ *Hipólito Yrigoyen 1390, Congreso* ☎ *11/4382-8492* ⊙ *Tues.–Sun. noon–4 pm and 8 pm–12:30 am* Ⓜ *A to Sáenz Peña.*

La Morada. Local office workers know where to find the best empanadas. Photos of Argentine celebrities are hung so close you can barely see the walls. ⊠ *Hipólito Yrigoyen 778, Plaza de Mayo* ☎ *11/4343-3003* ⊕ *www.lamorada.com.ar* ⊙ *Mon.–Thurs. 10–4, Fri. 10–4 and 6–midnight* Ⓜ *A to Plaza de Mayo; D to Catedral; E to Bolívar.*

La Giralda. Don't let the small tables or surly waiters put you off—La Giralda's signature *chocolate con churros* (hot chocolate with crisp cigar-shaped donuts) are to die for. ⊠ *Av. Corrientes 1453, Centro* ☎ *11/4371-3846* ⊙ *Mon.–Thurs. 8 am–midnight, Fri. and Sat. 7 am–2 am, Sun. 4 pm–midnight* Ⓜ *B to Uruguay.*

GETTING AROUND

The quickest way into Centro is by subte. For Microcentro, get off at Florida (Línea B) or Lavalle (C). Retiro and Plaza San Martín have eponymous stations on Línea C. Stations Avenida de Mayo (A), Catedral (D), and Bolívar (E) all serve Plaza de Mayo. Línea A has stops along de Mayo, including at Congreso. Lines B, C, and D intersect at Carlos Pellegrini/Diagonal Norte/9 de Julio. Change lines here only if you're going more than one stop. Otherwise, walking is quicker. Puerto Madero is close to L. N. Alem on Línea A, and is connected by the Tren del Este, a light-rail service running parallel to Avenida Alicia Moreau de Justo.

You can take a taxi or bus to Microcentro, but walking is the best way to move within it. Bus nos. 17, 24, 28, and 59 run between San Telmo and Microcentro; nos. 17 and 59 also stop in Recoleta and Palermo, while No. 24 continues on to Almagro. Bus No. 29 starts in La Boca and passes San Telmo and Centro before moving on to Almagro and Palermo. Bus No. 130 connects Centro with the southern end of Puerto Madero.

scholars who once worked within. Most of the site can be visited only on guided tours led by excellent professional historians. Regular departures are in Spanish, but they provide brochures with English summaries of each stage.

The earliest occupant of the site was the controversial Jesuit order, which began construction here in 1661. The only survivor from this first stage is the galleried **Procuraduría**, the colonial administrative headquarters for the Jesuits' vast land holdings in northeastern Argentina and Paraguay (think: *The Mission*). Secret tunnels, still undergoing archaeological excavation, linked it to area churches, the Cabildo, and the port. Guided visits include a glimpse of a specially reinforced section. After the Jesuits' expulsion from Argentina in 1767 (the Spanish crown saw them as a threat), the simple brick-and-mud structure housed the city's first school of medicine and then the University of Buenos Aires. Fully restored, it's now home to a school for stringed-instrument makers and a rather tacky crafts market.

The Jesuits honored their patron saint at the **Iglesia de San Ignacio de Loyola** (Church of Saint Ignatius of Loyola), at the intersection of Alsina and Bolívar. It's the only building in the block you can visit without going on a tour. The original sanctuary here was built of adobe in 1675; within a few decades it was rebuilt in stone.

Argentina's first congress convened within another building on the site, the **Casas Virreinales** (Viceroyal Residences)—ironic, given that it was built to house colonial civil servants. The remaining historic building is the neoclassical **Colegio Nacional**, a top-notch public school and a hotbed of political activism that replaced a Jesuit-built structure. The president often attends graduation ceremonies, and Einstein gave a lecture here in 1925. ✉ *Entrance at Perú 272, Plaza de Mayo* ☎ *11/4342–6973* ⊕ *www.manzanadelasluces.gov.ar* 🖃 *20 pesos* ☉ *Visits by guided tour only; Spanish-language tours weekdays at 3, weekends at 4:30 and 6; call 2 wks ahead to arrange tours in English* Ⓜ *A to Plaza de Mayo; D to Catedral; E to Bolívar.*

Museo del Bicentenario. Today, the River Plate is nowhere in sight, but the humming traffic circle that overlooks this underground museum behind the Casa Rosada was once on the waterfront. The brick vaults, pillars, and wooden pulley mechanisms are the remains of the 1845 Taylor Customs House and jetty, discovered after being buried for almost a century. In honor of Argentina's 2010 bicentenary celebrations the structure was restored and capped with a glass roof.

Each vault covers a portion of Argentina's political history, recalling it through artifacts (often personal possessions of those who governed from the house overhead), paintings, photographs, film reels, and interactive screens. Temporary art exhibitions run on the other side of the museum courtyard.

The large glass structure in the center contains the star attraction: a 360-degree masterpiece by Mexican muralist David Alfaro Siqueiros, which originally covered the walls, floor, and ceiling of a basement room in a client's home. When the house was demolished in the early 1990s, the mural was carefully removed in pieces, only to languish in

DID YOU KNOW?

La Puente de la Mujer connects the Microcentro with Puerto Madero. The whole middle section of the bridge, including the skyward-reaching arm, swings like a door on a hinge to let boats pass.

a shipping container for 17 years. Thankfully, Siqueiros's innovative use of industrial paint meant that damage was minimal. Prompted by the campaigns of committed art activists, President Cristina Fernández intervened and the mural has now been fully restored and reassembled here. After donning protective shoes, you cross a small passageway into the work, which represents an underwater scene, against which the feet and faces of swimmers seem to press. The only male figure (swimming upwards on the wall opposite the entrance) is said to represent the artist.

A café at the back of the museum offers coffee, sandwiches, salads, and a set lunch menu. ⊠ *Paseo Colón 100, at Hipólito Yrigoyen, Plaza de Mayo* ☎ *11/4344–3802* ⊕ *www.museobicentenario.gob.ar* ⊠ *Free* ☉ *Apr.–Nov., Wed.–Sun. 10–6; Dec.–Mar., Wed.–Sun. 11–7* Ⓜ *A to Plaza de Mayo, D to Catedral, E to Bolívar.*

Museo Etnográfico Juan B. Ambrosetti (*Ethnographic Museum*). Until 2012, the 100-peso bill still honored General Roca—the man responsible for the massacre of most of Patagonia's indigenous population—so it's not surprising that information on Argentina's original inhabitants is sparse. This fascinating but little-visited museum is a welcome remedy.

Begun by local scientist Juan Bautista Ambrosetti in 1904, the collection originally focused on so-called exotic art and artifacts, such as the Australasian sculptures and Japanese temple altar showcased in the rust-color introductory room. The real highlights, however, are the Argentine collections: if you're planning to visit Argentina's far north or south, they'll provide an eye-opening introduction.

The ground-floor galleries trace the history of human activity in Patagonia, underscoring the tragic results of the European arrival. Dugout canoes, exquisite Mapuche silver jewelry, and scores of archival photos and illustrations are the main exhibits.

In the upstairs northwestern Argentina gallery the emphasis is mainly archaeological. Displays briefly chronicle the evolution of Andean civilization, the heyday of the Inca empire, and postcolonial life. Artifacts include ceramics, textiles, jewelry, farming tools, and even food: anyone for some 4,000-year-old corn?

The collection is run by the University of Buenos Aires' Faculty of Philosophy and Letters. Although their insightful labels and explanations are all in Spanish, you can ask for a photocopied sheet with English versions of the texts. It's a pleasure just to wander the quiet, light-filled 19th-century town house that contains both the collection and an anthropological library. The peaceful inner garden is the perfect place for some post-museum reflection. ⊠ *Moreno 350, Plaza de Mayo* ☎ *11/4345–8197* ⊕ *www.museoetnografico.filo.uba.ar* ⊠ *20 pesos* ☉ *Tues.–Fri. 1–7, weekends 3–7* Ⓜ *A to Plaza de Mayo; D to Catedral; E to Bolívar.*

Museo Histórico Nacional del Cabildo y de la Revolución de Mayo (*Cabildo*). Plaza de Mayo's only remaining colonial edifice was built in 1765 as the meeting place for the city council, now based in the ornate wedge-shape building on the southwest corner of the square. The center of the May Revolution of 1810, where patriotic citizens gathered to vote against Napoleonic rule, the hall is one of Argentina's national shrines.

However, this hasn't stopped successive renovations to its detriment, including the demolition of the whole right end of the structure to make way for the new Avenida de Mayo in 1894 and of the left end for Diagonal Julio Roca in 1931. The small museum of artifacts and documents pertaining to the events of the May Revolution is less of an attraction than the building itself. Thursday and Friday from 11 to 6, a tiny craft market takes place on the patio behind the building. ⌧ *Bolívar 65, Plaza de Mayo* ☎ *11/4334–1782* ⊕ *www.cabildonacional.gob.ar* ✉ *4 pesos* ⊙ *Wed.–Fri. 10:30–5, weekends 11:30–6* Ⓜ *A to Plaza de Mayo; D to Catedral; E to Bolívar.*

Fodor'sChoice
★ **Plaza de Mayo.** Since its construction in 1580, this has been the setting for Argentina's most politically turbulent moments, including the uprising against Spanish colonial rule on May 25, 1810—hence its name. The square was once divided in two by a *recova* (gallery), but this reminder of colonial times was demolished in 1883, and the square's central monument, the Pirámide de Mayo, was later moved to its place. The pyramid you see is actually a 1911 extension of the original, erected in 1811 on the anniversary of the Revolution of May, which is hidden inside. The bronze equestrian statue of General Manuel Belgrano, the designer of Argentina's flag, dates from 1873, and stands at the east end of the plaza.

The plaza remains the traditional site for ceremonies, rallies, and protests. Thousands cheered for Perón and Evita here; anti-Peronist planes bombed the gathered crowds in 1955; there were bloody clashes in December 2001 (hence the heavy police presence and crowd-control barriers); but the mood was jubilant when revelers thronged in to celebrate the nation's bicentenary in 2010. The white headscarves painted around the Pirámide de Mayo represent the Madres de la Plaza de Mayo (Mothers of May Square) who have marched here every Thursday at 3:30 for nearly four decades. Housewives and mothers-turned-militant-activists, they demand justice for *los desaparecidos*—the people who were "disappeared" during the rise to power and reign of Argentina's dictatorial military government (1976–1983). Ⓜ *A to Plaza de Mayo; D to Catedral; E to Bolívar.*

Fodor'sChoice
★ **Teatro Colón.** Its magnitude, magnificent acoustics, and opulence earn the Teatro Colón (Colón Theater) a place among the world's top five opera theaters. An ever-changing stream of imported talent bolsters the well-regarded local lyric and ballet companies.

After an eventful 18-year building process involving the death of one architect and the murder of another, the sublime Italianate structure was finally inaugurated in 1908 with Verdi's *Aïda*. It has hosted the likes of Maria Callas, Richard Strauss, Arturo Toscanini, Igor Stravinsky, Enrico Caruso, and Luciano Pavarotti, who said that the Colón has only one flaw: the acoustics are so good that every mistake can be heard. The theater was closed in 2008 for controversial renovations which ran way over schedule and budget, but reopened on May 24, 2010, to coincide with Argentina's bicentenary celebrations. Much of the work done was structural, but its stone facade and interior trimmings are now scrubbed and gleaming.

The theater's sumptuous building materials—three kinds of Italian marble, French stained glass, and Venetian mosaics—were imported from Europe to create large-scale lavishness. The seven-tier main theater is breathtaking in size, and has a grand central chandelier with 700 lights to illuminate the 3,000 mere mortals in its red-velvet seats.

> **DID YOU KNOW?**
>
> Roughly 85% of the Argentine population is of European origin. Indeed, Buenos Aires locals refer to themselves as porteños because many of their forebears arrived by ship to this *port* town.

Nothing can prepare you for the thrill of seeing an opera or ballet here. The seasons run April through December, but many seats are reserved for season-ticket holders. Shorter options in the main theater include symphonic cycles by the stable orchestra as well as international orchestral visits. Chamber music concerts are held in the U-shape Salón Dorado (Golden Room), so named for the 24-karat goldleaf that covers its stucco molding. Underneath the main building is the ultra-minimal Centro Experimental, a tiny theater showcasing avant-garde music, opera, and dramatic performances.

You can see the splendor up close and get in on all the behind-the-scenes action with the theater's extremely popular guided tours. The whirlwind visits take you up and down innumerable staircases to rehearsal rooms and to the costume, shoe, and scenery workshops, before letting you gaze at the stage from a sought-after box. (Arrive at least a half hour before the tour you want to take starts, as they fill up very quickly.)

Buy tickets from the box office on Pasaje Toscanini. If seats are sold out—or beyond your pocket—you can buy 10-peso standing-room tickets on the day of the performance. These are for the lofty upper-tier *paraíso*, from which you can both see and hear perfectly, although three-hour-long operas are hard on the feet. ☒ *Main entrance: Libertad between Tucumán and Viamonte; box office: Pasaje Toscanini 1180, Centro* ☎ *11/4378–7100 for tickets, 11/4378–7127 for tours* ⊕ *www.teatrocolon.org.ar* ☒ *Guided tours 130 pesos* ☉ *Daily 9–5, tours every hr on the hr* Ⓜ *D to Tribunales.*

WORTH NOTING

Calle Florida. Nothing sums up the chaotic Microcentro better than this pedestrian axis, which has fallen from grace and risen from the ashes at least as many times as Argentina's economy. It's a riotous spot on weekdays, when throngs of office workers eager for a fast-food or high-street retail fix intermingle with buskers and street vendors who busily hawk souvenirs and haggle over leather goods. You can wander it in less than an hour: start at the intersection with Avenida de Mayo and a bench or patch of grass in shady **Plaza San Martín** will be your reward at the other end.

En route, lift your gaze from the brash shop fronts to take in the often noteworthy buildings that house them. At the ornate **Edificio Bank Boston** (No. 99) attention tends to focus on the battered, paint-splattered 4-ton bronze doors—unhappy customers have been taking out their

The Casa Rosada sits on the eastern end of Plaza de Mayo.

anger at *corralitos* (banks retaining their savings) since the economic crisis of 2001–02.

The restoration process at **Galería Güemes** has left the soaring marble columns and stained-glass cupola gleaming. The tacky shops that fill this historic arcade do nothing to lessen the wow factor. Witness Buenos Aires' often cavalier attitude to its architectural heritage at Florida's intersection with Avenida Corrientes, where the neo-Gothic **Palacio Elortondo-Alvear** is now home to Burger King. Buy a soda and drink it upstairs to check out the plaster molding and stained glass.

Milan's Galleria Vittorio Emanuele served as the model for **Galerías Pacífico,** designed during Buenos Aires' turn-of-the-20th-century golden age. Once the headquarters of the Buenos Aires–Pacific Railway, it's now a posh shopping mall and cultural center. Head to the central stairwell to see the allegorical murals painted by local greats Juan Carlos Castagnino, Antonio Berni, Cirilo Colmenio, Lino Spilimbergo, and Demetrio Urruchúa. The Centro Cultural Borges, which hosts small international exhibitions and musical events, is on the mezzanine level.

Past the slew of leather shops in the blocks north of Avenida Córdoba is **Plaza San Martín,** where you'll see a bronze statue of the namesake saint atop a rearing horse. It's overlooked by several opulent Italianate buildings and South America's tallest art deco structure, the **Edificio Kavanagh.** ⊠ *Microcentro* Ⓜ *A to Plaza de Mayo; D to Catedral; B to Florida (southern end); C to Plaza San Martín (northern end).*

Catedral Metropolitana. The columned neoclassical facade of the Metropolitan Cathedral makes it seem more like a temple than a church, and its history follows the pattern of many structures in the Plaza de

Mayo area. The first of six buildings on this site was a 16th-century adobe ranch house; the current structure dates from 1822, but has been added to several times.

There's been a surge of interest in it since February 2013, when Cardinal Jorge Bergoglio, then archbishop of Buenos Aires, was elected Pope Francis. The sanctuary now includes a small commemorative display of the pope's personal objects, watched over by a grinning life-size fiberglass statue of the pontiff in full regalia.

The embalmed remains of another local hero, General José de San Martín—known as the Liberator of Argentina for his role in the War of Independence—rest here in a marble mausoleum lighted by an eternal flame. Soldiers of the Grenadier Regiment, an elite troop created and trained by San Martín in 1811, permanently guard the tomb. Guided tours (in Spanish) of the mausoleum and crypt leave Monday to Saturday at 11:45 am. ⊠ *San Martín 27, at Rivadavía, Plaza de Mayo* 🕾 *11/4331–2845* ⊕ *www.catedralbuenosaires.org.ar* ▣ *Free* ⊘ *Weekdays 7–7, weekends 9–7:30* Ⓜ *A to Plaza de Mayo; D to Catedral; E to Bolívar.*

Centro Cultural Borges. There's something very low-key about this cultural center, despite its considerable size and prime location above the posh Galerías Pacífico mall. With a minimum of pomp and circumstance it has hosted exhibitions of Warhol, Kahlo and Rivera, Man Ray, Miró, Picasso, Chagall, and Dalí, as well as local greats Seguí, Berni, and Noé. Occasional mass shows focus on new local artists and art students. Small, independent theater and dance performances are also staged here. ⊠ *Viamonte 525, at San Martín, Centro* 🕾 *11/5555–5359* ⊕ *www.ccborges.org.ar* ▣ *30 pesos* ⊘ *Mon.–Sat. 10–9, Sun. noon–9* Ⓜ *B to Florida.*

Museo de Arte Hispanoamericano Isaac Fernández Blanco (*Isaac Fernández Blanco Hispanic-American Art Museum*). The distinctive Peruvian neocolonial-style Palacio Noel serves as the perfect backdrop for this colonial art and craft museum, which was built in 1920 as the residence of architect Martín Noel. He and museum founder Fernández Blanco donated most of the exquisite silver items, religious wood carvings, inlaid furnishings, and paintings from the Spanish colonial period that are on display. Guided tours in English can be arranged by calling ahead. Shaded benches in the lush walled gardens provide welcome respite for your feet, and the rustling leaves and birdcalls almost filter out the busy Retiro traffic noises. The museum is an easy five-block walk from Estación San Martín on Línea C: From there go west along Avenida Santa Fe and then turn right into Suipacha and continue four blocks. ⊠ *Suipacha 1422, at Av. Libertador, Retiro* 🕾 *11/4327–0228* ⊕ *www.museofernandezblanco.buenosaires.gob.ar* ▣ *5 pesos (free Tues. and Thurs.)* ⊘ *Tues.–Fri. 2–7, weekends 1–7* Ⓜ *C to San Martín.*

PUERTO MADERO

A forest of skyscrapers designed by big-name architects like Sir Norman Foster and César Pelli is sprouting up in Puerto Madero, a onetime port area that's now notable for its chic hotels, restaurants, and boutiques.

Original dockland structures have been repurposed: former grain silos now house luxury lodgings, and high-end cafés line the waterside walkways where cargo was once offloaded.

The neighborhood's upswing has even extended to the 865-acre Reserva Ecológica, a nature preserve built on land reclaimed from the river using rubble from major construction projects in the 1970s and '80s.

PLANNING YOUR TIME

Puerto Madero has a few sights, but the best reason to come here is a leisurely stroll along the waterfront. You might want to enjoy a morning excursion to Puerto Madero, then cross the Puente de la Mujer to spend your afternoon in El Centro.

TOP ATTRACTIONS

Colección de Arte Amalia Lacroze de Fortabat (Museo Fortabat). The late Amalia Fortabat was a cement heiress, so it's not surprising that the building containing her private art collection is made mostly of concrete. It was completed in 2003, but after-effects from Argentina's 2001–02 financial crisis delayed its opening until 2008. Amalita (as she was known locally) was closely involved in the design, and the personal touch continues into the collection, which includes several portraits of her—a prized Warhol among them—and many works by her granddaughter, Amalia Amoedo. In general, more money than taste seems to have gone into the project. The highlights are lesser works by big names both local (Berni, Xul Solar, Pettoruti) and international (Brueghel, Dalí, Picasso), hung with little aplomb or explanation in a huge basement gallery that echoes like a high-school gym. The side gallery given over to Carlos Alonso's and Juan Carlos Castagnino's figurative work is a step in the right direction, however. So are the luminous paintings by Soldi in the glass-wall upper gallery. They're rivaled by the view over the docks below—time your visit to end at sunset when pinks and oranges light the redbrick buildings opposite. Views from the dockside café come a close second. ⊠ *Olga Cossettini 141, Puerto Madero* ☎ *11/4310–6600* ⊕ *www.coleccionfortabat.org.ar* ⚏ *45 pesos* ⊙ *Tues.–Sun. noon–8* Ⓜ *B to L. N. Alem (13 blocks away).*

WORTH NOTING

Buque Museo Corbeta Uruguay (*Uruguay Corvette Ship Museum*). Bought from England in 1874, the oldest ship in the Argentine fleet has been around the world several times and was used in the nation's Antarctic campaigns at the turn of the 20th century. You can see what the captain's cabin and officers' mess looked like at that time; there are also displays of artifacts rescued from shipwrecks. A stroll around the decks affords views of the vessel and of Puerto Madero. ⊠ *Dique 4, Alicia M. de Justo 500-block, Puerto Madero* ☎ *11/4314–1090* ⊕ *www.ara.mil. ar/pag.asp?idItem=113* ⚏ *2 pesos* ⊙ *Daily 10–7* Ⓜ *B to L. N. Alem.*

Buque Museo Fragata A.R.A. Presidente Sarmiento (*President Sarmiento Frigate Museum*). The navy commissioned this frigate from England in 1898 to be used as an open-sea training vessel. The 280-foot boat used up to 33 sails and carried more than 300 crew members. The beautifully restored cabins include surprisingly luxurious officers' quarters that feature parquet floors, wood paneling, and leather armchairs; cadets had to make do with hammocks. ✉ *Dique 3, Alicia M. de Justo 980, Puerto Madero* ☏ *11/4334–9386* ⊕ *www.ara.mil.ar/pag.asp?idItem=112* 🎟 *2 pesos* ☉ *Daily 10–7* Ⓜ *B to L. N. Alem (9 blocks away).*

Puente de la Mujer. Tango dancers inspired the sweeping asymmetrical lines of Valencian architect Santiago Calatrava's design for the pedestrian-only Bridge of the Woman. Puerto Madero's street names pay homage to famous Argentine women, hence the bridge's name. (Ironically its most visible part—a soaring 128-foot arm—represents the man of a couple in mid-tango.) The $6 million structure was made in Spain and paid for by local businessmen Alberto L. González, one of the brains behind Puerto Madero's redevelopment; he also built the Hilton Hotel here. Twenty engines rotate the bridge to allow ships to pass through. ✉ *Dique 3, between Pierina Dealessi and Manuela Gorriti, Puerto Madero* Ⓜ *A to Plaza de Mayo; B to L. N. Alem; D to Catedral; E to Bolívar (all about 10 blocks away).*

Reserva Ecológica. Built over a landfill, the 865-acre Ecological Reserve is home to more than 500 species of birds and a variety of flora and fauna. On weekends thousands of porteños vie for a spot on the grass, so come midweek if you want to bird-watch and sunbathe in peace or use the jogging and cycling tracks. A monthly guided "Walking under the Full Moon" tour in Spanish begins at 7:30 pm April through October and at 8:30 pm November through March. Even if you don't speak Spanish it's still a great way to get back to nature at night; otherwise avoid the area after sunset. The main entrance and visitor center is across from the traffic circle where Avenida Tristán Achával Rodríguez intersects with Avenida Elvira Rawson de Dellepiane, a short walk from the south end of Puerto Madero; you can also enter and leave the reserve at its northern end, across from the intersection of Mariquita Sánchez de Thompson and Avenida Hernán M. Giralt. ✉ *Av. Tristán Achával Rodríguez 1550, Puerto Madero* ☏ *11/4315–4129, 11/4893–1853 for tours* ⊕ *www.buenosaires.gov.ar/areas/med_ambiente/reserva* 🎟 *Free* ☉ *Apr.–Oct., Tues.–Sun. 8–6; Nov.–Mar., Tues.–Sun. 8–7; guided visits in Spanish weekends at 10:30 and 3:30.*

SAN TELMO AND LA BOCA

Sightseeing
★★★★

Dining
★★★

Lodging
★★★★

Shopping
★★★★

Nightlife
★★★

"The south also exists," quip residents of bohemian neighborhoods like San Telmo and La Boca, which historically played second fiddle to posher northern barrios. No more. The hottest designers have boutiques here, new restaurants are booked out, an art district is burgeoning, and property prices are soaring. The south is also the linchpin of the city's tango revival, appropriate given that the dance was born in these quarters.

SAN TELMO

San Telmo, Buenos Aires' first suburb, was originally inhabited by sailors, and takes its name from their wandering patron saint. All the same, the mariners' main preoccupations were clearly less than spiritual, and San Telmo became famous for its brothels.

That didn't stop the area's first experience of gentrification: wealthy local families built ornate homes here in the early 19th century, but ran for Recoleta when a yellow-fever epidemic struck in 1871. Newly arrived immigrants crammed into their abandoned mansions, known as *conventillos* (tenement houses). Today these same houses are fought over by foreign buyers dying to ride the wave of urban renewal—the *reciclaje* (recycling), as porteños call it—that's sweeping the area and transforming San Telmo into Buenos Aires' hippest 'hood.

Although San Telmo does have its share of sites, the barrio itself is the big attraction. Simply watching the world go by as you linger over coffee is one quintessential experience. Soaking up some history by wandering down cobbled streets edged with Italianate townhouses is another. You can get closer to the past at two small museums, or even take a piece of it home from the shops and stands selling antiques and

Caminito, the main pedestrian street in La Boca

curios. However, there's plenty of contemporary culture on offer in the neighborhood's art museums, cutting-edge galleries, and bars.

PLANNING YOUR TIME

San Telmo thrives on Sunday, thanks to the art and antiques market in Plaza Dorrego. During the week a leisurely afternoon's visit is ideal. Start with lunch in a café at the northern or southern end of San Telmo, then spend an hour or two wandering the cobbled streets. You still have time for some shopping before winding up with a coffee or a drink.

TOP ATTRACTIONS

Fodor's Choice
★

El Zanjón de Granados. All of Buenos Aires' history is packed into this unusual house. The street it's on was once a small river—the *zanjón*, or gorge, of the property's name—where the first, unsuccessful attempt to found Buenos Aires took place in 1536. When the property's current owner decided to develop what was then a run-down conventillo, he began to discover all sorts of things beneath it: pottery and cutlery, the foundations of past constructions, and a 500-foot network of tunnels that has taken over 20 years to excavate. These were once used to channel water, but like the street itself, they were sealed after San Telmo's yellow-fever outbreaks. With the help of historians and architects, they've now been painstakingly restored, and the entire site has been transformed into a private museum, where the only exhibit is the redbrick building itself. Excellent hour-long guided tours in English and Spanish take you through low-lighted sections of the tunnels. The history lesson then continues aboveground, where you can see the surviving wall of a construction from 1740, the 19th-century mansion built around it, and traces of the conventillo it became. Expect few visitors

and plenty of atmosphere on weekdays; cheaper, shorter tou
day draw far more people. If you want to spend even more ti.
you can rent the whole place (including an adjacent building reach
the tunnels) for functions. ⊠ *Defensa 755, San Telmo* ☎ *11/4361–3*
⊕ *www.elzanjon.com.ar* ✉ *Guided tours weekdays 120 pesos (1 hr),
Sun. 75 pesos (30 mins)* ⊘ *English tours weekdays at 12, 2 and 3, Sun.
1–6 every 30 mins. Closed Sat.* Ⓜ *C or E to Independencia.*

Museo de Arte Moderno de Buenos Aires (MAMBA) (*Museum of Modern
Art of Buenos Aires*). Some 7,000 contemporary artworks make up
the permanent collection at this newly renovated, block-long museum.
Formerly the site of a tobacco company, the MAMBA retains its original exposed-brick facade and fabulous wooden doors with wrought-
iron fixtures. Inside, galleries showcasing a carefully curated selection
of paintings, sculptures, and new media are complemented by large
temporary exhibitions of local or Latin American works as well as
smaller installations. Recent highlights include the unusual portraits of
superstar collective Grupo Mondongo, who eschew paint in favor of
materials like crackers, sliced ham, and chewing gum. ⊠ *Av. San Juan
350, San Telmo* ☎ *11/4341–3001* ⊕ *www.museos.buenosaires.gob.ar/
mam.htm* ✉ *10 pesos (free Tues. and Thurs.)* ⊘ *Tues.–Fri. 11–7, weekends 11–8* Ⓜ *C to San Juan.*

Pasaje de la Defensa. Wandering through this well-preserved house
affords a glimpse of life in San Telmo's golden era. Behind an elegant but
narrow stone facade, the building extends deep into the block around
a series of internal courtyards. This type of elongated construction—
known as a *casa chorizo* or "sausage house"—is typical of San Telmo.
Once the private residence of the well-to-do Ezeiza family, it became a
conventillo (tenement), but is now a picturesque spot for antiques and
curio shopping. The stores here are open from 10 to 6 daily. ⊠ *Defensa
1179, San Telmo* Ⓜ *C to San Juan.*

Plaza Dorrego. During the week a handful of craftspeople and a few
scruffy pigeons are the only ones enjoying the shade from the stately
trees in the city's second-oldest square. Sunday couldn't be more different: scores of stalls selling antiques, collectibles, and just plain old stuff
move in to form the Feria de San Pedro Telmo (San Pedro Telmo Fair).
Tango dancers take to the cobbles, as do hundreds of shoppers (mostly
tourists) browsing the tango memorabilia, antique silver, brass, crystal,
and Argentine curios. Note that prices are high at stalls on the square
and astronomical in the shops surrounding it, and vendors are immune
to bargaining. ⚠ **Pickpockets work as hard as stall owners on Sundays,
so keep a firm hold on bags and purses or—wiser still—leave them at
home.** More affordable offerings—mostly handicrafts and local artists'
work—are on the ever-growing web of stalls along nearby streets like
Defensa. ■ **TIP➔ Be on the lookout for antique glass soda siphons that
once adorned every bar top in Buenos Aires. Classic colors are green
and turquoise.** Be sure to look up as you wander Plaza Dorrego, as the
surrounding architecture provides an overview of the influences—Spanish colonial, French classical, and ornate Italian masonry—that shaped
the city in the 19th and 20th centuries. ⊠ *Defensa and Humberto I, San
Telmo* Ⓜ *C to San Juan.*

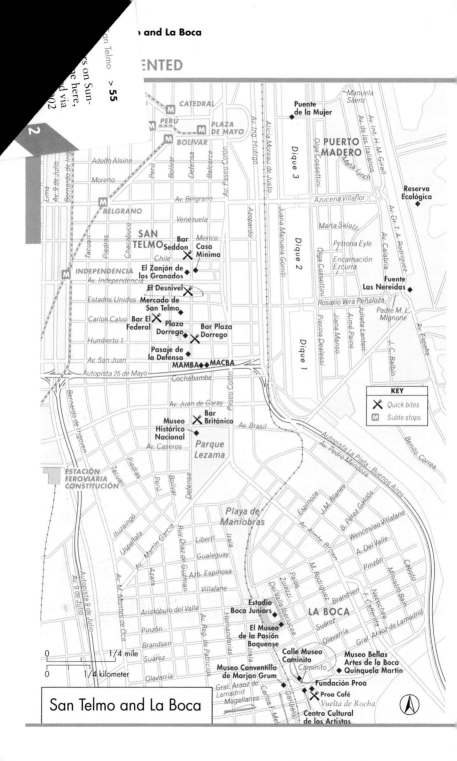

San Telmo and La Boca

THE TERRITORY

San Telmo, south of the Centro, is bordered by Avenida Madero to the east, Avenidas Brasil and Caseros to the south, Piedras to the west, and—depending on whom you ask—Chile or Belgrano to the north. The main drag is north–south Defensa, part of which is pedestrian-only. It forms one side of Plaza Dorrego, the area's tourist hub.

South of Avenida Brasil lies La Boca, whose westernmost edge is Avenida Patricios. The Riachuelo River forms a curving border; Avenida Don Pedro de Mendoza runs beside it.

GETTING AROUND

The subte takes you within about half a mile of San Telmo. The closest stations to the southern end are Independencia (Línea C or E) and San Juan (Línea C). Be prepared to walk nine blocks east along Avenidas Independencia, Estados Unidos, or San Juan to get to Defensa, the main street. To approach San Telmo from the north, get off at Bolívar (Línea E) or Catedral (Línea D) and walk eight blocks south along Bolívar. Buses nos. 17, 24, 28, and 59 connect San Telmo to Centro; No. 24 also stops in Almagro, while nos. 17 and 59 stop in Recoleta and Palermo. A taxi from Centro costs around 20 pesos.

There's no subte to La Boca, so taxi travel is a good bet, especially after dark: expect to pay 40–50 pesos to or from Centro.

SAFETY AND PRECAUTIONS

San Telmo's popularity with visitors has led to increased police presence in the busiest areas (especially near Defensa). Still, instances of petty crime are common. After dark, stick to busy, well-lighted streets close to Defensa.

La Boca is far sketchier, and you'd do best not to stray from the Caminito area. Avoid the neighborhood after dark; take radio taxis if you must visit then.

TOP EXPERIENCES

Photographing: cobbled streets and stunning facades, then comparing your work with that of the pros at the MAMBA or Fundación Proa.

Descending: into El Zanjón de Granados's restored tunnels for a different perspective.

Drinking: in the atmosphere—and a cortado—at a time-honored café like La Perla.

Wandering: Caminito (and adjacent Garibaldi and Magallanes), to tick the sightseeing boxes, or Defensa to cruise the boutiques and Sunday antiques stalls.

QUICK BITES

El Desnivel. At this classic *parrilla* (grill) the trimmings don't go beyond a mixed salad and fries, and surly waiters virtually fling food at you—but it's all part of the experience. ⊠ *Defensa 855, San Telmo* ☎ *11/4300–9081* ⊕ *www.parrillaeldesnivel.com. ar* ⊗ *Mon. 7 pm–1 am, Tues.–Sun. noon–1 am* Ⓜ *C or E to Independencia.*

La Perla. Right opposite Caminito, this colorful old-time café is *the* place for a *licuado* (milk shake) or *tostado mixto* (a local take on the croque-monsieur). ⊠ *Av. Pedro de Mendoza 1899, La Boca* ☎ *11/4301–2985* ⊗ *Daily 7 am–8 pm.*

SAN TELMO'S TRADITIONAL BARS

Get a taste of traditional San Telmo life at the worn wooden tables of its vintage bars (most are open from breakfast right through to the wee hours).

Bar Británico. When they tried to shut down ultravintage Bar Británico, the whole city rallied to its defense. Rub elbows with bohemian students and wizened old-timers as you perk up with a *cortado* (espresso "cut" with a dash of milk) or unwind with a *ginebra* (ginlike spirit). The area can be sketchy, so it's best to grab a cab. ⊠ *Brasil 399, at Defensa, San Telmo* ☎ *11/4361–2107* ⊙ *Mon. 8 am–midnight, Tues.–Sun. 24 hrs* Ⓜ *C to San Juan.*

Bar Plaza Dorrego. Wood-paneled, dust-festooned Bar Plaza Dorrego is right on San Telmo's main square. Sip your *cafecito* (espresso) or icy beer at one of its window tables for some prime people-watching, all the while shelling your pile of peanuts. ⊠ *Defensa 1098, at Humberto I, San Telmo* ☎ *11/4361–0141* ⊙ *Sun.– Thurs. 8 am–1 am, Fri. and Sat. 8 am–5 am* Ⓜ *C or E to Indepencia.*

Bar Seddon. Tango musicians often perform at Bar Seddon, an otherwise quiet bar with a beautiful checkered floor and old-fashioned cash register. ⊠ *Defensa 695, at Chile, San Telmo* ☎ *11/4342–3700* ⊕ *www.barseddon. com.ar* ⊙ *Sun.–Thurs. 10 am–3 am, Fri. and Sat. 10 am–5:30 am* Ⓜ *C or E to Independencia.*

El Federal. Regulars insist that the *picadas* (snacks such as cold cuts and bread) at El Federal are some of the best in town—and you can linger over them for hours, no questions asked. ⊠ *Carlos Calvo 599, at Perú, San Telmo* ☎ *11/4300–4313* ⊕ *www. elfederalrestaurante.com* ⊙ *Mon.– Sat. 10 am–midnight* Ⓜ *C or E to Independencia.*

WORTH NOTING

Museo de Arte Contemporáneo de Buenos Aires (MACBA). Geometric abstraction is the guiding principle for both the collection and the construction of Buenos Aires' newest museum. Sharply sloped walkways connect four floors of concrete-walled galleries, creating an austere backdrop for the bright lines and shapes of local financier Aldo Rubin's private collection. Regularly changing exhibitions may include pieces by contemporary local stars like Pablo Siquier and Guillermo Kuitca. ⊠ *Av. San Juan 328, San Telmo* ☎ *11/5299–2010* ⊕ *www.macba.com.ar* ▭ *25 pesos (15 pesos Wed.)* ⊙ *Mon. and Wed.–Fri. noon–7, weekends 11–7:30* Ⓜ *C to San Juan.*

Museo Histórico Nacional. What better place for the National History Museum than overlooking the spot where the city was supposedly founded? Once owned by entrepreneur and horticulturalist Gregorio Lezama, the beautiful chestnut-and-white Italianate mansion that houses it later did duty as a quarantine station during the San Telmo cholera and yellow-fever epidemics before morphing into a museum in 1897. Due to ongoing renovation work, much of the building remains closed at the time of writing; three rooms, however, reopened to the public in 2013. Personal possessions and thoughtful explanations (in Spanish) chronicle the rise and fall of Argentina's liberator José de San

Martín. Other galleries celebrate the heroes of independence and foreign forces' unsuccessful attempts to invade Argentina. ⊠ *Calle Defensa 1600, San Telmo* ☎ *11/4307–1182* ⊕ *www.cultura.gob.ar/museos/museo-historico-nacional* 🎫 *10 pesos* ⊙ *Wed.–Sun. 11–6.*

LA BOCA

Although La Boca is more touristy, it shares much of San Telmo's gritty history. La Boca sits on the fiercely polluted—and thus fiercely smelly—Riachuelo River, where rusting ships and warehouses remind you that this was once the city's main port. The immigrants who first settled here built their houses from corrugated metal and brightly colored paint left over from the shipyards. Today you'll see imitations of these vibrant buildings forming one of Buenos Aires' most emblematic sights, the Caminito.

The waterfront near the iconic Caminito area may be the most unashamedly touristy part of town, but the neighborhood surrounding it is the most fiercely traditional. Cafés, pubs, and general stores that once catered to passing sailors (and now reel in vacationers) dot the partially renovated area. For high-brow hipsters, the gallery of the Fundación Proa is the main draw.

Two quite different colors have made La Boca famous internationally: the blue and gold of the Boca Juniors soccer team, whose massive home stadium is the barrio's unofficial hub. For many local soccer devotees, the towering Boca Juniors stadium makes La Boca the center of the known world.

PLANNING YOUR TIME

In La Boca, allow two or three hours to explore Caminito and do a museum or two. It's busy all week, but expect extra crowds on weekends.

TOP ATTRACTIONS

Calle Museo Caminito.

See the highlighted listing in this chapter.

Fundación Proa. For more than a decade, this thoroughly modern art museum has been nudging traditional La Boca into the present. After major renovation work, its facade alone reads like a manifesto of local urban renewal: part of the original 19th-century Italianate housefront has been cut away, and huge plate-glass windows accented by unfinished steel stand alongside it. The space behind them now includes three adjacent properties. The luminous main gallery retains the building's original Corinthian-style steel columns, artfully rusted, but has sparkling white walls and polished concrete floors. With every flight of stairs you climb, views out over the harbor and cast-iron bridges get better. On the first floor, you can browse through one of Buenos Aires' best art bookshops (it has a particularly strong collection of local artists' books and photography tomes displayed on trestle tables). On the roof, an airy café serves salads, sandwiches, and cocktails. Bag one of the outdoor sofas around sunset and your photos will rival the work below. English versions of all exhibition information are available. The

CALLE MUSEO CAMINITO

✉ *Caminito between Av. Pedro de Mendoza (La Vuelta de Rocha promenade) and Gregorio Aráoz de Lamadrid, La Boca* 🎫 *Free* ☉ *Daily 10–6.*

TIPS AND TRIVIA

■ "Caminito" comes from a 1926 tango by Juan de Dios Filiberto, who is said to have composed it while thinking of a girl leaning from the balcony of a ramshackle house like those here. It was chosen by local artist Benito Quinquela Martín, who helped establish the street as an open-air museum.

■ Expect to be canvassed aggressively by rival restaurant owners touting overpriced, touristy menus near the start of Caminito and along every other side street. Each restaurant has its own outdoor stage—competing troupes of stamping gauchos make meals a noisy affair. The best tactic to get by them is to accept their leaflets with a serene smile and "gracias."

■ The Caminito concept spills over into nearby streets Garibaldi and Magallanes, which form a triangle with it. The strange, foot-high sidewalks along streets like Magallanes, designed to prevent flooding, show how the river's proximity has shaped the barrio.

Cobblestones, tango dancers, and haphazardly constructed, colorful conventillos have made Calle Museo Caminito the darling of Buenos Aires' postcard manufacturers since this pedestrian street was created in 1959. Artists fill the block-long street with works depicting port life and the tango, which is said to have been born in La Boca. These days it's painfully commercial, and seems more a parody of porteño culture than anything else, but if you're willing to embrace the out-and-out tackiness it can make a fun outing.

Highlights

Conventillos. Many of La Boca's tenements are now souvenir stores. The plastic Che Guevaras and dancing couples make the shops in the Centro Cultural de los Artistas (*Magallanes 861 Mon.–Sat. 10:30–6*) as forgettable as all the others on the street, but the uneven stairs and wrought-iron balcony hint at what a conventillo interior was like. You get a clearer vision at the Museo Conventillo de Marjan Grum (*Garibaldi 1429 30 pesos 11/4302–2472 Daily 10:30–5:30*), which the eponymous sculptor-owner has converted into an art gallery.

Local art. Painters, photographers, and sculptors peddle their creations from stalls along Caminito. Quality varies considerably; if nothing tempts you, focus on the small mosaics set into the walls, such as Luis Perlotti's *Santos Vega*. Another local art form, the brightly colored scrollwork known as *fileteado*, adorns many shop and restaurant fronts near Caminito.

Tangueros. Competition is fierce among the sultry dancers dressed in split skirts and fishnets. True, they spend more time trying to entice you into photo ops than actually dancing, but linger long enough (and throw a big enough contribution in the fedora) and you'll see some fancy footwork.

museum also runs guided tours in English, with two days' notice. ⊠ *Av. Pedro de Mendoza 1929, La Boca* ☎ *11/4104–1000* ⊕ *www.proa.org* 🎫 *20 pesos (free Tues.)* ☉ *Tues.–Sun. 11–7.*

Museo de la Pasión Boquense. Inside Estadio Boca Juniors (aka La Bombonera), this modern, two-floor museum is heaven for fútbol fans. It chronicles Boca's rise from a neighborhood club in 1905 to its current position as one of the best teams in the world. Among the innovative exhibits is a giant soccer ball that plays 360-degree footage of an adrenaline-fueled match, recreating all the excitement (and the screaming) for those too faint-hearted to attend the real thing. Jerseys, trophies, and more are also on display. A huge mural of Maradona (the team's most revered player) and a hall of fame complete the rest of the circuit. Everything you need to Boca up your life—from official team tees to bed linens, school folders to G-strings—is available in the on-site gift store (shops and stalls outside La Bombonera sell cheaper copies). For the full-blown experience, buy a combo ticket that includes museum entry plus an extensive tour of the beloved "Candy Box" stadium. ⊠ *Brandsen 805, La Boca* ☎ *11/4362–1100* ⊕ *www.museoboquense. com* 🎫 *65 pesos, 80 pesos with stadium tour* ☉ *Daily 10–6.*

2

RECOLETA AND ALMAGRO

Sightseeing
★★★★★
Dining
★★★
Lodging
★★★★
Shopping
★★★★
Nightlife
★★

For Buenos Aires' most illustrious families, Recoleta's boundaries are the boundaries of the civilized world. The local equivalents of the Vanderbilts are baptized and married in the Basílica del Pilar, throw parties in the Alvear Palace Hotel, live in spacious 19th-century apartments nearby, and wouldn't dream of shopping anywhere but Avenidas Quintana and Alvear. Ornate mausoleums in the Cementerio de la Recoleta promise an equally stylish afterlife. In nearby Almagro, the spirit of tango legend Carlos Gardel, whose former home has been turned into a museum, lives on in the tango performance venues scattered through the otherwise residential area.

RECOLETA

Recoleta wasn't always synonymous with elegance. Colonists, including city founder Juan de Garay, farmed here. So did the Franciscan Recoleto friars, whose 1700s settlement here inspired the district's name. Their church, the Basílica del Pilar, was almost on the riverbank then: tanneries grew up around it, and Recoleta became famous for its *pulperías* (taverns) and brothels. Everything changed, though, with the 1871 outbreak of yellow fever in the south of the city.

The elite swarmed to Recoleta, building the *palacios* and stately Parisian-style apartment buildings that are now the neighborhood's trademark. They also laid the foundations for Recoleta's concentration of intellectual and cultural activity: the Biblioteca Nacional (National Library), a plethora of top-notch galleries, and three publicly run art

museums are based here. Combine all of that with Recolet
boutiques and its beautiful parks and squares—many filled
pooches and their walkers—and sightseeing becomes a visual fe
unofficial subdistrict, Barrio Norte, is one step south of Recoleta pr
and one small step down the social ladder. Shopping is the draw: loc
chains, sportswear flagships, and minimalls of vintage clothing and
clubwear line Avenida Santa Fe between 9 de Julio and Puerreydón.

PLANNING YOUR TIME

Despite the luxury around you, many of Recoleta's sights are free. Blitz
through the main ones in half a day, or spend a full morning or afternoon in the cemetery or museums alone. Come at midweek for quiet
exploring, or on the weekend to do the cemetery and crafts market on
Plaza Francia in one fell swoop.

TOP ATTRACTIONS

Fodor's Choice   **Cementerio de la Recoleta.**
★   *See the highlighted listing in this chapter.*

Feria de Artesanos de Plaza Francia (*Feria de Plaza Francia*). On weekends
artisans' stalls line the small park outside Recoleta Cemetery, forming
the open-air market known as La Feria de Artesanos de Plaza Francia.
It's usually teeming with shoppers eager to stock up on quality crafts—
including leather goods, pottery, table linens, and other textiles, plus
lovely pieces of handmade jewelry. Although the market officially opens
at 11, many stalls aren't properly set up until after 1. ⊠ *Pl. Francia, at
avs. Libertador and Pueyrredón, Recoleta ⊕ www.feriaplazafrancia.
com ⊙ Weekends 11–8.*

Floralis Genérica. The gleaming steel and aluminum petals of this giant
flower look very space age, perhaps because they were commissioned
from the Lockheed airplane factory by architect Eduardo Catalano,
who designed and paid for the monument. The 66-foot-high structure
is supposed to open at dawn and close at dusk, when the setting sun
turns its mirrored surfaces a glowing pink. It's been stuck in open mode
for several years due to a faulty petal that no one can afford to fix, but
even static it seems stylish. The flower stands in the Plaza Naciones Unidas (behind El Museo Nacional de Bellas Artes over Avenida Figueroa
Alcorta), which was remodeled to accommodate it. ⊠ *Pl. Naciones Unidas, at avs. Figueroa Alcorta and J. A. Biblioni, Recoleta ⊙ Dawn–dusk.*

Museo Nacional de Arte Decorativo. The harmonious, French neoclassical
mansion that houses the National Museum of Decorative Art is as much
a reason to visit as the period furnishings, porcelain, and silver within it.
Ornate wooden paneling in the Regency ballroom, the imposing Louis
XIV red-and-black-marble dining room, and a lofty Renaissance-style
great hall are some of the highlights in the only home of its kind open to
the public here. There are excellent English descriptions of each room,
and they include gossipy details about the original inhabitants, the well-
to-do Errázuriz-Alvear family. The museum also contains some Chinese
art. Guided tours include the Zubov Collection of miniatures from
Imperial Russia. ⊠ *Av. del Libertador 1902, Recoleta ☎ 11/4801–8248
⊕ www.mnad.org ☞ 15 pesos (free Tues.), guided tours in English 15
pesos ⊙ Jan., Tues.–Sat. 2–7; Feb.–Dec., Tues.–Sun. 2–7.*

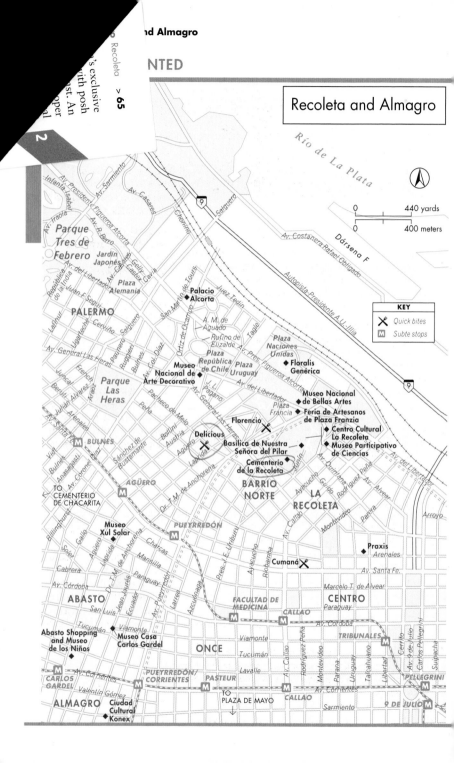

THE TERRITORY

The River Plate borders Recoleta to the north. Uruguay and Montevideo join to form the eastern border; the jagged western edge is made up of Mario Bravo, Coronel Díaz, and Tagle. The area between Juncal and Córdoba—Recoleta's southern boundary—is known as Barrio Norte, whose main thoroughfare is Santa Fe. In Recoleta proper, Avenidas Alvear and Quintana are the key streets.

Almagro is officially bordered by Avenidas Córdoba and Estado de Israel to the north, Río de Janeiro to the west, Independencia to the south, and Sánchez de Bustamente and Gallo to the east. The Abasto subdistrict, which centers on Gallo and Corrientes, stretches a few blocks farther east into neighboring Balvanera.

GETTING AROUND

True to its elite roots, Recoleta has no subway, so taxis are your best option. Expect to pay around 30 pesos from downtown or 40 from Palermo. Bus nos. 17 and 59 run to Recoleta from Palermo, San Telmo, and Centro; No. 92 connects Retiro and Recoleta, then continues to central Palermo and Almagro.

Heavy traffic means Almagro is best reached by subte. Línea B runs along Avenida Corrientes through Almagro; Carlos Gardel station leads right into the Abasto mall. Bus No. 24 connects Almagro with Centro and San Telmo; No. 168 goes west to Palermo Viejo.

SAFETY AND PRECAUTIONS

Recoleta and Barrio Norte are relatively safe in the daytime, but stick to well-lighted streets at night. Bag snatching is opportunist rather than systematic here: keep a firm grip on your purse in the crowded weekend market and in busy restaurants. Although Almagro is on the upswing, wander with caution.

TOP EXPERIENCES

Admiring: the to-die-for tombs in Cementerio de la Recoleta, one of the world's most beautiful burial grounds.

Window-shopping: on Avenida Quintana for haute designs and finding bargains on Avenida Santa Fe.

Comparing: 19th-century Argentine and European art on the first floor of the Museo Nacional de Bellas Artes.

Wandering: along Avenida Alvear to ogle the gorgeous late-19th- and early-20th-century mansions.

QUICK BITES

Cumaná. The hearty stews, steaks, and empanadas at chaotic Cumaná are a far cry from Recoleta's European pretensions. Skip dessert, though (nearby ice-creameries are better). ⊠ *Rodríguez Peña 1149, Barrio Norte* 🖀 *11/4813-9207* 🕓 *Daily noon–12:30 am* Ⓜ *D to Callao.*

Delicious. It's a hard name to live up to, but there's no doubt this casual café pulls it off. Delicious does super fresh sandwiches, salads, and smoothies. ⊠ *Laprida 2015, Recoleta* 🖀 *11/4803-1151* ⊕ *www.deliciouscafe.com.ar* 🕓 *Tues.–Fri. 9–8, weekends 10–8* Ⓜ *D to Agüero.*

CEMENTERIO DE LA RECOLETA

✉ *Junín 1760, Recoleta*
☎ *11/4803–1594* 🔖 *Free*
🕐 *Daily 7–6.*

TIPS AND TRIVIA

■ The city government runs free guided visits to the cemetery in English on Tuesday and Thursday at 11; visits in Spanish operate Tuesday through Sunday at 9:30, 11, 2, and 4. Groups gather at the entrance.

■ If you prefer an independent tour, the administrative offices at the entrance can usually provide a free photocopied map, and caretakers throughout the grounds can help you locate the more intriguing tombs. These are also labeled on a large map at the entrance.

■ It's easy to get lost in the cemetery, so start your independent tour well before closing time.

■ Look out for such intriguing statues such as the life-size likeness of boxer Luis Angel Firpo, who lost the world heavyweight title to Jack Dempsey in 1923. It stands on guard outside his tomb at the back of the cemetery, wearing a robe and boxing boots.

■ The cemetery had its blessing withdrawn by the Catholic Church in 1863, when President Bartolomé Mitre ordered that a suicide be buried there.

The ominous gates, Doric-columned portico, and labyrinthine paths of the city's oldest cemetery may leave you with a sense of foreboding. Founded in 1822, it's the final resting place for the nation's most illustrious figures, and covers 13½ acres that are rumored to be the most expensive real estate in town. The cemetery has more than 6,400 elaborate vaulted tombs and majestic mausoleums, 70 of which have been declared historic monuments. The mausoleums resemble chapels, Greek temples, pyramids, and miniature mansions.

Highlights

Evita. The embalmed remains of Eva Duarte de Perón, who made it (almost intact) here after 17 years of posthumous wandering, are in the Duarte family vault. Around July 26, the anniversary of her death, flowers pile up here.

Late Greats. If the tomb of brutal *caudillo* (dictator) Facundo Quiroga looks small, it's because he's buried standing—a sign of valor—at his request. Prominent landowner Dorrego Ortíz Basualdo resides in Recoleta's most monumental sepulchre, complete with chandelier. The names of many key players in Argentina's history are chiseled over other sumptuous mausoleums: Alvear, Quintana, Sáenz Peña, Lavalle, Sarmiento.

Spooky Stories. Rufina Cambaceres is known as the girl who died twice. She was thought dead after suffering a cataleptic attack, and was entombed on her 19th birthday in 1902. Rufina awoke inside her casket and clawed the top open but died of a heart attack before she could be rescued. When Alfredo Gath heard of Rufina's story, he was appalled and commissioned a special mechanical coffin with an opening device and alarm bell. Gath successfully tested the coffin in situ 12 times, but on the 13th the mechanism failed and he died inside.

Ce[...]
la[...]

Azcuénaga

Vicente López

Guido

[...]deyrredón

Luis Ángel Firpo ◆

Roque
Sáenz Peña ◆

Juan Lavalle ◆

Evita ◆

Dorrego Ortiz
Basualde ◆

Domingo
Faustino
Sarmiento ◆

Rufina
Cambaceres ◆

Vicente López

Nuestra
Señora
de Pilar

Facundo Quiroga ◆

Carlos M. de Alvear ◆

Office

Capilla

Administration

Junín

ENTRANCE

Junín

Plaza Intendente
Torcuato de Alvear

Guido

Pres. Roberto M. Ortiz

Av. Alvear

Ayacucho

| 0 | | 50 yards |
| 0 | | 50 meters |

Recoleta Cemetery is a good place for a rest, whether eternal or momentary.

Fodor's Choice **Museo Nacional de Bellas Artes.**

★ *See the highlighted listing in this chapter.*

WORTH NOTING

Basílica de Nuestra Señora del Pilar. This basilica beside the famous Cementerio de la Recoleta is where Buenos Aires' elite families hold weddings and other ceremonies. Built by the Recoleto friars in 1732, it is considered a national treasure for its six German baroque–style altars. The central one is overlaid with Peruvian engraved silver; another, sent by Spain's King Carlos III, contains relics. The basilica's cloisters house the **Museo de los Claustros del Pilar,** a small museum that displays religious artifacts as well as pictures and photographs documenting Recoleta's evolution. There are excellent views of the cemetery from upstairs windows. ⊠ *Junín 1904, Recoleta* ☎ *11/4806–2209* ⊕ *www. basilicadelpilar.org.ar* 🎟 *Basílica free, museum 8 pesos* ⊗ *Basílica daily 9–9:30; museum Mon.–Sat. 10:30–6:30, Sun. 2:30–6:10.*

Centro Cultural La Recoleta. Art exhibitions, concerts, fringe theater performances, and workshops are some of the offerings at this cultural center. The rambling building it occupies was converted from the cloister patios of the Franciscan monks. ⊠ *Junín 1930, Recoleta* ☎ *11/4803–1040* ⊕ *www.centroculturalrecoleta.org* ⊗ *Tues.–Fri. 1–8, weekends 11–8.*

FAMILY **Museo Participativo de Ciencias.** The motto of this mini science museum inside the Centro Cultural La Recoleta is *"Prohibido No Tocar"* ("Not Touching Is Forbidden"), which says it all. Ten hands-on rooms aim to teach kids how things like electricity, music, light, and computers work through thoughtful interactive displays that include giant musical

MUSEO NACIONAL DE BELLAS ARTES

✉ *Av. del Libertador 1473,*
Recoleta ☎ *11/5288–9900*
⊕ *www.mnba.gob.ar* 🎫 *Free*
⊙ *Tues.–Fri. 12:30–8:30,*
weekends 9:30–8:30.

TIPS AND TRIVIA

■ Information about most works is in Spanish only; free one-hour guided visits in English are offered Tuesday, Thursday, and Friday at 12:30, and Saturday at 2. Alternately, you can rent an MP3 audio guide (50 pesos) or purchase a printed guide (30 pesos); collection maps may be downloaded for free on the museum website.

■ You wouldn't know it by looking at the museum's elegant columned front, but the building was once the city's waterworks. Famed local architect Alejandro Bustillo oversaw its conversion into a museum in the early 1930s.

■ The museum owns more than 11,000 works, but restricted space means only 10% of them are ever on display.

■ The large modern pavilion behind the museum hosts excellent temporary exhibitions, often showcasing top local artists little known outside Argentina.

The world's largest collection of Argentine art is contained in this neoclassical wine-color building. It also houses many lesser works by big-name European artists from the 12th through 20th century and hosts several high-profile temporary exhibitions per year.

Since 2010, alternating parts of the museum have been shut for renovation. At this writing, the European collection and 19th-century Argentine works are on display in the 24 ground-floor galleries; the upper floor, currently closed, will eventually hold the 20th-century collection.

Highlights

War and peace. Cándido López painted the panoramic battle scenes with his left hand after losing his right arm in the 1870s during the War of the Triple Alliance. His work spearheaded contemporary primitive painting and is showcased in Gallery 23. Local master Eduardo Sívori's tranquil landscapes (in Gallery 24) portray less turbulent times.

European masters. A whole room (Gallery 8) is given over to Goya's dark, disturbing works. Nearby are minor works by El Greco, Rubens, Tiepolo, Titian, and Zurbarán. The room behind the entrance hall (Gallery 10) contains Rodin sculptures. The right wing includes paintings by Manet, Degas, Monet, Pissarro, Gaugin, and Toulouse-Lautrec.

instruments and DIY whirlpools. Explanations are entirely in Spanish, so your little ones may not get the full educational experience, but there's so much to touch and try that they probably won't mind. ⊠ *Centro Cultural La Recoleta, Junín 1930, Recoleta* ☎ *11/4807–3260* ⊕ *www.mpc.org.ar* ✉ *50 pesos* ⊙ *Jan. and Feb., daily 3:30–7:30; Mar.–Dec., Tues.–Fri. 10–5, weekends 3:30–7:30; school holidays (approx. last 2 wks of July.), Tues.–Fri. 12:30–7:30, weekends 3:30–7:30.*

ALMAGRO

Almagro lies southwest of Recoleta but feels like a different world. Traditionally a gritty, working-class neighborhood, it spawned many tango greats, including the legendary Carlos Gardel. The Abasto subdistrict has long been the heart of the barrio: it centers on the massive art deco building (at Corrientes and Agüero) that was once the city's central market. The abandoned structure was completely overhauled and reopened in 1998 as a major mall, spearheading the redevelopment of the area, which now has several top hotels and an increasing number of restaurants and tango venues. More urban renewal is taking place a few blocks away at Sarmiento and Jean Jaurés, where the Konex Foundation has transformed an old factory into a cutting-edge cultural venue.

PLANNING YOUR TIME

In Almagro a couple of hours will suffice if you want to pay homage to Carlos Gardel—tango's greatest hero—and get a feel for the district.

TOP ATTRACTIONS

Museo Casa Carlos Gardel. Hard-core tango fans shouldn't pass up a quick visit to the home of tango's greatest hero, Carlos Gardel. The front rooms of this once-crumbling casa chorizo contain extensive displays of Gardel paraphernalia—LPs, photos, and old posters. The maestro's greatest hits play in the background. The back of the house has been restored with the aim of recreating as closely as possible the way the house would have looked when Gardel and his mother lived here, right down to the placement of birdcages on the patio. Concise but informative texts in Spanish and English talk you through the rooms and the history of tango in general. Short guided visits in English are usually available on request on weekdays. ⊠ *Jean Jaurés 735, Almagro* ☎ *11/4964–2015* ⊕ *www.museocasacarlosgardel.buenosaires.gob.ar* ✉ *5 pesos (free Wed.)* ⊙ *Mon. and Wed.–Fri. 11–6, weekends 10–7* Ⓜ *B to Carlos Gardel.*

WORTH NOTING

Cementerio de Chacarita. This cemetery is home to Carlos Gardel's tomb, which features a dapper, Brylcreemed statue and dozens of tribute plaques. It's treated like a shrine by hordes of faithful followers who honor their idol by inserting lighted cigarettes in the statue's hand. On June 24, the anniversary of his death, aging *tangueros* in suits and fedoras gather here to weep and sing. Fellow tango legends Aníbal Troilo and Osvaldo Pugliese are also buried in this cemetery, which is about equidistant from Palermo and Almagro. If you're heading from Almagro, hop Línea B at the Carlos Gardel station for a 10- to 15-minute ride west to the Federico Lacroze stop. Depending on where you are in Palermo, a cab here will cost 40 to 50 pesos. ⊠ *Guzmán 680, at Corrientes, Chacarita* ☎ *11/4553–9338* ✉ *Free* ☉ *Daily 7–5* Ⓜ *B to Federico Lacroze.*

FAMILY **Museo de los Niños.** The real world is scaled down to kiddie size at this museum in Abasto Shopping. Children can play at sending letters, going to a bank, acting in a mini TV studio, or making a radio program. You need to speak Spanish to participate in most activities, but the play areas and giant pipes that replicate the city's water system are internationally comprehensible. ⊠ *Abasto Shopping, Level 2, Av. Corrientes 3247, Almagro* ☎ *11/4861–2325* ⊕ *www.museoabasto.org.ar* ✉ *30 pesos* ☉ *Tues.–Sun. 1–8* Ⓜ *B to Carlos Gardel.*

PALERMO

Sightseeing
★★★★
Dining
★★★★★
Lodging
★★★★
Shopping
★★★★★
Nightlife
★★★

Trendy shops, bold restaurants, elegant embassies, acres of parks—Palermo really does have it all. Whether your idea of sightseeing is ticking off museums, flicking through clothing racks, licking your fingers after yet another long lunch, or kicking up a storm on the dance floor, Palermo can oblige. The city's largest barrio is subdivided into various unofficial districts, each with its own distinct flavor.

Some say Palermo takes its name from a 16th-century Italian immigrant who bought land here, others from the abbey honoring Saint Benedict of Palermo. Either way, the area was largely rural until the 1830s, when national governor Juan Manuel de Rosas built an estate in Palermo. After the dictatorial Rosas was overthrown, his property north of Avenida del Libertador was turned into a huge patchwork of parks and dubbed Parque Tres de Febrero—a reference to February 3, 1852, the day he was defeated in battle. More commonly known as Los Bosques de Palermo (the Palermo Woods), the green space provides a peaceful escape from the rush of downtown. The zoo and botanical gardens are at its southern end.

Plastic surgery and imported everything are the norm further east in Palermo Chico (between avenidas Santa Fe and Libertador), where ambassadors and rich local celebs live in Parisian-style mansions. Higher-brow culture is provided by the gleaming Museo de Arte de Latinoamericano (Museum of Latin American Art) on Avenida Figueroa Alcorta.

If a week away from your analyst is bringing on anxiety attacks, the quiet residential district around Plaza Güemes might offer some relief: it's nicknamed Villa Freud, for the high concentration of psychoanalysts who live and work here. But if it's retail therapy you need, Palermo delivers in that department, too. The streets around the intersection of avenidas Santa Fe and Coronel Díaz are home to mainstream clothing stores and the mid-range Alto Palermo mall. More upscale alternatives,

GETTING ORIENTED

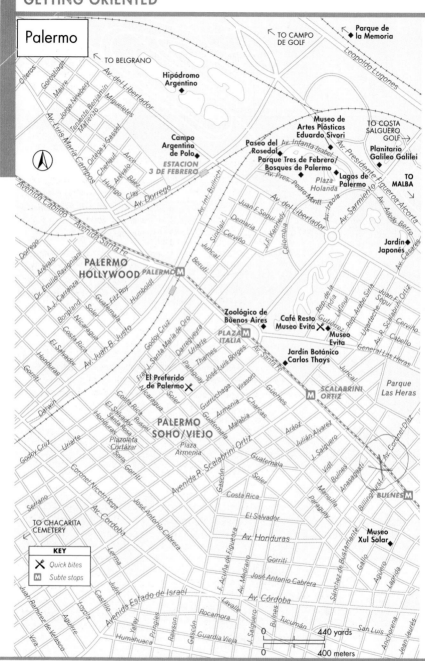

Palermo

TO BELGRANO

TO CAMPO
DE GOLF

Parque de
la Memoria

Leopoldo Lugones

Oteros

Gorostiaga

Maure

Jorge Newbery

Teniente Benjamín
Matienzo

Migueletas

Av. del Libertador

Hipódromo
Argentino

Av. Luis María Campos

Ortega y Gasset

Chenaut

Arévalo

Arce

Baéz

Huergo

Clay

Campo
Argentino
de Polo

ESTACIÓN
3 DE FEBRERO

Av. Dorrego

Museo de
Artes Plásticas
Eduardo Sívori

Paseo del
Rosedal

Av. Infanta Isabel

Parque Tres de Febrero/
Bosques de Palermo

Av. Pres. Pedro Montt

Plaza
Holanda

Lagos de
Palermo

TO COSTA
SALGUERO
GOLF

Planitario
Galileo Galilei

Av. Presidente Figueroa Alcorta

TO
MALBA

Av. Int. Bullrich

Juan F. Seguí

Demaria

Cerviño

J.F. Kennedy

Av. del Libertador

Colombia

Av. Sarmiento

Av. Adolfo Berro

Jardín
Japonés

Avenida Cabildo

Avenida Santa Fe

Dorrego

Arévalo

Dr. Emilio Ravignani

A.J. Carranza

Bonpland

Nicaragua

Costa Rica

El Salvador

Honduras

Gorriti

Fitz Roy

Humboldt

Soler

Guatemala

Av. Juan B. Justo

Godoy Cruz

Fray J. Santa María de Oro

PALERMO
HOLLYWOOD

PALERMO M

Berutti

Juncal

Sánchez

Av. Santa Fe

Rep. de la
India

Rep. Árabe Siria

Lafinur

Ugartecha

Cavia

Juan F. Ortíz

Seguí

Scalabrini Cerviño

J. Cabello

General Las Heras

Zoológico de
Buenos Aires

PLAZA
ITALIA M

Darregueyra

Uriarte

Thames

Av. Santa Fe

Café Resto
Museo Evita ✕

Gutiérrez

Museo
Evita

Padilla

Paraguay

Darwin

El Preferido
de Palermo ✕

Jorge Luis Borges

Virasoro

Gurruchaga

Armenia

Chacras

Güemes

Jardín Botánico
Carlos Thays

Juncal

Parque
Las Heras

Godoy Cruz

El Salvador

Santa Rosa

Honduras

Costa Rica

Russel

Nicaragua

Soler

PALERMO
SOHO/VIEJO

Plazoleta
Cortázar

Plaza
Armenia

Soria

Gorriti

Cnel. Niceto Vega

Avenida R. Scalabrini Ortíz

Guatemala

Malabia

SCALABRINI
ORTIZ M

Aráoz

Julián Álvarez

J. Salguero

Vidt

Bulnes

Ansesagasti

Marsilla

Billinghurst

Av. Coronel Díaz

BULNES M

Serrano

Av. Córdoba

José Antonio Cabrera

Uriarte

Gascón

Costa Rica

Soler

El Salvador

Paraguay

Guatemala

TO CHACARITA
CEMETERY

Lerma

Juan Ramírez de Velasco

Aguirre

Loyola

Castillo

Avenida Estado de Israel

Jufré

Pringles

Bulnes

Gascón

Guardia Vieja

Humahuaca

Rocamora

Lavalle

Av. Acuña de Figueroa

F. Acuña de Figueroa

Av. Medrano

Av. Honduras

Gorriti

José Antonio Cabrera

Av. Córdoba

Tucumán

J. Salguero

Sánchez de Bustamante

Museo
Xul Solar

Gallo

Agüero

Laprida

San Luis

Anchorena

Jean Jaurés

KEY
✕ Quick bites
M Subte stops

0   440 yards

0   400 meters

2

TOP EXPERIENCES

Gazing: at the Latin American masterpieces on the walls of the MALBA or at the beautiful people who frequent the Palermo bar scene.

Exercising: your arms in Palermo Viejo carrying bags on a boutique crawl or lifting cocktails on a bar crawl.

Learning: how young Eva Duarte morphed into the iconic Evita, Argentina's most famous first lady, at the museum that bears her name.

Wandering: on the winding paths of Parque Tres de Febrero, to smell the roses, or along Honduras for boutiques, bars, and restaurants.

QUICK BITES

El Preferido de Palermo. Trends come and go, but nothing changes these tall Formica tables. A plate of cold cuts and pickles or delicious sandwiches are the way to go. ⊠ *Jorge L. Borges 2108, Palermo Viejo* ☎ *11/4774–6585* ⊗ *Mon.–Sat. noon–12:30 am* Ⓜ *D to Plaza Italia.*

Café Resto Museo Evita. These checker floors and glossy black tables as stylish as the great lady herself. Sticky and flaky, the *medialunas* here are some of the best in town. ⊠ *J. M. Gutiérrez 3926, Palermo Botánico* ☎ *11/4800–1599* ⊕ *www.museoevitaresto.com. ar* ⊗ *Mon.–Sat. 9 am–midnight, Sun. 9–7* Ⓜ *D to Plaza Italia.*

THE TERRITORY

The city's biggest barrio stretches from Avenida Costanera R. Obligado, along the river, to Avenida Córdoba in the south. Its other boundaries are jagged, but include Avenida Coronel Díaz to the east and La Pampa and Dorrego to the west. Avenida Santa Fe cuts the neighborhood roughly in half. Palermo's green spaces and Palermo Chico lie north of it. To the south are Palermo Viejo and Palermo Hollywood, east and west of Avenida Juan B. Justo, respectively.

GETTING AROUND

Subte Línea D runs along Avenida Santa Fe, but doesn't always bring you to the doorstep of Palermo's attractions, so you may need to combine it with a taxi or some walking. Indeed, weekday traffic makes this combination a better idea than coming all the way from Centro by cab (which costs 40–50 pesos). Get off the subte at Bulnes or Scalabrini Ortíz for Palermo Chico; Plaza Italia for Palermo Viejo and the parks; and Ministro Carranza for Palermo Hollywood.

A more scenic route to Palermo Viejo and Hollywood from Centro is Bus No. 39 (Route 3, usually with a windshield sign "Palermo Viejo"). It takes 30 to 60 minutes, running along Honduras on the way to Palermo and along Gorriti on the way back. Bus No. 59 serves Palermo via Centro, San Telmo, and Recoleta. Bus nos. 29 and 64 link La Boca, San Telmo, and Centro with the northern end of Palermo; Bus No. 152 connects La Boca and Palermo more directly. Once you're in Palermo, walking is the best way to get around: much of the district is leafy, and there's little traffic on its smaller streets.

SAFETY AND PRECAUTIONS

Pickpocketing is the biggest threat, especially on crowded streets on weekends. Palermo Viejo's cobbled streets aren't well lighted at night, so avoid walking along any that look lonely. Although locals usually hail cabs on the street, it's safer to ask a restaurant or bar to call one for you.

meanwhile, abound in Palermo Viejo. Top boutiques—along with minimalist lofts, endless bars, and the most daring restaurants in town—have made Palermo Viejo (and its unofficial subdistrict, Palermo Soho) the epicenter of Buenos Aires' design revolution.

Many of these establishments occupy beautifully restored townhouses built in the late 19th century, when Palermo became a popular residential district. Trendsetters gravitate to the cobbled streets around Plazoleta Cortázar. The action also spills over into neighboring Palermo Hollywood, where streets like Honduras are lined with hip hotels and cocktail bars. Many patrons are local starlets or media types from the TV production centers that give the area its moniker.

PLANNING YOUR TIME

Palermo is so big that it's best to tackle it in sections. An even-paced ramble through Parque Tres de Febrero should take no more than two hours, though you could easily spend an entire afternoon at the zoo, Japanese Garden, and Botanical Garden. In architectural and geographic terms, Palermo Chico and the MALBA tie in nicely with a visit to Recoleta: allow at least a couple of hours for such an experience.

TOP ATTRACTIONS

FAMILY **Jardín Japonés** (*Japanese Garden*). Like the bonsais in the nursery within it, this park is small but perfectly formed. A slow wander along its arched wooden bridges and walkways is guaranteed to calm frazzled sightseeing nerves during the week; crowds on the weekend make for a less-than-soothing experience. A variety of shrubs and flowers frame ornamental ponds that are filled with friendly koi carp—you can actually pet them if you feel so inclined (kids often do). The traditional teahouse, where you can enjoy sushi, adzuki-bean sweets, and tea, overlooks a zen garden. ⊠ *Av. Casares at Av. Figueroa Alcorta, Palermo* ☎ *11/4804–4922* ⊕ *www.jardinjapones.org.ar* ☜ *32 pesos* ☉ *Daily 10–6.*

Fodor's Choice ★ **Museo de Arte de Latinoamericano de Buenos Aires** (MALBA, Museum of Latin American Art of Buenos Aires).
See the highlighted listing in this chapter.

Museo Evita.
See the highlighted listing in this chapter.

FAMILY **Parque Tres de Febrero.** Known locally as Los Bosques de Palermo (the Palermo Woods), this 400-acre green space is really a crazy quilt of smaller parks. Lush grass and shady trees make it an urban oasis, although the busy roads and horn-honking drivers that crisscross the park never let you forget what city you're in. Near the lakes in the northwestern part, some 12,000 rosebushes (more than 1,000 different species) bloom seasonally in the **Paseo del Rosedal**. A stroll along the paths takes you through the Jardín de los Poetas (Poets' Garden), dotted with statues of literary figures, and to the enchanting **Patio Andaluz** (Andalusian Patio), where majolica tiles and Spanish mosaics sit under a vine-covered pergola.

South of Avenida Figueroa Alcorta, you can take part in organized tai chi and exercise classes as well as impromptu soccer matches. You can

MALBA

✉ *Av. Presidente Figueroa Alcorta 3415, Palermo* ☎ *11/4808–6500* ⊕ *www.malba.org.ar* 🎫 *50 pesos (25 pesos Wed.)* ⊙ *Thurs.–Mon. noon–8, Wed. noon–9* Ⓜ *D to Bulnes.*

2

TIPS AND TRIVIA

■ MALBA also has a great art cinema showing restored copies of classics, never-released features, and silent films with live music, as well as local films of note.

■ Kids love hands-on kinetic works like Julio Le Parc's Seven Unexpected Movements, a sculpture with gleaming parts that move at the press of a button.

■ Leave time to browse the art books and funky design objects in the museum's excellent gift shop.

■ Young, enthusiastic guides give great tours of the permanent collection in Spanish on Wednesday and Sunday at 4.

■ Give your feet—and eyes—a rest on the first-floor sculpture deck, with views over Belgrano and Barrio Norte.

■ Córdoba-based studio AFT Arquitectos' triangular construction in creamy stone and steel is one of the museum's draws. The main galleries run along a four-story atrium, flooded in natural light from a wall of windows.

The fabulous Museum of Latin American Art of Buenos Aires (MALBA) is one of the cornerstones of the city's cultural life. Its centerpiece is businessman and founder Eduardo Constantini's collection of more than 220 works of 19th- and 20th-century Latin American art in the main first-floor gallery.

Highlights

Europe vs. Latin America. Early works in the permanent collection reflect the European avant-garde experiences of artists such as Diego Rivera, Xul Solar, Roberto Matta, and Joaquín Torres García. These, in turn, gave rise to paintings like *Abaporu* (1928) by Tarsila do Amaral, a Brazilian involved in the "cannibalistic" Movimento Antropofágico (rather than actually eating white Europeans, proponents of the movement proposed devouring European culture and digesting it into something new). Geometric paintings and sculptures from the 1940s represent movements such as Arte Concreto, Constructivism, and Arte Madí.

Argentine Art. Argentina's undisputed modern master is Antonio Berni, represented by a poptastic collage called *The Great Temptation* (1962) and the bizarre sculpture *Voracity or Ramona's Nightmare* (1964): both feature the eccentric prostitute Ramona, a character Berni created in this series of works criticizing consumer society. Pieces by local greats Liliana Porter, Marta Minujín, Guillermo Kuitca, and Alejandro Kuropatwa form the end of the permanent collection.

Temporary Exhibitions. World-class temporary exhibitions are held on the second floor two or three times a year, and two small basement galleries show art by cutting-edge Argentines.

MUSEO EVITA

✉ *Lafinur 2988, 1 block north of Av. Las Heras, Palermo* ☎ *11/4807–0306* ⊕ *www.museoevita.org* 🎫 *60 pesos* 🕐 *Tues.–Sun. 11–7* Ⓜ *D to Plaza Italia.*

TIPS AND TRIVIA

■ Laminated cards with just-understandable English translations of the exhibits are available in each room and at the ticket booth.

■ Take a postmuseum coffee or lunch break at the on-site café (its outside tables are shaded by classy black umbrellas). There's also a small museum gift shop.

■ The gray-stone mansion dates from 1909. It was purchased in 1948 by the Fundación de Ayuda Social Eva Perón (Eva Perón Social Aid Foundation) and converted into a home for single mothers, to the horror of the rich, conservative families living nearby.

■ The Evita myth can be baffling to the uninitiated. The museum's excellent guided visits shed light on the phenomenon and are available in English for groups of six or more, but must be arranged by phone in advance.

Eva Duarte de Perón, known universally as Evita, was the wife of populist president Juan Domingo Perón. She was both revered by her working-class followers and despised by the Anglophile oligarchy of the time. The Museo Evita shies from pop-culture clichés and conveys facts about Evita's life and works, particularly the social aid programs she instituted and her role in getting women the vote. Knowledgeable staffers answer questions enthusiastically.

Highlights

Photographic evidence. The route through the collection begins in a darkened room, where 1952 footage showing hundreds of thousands of mourners lined up to view their idol's body is screened. Family photos and magazine covers document her humble origins and time as a B-list actress. Upstairs there are English-subtitled film clips of Evita making incendiary speeches to screaming crowds: her impassioned delivery beats Madonna's hands down.

Death becomes her. The final rooms follow the First Lady's withdrawal from political life and her death from cancer at age 33. A video chronicles the fate of Evita's cadaver: embalmed by Perón, stolen by political opponents, and moved and hidden for 17 years before being returned to Argentina, where it now rests in the Recoleta Cemetery.

Fabulous clothes. Evita's reputation as a fashion plate is reflected in the many designer outfits on display, including her trademark suits and some gorgeous ball gowns.

also jog or rent bikes, in-line skates, and pedal boats. The park gets crowded on sunny weekends, as this is where families come to play and have picnics. If you like the idea of the latter, take advantage of the street vendors who sell refreshments and *choripan* (chorizo sausage in a bread roll) within the park. There are also several posh cafés lining the Paseo de la Infanta (running from Libertador toward Sarmiento in the park). ⊠ *Bounded by avs. del Libertador, Sarmiento, Leopoldo Lugones, and Dorrego, Palermo* Ⓜ *D to Plaza Italia.*

WORTH NOTING

FAMILY **Jardín Botánico Carlos Thays.** Wedged between three busy Palermo streets, this unexpected haven has 18 acres of gardens filled with 5,500 varieties of exotic and indigenous flora. Different sections recreate the environments of Asia, Africa, Oceania, Europe, and the Americas. An organic vegetable garden aims to teach children healthy eating habits. Winding paths lead to hidden statues and a brook that's watched over by an ever-growing population of cats (the gardens are the traditional dumping ground for unwanted porteño pets). The central area contains an exposed-brick botanical school and library, plus a beautiful greenhouse brought from France in 1900 but sadly not open to the public. ⊠ *Av. Santa Fe 3951, Palermo* ☎ *11/4832–1552* ⊕ *www.buenosaires.gob.ar/ jardin-botanico-carlos-thays* ☞ *Free* ⊙ *Sept.–Mar., weekdays 8–6:45, weekends 9:30–6:45; Apr.–Aug., weekdays 8–5:45, weekends 9:30– 5:45.* Ⓜ *D to Plaza Italia.*

Museo de Artes Plásticas Eduardo Sívori (*Eduardo Sívori Art Museum*). If you're looking for respite from the sun or sports in Parque Tres de Febrero, try this sedate museum. Focused on 19th- and 20th-century Argentine art, its collection includes paintings by local masters like Emilio Petoruti, Lino Eneo Spilimbergo, Antonio Berni, and the museum's namesake Sívori. The shaded sculpture garden is the perfect combination of art and park. ⊠ *Av. Infanta Isabel 555, Palermo* ☎ *11/4774–9452* ⊕ *museos.buenosaires.gob.ar/sivori.htm* ☞ *5 pesos (free Wed.)* ⊙ *Tues.–Fri. noon–8, weekends 10–8* Ⓜ *D to Plaza Italia.*

Museo Xul Solar. Avant-garde artist, linguist, esoteric philosopher, and close friend of Borges, Xul Solar is best known for his luminous, semi-abstract watercolors. They glow against the low-lighted concrete walls of this hushed museum. Solar's wacky but endearing beliefs in universalism led him to design a pan-language, pan-chess (a set is displayed here), and the Pan Klub, where these ideas were debated. One of its former members, architect Pablo Beitia, masterminded the transformation of the townhouse where Solar lived and worked. Open stairways crisscross the space, an homage to one of Solar's favorite motifs. ⊠ *Laprida 1212, Palermo* ☎ *11/4824–3302* ⊕ *www.xulsolar.org.ar* ☞ *20 pesos* ⊙ *Tues.– Fri. noon–7:30, Sat. noon–6:30* Ⓜ *D to Agüero.*

Planetario Galileo Galilei (*Galileo Galilei Planetarium*). One of the city's most iconic buildings, the Planetario Galileo Galilei is a great orb positioned on a massive concrete tripod in the middle of Palermo's Parque Tres de Febrero. Built in the early 1960s, it looks like something out of *Close Encounters of the Third Kind*—especially at night, when the dome glows with eerie blue lighting. It reopened after major renovation in 2012 with a state-of-the-art projector, new sound system, and vibrating seats for the twice-daily sky shows, narrated in Spanish. Tickets go on sale at 9:30 Tuesday through Friday and 11:30 on weekends; note that they usually sell out fast. Three meteorites that landed in northern Argentina 4,000 years ago guard the entrance. The nearby pond with swans, geese, and ducks is always a hit with kids. ⊠ *Avs. Sarmiento and Figueroa Alcorta, Palermo* ☎ *11/4771–9393* ⊕ *www.planetario.gov.ar* 🎟 *30 pesos* Ⓜ *D to Plaza Italia.*

FAMILY **Zoológico de Buenos Aires.** The grandiose stone pens and mews—many dating from the zoo's opening in 1874—are as much an attraction at the 45-acre city zoo as their inhabitants. Jorge Luis Borges said the recurring presence of tigers in his work was inspired by time spent here. Today, the six rare white Bengal tigers (four of which were born at the zoo in 2013) may inspire you to pen a few lines of your own. South American animals you might not have seen before include the *aguará guazú* (a sort of fox), the *coatí* (a local raccoon), anteaters, and the black howler monkey. Some smaller animals roam freely, and there are play areas for children, a petting farm, and a seal show. *Mateos* (traditional, decorated horse-drawn carriages) stand poised at the entrance to whisk you around the nearby parks. ⊠ *Avs. General Las Heras and Sarmiento, Palermo* ☎ *11/4011–9900* ⊕ *www.zoobuenosaires.com.ar* 🎟 *90 pesos* ⊙ *Tues.–Sun. 10–6 (last entry at 5)* Ⓜ *D to Plaza Italia.*

BELGRANO

Once rural villages far removed from urban life, Belgrano and neighboring Núñez now mark the transition from the city proper to the sprawling northern suburbs of Greater Buenos Aires. The stolid storefronts and safe menus of Belgrano's clothing stores and restaurants cater to its well-to-do but conservative residents. They're the reason that the soccer fans are known as *millonarios* (millionaires); adjacent Núñez is home to the club's huge stadium, La Monumental. Away from the crazy traffic of Avenida Cabildo, Belgrano's tree-lined streets are pleasant, if lacking in tourist attractions.

COSTANERA NORTE

It's said that Buenos Aires was built with its back to the Río de la Plata, but the exception is the riverside strip of Costanera Norte, where a promenade borders the choppy brown waters. By day, the drone of engines and the smell of jet fuel fill the air above this strip of land along the river: Aeroparque Jorge Newbery, the hub for domestic flights, is here. Wishful fishermen often cast a line from the wide waterfront promenade, but a steak or chorizo sandwich from the many *carritos* (food stands) is a surer meal ticket. At night, the soundtrack is pounding beats and guitar riffs coming from long-standing dance clubs. Respectful silence reigns a little farther north at the haunting Parque de la Memoria, a monument to victims of Argentina's last dictatorship.

Continued on page 92

ARGENTINE ICONS

SAINTS, SINNERS & PRODIGAL SONS by Victoria Patience

One minute Argentinians are cursing their country's shortcomings; the next they're waving a flag and screaming "Ar-gen-tina" as their soccer team chalks up a victory. But when it comes to their famous sons and daughters, most Argentinans are resolutely proud.

Were it not for the heroics of one man, José de San Martín, Argentina might not exist at all. Raised in Spain, he was a passionate believer in Latin American independence.

You could say that in modern Argentine politics, it takes two to tango. The original political double act was Juan Domingo Perón and his wife, Evita, who were revered and reviled in equal measure.

Indeed, passionate hatred of Perón and serious literary genius were among the few things shared by two great Argentine writers: erudite Anglophile Jorge Luis Borges and bearded bohemian Julio Cortázar.

Revolution was the passion of Ernesto Guevara, or rather, El Che. This middle-class med student was instrumental in the building of Castro's Cuba, and remains the figurehead of many left-wing student movements. You'll find Che's face tattooed on the arm of a different secular saint: Diego Armando Maradona, voted the 20th century's best soccer player by FIFA (International Football Association). The toughest local machos have been brought to tears by his goals.

(top) Eva Perón and Che Guevara posters. (bottom) Diego Maradona during the 1979 World Youth Championship in Japan.

POLITICAL FIGURES

AKA: El Libertador
de America
BORN: February 25, 1778,
in Yapeyú, Argentina
DIED: August 17, 1850, in
Boulogne-sur-Mer, France
QUOTE: "Let us be free.
Nothing else matters."
REMEMBERED: A
national public holiday
commemorates the
anniversary of his death.

JOSÉ DE SAN MARTÍN

TOP 3 SAN MARTÍN SIGHTS

Plaza San Martín, named in his honor, contains a monument to the general, who looks dashing atop his horse.

Museo Histórico Nacional, which has recreated San Martín's bedroom at the time he died.

Catedral de Buenos Aires, home to his mausoleum.

BIO: Ironically, the man who freed Argentina from Spanish colonial shackles spent his formative years in Spain. But when news of Argentina's May 1810 revolution reached him, he abandoned an illustrious career in the Spanish army and rushed back to the country of his birth. His flamboyant military campaigns were instrumental in the independence of the Viceroyalty of the Río de la Plata (Argentina, Paraguay, Bolivia, and Uruguay). He then led his forces across the Andes to liberate Chile and Peru.

Today, San Martín's selfless idealism is universally lauded. However, he fell from favor in his lifetime by refusing to spill a fellow Argentine's blood and participate in Argentina's civil war. His military pension was never honored, and he died in France in severe financial straits, far from the country he'd fought so hard for.

POSTHUMOUS ADVENTURES: San Martín expressly requested in his will that his heart be buried in Buenos Aires. Political disagreements and red tape meant 30 years went by before his body was repatriated and he was finally laid to rest in a mausoleum in Buenos Aires Cathedral. The urn-like structure designed to contain his coffin was built too short, so he was placed in it on an angle (head down, local legend says) to fit.

(top) General José de San Martín engraving; (bottom) Monument to the Libertador General San Martín, by Frances Louis Joseph Daumes in Plaza San Martín, Buenos Aires, Argentina

2

AKA: El General; The Father of the Nation
BORN: October 8, 1895, in Lobos, Argentina
DIED: July 1, 1974, in Olivos, Argentina
QUOTE: "Better than saying is doing; better than promising, achieving."
REMEMBERED: Union members and fiercely loyal Peronists recreate the demonstrations in Plaza de Mayo that got Perón freed on October 17, 1945, the so-called Día de la Lealtad (Day of Loyalty).

POSTHUMOUS ADVENTURES: In 1987, thieves stole Perón's hands from his tomb in Buenos Aires' Chacarita Cemetery. Some say they demanded an $8 million ransom, others that they needed his fingerprints to access a bank deposit box in Switzerland. When the body was moved to a special mausoleum in 2006, scuffles between police and Peronist demonstrators led to 40 injuries.

JUAN DOMINGO PERÓN

BIO: Perón is a complex figure, even for Argentinians. Although he was an army general, Perón reached the presidency through a landslide election victory. He revolutionized worker's rights, nationalized Argentina's services, championed local industry, expanded the country's health and education, and instigated a huge social aid program. Despite these left-leaning policies, he loathed communism, and even secretly facilitated the entry of Nazi war criminals into Argentina.

The General and Evita were the people's pin-ups, but things began to fall apart after her death. Ousted by a coup in 1955, Perón went into an 18-year exile, during which Peronism was made illegal in Argentina. He made a glorious comeback in 1973, but party infighting soon soured things. He died in office in 1974 and was briefly and disastrously succeeded by the vice president, his third wife. Argentina's most horrific dictatorship soon followed. The Peronist party is riddled with contradictions—it spawned both the right-wing government of Carlos Menem and the center-left Kirchners—but Argentine politics still live in its shadow.

(top) Juan Domingo Perón (1895–1974), president of Argentina, addressing the parliament, May, 1952; (bottom) Perón and Evita

SANTA EVITA

AKA: Evita, mother of the nation, Spiritual Leader of the Nation, Santa Evita (Saint Evita), *esa mujer* (that woman)

BORN: May 17, 1919, in Los Toldos, Argentina

DIED: July 26, 1952, in Buenos Aires

QUOTE: "I have only one thing that counts, and I carry it in my heart. It burns my soul, it aches in my flesh, and it stings my nerves, and that is my love for the people and for Perón. I never wanted anything for myself, nor do I want it now. My glory is and will always be Perón and the flag of my people."

REMEMBERED: Loyal Peronists cover Evita's tomb with flowers and hold candlelight vigils on the anniversary of her death.

EVA MARÍA DUARTE DE PERÓN

BIO: Evita was revered long before musicals and Hollywood films made her internationally famous. Born in the provinces, she left home for Buenos Aires at 17, and soon became a B-movie actress. However, her loyalties switched from showbiz to politics upon meeting Perón, and they married during his first presidential campaign. Her campaign for female suffrage helped his re-election in 1951. Until her untimely death from cancer at the age of 33, Evita and Perón were a duo of unprecedented popularity. However, Evita is a contradictory figure: despite her designer frocks and perfect blonde chignon, her politics were radical, to the horror of the conservatives of the time. Her activism championed the working class as well as the poor and such marginalized groups as single mothers, and brought her millions of fanatical followers, who, more than 60 years on, still campaign for her to be made a saint.

POSTHUMOUS ADVENTURES: When a coup overthrew Perón in 1955, Evita's embalmed body was stolen by the opposition. The casket was stored in several army offices, hidden in an embassy garden in Bonn, buried under a false name in Italy, and put on display by Perón's third wife before it was finally laid in the family vault in Recoleta cemetery in 1977.

(top) 1950, Eva Perón being presented with an insignia by volunteer workers of the Institute for Work of Argentina

EVITA PILGRIMAGE

"¡Evita vive!" ("Evita lives"), her faithful followers never tire of saying. It's not just the national psyche she's left a lasting impression on: the city itself is full of places inextricably linked to her. Here's how to see them all during one day in Buenos Aires.

Start your pilgrimage in morbid Argentine style, at her tomb in **Recoleta Cemetery** (Junín 1760, Recoleta). If you come near the anniversary of her death, July 26, expect tearful crowds and piles and piles of flowers.

Intrigued? Catch a taxi or buses 37, 59, or 60 north along nearby Av. Las Heras to the 3900 block in Palermo to get the Evita 101 at the excellent **Museo Evita** (Lafinur 2988, 1 block north of Av. Las Heras, Palermo). Its classy, all-day restaurant is a good bet for coffee or lunch.

Then catch the subte from nearby Plaza Italia to Belgrano station on Línea C. Two 100-foot high portraits of Evita decorate the north and south faces of building in the center of Av. 9 de Julio. In 1951, Evita renounced her vice-presidential candidacy from a stage here before two million passionate supporters.

It's a short taxi ride or a 12-block walk east along Av. Belgrano then south on Paseo Colón

to the monumental **Facultad de Ingeniería** (Faculty of Engineering; Paseo Colón 850, San Telmo). This rather totalitarian-looking building was originally designed for the Fundación Eva Perón, Evita's aid organization. Before being stolen by anti-Peronists, Evita's embalmed body lay in state for three years at the **Edificio de la CGT** (Building of the General Confederation of Labor; Azopardo 802, San Telmo), just around the corner from the Facultad de Ingeniería.

You can pick up Evita-print packing tape and other collectibles at **Tienda Palacio** (Defensa 926, San Telmo), two blocks west of the Edificio de la CGT along Av. Independencia and two blocks south along Defensa.

Next, head to Plaza de Mayo. Here, thousands of Perón's supporters protested his imprisonment in 1945 and were moved to tears by Evita's speeches from the balcony of the Casa Rosada.

Now the only thing left to do is throw back your head and sing "Don't Cry for me, Argentina."

(left) Burial plaque at Recoleta; (right) nursing school uniform at Museo Evita

LITERARY GIANTS

AKA: Georgie (his family nickname); H. Bustos Domecq (the pseudonym he and friend Adolfo Bioy Casares used for their collaborations).

BORN: August 24, 1899, in Buenos Aires

DIED: June 14, 1986, in Geneva, Switzerland

QUOTES: "To me it seems impossible that Buenos Aires once began / I judge her as eternal as the water and the air." "Reading… is an activity subsequent to writing: more resigned, more civil, more intellectual."

POLITICAL LEARNINGS: Extreme conservative, so much so that he initially praised the 1976 military coup, but ended up petitioning General Videla over disappearances.

DAY JOBS: Librarian; first in a small neighborhood library where his anti-Peronist sentiments got him fired; and eventually director of the National Library, courtesy of a military government he supported.

MARRIAGES: Two: Elsa Astete Millán, a one-time childhood sweetheart, in 1967. Borges described the marriage as "total incompatibility," and they divorced in 1970. María Kodama, a former student, 45 years his junior, shortly before his death in 1985. She had been his secretary, travel companion, and then partner for 10 years.

JORGE LUIS BORGES

BIO: Borges claimed all his life to belong far more to the 19th century than the 20th. A lifelong Anglophile, his conservative politics were probably what denied him the Nobel Prize many feel he deserved. His political ideas also earned him the passionate hatred of many Argentine intellectuals, although lots of them were eventually sufficiently overcome by his literary brilliance to forgive him.

LINGUISTIC TRIVIA: Legend has it Borges first read that greatest of Spanish works, *Don Quixote*, in English translation, and when faced with the Spanish original, thought it inferior. For, ironically, although Borges was a magician of the Spanish language, the first language he learned to read in was English, thanks to his English grandmother.

NOW READ ON: BORGES

- The Aleph and Other Stories
- Fictions
- Brodie's Report

Penguin

(top) Jorge Luis Borges, at home, Buenos Aires, 1983

AKA: Julio Denis, the pseudonym he published early work under.

BORN: August 26, 1914, in Argentine Embassy of Brussels, Belgium

DIED: February 12, 1984, in Paris, France

QUOTE: "Nothing is lost if we have the courage to admit that everything is lost and that we have to start again."

POLITICAL LEARNINGS: Very left-wing, he was a committed supporter of the Cuban revolution but was rejected by Castro when he protested the arrest of a Cuban poet for political reasons.

DAY JOBS: High-school teacher, but resigned when Perón came to power; translator for UNESCO; also translated Edgar Allan Poe and G.K. Chesterton, among others, into Spanish.

MARRIAGES: Three: Aurora Bernárdez, an Argentine translator, in 1955. Ugné Karvelis, a Lithuanian activist, whom he met in 1967. Carol Dunlop, a Canadian poet, in 1979.

JULIO CORTÁZAR

BIO: Cortázar's semi-surreal prose and flamboyant bohemian lifestyle have long made him the intellectual pin-up for idealistic students throughout Latin America. He began to publish in earnest after 1951, when a scholarship took him to Paris. He lived in that city for the rest of his life but always wrote in Spanish. His most famous works appeared in the 1960s, including the highly experimental *Hopscotch*, a story of Argentine beatniks afloat in Paris, the chapters of which can be read in any order. Stories from his several collections were published in English as *Blow-Up: And Other Stories*; Michelangelo Antonioni based his award-winning film on the title story. Jazz, boxing, and politics were also big passions, and he signed over the royalties of two books to Argentine political prisoners and the Sandinista movement in Nicaragua. Ironically for one who was also a brilliant translator, the English-language versions of his work have yet to gain him the respect he commands in Spanish.

LINGUISTIC TRIVIA: His early childhood in Belgium left him incapable of pronouncing the Spanish "r."

NOW READ ON: CORTÁZAR

- Hopscotch
- "Blow-Up": And Other Stories
- 62: A Model Kit

Pantheon

(left) June 1967, Paris, France; (right) Mature Cortázar and cat

SOUL STIRRERS

AKA: Fuser (the nickname his rugby teammates gave him), El Che ("che" is a typically Argentinean interjection, an old-fashioned version of "man" or "dude" or just "hey." His constant use of the word caused coworkers to start calling him by it. It stuck.)

BORN: June 14, 1928, in Rosario, Argentina

DIED: October 9, 1967, in La Higuera, Bolivia

QUOTES: *"Hasta la victoria siempre"* (Always toward victory). "I am not a liberator. Liberators do not exist. The people liberate themselves."

SUPPORTED: Rugby: San Isidro Club, of which his father was one of the founders. Soccer: Rosario Central.

HEALTH PROBLEMS: Chronic asthma

ERNESTO "CHE" GUEVARA DE LA SERNA

BIO: Ironically, this socialist figurehead started life in an upper-middle class family and was a keen player of rugby, considered a posh sport. Soon, his horror at the plight of Latin American peasants and workers and a chance meeting with the young Fidel Castro in Mexico led to his well-known participation in the Cuban revolution, first as a guerrilla and eventually as President of the National Bank and Minister of Industries.

Darker allegations also surround this time in Che's life: some say the trials—and executions—of Batista followers he oversaw in La Cabaña prison in 1959 were unfair. Che soon realized that he was more suited to fighting oppression than to pushing paper at the ministry. He led guerrilla campaigns in the Congo and Bolivia, where he was executed by Bolivian soldiers on October 9, 1967. His ideals, ascetic lifestyle, and, more than anything, a lot of very dramatic photographs have transformed him into a pop icon.

DID YOU KNOW?

Mario Terán, the Bolivian army sergeant who fired the shots that killed Che, benefited greatly from the Cuban health system. Just shy of the 40th anniversary of Che's death, Terán had cataracts removed by Cuban doctors in Bolivia as part of Operation Milagro, a program offering eye surgery to Latin Americans in need of free treatment.

(top left) Argentinian revolutionary portrait; (top right) posters; (bottom) Che Guevara and Fidel Castro

2

IN FOCUS ARGENTINE ICONS

AKA: El 10 (Number 10), El Diego de la Gente (The Diego of the People), La Mano de Dios (The Hand of God).

BORN: October 30, 1960, in Buenos Aires

QUOTE: "It was the hand of God!" in defense of his supposed hand-goal in the 1986 World Cup.

SUPPORTS: Boca Juniors

DEFINING MOMENT: 1986 soccer World Cup quarter-final against England, when he scored his goal after dribbling down half the field and dodging round five players and the goalkeeper. FIFA voted it the Goal of the Century.

HEALTH PROBLEMS: Recurring cocaine addiction and obesity.

MARADONA SPOTTING

He might not be making the headlines, but you might see him...

■ ...cheering on Boca Juniors or the Argentinian soccer team with his daughters from a special box. He's often in the crowds at international tennis and polo matches, too.

■ ...in TV interviews giving his opinion on everything from soccer coaching to Latin American politics (in 2007 he was a guest on Venezuelan president Hugo Chávez's show, *Aló Presidente*).

DIEGO ARMANDO MARADONA

BIO: Ask any local soccer fan what nationality God is, and their answer will be "Argentinian," in clear reference to Diego Armando Maradona, whose status as national sporting idol can't get any higher. A football prodigy, Maradona grew up in one of Buenos Aires' shantytowns, but started playing professionally at the age of 10. He shot to fame in the early '80s playing for Boca Juniors and then Italian team Napoli, before his 1986 goal against England won the World Cup for Argentina and immortality for Maradona. Too much time at the top took its toll, though: after retiring Maradona's cocaine addiction bloomed and his weight skyrocketed, and for a while it looked like Argentina's greatest hero was on his way out. However, a clean, slimmed-down Maradona returned to become manager of the Argentina team for the 2010 FIFA World Cup. They only reached the quarterfinals but Maradona's status as national *fútbol* legend remains intact.

(top) Diego Maradona before the 1987 Xerox Super Soccer match in Tokyo, Japan; (bottom) World Cup, 1990

WORTH NOTING

Parque de la Memoria. Between 1969 and 1983, 30,000 civilians were illegally detained, tortured, and "disappeared" in Argentina by the military dictatorship and the paramilitary operations that preceded their coup. The 35-acre site of the country's first memorial park was chosen because it borders the River Plate, into which many of the *desaparecidos* (disappeared) were thrown—heavily drugged but still alive—from military aircraft. The park is designed to look toward the city skyline as a reminder of citizens' widespread collusion with the government. The chilling stone walls slicing down through the park to the river form the **Monumento a las Víctimas del Terrorismo del Estado** (Monument to the Victims of State-Organized Terrorism). Engraved on it are the names and ages of roughly 9,000 identified victims, organized by the year they vanished. You reach the park and the monument via a square containing sculptures such as Roberto Aizenberg's untitled piece representing his three disappeared stepchildren, and Dennis Oppenheim's *Monument to Escape*. The small information booth usually has leaflets in English. ⊠ *Av. Costanera Norte Rafael Obligado 6745, Costanera* ☎ *11/4787–0999* ⊕ *www.parquedelamemoria.org.ar* ⊠ *Free* ⊙ *Weekdays 10–6, weekends 11–6.*

> **DID YOU KNOW?**
>
> Porteños speak a very local version of Spanish. Instead of *"tú"* for "you," the archaic *"vos"* form is used, and "ll" and "y" are pronounced like "sh." A singsong accent owes a lot to Italian immigrants; indeed, an Italian-influenced slang—called *lunfardo*—is ever-present.

LAS CAÑITAS

Not quite as cool as Palermo but much less staid than Belgrano, Las Cañitas sits between the two both geographically and conceptually. In the late 1990s, the in-your-face bars and clubs of this outpost northwest of Palermo were the epitome of cool. Its star has since faded, but Las Cañitas remains a fond favorite among local models, aging TV divas, and others dying to be seen.

3

SHOPPING

WHAT TO SHOP FOR IN BUENOS AIRES

Where there's steak, there's leather—and in Argentina it comes in all colors, shapes and sizes. But that's just the beginning: local shops are laden with trinkets and treasures that evoke *porteño* life.

DULCE DE LECHE

Thick, sticky, and oh-so sweet, *dulce de leche* (a spread made from sweetened condensed milk) is highly addictive. Stock up on brands like La Serenísima at supermarkets and corner stores, or opt for posh glass jars of La Salamandra, which isn't quite as sugary. Another way to get your fix is by going to the nearest Havanna coffee shop (there is one on practically every corner) for a supply of *alfajores*: these chocolate-covered dulce de leche–filled cookies can also provide a small, perfectly rounded taste of Argentina for friends and colleagues back home.

EVITA MEMENTOS

Argentina's most famous first lady not only graces 100-peso bills and the banners waved at political rallies, she also appears on loads of merchandise. Score a kitschy plastic bust of Mrs. Perón at the Feria de San Pedro Telmo, which also sells used stamps bearing her image. Evita screenprints adorn notebooks at Papelera Palermo, while Marcelo Toledo carries a whole range of Evita-inspired jewelry, including replicas of pieces she wore. For a perfect finishing touch, invest in some Evita-print packing tape from Tienda Palacio to wrap your goodies in.

KNIVES

Can't kick your Argentine beef habit? Remind yourself of all those delicious steaks you devoured by returning home with a traditional *asado* knife. Practical wood- or horn-handle models are

available at most markets, and they are sometimes bundled in a carrying case with a sturdy cutting board. Upper-crust carnivores might prefer the more elaborate renditions—complete with silver- and alpaca-adorned hilts and sheaths—that silversmiths sell. Just don't forget to pack them in your suitcase (not in your carry-on bag) to avoid complications at airport security.

LEATHER

If you can't take a real-life gaucho home with you, the next best thing is to accessorize your home—or yourself—with some leather or cowhide. Rugs are easily transportable (check out the wholesalers on Avenida Boedo in Amagro); a broad range of jackets can be found along Calle Murano in Villa Crespo; and you can buy wallets, purses, iPad cases, and such virtually everywhere. For a different take on the gaucho tradition, look for an illustrated, leather-bound edition of *Martín Fierro,* the epic tale of Argentina's favorite folk hero, at El Ateneo.

SHOES

The Latino answer to European espadrilles, *alpargatas* are comfy, casual shoes that can take you from a day mucking around in the countryside to an urban bar come nightfall. While the most basic pairs (picture black or burgundy fabric uppers) can be bought relatively cheaply at shoe repair stores, hold out for Paez ones: the brand has

reinvigorated this classic gaucho shoe, producing it in a kaleidoscope of colors and patterns, from stripes and checks to funky dots.

SOCCER GEAR

In Argentina there are two colors that can be worn together on pretty much any occasion—light blue and white. If you've been to a live match at the soccer stadium, chanted the songs, and howled at missed goals, all that's lacking is showing your allegiance on your chest. The vertical *celeste y blanco* stripes don't just apply to the "beautiful game," though. The Leonas ladies field hockey team (Olympic silver-medal winners) also sport the colors, while the Pumas rugby squad wears them arranged diagonally. Almost all sports stores will stock original *camisetas.*

TANGO CLOTHES

Need we remind you that Buenos Aires is the best place in the world to stock up on tango music, memorabilia, and serious dance wear? There are plenty of shops in El Centro, including Flabella and Segunda Generación, where you

can pick up designer duds perfect for the dance floor. If you're looking for vintage items, head to the open-air flea market at the Feria de San Pedro Telmo. As you shop, you can watch couples dance on the cobblestone streets.

WINE

Although award-winners from wineries such as Catena Zapata and Achaval Ferrer can cost hundreds of dollars per bottle, a great malbec is a bargain in the motherland. So why not snap some up at Grand Cru? The store sells lovely leather carrying cases, too. If you fell in love with *pingüinos* (the penguin-shape wine jugs used at traditional eateries), purchase a cute pastel version at Bartolomea. Malbec bath gel and body cream from Universo Garden Angels or "sacred grape" soap from Sabater Hermanos also fulfill oenophiles' wine-infused fantasies.

YERBA MATÉ

You might not immediately fall for the bitter regional tea that is the backbone of Argentine culture, but its paraphernalia makes unusual souvenirs. Colonial-style silver vessels with sipping straws are fit for royalty and priced accordingly; however, more humble (and affordable) gourds made out of dried pumpkin are frequently available at local markets. Look out for bright, breezy ones that come in a rainbow of colors. True libation lovers can even wear the drink: Elementos Argentinos sells hand-woven llama shawls dyed pale green using yerba maté.

3

By Sorrel Moseley-Williams

Whether you're looking for a unique handicraft, the latest boutique-vineyard malbec, a one-off pair of rhodochrosite earrings, or jeans no one's got back home, you're bound to leave Buenos Aires with your suitcases full. Argentina's designers inject their wares with creativity, and innovative items can be found everywhere from elite boutiques to neighborhood street fairs.

If you love the hustle and bustle, elbow your way through the city's outdoor ferias. The array of open-air markets testifies to the fact that locals enjoy stall-trawling as much as visitors do. Crafts—whether traditional or contemporary—often take center stage, with artisans proudly selling their own creations; however, the selection can also include art, antiques, curios, clothing, jewelry, and assorted household goods.

At the other end of the spectrum, this city certainly isn't lacking in high-end couture. During Fashion Weeks (⊕ *www.bafweek.com.ar*) in February and August, Buenos Aires turns the spotlight on both its world-class designers and its talented up-and-comers. But at any time of year you can swank it up at Patio Bullrich or at posh Recoleta boutiques where the security is as tight as an airport.

Clothing bargains are harder to find than they once were, but that doesn't mean visitors should pay through the nose. Although haggling isn't commonplace, do ask for a discount if paying in cash, especially if you decide to snap up leather wrist cuffs for all your cousins at a sidewalk stall. Also look out for the tax refund sticker in many shop windows.

Argentina is cow central, and leather goods—from boots to jackets to polo saddles—are an excellent value. Buenos Aires' well-established antiques trade is also thriving, but modern houseware shops are putting up some fierce competition. On the wine front, many local vintages still aren't exported, so this may be your only chance to try wines from regions other than Mendoza.

It's not just about retail therapy, either. Part of the Buenos Aires experience can be wandering around and stepping, unexpectedly, into a restored mansion selling silk frocks and vertigo-inducing heels, then taking a break at a bistro or juice bar. People-watching is the name of the game. Known for their good looks, Argentineans like to watch and be watched from the café sidelines.

PLANNING

DOING BUSINESS

Some stores give discounts for paying cash (although check before you get to the till); others charge a premium for using credit cards. Carry both, and keep your options open. Tourist-area shops may try to charge you in dollars or euros what they charge Argentineans in pesos. Always confirm which currency you're dealing with. Bargaining is accepted only in some leather-goods shops on Calle Florida. Elsewhere—even in markets—prices are fixed, although it is worth asking for a small discount if you're buying several of the same item.

"Refund" is a dirty word. No shop will give you back your money just because you change your mind. Even if a product is faulty, exchanges or credit notes are the norm. Many shops won't process exchanges on Saturday, a busy shopping day.

Keep receipts: the 21% V.A.T. tax, included in the sale price, is refundable for purchases over 70 pesos at stores displaying the Global Blue tax-refund sign. Visit the return desk at the airport to obtain your refund, but remember to have the goods on you in order to present them to officials.

TIMING

Malls are typically open from 10 to 9 daily. Shops that aren't in a mall or part of a chain may open an hour or so later and close an hour earlier; they also tend to be shut on either Sunday or Monday.

GET BUZZED IN

Locked shop doors are standard anti-theft practice, so don't be surprised (or intimidated) by having to ring a doorbell and be buzzed in. Once inside, you'll find that sloppily dressed customers usually get sloppy service. Porteños (as residents of Buenos Aires are called) take shopping seriously, and they dress for the occasion. You should, too: ditch the sneakers and fanny pack and look like you mean business.

VALUE FOR MONEY

Clothing in Buenos Aires is fairly cheap and plentiful, but bear in mind that the quality may match the price. Pay particular attention to seams and hems; stitching isn't always superlative. This is true even with international-brand items, which are often labeled "Made in Argentina."

Local brands come at even lower prices in the discount outlets on Avenida Córdoba (4400 to 5000) and in the unofficial new shopping zone, Palermo Outlets, between Malabia and Serrano—most chain stores have a branch here. End-of-season sales can work to your advantage, too. Remember, when summer is ending in Buenos Aires, it's just beginning in North America and Europe.

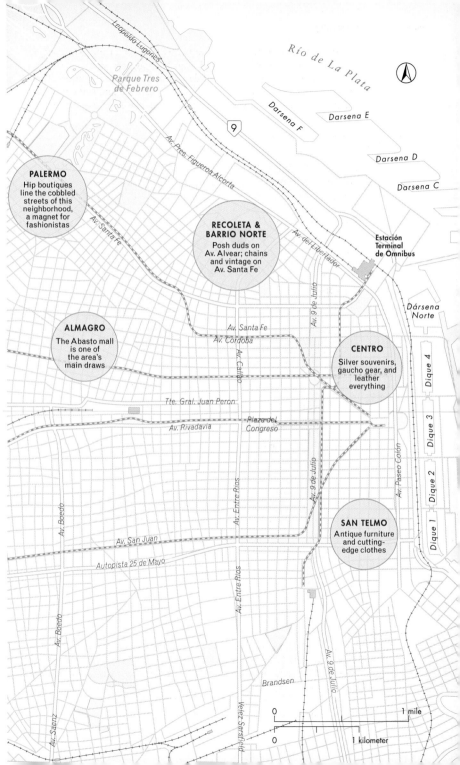

CLOTHING SIZES

Porteños are, on average, smaller than Europeans and North Americans. Chic women's boutiques often don't carry clothes in sizes larger than a U.S. 8. It doesn't get any better for men: a porteño men's large will seem more like a small to many visitors, and trousers rarely come in different lengths.

CENTRO

BEAUTY

Universo Garden Angels. Despite the New Age brand name and emphasis on inner beauty, these cosmetics mix hard science with color and aromatherapy to create aromacolortherapy. One of the top lines is the lemongrass-based Spa collection, which includes scrubs perfect for revitalizing weary feet after a day's sightseeing. ⊠ *Av. Santa Fe 1355, Microcentro* ☎ *11/4816–6780* ⊕ *www.universogardenangels.com* Ⓜ *C to Gral. San Martín.*

CLOTHING

La Martina. Feel part of the jet set when you browse the clothing line of Argentine polo team La Martina. It's not just about boots and jodhpurs; there are also corduroy pants and cashmere sweaters perfect for lounging around your country house. Screen-printed tees—including the country's national polo-team shirt—are a must-have. ⊠ *Paraguay 661, Microcentro* ☎ *11/4311–5963* ⊕ *www.lamartina.com* Ⓜ *C to San Martín* ⊠ *Arribeños 2632, Belgrano* ☎ *11/4576–0010.*

Mickey. You won't see any billboards around town for Mickey: reputation is a far better way of advertising. Generations of porteños have been coming here for top-quality shirts, suits, and footwear at reasonable prices. Young, energetic assistants are as happy to show you wide-collar shirts in splendidly patterned Italian cotton as well as classic button-downs. ⊠ *Perón 917, Microcentro* ☎ *11/4326–7195* ⊕ *www.camisasmickey.com.ar* Ⓜ *C to Diagonal Norte; D to 9 de Julio.*

Ona Saez. The ultrafitted jeans at Ona Saez are designed to be worn with sky-high heels and slinky tops for a sexy night out. The menswear is equally slick, mixing dressed-down denim with cool cotton shirts and tees. ⊠ *Florida 789, #203, Centro* ☎ *11/5555–5203* ⊕ *www.onasaez.com* Ⓜ *C to San Martín* ⊠ *Santa Fe 1609, Barrio Norte* ☎ *11/4815–0029.*

Segunda Generación. For custom-made, haute-couture tango wear and accessories (including fabulous feather hairpieces), visit the family-run Segunda Generación. ⊠ *Esmeralda 1249, Microcentro* ☎ *011/4312–7136* ⊕ *www.2gen.com.ar* Ⓜ *C to Retiro.*

HOME DECOR

Falabella Hogar. A block away from Falabella (the excellent Chilean department store) is its housewares branch, Falabella Hogar. It does a roaring trade in cheap 'n' stylish crockery, kitchenware, and textiles, mostly imported from China and India. The store is crowded with office workers from noon to 2:30. ⊠ *Florida 343, Microcentro*

☎ *0810/555–3252* ⊕ *www.falabella.com.ar* Ⓜ *B to Florida; C to Lavalle; D to Catedral.*

JEWELRY AND ACCESSORIES

Autoría Bs As. Fashion meets art at Autoría Bs As. After browsing the ready-to-wear women's collections by Mariana Dappiano, Min Agostini, and Vero Ivaldi, head to jewelry and accessories. Necklaces may be made of coiled silver by María Medici or crochet by Tatiana Pini. Some handbags have been fashioned from car tires, others from top-quality leather or organic wool. This is one of the few places to pick up a daring one-of-a-kind Manto Abrigo coat, handwoven in luminous colors in northern Argentina. ⊠ *Suipacha 1025, Microcentro* ☎ *11/5252–2474* ⊕ *www.autoriabsas.com.ar* Ⓜ *C Line to San Martín.*

Cousiño. Veined pinky-red rhodochrosite (Argentina's national stone) comes both in classic settings and as diminutive sculptures at this second-generation goldsmith's shop. Cousiño's sculptures of birds in flight are also exhibited in the National Museum of Decorative Arts. ⊠ *Sheraton Buenos Aires Hotel, San Martín 1225, Retiro* ☎ *11/4318–9000* ⊕ *www.rodocrosita.com* Ⓜ *C to Retiro.*

Plata Nativa. Tucked into an arcade, this tiny shop is filled with delights for both boho chicks and collectors of singular ethnic jewelry. Complex, chunky necklaces with turquoise, amber, and malachite—all based on original Araucanian (ethnic Argentine) pieces—and Mapuche-style silver earrings and brooches are some of the offerings. Happy customers include Sharon Stone, Pedro Almodóvar, and the Textile Museum in Washington, D.C. ⊠ *Galería del Sol, Shop 41, Florida 860, Centro* ☎ *11/4312–1398* ⊕ *www.platanativa.com* Ⓜ *C to San Martín.*

MALLS AND SHOPPING CENTERS

Falabella. There's no love lost between Argentina and its neighbors, but when this Chilean department store opened, the affordable prices soon had locals swallowing their pride. The busy corner store's ground floor contains accessories, perfumes, and cosmetics such as MAC and Lancôme. Falabella also has three clothing lines: Sybila does low-cost (and low-quality) street wear; University Club is preppier and harder-wearing; Basement includes better-quality casual and work clothes. The overworked staff at both Falabella and its nearby housewares branch, Falabella Hogar, don't give much guidance, but the prices make up for it. Avoid lunchtime, when it is packed with office workers looking for retail diversion. ⊠ *Florida 202, at Sarmiento, Microcentro* ☎ *0810/555–3252* ⊕ *www.falabella.com.ar* Ⓜ *B to Florida; C to Lavalle; D to Catedral.*

Galerías Pacífico. Upscale shops line the three levels of this beautiful building, designed during the city's turn-of-the-20th-century golden age. Stores are organized along four glass-roof passages, which branch out in a cross from the central stairwell; the cupola above it is decorated by five Argentine greats, including muralist Antonio Berni. Top local, polo-inspired, menswear brands Etiqueta Negra and La Martina have large stores, while Jazmín Chebar, Ona Saez, and Vitamina's collections are aimed at younger women. Check out Janet Wise and Las Oreiro for more sophisticated looks among international brands such as Chanel

DID YOU KNOW?

Some claim that there are more psychoanalysts in Buenos Aires per capita than any other city in the world. This might just apply to shoe stores, too. Here, a zapatería in La Boca.

and Christian Lacroix. For a respite from the retail, head down to the basement's bustling food court or up to the second floor, where the Centro Cultural Borges stages tango shows and hosts small art exhibitions that feature international stars like Andy Warhol and Salvador Dalí. ⊠ *Calle Florida 737, at Av. Córdoba, Microcentro* ☎ *11/5555–5110* ⊕ *www.galeriaspacifico.com.ar* Ⓜ *B to Florida.*

SHOES, HANDBAGS, AND LEATHER GOODS

Carpincho. As its name suggests, this spot specializes in supersoft, stippled *carpincho* leather from the capybara—the world's largest rodent, native to Argentina. Gloves (which also come in more conventional kidskin) are the main attraction, and there's a wide variety of lengths and colors to choose from. ⊠ *Esmeralda 775, Centro* ☎ *11/4322–9919* ⊕ *www.carpinchonet.com.ar* Ⓜ *C to Lavalle.*

Casa López. Don't let the drab storefront put you off: you're as likely to find a trouser suit in floral-print suede as a staid handbag for grandma at this two-part place. The right-hand shop (No. 658) has totes in chestnut- and chocolate-color leather that look good enough to eat; there are also classic jackets. More unusual fare—including fur sacks with wool fringes, black cowhide baguettes, and tangerine purses—are sold next door at No. 640. ⊠ *Marcelo T. de Alvear 640 and 658, Centro* ☎ *11/4311–3044* ⊕ *www.casalopez.com.ar* Ⓜ *C to San Martín.*

Flabella. Some of the finest tango shoes in town—including classic spats, 1920s T-bar designs, and glitzier numbers for men and women—are all handmade and custom fitted at Flabella. ⊠ *Suipacha 263, Microcentro* ☎ *11/4322–6036* ⊕ *www.flabella.com* Ⓜ *B, C, D to 9 de Julio.*

WINE

Ligier. Ligier has a string of wine stores across town and lots of experience guiding bewildered drinkers through their impressive selection. Although they stock some boutique-vineyard wines, they mostly carry big names such as Rutini, Catena, and Luigi Bosca, as well as more modest mass-produced wines. ⊠ *Callao 1111, Recoleta* ☎ *11/5353–8050* ⊕ *www.ligier.com.ar* Ⓜ *C to San Martín.*

SAN TELMO

The city's oldest neighborhood has long been the place to shop for antiques and collectibles. But now you're as likely to buy a shirt as a chandelier: following the lead of local fashion god Pablo Ramírez, other retailers have arrived to make San Telmo the new epicenter of porteño cool.

ANTIQUES AND COLLECTIBLES

Gabriel del Campo. Gabriel's good taste means 50-year-old Louis Vuitton trunks don't look out of place beside wooden church statues or scale-model ships with canvas sails. Ceramic rubber-glove molds, one of his specialties, are some of the more accessible conversation pieces. The flagship store takes up a sizable patch of Plaza Dorrego shop front. ⊠ *Bethlem 427, on Pl. Dorrego, San Telmo* ☎ *11/4307–6589* Ⓜ *C to San Juan (walk 6 blocks along Humberto I).*

Gil Antigüedades. Sequined flapper dresses, dashing white-linen suits, and creamy lace wedding veils are some of the items you might stumble across in this *casa chorizo* (colonial-style house). Period accessories include Castilian hair combs and lacy fans that beg you to bat your lashes from behind them. ⊠ *Humberto I 412, San Telmo* ☎ *11/4361–5019* ⊕ *www.gilantiguedades.com.ar* Ⓜ *C to San Juan (walk 6 blocks along Av. San Juan).*

HB Anticuario. White-leather trefoil chairs and gleaming walnut side tables with black-lacquer details are among the many heavenly furniture items in this art deco emporium. Much more packable (though not cheap) are the Clarice Cliff dinner services or French rosewood cigar boxes. ⊠ *Defensa 1016/18, San Telmo* ☎ *11/4361–3325* ⊕ *www.hbantiques.com.ar* Ⓜ *C or E to Independencia (walk 6 blocks along Estados Unidos).*

La Candelaria. A Spanish-style abode built in 1745 contains several tempting shops. One is filled with enough miniature wooden furniture to fill several dollhouses; another sells golden-age Argentine cinema posters. Wind-up monkeys, brass fittings, old apothecary bottles, and vintage leather suitcases are other interesting finds. ⊠ *Defensa 1170, San Telmo* Ⓜ *C to San Juan (walk 6 blocks along Av. San Juan).*

Remates La Maja. This cavernous auction warehouse is crammed with furniture, mirrors, statues, rugs, dinner sets, and even salvaged doors and windows. Scores of chandeliers glitter overhead, and glassware is packed into cabinets along the edges. Some pieces are antique, others are simply old—size them up during the week, then return for the auction. Alternatively, you can make an advance offer which opens bidding in your absence. ⊠ *Humberto I 236, San Telmo* ☎ *11/4361–6097* ⊕ *www.lamajaremates.com.ar* Ⓜ *C Line to San Juan (7 blocks away).*

Silvia Petroccia. Despite being crammed with furniture, this corner store looks extravagant rather than chaotic. It's probably due to the alluring European collectibles, ranging from terracotta amphoras and gilt-wood church candles to Louis XV–style chairs reupholstered in buttercup-yellow silk. ⊠ *Defensa 1002, San Telmo* ☎ *11/4362–0156* ⊕ *www.sp-antiques.com* Ⓜ *C or E to Independencia.*

BOOKS AND MUSIC

Walrus Books. A peaceful sanctuary away from the busy Sunday street market, Walrus stocks more than 4,000 good quality books in English. American owner Geoff and his English-speaking staff are helpful yet unobtrusive when it comes to selecting a translation of local masters or some contemporary fiction. Slide open the bargain drawer at the front of the store to uncover more reads perfect for flight delays or long bus journeys. ⊠ *Estados Unidos 617, San Telmo* ☎ *11/4300–7135* ⊕ *www.walrus-books.com.ar* Ⓜ *C to Independencia.*

CLOTHING

Fodor'sChoice
★
Pablo Ramírez. His tiny shop front is unadorned except for "Ramírez" printed on the glass over the door—when you're this big, why say more? Voted Argentina's best designer by the fashion blogger Scott Schuman, Ramírez's couture doesn't come cheap, but these perfectly tailored numbers are worth every *centavo*. He favors black or white for both

waspishly waisted women's wear and slick gent's suits, though a few other shades are creeping in. ✉ *Perú 587, San Telmo* ☎ *11/4342–7154* ⊕ *www.pabloramirez.com.ar* Ⓜ *E to Belgrano.*

GIFTS AND SOUVENIRS

Artepampa. An artist-and-architect duo is behind these singular works, which are inspired by native Argentine art. They use an unusual papier-mâché technique to create boxes, frames, tapestries, and free-standing sculptures. The primitive-looking pieces, a vision of rich rusts and earthy browns, make highly original gifts. ✉ *Defensa 917, on Pl. Dorrego, San Telmo* ☎ *11/4362–6406* ⊕ *www.artepampa.com* Ⓜ *C to San Juan.*

Cualquier Verdura. Set up like the 19th-century home it once was, Cualquier Verdura gives the otherwise antiques-dominated neighborhood a much-needed kitsch injection. Check out furniture designed by Philippe Starck for Kartell, fun animal-shape placemats, vinyl records, glow-in-the-dark toys, old-yet-functioning kitchen implements, and books by local photographers and artists calling out for a coffee table. ✉ *Humberto I 517, San Telmo* ☎ *11/4300–2474* ⊕ *www.cualquierverdura.com.ar* ⊙ *Closed Mon.–Wed.* Ⓜ *C to San Juan (6 blocks away).*

Juan Carlos Pallarols Orfebre. Argentina's legendary silversmith has made pieces for a mile-long list of celebrities that includes Frank Sinatra, Sharon Stone, Antonio Banderas, Bill Clinton, Nelson Mandela, the king and queen of Spain, and Queen Máxima Zorrequieta (a local export now integrated into the Dutch royal family). A set of ornate silver-handle steak knives is the perfect memento of cow country—although it will set you back a few grand. ✉ *Defensa 1039, San Telmo* ☎ *11/4361–7360* ⊕ *www.pallarols.com.ar* Ⓜ *C or E to Independencia (walk 6 blocks along Estados Unidos).*

Fodor's Choice ★ **Marcelo Toledo.** Sunlight and the smell of solder fill the rooms of this old San Telmo house, which doubles as a store and open workshop for celebrity silversmith Marcelo Toledo. A huge silver mosaic of Evita gives away who Toledo's main muse is: he has created replicas of her own jewelry (and is the only silversmith authorized by her estate to do so) as well as pieces inspired by her. Eva Duarte Perón isn't the only crowd-pleasing politician Toledo's been associated with: a local magnate commissioned cuff links as an inauguration gift for President Obama. He also designed a maté gourd especially for Prince William and his bride, the Duchess of Cambridge. ✉ *Humberto I 458, San Telmo* ☎ *11/4362–0841* ⊕ *www.marcelotoledo.net* Ⓜ *C to San Juan (6 blocks away).*

Marcelo Toledo is the place to go for beautifully crafted silver, like this *bombilla* (maté straw) set.

Materia Urbana. The quirky, postmodern souvenirs this store specializes in are a welcome variation from classic maté gourds or gaucho knives. Take the ubiquitous cow, which has been reformed into a leather vampire-bat key holder, or the piglet change purse. Beautiful bags, silver and steel bijouterie as well as tango-themed soaps are cute gift options. Head upstairs to browse clothes by a variety of designers. ⊠ *Defensa 702, San Telmo* ☎ *11/4361–5265* ⊕ *www.materiaurbana.com* Ⓜ *C to Independencia (7 blocks away).*

JEWELRY AND ACCESSORIES

Abraxas. "Yes" is pretty much guaranteed if you propose with one of the period engagement rings that dazzle in the window of this antique jeweler. If you're not planning on popping the question any time soon, surely you can find a home for a pair of art deco earrings with the tiniest of diamonds or a gossamer-fine bracelet? ⊠ *Defensa 1092, San Telmo* ☎ *11/4361–7512* ⊕ *www.abraxasantiques.com* Ⓜ *C to San Juan (walk 6 blocks along Humberto I).*

Midas Antigüedades. Everything a gentleman needs to accessorize like a lord is arrayed in the minimalist storefront. Vintage timepieces are the specialty, from turn-of-the-20th-century pocket watches to a 14k-gold 1950s Longines wristwatch with a snakeskin strap. Jeweled tiepins, cuff links, cigarette cases, and even an evil dog-head walking cane round out the stock. ⊠ *Defensa 1088, San Telmo* ☎ *11/4307–1314* ⊕ *www. relojeriamidas.com* Ⓜ *C to San Juan (walk 6 blocks along Humberto I).*

MARKETS

Feria de San Pedro Telmo. Plaza Dorrego is the heart of the Feria de San Pedro Telmo—an open-air market that stretches for more than a kilometer (½ mile) along Calle Defensa each Sunday. Thrust your way through the crowds to pick through antiques and curios of varying vintages as well as tango memorabilia, or watch dolled-up professional tango dancers perform on the surrounding cobbled streets. The unofficial "stalls" (often just a cloth on the ground) of young craftspeople stretch several blocks up Defensa, away from the market proper. As it gets dark, the square turns into a milonga, where quick-stepping locals show you how it's done. ⊠ *Pl. Dorrego, Humberto I and Defensa, San Telmo* ⊕ *www.feriadesantelmo.com* ☉ *Sun. 10–dusk* Ⓜ *C to San Juan.*

RECOLETA

The most upscale neighborhood in B.A. won't disappoint seriously big spenders. Top-name Argentine designers rub shoulders here with the biggest and best international luxury brands; however, high-street stores located in the Recoleta Mall and dotted around the Barrio Norte district mean no one needs to leave empty-handed.

BOOKS AND MUSIC

El Ateneo. An imposing theater dating from 1919 provides a fabulous backdrop for this bookshop. The former foyer holds a small selection of CDs and DVDs; the orchestra seating area has art books and fiction (including some English works); specialist subjects are arrayed in the circle; and you pay at the box office. Argentine cookbooks, illustrated gaucho classics, and coffee-table tomes are some of the weighty souvenirs. There are similar offerings at the less dramatic store in El Centro. ⊠ *Ateneo Grand Splendid, Santa Fe 1860, Recoleta* ☎ *11/4813–6052* ⊕ *www.tematika.com* Ⓜ *D to Callao.*

Notorious. Intrigued by the sounds you've heard on your trip? Take some home with you from Notorious, which has a strong selection of local rock, folk, jazz, and tango. Friendly staff will happily make suggestions. The shop is small, but there are plenty of listening stations, so you can try before you buy. ⊠ *Av. Callao 966, Barrio Norte* ☎ *11/4813–6888* ⊕ *www.notorious.com.ar* Ⓜ *D to Callao* ⊠ *Estados Unidos 488, San Telmo* ☎ *11/4361–6189.*

CLOTHING

Giesso. A classic gents' tailor for more than 130 years, Giesso has pulled a Thomas Pink by adding jewel-color ties and shirts to its range of timeless suits and corduroy jackets. A women's line includes gorgeous linen suits and cashmere overcoats. ⊠ *Av. Alvear 1882, Recoleta* ☎ *11/4804–8288* ⊕ *www.giesso.com.ar* Ⓜ *D Line to Tribunales (12 blocks away)* ⊠ *Florida 997, Centro* ☎ *11/4312–7606.*

Kosiuko. Branches of Kosiuko, the ultimate local teen brand, are always packed with trendy adolescents served by hip-wiggling staff not much older than they are. The girls come for the improbably small, low-cut denim, the guys for budding metrosexual-wear under the Herencia brand. Kosiuko's fragrances and deodorant are a favorite with the population's most perspiring age group. ⊠ *Av. Santa Fe 1756, Barrio Norte* ☎ *11/4815–2555* ⊕ *www.kosiuko.com.ar* Ⓜ *D to Callao* ⊠ *Abasto Mall, Av. Corrientes 3247, Almagro.*

CLOTHING: MEN'S

La Dolfina. Being a number-one polo player wasn't enough for Adolfo Cambiaso—he founded his own team in 1995, then started a clothing line which he also models for. If you think polo is all about knee-high boots and preppy chinos, think again: Cambiaso sells some of the best urban menswear in town. The Italian-cotton shirts, sharp leather jackets, and to-die-for totes are perfect for any occasion. ⊠ *Av. Alvear 1751, Recoleta* ☎ *11/4811–1066* ⊕ *www.ladolfina.com* Ⓜ *D to Tribunales (12 blocks away).*

Tienda Rethink. Bored of drab utility-wear? Rethink has, well, rethought the issue. Grown-up skaters and sophisticated rockers love its well-made jeans, hoodies, and tees. Simple in cut, they come alive with graffiti-inspired designs, which spill over onto the shop walls. ⊠ *Marcelo T. de Alvear 1187, Barrio Norte* ☎ *11/4815–8916* ⊕ *www.7rethink.com* Ⓜ *D to Tribunales (walk 4 blocks along Libertad).*

CLOTHING: WOMEN'S

Cora Groppo. A queen of the porteño haute-couture scene, Cora Groppo made her name designing flirty cocktail dresses with lots of cleavage and short flared or bell-shaped skirts. These continue to be the main attraction at her Recoleta branch. The lower-key Palermo store at El Salvador 4657 sells skinny pants and shorts best accompanied by draped tops, although the whisper-thin cotton jersey that most are made of doesn't do much for clients without catwalk figures. ⊠ *Uruguay 1296, Recoleta* ☎ *11/4815–8516* ⊕ *www.coragroppo.com* Ⓜ *D to Tribunales (8 blocks away)* ⊠ *El Salvador 4696, Palermo Viejo* ☎ *11/4833–7474.*

Evangelina Bomparola. Evangelina takes her clothes very seriously, and it's easy to see why. Top-of-the-line materials and detailed attention to the way they hang translate into designs that are simple but never dull. This is *the* place to come for a little (or long) black dress; wilder items—such as a '60s-style funnel-neck coat or a colorful raw-silk jumpsuit—also line the minimalist boutique's racks. ⊠ *Alvear 1920, Recoleta* ☎ *11/4802–8807* ⊕ *www.evangelinabomparola.com* Ⓜ *D to Callao (12 blocks away).*

Holi. Model-turned-designer Dolores Barreiro provides a fresh take on tribal prints by injecting them with bold colors. Acid oranges and yellows fuse comfortably with turquoise and lavender: the result is a fun collection of Indian- and African-inspired beach frocks, wraps, and skirts. ⊠ *Rodriguez Peña 2050, Recoleta* ☎ *11/4814–4379* ⊕ *holipordoloresbarreiro.com* Ⓜ *C to Retiro (10 blocks away).*

Luz Ballestero. Each collection by Luz Ballestero has a different inspiration: summer might reflect contemporary dance while winter takes shelter and protection as its muse. The result is a simple yet eclectic brand that is both modern and urban. Blushing brides should make an appointment to check out her gowns, too. ⊠ *Vicente López 1661, Pasaje del Correo 5, Recoleta* ☎ *11/4812–2670* ⊕ *www.luzballestero. com* Ⓜ *D to Tribunales (8 blocks away).*

Tramando, Martín Churba. The name of this hushed town-house store means both "weaving" and "plotting"—and designer Martín Churba is doing plenty of both. Unique evening tops made of layers of draped and pleated sheer fabric adorned with circular beads and irregular embroidery look fit for an urban mermaid. Asymmetrical shrugs, screen-printed tees, and even vases are some of the other woven wonders that represent a fusion of art and fashion. ⊠ *Rodríguez Peña 1973, Recoleta* ☎ *11/4811-0465* ⊕ *www.tramando.com* Ⓜ *C to Retiro (10 blocks away).*

Trosman. Highly unusual beadwork is the only adornment on Trosman designs. There's nothing small and sparkling about it: beads are smooth, inch-wide acrylic orbs that look futuristic yet organic. You might balk at the price tags, considering that most of the clothes are made of T-shirting, but that hasn't stopped Tokyo or Paris from stocking wares. Note that the brand is now under new ownership: you can check out original designer Jessica Trosman's latest, more urban offerings at JT in Palermo. ⊠ *Patio Bullrich Mall, Av. del Libertador 750, Store 1, Recoleta* ☎ *11/4814-7414* ⊕ *www.trosman.com* Ⓜ *C to Retiro (8 blocks away)* ⊠ *Armenia 1998, Palermo Viejo* ☎ *11/4833-3058.*

Varanasi. The structural perfection of Varanasi's clothes is a clue that the brains behind them trained as architects. Find A-line dresses built from silk patchwork and unadorned bias cuts, some of the night-out joys that local celebs shop for. ⊠ *Juncal 1280, Recoleta* ☎ *11/4812-4282* ⊕ *www.varanasi-online.com* Ⓜ *C to Retiro.*

Zitta. It may be easy to pass by this unprepossessing Recoleta shop, but there's no way Fabián Zitta's evening dresses could go unnoticed. Local starlets love his bold designs, notable for their volume: picture balloon skirts, puffball sleeves, or organic-looking ruffled tubes snaking over severely tight bodices. Each collection includes black, white, and one other (usually blinding) color. Brides-to-be must give his wedding collection a whirl. ⊠ *Av. Quintana 10, Recoleta* ☎ *11/4811-2094* ⊕ *www. zittacostura.com* Ⓜ *C to Retiro (8 blocks away).*

GIFTS AND SOUVENIRS

Fueguia. It makes perfect scents to visit Fueguia's perfume and candle-making laboratory to create your own *eau de*. Named after the nine-year-old native Patagonian girl who was abducted by *HMS Beagle* captain Robert FitzRoy, Fueguia has more than 100 fragrances to choose from, including Uruguayan jasmines, Tucumán lemons, and Neuquén roses. ⊠ *Av. Alvear 1680, Recoleta* ☎ *11/4311-5360* ⊕ *www. fueguia.com* Ⓜ *C to Retiro.*

Fundación Silataj. This small handicraft shop is run by a non-profit organization that trades fairly with more than two-dozen indigenous communities in Argentina. The shop smells like the aromatic *palo santo* wood used to make the trays, platters, cutting boards, and hair combs they carry. Other offerings include carnival masks, handwoven textiles, beaten tin ornaments, and alpaca jewelry. Prices, though higher than in markets, are reasonable; quality is excellent (hence the name, meaning "the best" in the Wichi Indian language); and you know your money is going to the artisans. There's also a store in Belgrano at Vuelta de

Obligado 1933. ⊠ *Libertad 948, Recoleta* ☎ *11/4816–4351* ⊕ *www. fundacionsilataj.org.ar* Ⓜ *D to Tribunales.*

Plata Lappas. Classic silver trays, cutlery sets, tea sets, and ice buckets have been favorites on porteño high-society wedding lists for more than 125 years. Department stores worldwide stock Lappas silverware, but why pay export prices? ⊠ *Santa Fe 1381, Recoleta* ☎ *11/4811–6866* ⊕ *www.lappas.com* Ⓜ *D to Tribunales.*

JEWELRY AND ACCESSORIES

FodorśChoice **Celedonio.** Local design hero Celedonio Lohidoy has created pieces—
★ often with frothy bunches of natural pearls—for Kenzo and Emanuel Ungaro; his work has even been slung around Sarah Jessica Parker's neck on *Sex in the City.* He favors irregular semiprecious stones, set in asymmetrical, organic-looking designs such as butterflies and daisies. ⊠ *Uruguay 1223, #8, Recoleta* ☎ *11/4803–7598* ⊕ *www.celedonio. com.ar* ⊙ *Closed weekends* Ⓜ *D to Tribunales (6 blocks away).*

Fahoma. This small boutique has enough accessories to make the rest of your outfit a mere formality. Berry-size beads go into chunky but afford-able necklaces, which take flora and fauna as their inspiration, while all manner of handbags line the back wall. Need a royal seal of approval? Queen Máxima of the Netherlands has been photographed wearing their fun, oversize earrings. ⊠ *Libertad 1169, Recoleta* ☎ *11/4813–5103* ⊕ *www.fahoma.es* Ⓜ *D to Tribunales (5 blocks away).*

Homero. Previously known for innovative, beautifully designed neck-laces and rings, Homero has taken a new turn by adding heirloom pieces to its selection: choose from jewels (including complete sets), watches, and other unique items—each with its own story. ⊠ *Patio Bull-rich, Av. Libertador 750, #2007, Recoleta* ☎ *11/4812–9881* ⊕ *www. homerocompra.com* Ⓜ *C to Retiro (7 blocks away).*

MALLS AND SHOPPING CENTERS

Galería Bond Street. This is a preferred address for skaters, clubbers, and alternative-minded teens. The stores downstairs sell club wear, punky T-shirts, and band pins, while those on the top floor have slightly class-ier offerings from local designers who aren't big enough to set up in Palermo. If you're in the mood for a tattoo, you can take your pick from a large selection of ground-floor studios. ⊠ *Av. Santa Fe 1607, Barrio Norte* ☎ *11/4812–8744* ⊕ *galeriabondstreet.com* Ⓜ *D to Callao (4 blocks away).*

Galería Quinta Avenida. Vintage vultures should swing by Galería Quinta Avenida, which has a host of dusty boutiques ideal for a few hours of rack-roaming. There's a particularly good selection of leather jackets, as well as accessories like specs from the 1950s and '60s. Keep an eye out for irregular *ferias americanas,* impromptu flea market sales. ⊠ *Av. Santa Fe 1270, Recoleta* ☎ *11/4816–0451* Ⓜ *D to Tribunales.*

Patio Bullrich. The city's most upscale mall was once the headquarters for the Bullrich family's meat-auction house, and stone cow heads mounted on pillars still watch over the clientele. A colonnaded front and glass-dome ceiling are further reminders of a past age. Fashion fans can check out international brands such as Salvatore Ferragamo, Cacharel,

Lacoste, and Carolina Herrera; on the local design front, urban leather-ware brand Besha has a shop here, as does Ricky Sarkany (the *enfant terrible* of Argentine footwear, who sells dangerously pointed stilettos in colors that walk the line between exciting and kitsch). The edgy but elegant menswear brand Etiqueta Negra opened its first store outside the snooty northern suburbs here, and La Martina gives it fierce competition. When the bags begin to weigh you down, stop for cake at Nucha, on the Avenida del Libertador side of the building. ⊠ *Enter at Posadas 1245 or Av. del Libertador 750, Recoleta* ☎ *11/4814–7400* ⊕ *www.shoppingbullrich.com.ar* Ⓜ *C to Retiro (walk 7 blocks up Av. del Libertador).*

Recoleta Mall. This modern glass-and-steel construction may be smaller than most of its Buenos Aires counterparts, but it's not lacking in stores. Most classic Argentine high-street brands are represented, including Ayres, A.Y. Not Dead, and Delaostia for women and Key Biscayne for men. There's also an impressive movie theater on site. Offering fabulous views of the famous Recoleta Cemetery, the mall breathes added life into an area mainly inhabited by corpses. ⊠ *Vicente López 2050, between Junín and Uriburu, Recoleta* ☎ *0810/810–2463* ⊕ *www.recoletamall. com.ar* Ⓜ *D to Pueyrredon.*

MARKETS

Feria de Artesanos de Plaza Francia (*Feria Plaza Francia*). The sprawling open-air market winds through several linked squares outside the Recoleta Cemetery. Each weekend, artisans sell handmade clothes, jewelry, and housewares as well as traditional crafts. ⊠ *Avs. Libertador and Pueyrredón, La Recoleta* ⊕ *www.feriaplazafrancia.com* ⊗ *Weekends 11–dusk.*

SHOES, HANDBAGS, AND LEATHER GOODS

Arandú. This three-story Recoleta town house sells chaps and bridles alongside asado steak knives, maté gourds, and silver jewelry. Racks stuffed with boots begging to be scuffed up gleam temptingly at the back of the shop, and if you find the supple canvas and leather sports bags too conventional, check out such novelties as leather rifle cases. Price tags are sky high, but the quality is superlative. ⊠ *Ayacucho 1924, Recoleta* ☎ *11/4800–1575* ⊕ *www.arandu.com.ar* Ⓜ *D to Callao (13 blocks away).*

Cardon. Pine floors, pine walls, pine cabinets: it's all very country at Cardon, where you can get the *estancia* look at reasonable high-street prices. The horsey set comes here for no-nonsense sheepskin jackets and riding boots. Cowboy hats and other traditional gaucho-style leather items from the *talabartería* line make great gifts. ⊠ *Av. Alvear 1750, Recoleta* ☎ *11/4816–0049* ⊕ *www.cardon-ecommerce.com.ar* Ⓜ *C to Retiro (13 blocks away)* ⊠ *Honduras 4755, Palermo Viejo* ☎ *11/4832–5925.*

Comme Il Faut. For foxier-than-thou footwear that's kicking up storms on milonga floors worldwide, head to Comme Il Faut; dedicated dancers love its combination of top-notch quality and gorgeous, show-stopping colors like teal or plum, usually with metallic trims. Animal-print suede, fake snakeskin, and glittering ruby take-me-home-to-Kansas numbers are some of the wilder options. ☒ *Arenales 1239, 3M, Barrio Norte* ☎ *11/4815–5690* ⊕ *www.commeilfaut.com.ar* Ⓜ *C to San Martín.*

Guido. In Argentina loafers mean Guido, whose retro-looking logo has been the hallmark of quality footwear since 1952. Try on timeless hand-made Oxfords and wingtips; there are also fun items like a tomato-red handbag or a cow-skin tote. Accessories include simple belts and suede wallets. ☒ *Av. Quintana 333, Recoleta* ☎ *11/4811–4567* ⊕ *www. guidomocasines.com.ar* Ⓜ *C to San Martín (10 blocks away).*

Lonte. There's something naughty-but-oh-so-nice about Lonte's shoes. Chunky gold peep-toe heels are a dream, and the outré animal-print numbers are a favorite of local diva, TV presenter Susana Giménez. For more discreet feet there are patent-leather boots or classic heels in straightforward colors. ☒ *Quintana 470, Recoleta* ☎ *11/4806–7083* ⊕ *www.lonteshoes.com.ar* Ⓜ *D to Callao (11 blocks away).*

Prüne. Smart working chicks, busy moms, and older ladies who lunch all adore Prüne's chic yet practical leather bags, with thoughtful compartments and enough room for all your stuff. Colors tend to be rich and dark, while guest collections offer a brighter, quirkier alternative. Details such as studs and steel rings linking bags to straps lend urban touches. Leather jackets, belts, and footwear are also sold at Prüne locations citywide. ☒ *Santa Fe 1619, Recoleta* ⊕ *www.prune.com.ar* Ⓜ *D to Tribunales (5 blocks away).*

Rossi y Caruso. Top-quality workmanship and classic cuts are what have been bringing distinguished customers such as King Juan Carlos of Spain to Rossi y Caruso since 1878. This flagship store specializes in riding gear (think Marlborough fox-hunt rather than Marlboro man) but also carries luggage, leather jackets, gloves, and shoes. Should you require a saddle, those sold here are the best in town. ☒ *Posadas 1387, Recoleta* ☎ *11/4811–1965* ⊕ *www.rossicaruso.com* Ⓜ *C to Retiro (14 blocks away).*

Zapatos de María. María Conorti was one of the first young designers to set up shop in this swanky part of town, and she's still going strong. Wedge heels, satin ankle-ties, and abundant use of patent leather in pumps and boots are the trademark touches of her quirky designs. Head to the basement at the back of the store for discounted footwear from past seasons. ☒ *Libertad 1665, Recoleta* ☎ *11/4815–5001* ⊕ *www. zapatosdemaria.com.ar* Ⓜ *C to Retiro (6 blocks away).*

WINE

Grand Cru. Incredibly savvy staff, some trained as sommeliers, will guide you through Grand Cru's peerless selection; the vast range is dominated by high-end wines from small vineyards. ☒ *Rodríguez Peña 1886, Recoleta* ☎ *11/4816–3975* ⊕ *www.grandcru.com.ar* Ⓜ *D to Callao.*

ALMAGRO

Aside from tango stores and Peruvian restaurants, Almagro is known for its art deco–style Abasto Shopping mall. This converted market, originally constructed in 1892, is a real focal point in the neighborhood.

CLOTHING

Marcelo Senra. Irregular natural linen, hand-knit sweaters, cow-hair boots—it's all about texture at Marcelo Senra, a long-established local designer. Loose, flowing evening dresses come in raw silk or satin, off-set by belts or chunky wooden jewelry. Handwoven accessories that complement the clothes' earthy palette are reason enough to visit Senra's Almagro showroom. Make a reservation first. ✉ *Sánchez de Loria 51, #3E, Almagro* ☎ *11/4861–2762* ⊕ *www.marcelosenra.com* Ⓜ *A to Loria.*

Stock Center. The official light-blue-and-white shirts worn by the Argentine soccer team, the Pumas (the national rugby team), and the Leonas (the women's field hockey team) are bestsellers and make excellent souvenirs. You can also pick up Converse, Nike, Adidas, and Puma clothing and footwear as well as übertrendy Gola sneakers at this sporting megastore. ✉ *Corrientes 3247, Abasto* ☎ *11/4861–5467* ⊕ *www.stockcenter.com.ar* Ⓜ *B to Carlos Gardel.*

Topper. The cuts of their tank tops and sweatpants aren't quite as spacey as Nike or Reebok, but then this classic Argentine brand's prices are more down-to-earth, too. Tennis wear is a strong player, not surprising given that Topper sponsors '70s legend Guillermo Vilas as well as younger superstars such as Facundo Arguello and David Nalbandian. There's also off-court action: the black Converse-lookalike sneakers have been a fashion staple for teenage gig-goers for decades. ✉ *Corrientes 3247, Almagro* ☎ *11/4861–2687* ⊕ *www.topper.com.ar* Ⓜ *B to Carlos Gardel.*

MALLS AND SHOPPING CENTERS

FAMILY **Abasto Shopping.** The soaring art deco architecture of what was once the city's central market is as much a reason to come here as the 250 shops spread over its three levels. Although Abasto has many top local chains, it isn't as exclusive as other malls, so relative bargains await at retailers like Ver, Yagmour, and Markova. Women can dress up at Paula Cahen d'Anvers, Akiabara, and Rapsodia; while men can hit trendy shops such as Bensimon, Prototype, and Old Bridge, or go for the *estanciero* look with smart La Martina polo wear. When you need a break, there's a top-floor food court beneath the glass panes and steel supports of the building's original roof. The mall is also home to Museo de los Niños (a hands-on children's museum) and a 12-screen cinema; you can pick up tickets for entertainment elsewhere in town at the Ticketek booth near the food court, too. ✉ *Av. Corrientes 3247, Almagro* ☎ *11/4959–3400* ⊕ *www.abasto-shopping.com.ar* Ⓜ *B to Carlos Gardel.*

PALERMO

The hungry gazes of fashionistas on the prowl, the sublime townhouse shop windows, the sheer number of retailers per cobbled block: there's no question that this is the heart of the city's fashion scene. Palermo is brimming with hip boutiques, outlet stores, shopping malls, and street markets.

BEAUTY

Epoca Bella. Step back in time and get your soapy wares sliced and weighed before splashing the cash. Try the super-fresh Oceánico bubble bath or Té de Hojas Verdes, a warm and comforting room spray you'll wish came as a perfume. The line has recently widened to include luxurious candles and aromatherapy oils. Also check out the new store at Gorriti 4865. ⊠ *Gorriti 5037, Palermo Viejo* ☎ *11/4834–6306* ⊕ *www. epocabella.com.ar* Ⓜ *D to Plaza Italia.*

Sabater Hermanos. Third-generation Spanish soap makers are behind this shop that sells nothing but—let's come clean about it—soap. Get into a lather over the trays of no-nonsense rectangles made with chocolate, lavender, malbec, and more. You can also buy soap in brightly colored petals and balls, or printed with pithy messages like, "Don't wash away your conscience." ⊠ *Gurruchaga 1821, Palermo Viejo* ☎ *11/4833–3004* ⊕ *www.shnos.com.ar* Ⓜ *D to Plaza Italia (6 blocks away).*

BOOKS AND MUSIC

Dain Usina Cultural. Known to regulars as the DUC, this artsy spot combines a terrace café and a tiny music venue with a terrific bookstore. Browse the ground floor for artistic tomes and local literature while tapping your toes to some live jazz. ⊠ *Nicaragua 4899, Palermo Viejo* ☎ *11/4778–3554* ⊕ *www.dainusinacultural.com* Ⓜ *D to Plaza Italia (8 blocks away).*

Libros del Pasaje. If you don't feel inspired to put pen to paper for your epic novel after visiting this well-stuffed book boutique, it simply isn't meant to be. Wander through to the café at the back to peruse your purchase or attend one of the regular literary workshops hosted here. ⊠ *Thames 1762, Palermo Viejo* ☎ *11/4833–6637* ⊕ *www. librosdelpasaje.com.ar* Ⓜ *D to Plaza Italia.*

Papelera Palermo. Making paper funky, piles of handmade sheets and envelopes, leather-bound diaries, and vintage notebooks are arrayed on simple trestle tables. Writing implements range from old-world pens to chunky pencils. The store often showcases work by top engravers and graphic artists, who return the favor by designing covers for sketchbooks. ⊠ *Cabrera 5227, Palermo Viejo* ☎ *11/4833–3081* ⊕ *www. papelerapalermo.com.ar* Ⓜ *D to Palermo.*

Prometeo. Trendy design types and bearded literature students frequent this corner store, which shares an entrance with the Miles Discos record shop. Non–Spanish speakers can bridge the language gap with *Sin palabras,* an illustrated how-to dictionary of Argentine gestures. Quirky gift options include flipbooks like *El gol del siglo,* depicting Maradona's celebrated goal against England in the 1986 World Cup. ⊠ *Honduras 4912, Palermo Viejo* ☎ *11/4833–1771* ⊕ *www.prometeolibros.com.ar* Ⓜ *D to Plaza Italia (8 blocks away).*

CLOTHING

A.Y. Not Dead. Rainbow vinyl, fake snakeskin, truckloads of nylon, and faux fur: seen anywhere other than under a strobe light, the clothes here might be hard to take. Guys can check out the men's collection down the road at Gurruchaga 1715. ⊠ *Gurruchaga 1637, Palermo*

Viejo ☎ *11/4833–2999* ⊕ *www.aynotdead.com.ar* Ⓜ *D to Plaza Italia (8 blocks away).*

Adidas Originals. This is one of the few Adidas shops in the world to stock limited-edition items, though there may only be one in the shop at any given time. If you're less fussy about other people owning the same clothes as you, there's a great range of shimmering tops and gold-accent sneakers that would do you proud on the dance floor—and possibly at the gym as well. ⊠ *Malabia 1720, Palermo Viejo* ☎ *11/4831–0090* ⊕ *www.adidas.com/ar* Ⓜ *D to Scalabrini Ortiz.*

BlackMamba. Rarely deviating from the house color (you guessed it, black), the collection here appeals to tough chicks and tougher guys: imagine mohair spider-web sweaters and stylish goth-meets-sexy vampire garments that fuse leather with natural fibers. ⊠ *Soler 4502, Recoleta* ☎ *11/4832–5083* ⊕ *www.beblackmamba.com* Ⓜ *D to Scalabrini Ortiz (6 blocks away).*

Kostüme. It's all very space odyssey at Kostüme, a B.A. Fashion Week fave. Extra-brief dresses might be made of netting or bunched-up nylon and worn over drainpipe trousers. Many tops are asymmetrical, and pants come with saddlebag-like protrusions. Check out the Vader boots, a collaboration with Pony. ⊠ *Gurruchaga 1585, Palermo Viejo* ☎ *11/4833–3595* ⊕ *www.kostumeweb.net* Ⓜ *D to Plaza Italia.*

Nadine Zlotogora. Bring a sense of humor to Nadine Zlotogora, where you fight your way through giant knitted cacti to peruse way-out designs which are playful yet exquisitely put together. Sheer fabrics are embroidered with organic-looking designs, then worn alone or over thin cotton. Even the menswear gets the tulle treatment: military-look shirts come with a transparent top layer. ⊠ *El Salvador 4638, Palermo Viejo* ☎ *11/4831–4203* ⊕ *www.nadinez.com* Ⓜ *D to Plaza Italia.*

Nike Soho. The recycled rooms of an old town house are the unlikely backdrop for this brand's more exclusive lines. Ultratech women's tees and flexible yoga shoes contrast with riotous floral wallpaper and mauve lace curtains. Paint-striped walls and chicken wire offset swoosh wear for the guys. ⊠ *Gurruchaga 1615, Palermo Viejo* ☎ *11/4832–3555* ⊕ *www.nike.com/ar/es_ar* Ⓜ *D to Plaza Italia.*

Refans A+. Soccer players, soap-opera stars, clubbers: everyone seems to be wearing one of Refans' trademark T-shirts. They come in ultrabright colors, emblazoned with quirky Italian phrases like "*Siamo fuori*" ("We are out," a reference to the FIFA World Cup). Lucas Castromán, a local soccer star himself, is behind the brand. Anoraks, hoodies, jeans, and messenger bags round out the offerings. ⊠ *El Salvador 4577, Palermo Viejo* ☎ *11/4833–9689* ⊕ *www.refans.net* Ⓜ *D to Scalabrini Ortiz* ⊠ *Arévalo 2843, Las Cañitas* ☎ *11/4777–7251.*

CLOTHING: MEN'S

Balthazar. Everything a modern gent needs—and plenty he didn't know he wanted—is sold inside this discreet Palermo town house. Find top-notch shirts, suits, cuff links, and even driving gloves. The bright hand-woven alpaca scarves in color blocks or stripes are bestsellers. ⊠ *Gorriti 5131, Palermo Viejo* ☎ *11/4834–6235* ⊕ *www.balthazarshop.com* Ⓜ *D* *to Palermo* ✉ *Defensa 1008, 1st fl., San Telmo* ☎ *11/4300–6926* Ⓜ *C or E to Independencia (walk 6 blocks along Estados Unidos).*

Bokura. Wooden shelving and layers of Persian rugs make Bokura look part general store and part 1,001 nights. Levi's-style jeans are reasonably priced; match them with slick leather jackets, shirts, and screen-printed, aged tees. ✉ *El Salvador 4677, Palermo Viejo* ☎ *11/4833–3975* ⊕ *www.bokura.com.ar* Ⓜ *D to Plaza Italia.*

Bolivia. Porteño dandies know that Bolivia is *the* place for metrosexual fashion. Expect floral prints on shirts and leather belts. Aged denim, top-quality silk-screened T-shirts, vintage military jackets, and hand-knit slippers are among the items that fill this converted Palermo town house to bursting. A bright, breezy store nearby at Costa Rica 4670 stocks women's wear and accessories, too. ✉ *Gurruchaga 1581, Palermo Viejo* ☎ *11/4832–6284* ⊕ *www.boliviaonline.com.ar* Ⓜ *D to Plaza Italia* ✉ *Nicaragua 4908, Palermo* ☎ *11/4832–6409.*

El CID. Keep it casual at El CID, a men's store that covers most bases, from well-cut linen trousers to attractive button-down shirts. Hipster gentlemen will love the animal print pants, floral bowties, and flamboyant cotton scarves. ✉ *Gurruchaga 1732, Palermo Viejo* ☎ *11/4832–3339* Ⓜ *D to Plaza Italia (7 blocks away).*

El Burgués. From natty suits to slick leather jackets, the togs here appeal to thoroughly modern men who appreciate a touch of old-school class. The polos are a smart buy, as are the tailored cotton shirts; pair them with chinos in the traditional palette or more outrageously hued ones that seem geared to the golf course. ✉ *Gurruchaga 1743, Palermo Viejo* ☎ *11/4834–6880* ⊕ *www.elburgues.com* Ⓜ *D to Plaza Italia (7 blocks away).*

Félix. Hipster alert: waxed floorboards, worn rugs, exposed brick, and aging cabinets set the tone for the cool clothes at Félix. Beat-up denim, crisp flower-power shirts, and knits that look like a loving granny whipped them up are among the many delights. A kids' collection lets Mini-Me duplicate dad's look. ✉ *Honduras 4916, Palermo Viejo* ☎ *11/4832-2164* ⊕ *www.felixba.com.ar* Ⓜ *D to Plaza Italia.*

Gola. Pick up polo shirts, sweaters, and loose-cut trousers from über-cool British sportswear label Gola. You'll also find a small, incongruous selection of posh Etiqueta Negra clothing, the brand responsible for making Gola garments locally. ✉ *Gurruchaga 1606, Palermo Viejo* ☎ *11/4833–4179* ⊕ *www.golaclassics.com* Ⓜ *D to Plaza Italia (9 blocks away).*

Hermanos Estebecorena. The approach at this trendy streetwear store is 100% practical: dreamed up by brothers who are industrial designers, all of the flat-front shirts, pants, and rain jackets have pockets, seams, and buttons positioned for maximum utility. Everything looks great, too. With a product range that includes footwear and underwear, it's a one-stop guy shop. ✉ *El Salvador 5960, Palermo Hollywood* ☎ *11/4772–2145* ⊕ *www.hermanosestebecorena.com* Ⓜ *D to Carranza.*

CLOTHING: WOMEN'S

Allô Martínez. Trashy but attractive is the best way to describe Allô Martínez's designs. Skinny satin pants and studded layered tees with plenty of leopard print will get you ready to rock, but you could go glam or formal in full-skirt, slightly Gothic ball gowns. ✉ *Honduras 4725, Palermo Viejo* ☏ *11/4831–3733* ⊕ *www.allomartinez.com* Ⓜ *D to Plaza Italia.*

Benito Fernández. Eye-popping colors, big prints, and unusual texture combinations characterize the light-hearted looks of Benito Fernández. Fans of his dramatic dresses include Sarah Jessica Parker, who requested that his Etnia collection be included in the *Sex and the City 2* wardrobe. ✉ *Armenia 1460, Palermo Viejo* ☏ *11/4833–0303* ⊕ *www. benitofernandez.com.ar/en* Ⓜ *D to Scalabrini Ortiz.*

Caro Cuore. Argentina's favorite underwear brand does cute cotton panty and bra sets in bright colors as well as plenty of sexier fare. Although the stuff sold here is fun for flopping on the couch or spending the day in bed, don't come looking for support, whether it's structural or from the sales staff. Assistants look on, unsympathetic to the fact that bras have no cup size. ✉ *Córdoba 4716, Palermo Viejo* ☏ *11/4833–7914* ⊕ *www.carocuore.net* Ⓜ *D to Scalabrini Ortiz.*

Cecilia Gadea. The simple, almost stark, cuts Gadea favors are the perfect canvas for riotously pretty texture work—a dress, for instance, might be adorned with hundreds of hand-embroidered petals. Feast further on her skirts, suits, and well-cut cotton tops. The high-heeled Mary Janes here, specially designed by Belocca, are part girly, part sophisticated. ✉ *Serrano 1536, Palermo Viejo* ☏ *11/4831–5930* ⊕ *www.ceciliagadea. com* Ⓜ *D to Plaza Italia.*

DAM. Quirky prints are the standout feature at DAM, a small boutique led by designer Carola Bessasso. Stylewise, you can expect feminine cuts and 1950s flair (the halter dresses are especially flattering); best of all, since Bessasso mixes unconventional materials with vintage finds, every piece is truly one of a kind. ✉ *Thames 1780, Palermo Viejo* ☏ *011/4831–1264* ⊕ *www.damboutique.com.ar* Ⓜ *D to Plaza Italia (8 blocks away).*

Desiderata. Check out this popular women's wear brand for light and airy shirts, dresses, and tees. The well-cut jeans are merciful on the wallet—and on the hips (they're available up to a size 12, that's an Argentine 5). ✉ *Córdoba 4453, Palermo Viejo* ☏ *11/4511–4345* ⊕ *www. desiderata.com.ar* Ⓜ *B to Malabia.*

Didi Bandol. The A-line coats, shiny fabrics, and blocks of primary colors are clearly a nod to the '60s, but the look is very now when they're combined with perfect drainpipe pants and an overlength T-shirt. The deal maker? Quality that's higher than many places in Palermo, at prices that are lower. ✉ *Gurruchaga 1767, Palermo* ☏ *11/4831–8041* ⊕ *www. bandol.com.ar* Ⓜ *D to Plaza Italia.*

Garza Lobos. Rubén Troilo and Constanza von Niederhäusern's innovative, well-constructed ready-to-wear has been exciting fans since their brand launched in 2010. Combining exciting textures, colors, and prints, Garza Lobos makes great use of leather, silk, and cashmere.

Look for the capsule collection of purses made in collaboration with Lázaro. ✉ *El Salvador 4734, Palermo Viejo* ☎ *11/4833–5280* ⊕ *www. garzalobos.com* Ⓜ *D to Plaza Italia (9 blocks away).*

JT by Jessica Trosman. Jessica Trosman has left the helm of her eponymous brand and taken an urban turn, giving her new JT label a fresh minimalist look that fuses geometric and industrial elements. The Villa Crespo store combines a design studio, a dressmaking workshop, and a textile lab—all in open view. ✉ *Humboldt 291, Villa Crespo* ☎ *11/4857–6009* ⊕ *www.jtbyjt.com* Ⓜ *B to Dorrego.*

Las Oreiro. The brainchild of Uruguayan actress Natalia Oreiro and her sister, Las Oreiro focuses on casual glam. Feminine yet sexy, their garments can do double duty as daywear and early-evening cocktail attire. ✉ *Honduras 4780, Palermo Viejo* ☎ *11/4834–6161* ⊕ *www.lasoreiro. com/institucional* Ⓜ *D to Plaza Italia (9 blocks away).*

Lupe. The '80s are alive and well at Lupe, where the bright T-shirt dresses are all about draping and plunging necklines, with plenty of animal prints. Also check out the fitted shirts and effective use of color blocks. ✉ *El Salvador 4666, Palermo Viejo* ☎ *11/4832–6743* ⊕ *www. lupeba.com.ar* Ⓜ *D to Plaza Italia.*

Mäda. This store hails from posh Uruguayan beach resort Punta del Este, so it's no surprise that bikinis (picture floral appliqués, glitter, and ruffles) are the main attraction. A comfortable selection of tunics, tank tops, and trousers complete the collection. ✉ *El Salvador 4865, Palermo Viejo* ☎ *11/4833–9622* ⊕ *www.madastore.com.ar* Ⓜ *D to Plaza Italia.*

María Cher. Let the yards of racks draw you into this lanky shop, where simple cuts and swaths of natural fabrics make urban working clothes feel a touch Jedi-like. The earthy, deconstructed look is heightened by details such as unfinished hems or exposed seams. This is one of the most popular women's brands around. ✉ *El Salvador 4724, Palermo Viejo* ☎ *11/4833–4736* ⊕ *www.maria-cher.com.ar* Ⓜ *D to Plaza Italia.*

María Lizaso. A rising star on the style scene, Maria Lizaso's Palermo showroom is definitely worth a visit (reservations are recommended). Go nautical with stripy Brit-inspired seaside apparel, or opt for an uptown look with one of her sassy LBDs. Brides-to-be will also want to ogle the young designer's gorgeous wedding gowns. ✉ *Julián Alvarez 1791, Palermo Viejo* ☎ *11/4864–1114* ⊕ *www.marializaso.com* Ⓜ *D to Scalabrini Ortiz (8 blocks away).*

Min Agostini. Acres of skirts, structured wraps with oversize funnel necks, and loads of layers: yes, it's all very Yamamoto. These party clothes maxing out on volume are the result of architect-turned-designer Jazmín Agostini's "building" her garments on mannequins, rather than using patterns (her cutting table is the centerpiece of the Palermo shop). ✉ *Gorriti 5204, Palermo Viejo* ☎ *11/4833–7563* ⊕ *www.minagostini. com.ar* Ⓜ *D to Palermo* ✉ *Libertad 1532* ☎ *11/4813–0805.*

Pesqueira. The young at heart and their kiddy counterparts can thrill together at the quirky use of animals on Pesqueira's signature pieces, including jumpsuits, bags, purses, and accessories. Don't leave without at least picking up a leather bear-face sling purse. ✉ *Gurruchaga*

1750, Palermo Viejo ☎*11/4833–7218* ⊕ *www.pesqueiratm.com* Ⓜ *D to Plaza Italia.*

Seco. Singing in the rain is encouraged at Seco, where all the clothes are designed to get wet but keep you dry. See-through plastic numbers come with matching rain hats worth risking a soaking for. Pick up a pretty umbrella that will weather any unexpected shower; the bright, beautiful bikinis are also tempting. ✉ *Armenia 1646, Palermo Viejo* ☎*11/4833–1166* ⊕ *www.secorainwear.com* Ⓜ *D to Plaza Italia.*

GIFTS AND SOUVENIRS

Elementos Argentinos. A fair-trade agreement links this luminous Palermo town house to a team of craftswomen in northwest Argentina who spin, dye, and weave the exquisite woolen goods sold here. Some of the handmade rugs, blankets, and throws follow traditional patterns and use only natural pigments (such as yerba maté or beetroot juice); others are contemporary designs using brighter colors. Packable souvenirs include sheep-wool table runners, alpaca scarves, and knitted cacti. Ask about designing your own rug. ✉ *Gurruchaga 1881, Palermo Viejo* ☎*11/4832–6299* ⊕ *www.elementosargentinos.com.ar* Ⓜ *D to Plaza Italia.*

Tienda Palacio. The slogan here is "Cool Stuff," and it's spot on. From dress-up refrigerator magnet sets of Evita and El Che to traditional penguin-shape wine jugs, Tienda Palacio is full of the nifty Argentine paraphernalia with a heavy emphasis on kitsch meeting tongue in cheek. ✉ *Honduras 5272, Palermo Viejo* ☎*11/4833–9456* ⊕ *www. tiendapalacio.com.ar/esp* Ⓜ *D to Palermo* ✉ *Defensa 926, San Telmo* ☎*11/4361–4325.*

HOME DECOR

Arte Étnico Argentino. Naturally-dyed weavings and hand-hewn wooden basins are some of the items made by indigenous craftsmen at this shop-slash-gallery, which prides itself on being a socially responsible business. Owner Ricardo Paz handpicks pieces such as tables carved from a single tree trunk; exquisite woolen rugs are the most transportable of the shop's temptations. ✉ *El Salvador 4656, Palermo Viejo* ☎*11/4832–0516* ⊕ *www.arteetnicoargentino.com* Ⓜ *D to Plaza Italia.*

Bartolomea. The adorable collection of kitchen ceramics at Bartolomea is hard to resist. Pastels breathe new life into vintage-inspired dinnerware, while the colorful penguin wine jugs make unique (and useful) souvenirs. ✉ *Dorrego 2212, Palermo Hollywood* ☎*11/4772–7601* ⊕ *www. bartolomea.com* Ⓜ *D to Carranza (5 blocks away).*

Calma Chicha. The fun household items in this warehouselike shop are proudly Argentine: quirky cowhide chairs, patchwork placemats, funky leather rugs, and geometric cushions nestle alongside mini-*parrillas* (barbecues), maté gear, and retro pingüino wine jugs. ✉ *Honduras 4925, Palermo Viejo* ☎*11/4831–1818* ⊕ *www.calmachicha.com* Ⓜ *D to Plaza Italia.*

Casa Chic. A hotel-boutique hybrid, this charming housewares haven specializes in rustic chic. There's an emphasis on lace, velvet, and crocheted textiles; snap up a woolen rug or wonderfully potent handmade

CLOSE UP

Life Before Malls

No shopping trip is complete without browsing one of the city's many *galerías*. These quirky shopping arcades are the precursors of malls and were mostly built in the 1960s and '70s. Their boxy architecture often includes gloriously kitsch touches, and the unpredictable retail offerings of their small stores could include designer gear, no-name brands, used books, sex toys, cigars and pipes, tattoos, imported vinyl records, and other wonders. Though many galerías have closed down, they're still thick on the ground along Avenida Santa Fe (800 to 1500) and Avenida Cabildo (1500 to 2200). For an underground experience, try Paseo Obelisco Sur. Set up by an eccentric millionaire, it runs under the vast Avenida 9 de Julio.

lavender soap. ⊠ *El Salvador 4786, Palermo Viejo* ☎ *11/4897–2040* ⊕ *www.casa-chic.com* Ⓜ *D to Plaza Italia.*

Pehache. Replicating a private home, this classic two-story edifice is filled with eye-catching items sourced from 80 Argentine designers. Browse among the hand-painted pingüino wine jugs and chunky woolen rugs; then wander upstairs to discover one-off jewelry pieces in the boudoir or head out back for a well-deserved coffee on the pretty patio. ⊠ *Gurruchaga 1418, Palermo Viejo* ☎ *11/4832–4022* ⊕ *www.pehache.com* Ⓜ *D to Plaza Italia.*

JEWELRY AND ACCESSORIES

Compañia de Sombreros. Whether it's a Panama hat for the blazing sun or a flat cap complete with ear flaps for a rough winter, this store has your headwear needs covered. For an authentic Argentine touch, get the urban gaucho look with a tartan *boina.* ⊠ *Borges Jorge Luis 2089, Palermo Soho* ☎ *11/4831–4886* ⊕ *www.companiadesombreros.com. ar* Ⓜ *D to Plaza Italia.*

Infinit. Infinit's signature thick acrylic eyeglass frames are favored by graphic designers and models alike. If the classic black rectangular versions are too severe for you, the same style comes in a range of candy colors and two-tones. Bug-eye shades and oversize '70s-inspired designs are other options. ⊠ *Thames 1602, Palermo Viejo* ☎ *11/4831–7070* ⊕ *www.infinit.la* Ⓜ *D to Plaza Italia.*

La Mercería. This sumptuous haberdashery is a shrine to texture. Piles of floaty Indian scarves, ostrich-feather fans, and fur-lined leather gloves beg to be stroked, then purchased. Even more hands-on are the reels of lace trims and sequined edging that line the walls. ⊠ *Honduras 4795, Palermo Viejo* ☎ *11/4831–8558* ⊕ *www.lamerceriaonline.com* Ⓜ *D to Plaza Italia.*

Manu Lizarralde. Forget diamonds. In Manu Lizarralde's hands it's uncut emeralds, topaz, and rough tourmaline that are a girl's best friend. His trademark chunky rings and heavy necklaces combine irregular semiprecious stones in geometric silver settings. ✉ *Gorriti 5078, Palermo Viejo* ☎ *11/4832–6252* ⊕ *www.manulizarralde.com* Ⓜ *D to Plaza Italia.*

María Medici. Industrial-looking brushed silver rings and necklaces knitted from fine stainless-steel cables are some of the attractions at this tiny shop. Architect and sculptor María Medici also combines silver with primary-color resin to make unusual-looking rings. ✉ *Niceto Vega 4619, Palermo Viejo* ☎ *11/4773–2283* ⊕ *mariamedici.blogspot.com.ar* Ⓜ *B to Malabia.*

Positivo. Among the kitsch offerings at Positivo are button-covered satin handbags, metallic maté vessels, and thermos flasks in enough garish colors to match any outfit. ✉ *Honduras 4866, Palermo Viejo* ☎ *11/4831–8559* ⊕ *www.positivodesign.com.ar* Ⓜ *D to Plaza Italia.*

MALLS AND SHOPPING CENTERS

Alto Palermo. A prime location, choice shops, and an aggressive marketing campaign have turned Alto Palermo into a popular destination. Giggly teenage hordes are seduced by its long, winding layout; ladies who lunch, conversely, are drawn to the cafés in its top-level food hall. The 150-plus shops are strong on local street-wear brands—including Bensimon and Bowen for the boys and Akiabara, Ona Sáez, Las Pepas, and Rapsodia for the girls. Check out Argentine trendsetters María Vázquez and A.Y. Not Dead for way-out party clothes, and Kill for simple yet effective staples. Cristóbal Colón specializes in surfer- and skater-wear, while Cheeky has a great range of clothes for kids and babies. Paruolo, Sibyl Vane, and Lázaro are the best of the mall's many good shoe and handbag shops. ✉ *Av. Santa Fe 3253, at Av. Colonel Díaz, Palermo* ☎ *11/5777–8000* ⊕ *www.altopalermo.com.ar* Ⓜ *D to Bulnes.*

Paseo Alcorta. If you're a serious shopper with only enough time to visit a single mall, make it this one. Resident fashionistas favor Paseo Alcorta for its mix of high-end local chains and boutiques from some of the city's best designers. Trendsetters such as Jazmín Chebar and Allô Martinez make cool clothes for women, while María Cher and Chocolate offer more classic chic; the men can hold their own at Etiqueta Negra and Félix. The international presence is strong, too, with stores like Swarovski, Lacroix, Cacharel, and Zara, as well as the usual sports brands. There's even a personal-shopper service if it all gets too overwhelming. Complimentary hotel transfers, free Wi-Fi, and a classy food hall give you further reasons to drop in. ✉ *Jerónimo Salguero 3172, at Av. Figueroa Alcorta, Palermo* ☎ *11/5777–6500* ⊕ *www.paseoalcorta. com.ar* Ⓜ *D to Bulnes.*

MARKETS

Feria de Plaza Cortázar. The business conducted in hip Palermo Viejo's Feria de Plaza Cortázar (also known as Plaza Serrano) rivals that done in the neighborhood's trendy boutiques. In a small square—which is actually round—artisans sell wooden toys, ceramics, and funky jewelry made of stained glass or vintage buttons. This is also a great place to purchase art: the railings around a playground here act as an open-air gallery for Palermo artists, and organizers control the quality of art on display. The feria continues on the sidewalks of Honduras and Serrano, which intersect at the square, then down the former on weekends and inside the bars on the square itself, which push their tables and chairs aside to make room for clothing and accessory designers: expect to find anything from cute cotton underwear and one-off T-shirts to clubbing dresses. Quality is often low, but so are prices. ☒ *Plaza Cortázar (Pl. Serrano) at Honduras and Serrano, Palermo Viejo* ☉ *Weekends 11– dusk* Ⓜ *D to Plaza Italia.*

Mercado de las Pulgas (*Flea Market*). On the edge of Palermo Hollywood lies the large warehouse sheltering the Mercado de las Pulgas, packed with furniture on its second—or third or fourth—time around. You won't come across any Louis XV, but original pieces from the 1940s, '50s, and '60s may turn out to be (relative) bargains. Lighting up your life is a cinch: choose from the many Venetian-glass chandeliers, or go for a chrome-and-acrylic mushroom lamp. If your taste is more rustic, there's also a sizable selection of hefty farmhouse-style tables and cabinets in oak and pine. Don't be deceived by the stalls' simple-looking set-up: vendors are used to dealing with big-name local customers, and can often arrange overseas shipping. ☒ *Alvarez Thomas between Dorrego and Concepción Arenales, Palermo Hollywood* ☉ *Daily 10–dusk* Ⓜ *B to Dorrego.*

SHOES, HANDBAGS, AND LEATHER GOODS

28Sport. These leather bowling sneakers and boxing-style boots are the heart and, er, sole of retro. All the models are variations on a classic round-toe lace-up, but come with different-length legs. Plain black or chestnut uppers go with everything, but equally tempting are the two-tone numbers—in chocolate and orange, or black with curving white panels, for example. Even the store is a nod to the past, kitted out like a 1950s living room. ☒ *Gurruchaga 1481, Palermo Viejo* ☎ *11/4833– 4287* ⊕ *www.28sport.com* Ⓜ *D to Plaza Italia (10 blocks away).*

Divia. Step out in a pair of limited-edition Divias and it doesn't really matter what else you've got on. Designer Virginia Spagnuolo draws inspiration from travels to India, her own vintage shoe collection, and even her cat. The results are leather collages—suede, textured metallic, or patent leathers—in colors such as teal, ruby, or plum. Really go to town and order a custom-made pair. ☒ *Armenia 1489, Palermo Viejo* ☎ *11/4831–9090* ⊕ *www.diviashoes.com* Ⓜ *D to Plaza Italia.*

Doma. Doma's leather jackets are both hard-wearing and eye-catching. Military-style coats in olive-green suede will keep you snug in winter, while collarless biker jackets in silver, electric blue, or deep red offer a cooler summer option. ☒ *El Salvador 4693, Palermo Viejo* ☎ *11/4831– 6852* ⊕ *www.doma-leather.com* Ⓜ *D to Plaza Italia.*

Fodor'sChoice ★ **Humawaca.** Thanks to its innovative shapes and funky colors, Humawaca is the hippest leather name in town. Cowhide is a favorite here, as are lively combinations like chocolate-brown leather and moss-green suede, or electric blue nubuck with a floral lining. Along with the expected bags and purses, you can pick up stylish laptop or travel totes. Price tags will make you gulp, but there are wallets, gloves, and pencil cases for more demure budgets. ☒ *El Salvador 4692, Palermo Viejo* ☎ *11/4832–2662* ⊕ *www.humawaca.com* Ⓜ *D to Plaza Italia* ☒ *Posadas 1380* ☎ *11/4811–5995.*

Jackie Smith. The hit leather brand Jackie Smith is the brainchild (and perhaps alter ego) of designer Valeria Smith. Characterized by boisterous colors, it includes an extensive range of fun and fabulous purses, clutches, handbags, and shoulder bags for 30-something women. ⊠ *Gurruchaga 1660, Palermo Soho* ☎ *11/4833–2995* ⊕ *jackiesmith. com* Ⓜ *D to Plaza Italia (8 blocks away).*

Josefina Ferroni. Thickly wedged heels and points that taper beyond reason and are some of Ferroni's trademarks. Stacked heels in dark textured leather with metallic trim look like a contemporary take on something Evita might have worn. If all that height brings on vertigo, fear not: the three-tone boots and ballet pumps are pancake-flat. ⊠ *Armenia 1687, Palermo Viejo* ☎ *11/4831–4033* ⊕ *www.josefinaferroni. com.ar* Ⓜ *D to Plaza Italia.*

Lázaro. Some are classic, others are ultrahip, but all Lázaro handbags and purses are notable for their simple lines, minimal adornment, and high-quality workmanship. Check out specific collections which include fabulous futuristic totes, document holders, and bandolier bags; plenty of inner divisions make them truly travel-worthy. ⊠ *Av. Santa Fe 3253, Alto Palermo shopping mall, Palermo* ☎ *11/5777–8221* ⊕ *www. lazarocuero.com.ar* Ⓜ *D to Bulnes.*

Mishka. At this longtime Palermo favorite, your feet will go to the ball in high-heel lace-ups, kick some butt in metallic boots, or feel like a princess sporting ballet pumps. Footwear comes in leather as well as in fabrics like brocade; most styles run narrow. You can also check out the San Telmo location at Balcarce 1011. ⊠ *El Salvador 4673, Palermo Viejo* ☎ *11/4833–6566* ⊕ *www.mishkashoes.com.ar* Ⓜ *D to Scalabrini Ortiz.*

Uma. Light, butter-soft leather takes very modern forms here, with geometric stitching the only adornment on jackets and asymmetrical bags that might come in rich violet in winter and aqua-blue in summer. The top-quality footwear includes teetering heels and ultrasimple boots and sandals with, mercifully, next to no elevation. Ultra-tight jeans, leather boots and tops are also on offer. ⊠ *Paseo Alcorta Mall, Shop 1049, Jerónimo Salguero 3172, at Av. Figueroa Alcorta, Palermo* ☎ *11/5777–6535* ⊕ *www.uma.com.ar* Ⓜ *D to Bulnes* ⊠ *Galerías Pacífico Mall, Shop 229, Calle Florida 753, at Av. Córdoba, Microcentro* ☎ *11/5555–5229.*

TOYS

Sopa de Príncipe. This spot specializes in funky fabric toys; heavy stitching gives their dolls an appealingly punky look. Crates are filled with an ark-worthy selection of button-eye calico animals, including some that can be worn as scarves and backpacks. Check out the fun zebras and pigs, too. ⊠ *Thames 1749, Palermo Viejo* ☎ *11/4831–8505* ⊕ *www. sopadeprincipe.com.ar* Ⓜ *D to Plaza Italia.*

WINE

Pain et Vin. A spacious wine store that also includes a café and patio perfect for sipping your purchase, Pain et Vin is run by a savvy husband-and-wife team. This recent addition to the Palermo wine scene takes pride in boutique labels and offers tastings, accompanied by house-baked sourdough. ✉ *Gorriti 5132, Palermo Soho* ☎ *11/4832–5654* Ⓜ *D to Plaza Italia.*

Fodor's Choice ★ **Terroir.** Wine lovers' dreams come true inside this white-stone town-house. Expert English-speaking staffers are on hand to help you make sense of the massive selection of Argentine wine, which includes collector's gems such as the 1999 Angélica Zapata Cabernet Sauvignon. They even arrange private wine-tasting courses to get you up to speed on local vintages: call a week or two before you arrive. ✉ *Buschiazzo 3040, Palermo* ☎ *11/4778–3443* ⊕ *www.terroir.com.ar* Ⓜ *D to Palermo.*

NIGHTLIFE

By Sorrel Moseley-Wil-liams

Preparing for a night out in Buenos Aires has an element of marathon training to it. Rest up with a siesta, fortify yourself with some protein, and drink plenty of fluids before, during, and after. That's right, the key to *porteño* nightlife is longevity—after all, an early night means hailing a cab at 6 am.

The scene here rivals that of any capital city, so you'll find something to suit every taste. Trendy cocktail bars, secret speakeasies, classic tango haunts, artsy watering holes, and packed dance floors await. To make the most of them, try following the locals' lead.

Painting Buenos Aires red means looking sharp, going with the flow as you bar-hop, and not challenging your new B.A. buddies to raucous drinking games. Porteños adore going out with their friends, but it's not uncommon to see a large group sharing a liter bottle of beer and swigging from the same glass. Latino lightweights? Not at all. This is just how Argentines roll—and once a night gets really rocking, they'll move onto their favorite tipple, Fernet y Cola.

Hours are relaxed, but there are general guidelines. The smartest bars kick off an evening with happy hours that begin around 8 pm and often stretch way beyond 60 minutes; downtown drinking establishments start even earlier to lure workers to part with hard-earned pesos, spawning the "after-office" across the city, which is now a nightlife fixture almost any day of the week. Theater performances begin around 9 pm and the last movie begins after midnight. By that point, lines to get into popular bars have started forming, but clubs aren't buzzing until 4 am. If in doubt, turn up later than you consider reasonable when you're meeting a local (30 minutes after the appointed time is the norm). The subte (subway) closes between 10 and 11 pm, depending on the line and day. Monday through Saturday it reopens at 5 am; on Sunday, however, trains don't start running again until 8 am. So taking a cab to and from home is a good idea—it's also quicker than waiting for a *colectivo* bus very late at night.

PLANNING

WHAT IT COSTS

Wines are generally very good value, with bottles in reputable bars starting at around 100 pesos. A liter of local beer costs 40 to 50 pesos, while soft drinks approach the 25 peso mark; cocktails are usually 50 pesos and up. Concert tickets start at 200 pesos, rising with the act's reputation. Nightclubs can charge a cover of around 80 pesos, which might include a drink; the posher ones charge more. Tips are roughly 10% on top of the bill.

WHAT ARE THE OPTIONS?

Begin plotting your course by going to the Arts & Media section of the daily *Buenos Aires Herald* newspaper for up-to-date information on musical gigs, theater, and tango shows. What's Up Buenos Aires (⊕ *www.whatsupbuenosaires.com*) is a good source for indie options, while the Spanish-language website Vuenoz Airez (⊕ *www.vuenozairez. com*) makes daily recommendations covering everything from art to live music.

Bars: Porteños aren't the heaviest of drinkers, but they excel at everything else that the bar scene involves—talking at length, seeing and being seen, flirting, and staying out until dawn. There's a wide variety of places where they can indulge in such behavior. Cocktail bars are increasingly popular, and world-class mixologists take pride in their original *tragos*. Late-night bars—while late-night by most rational standards—should not be confused with the *late* late-night bars known as "afters." Spending the wee hours at one (or even hopping between several) rounds off the night-time routine, so pace yourself.

Dance Clubs: An influx of foreign DJs may be affecting the local flavor of Buenos Aires' electronic music scene, but it's also supporting a more diverse range of nightly parties. There's plenty to please, especially if you like your house music progressive and your dress code smart.

Gay and Lesbian Nightlife: With a gay-friendly attitude, Buenos Aires has a whole network of bars, clubs, meeting points, and milongas. Many free gay guides, found in hotels and boutiques, help you navigate the scene; GayBA (⊕ *www.gay-ba.com*) is available in bookshops and kiosks.

Live Music: *Rock nacional* (Argentine rock) makes up the majority of live music. There's a small but lively jazz scene, a buzzing indie/electro-pop circuit, and—for those who need reminding that they're in South America—folk *peñas* (meeting places), where guitars, pan pipes, and unpretentious singers conjure the spirit of the Andes.

Tango: The passion, drama, and nostalgia of tango is the most concise expression of the spirit of Buenos Aires—and a *milonga* (tango dance hall) should definitely be on every visitor's itinerary. Many offer reasonably priced early-evening classes for all levels. Whether you join in or not, spend some time at a floorside table to appreciate the ritual.

CENTRO

Chaotic during the workday, the downtown area can be deserted at night and on weekends. But you'll find some great bars and clubs here, if you know where to look.

BARS

BASA Basement Bar. A new kid in Retiro, BASA comes from great stock given that its owners founded the legendary Gran Bar Danzón. Look down and be drawn in by the bright bottles of spirits. Try a Moscow Mule (ginger beer, made in-house, gives it an appropriate kick), or ask Ludovico, the London-trained head barman, for suggestions. ✉ *Basavilbaso 1328, Centro* ☎ *11/4893–9444* ⊕ *www.basabar.com.ar* Ⓜ *C to Retiro.*

Dadá. Cozy and colorful, Dadá has a short but sweet list of classic cocktails and an ideal bar to perch at while sipping one. With its owners doubling as bar staff, Dadá sees an eclectic mix of locals and visitors popping in for dinner, a drink, or both. Grab a booth at the back for extra privacy. ✉ *San Martin 941, Centro* ☎ *11/4314–4787* Ⓜ *C to San Martín.*

Florería Atlántico. A flower shop and wine store combined with a whole lot of bar, this hip basement watering hole opened in 2013 and quickly became a fixture on the growing Retiro scene. The cocktail menu draws inspiration from Argentina's immigrant history (the Italians, Spaniards, English, and French have all played their part). Join the cool crowd and kick back with a Vinedo Italiano Spritz. ✉ *Arroyo 872, Centro* ☎ *11/4313–6093* ⊕ *www.floreriaatlantico.com.ar* Ⓜ *C to Retiro.*

The Kilkenny. A popular Irish pub that spawned a whole street of imitators, the Kilkenny serves surprisingly good food and has a well-stocked bar. Celtic or rock bands play nightly, entertaining an after-work crowd from nearby offices that comes for the extended happy hour and stays on into the wee hours. ✉ *Marcelo T. de Alvear 399, Centro* ☎ *11/4312–7291* ⊕ *www.thekilkenny.com.ar* Ⓜ *C to San Martín.*

La Cigale. After moving two blocks down the road, La Cigale has undergone a serious upgrade, proving that size does matter. Take advantage of happy hour until 10 pm at its curvaceously seductive first-floor bar, which leads to the streetside balcony and smokers' corner. Another flight of stairs winds up to the stage, ready and waiting for local indie, jazz, and acoustic bands any night of the week. ✉ *25 de Mayo 597, Centro* ☎ *11/4893–2332* ⊕ *www.lacigalebar.blogspot.com* Ⓜ *B to L. N. Alem.*

DANCE CLUBS

Fodor's Choice ★ **Bahrein.** Sheik—er, *chic* and super-stylish, this party palace is located in a former bank. The Funky Room is where beautiful, tightly clothed youth groove to pop, rock, and funk, while the basement Excess Room has electronic beats and dizzying wall visuals. For a more sophisticated dinner-before-dancing vibe, head upstairs to the Yellow Room. This is a great spot to catch local DJs in action. ✉ *Lavalle 345, Centro* ☎ *11/4314–8886* ⊕ *www.bahreinba.com* Ⓜ *B to Alem.*

Cocoliche. Cocoliche enjoys cult status in both the straight and gay communities. Upstairs is a diverse art gallery big on young locals; downstairs, underground house and techno drives one of the city's darkest dance floors, while DJs with huge followings line up to take on the decks. ⊠ *Rivadavia 878, Centro* ☎ *11/4342–9485* ⊕ *www. cocoliche.net* Ⓜ *A to Piedras.*

GAY AND LESBIAN NIGHTLIFE

Club One. Also fondly known by its previous name, Palacio Alsina, this enormous downtown club meets all the prerequisites for an excellent night out—especially when world-famous DJs make a guest appearance. Pop tunes attract a mixed-age gay and lesbian crowd on Friday and Sunday; Saturday delivers hard electronica for the dance-mad. ⊠ *Alsina 940, Centro* ☎ *11/4331–3231* ⊕ *www.clubonebsas.com. ar* Ⓜ *A to Piedras.*

Contramano. This was a pioneering gay disco when it opened in 1984, but—like its clientele—Contramano has grown up. Today it operates more as a small, laid-back bar with an older, male-only clientele. Occasionally there's live music and male strippers. ⊠ *Rodríguez Peña 1082, Centro* ⊕ *www.contramano.com* Ⓜ *D to Callao.*

Flux. It took a couple of expats to realize the gap in the market for early-evening gay bars. Their creation, Flux, is a smart, friendly, and sociable basement club that gets going for happy hour and keeps on until after midnight with decent pop music and an ample cocktail menu. ⊠ *Marcelo T. de Alvear 980, Centro* ☎ *11/5252–0258* ⊕ *www.fluxbar. com.ar* Ⓜ *C to San Martín.*

LIVE MUSIC

Bebop. Lurking beneath Aldo's Vinoteca Restorán, this new musical hot spot is led by sommelier and owner Aldo Graziani. A huge jazz fan, he makes sure that the offbeats are well paired with fine wine and tasty bar food. ⊠ *Moreno 364, Monserrat* ☎ *11/4331–3409* ⊕ *bebopclub. com.ar* Ⓜ *A to Plaza de Mayo.*

Gran Rex. Exquisite art deco theaters line Avenida Corrientes, but the rationalist-style Gran Rex—constructed by architect Alberto Prebisch, of the Obelisk fame—is a favorite venue for rock, pop, and jazz musicians. Recent acts that have tested its great acoustics include Coldplay and the legendary Peter Frampton. Tickets are available through Ticketek (⊕ *www.ticketek.com.ar*). ⊠ *Corrientes 857, Centro* ☎ *11/4322–8000* ⊕ *www.teatro-granrex.com.ar* ☺ *Box office daily 10–10* Ⓜ *B to Carlos Pellegrini.*

BIG-NAME CONCERTS

After years of relative isolation, Buenos Aires is becoming part of a South American tour circuit that includes São Paolo and Santiago, so big international acts visit fairly frequently and invariably play to packed audiences. Well-established artists tend to perform at large outdoor festivals or stadium shows in **Club Ciudad de Buenos Aires** (⊠ *Libertador 7501* ☎ *11/4702-7796* ⊕ *www. clubciudad.org.ar*) or **Estadio River Plate** (⊠ *Figueroa Alcorta 7597* ☎ *11/4789-1200* ⊕ *www. riverplate.com*), both in the Nuñez district.

TIPS FOR A GOOD NIGHT OUT

Don't be afraid to stand in line outside. Lines are generally quick and painless—and if there isn't one, the place might not be worth visiting.

Buy a ticket or make a reservation. For concerts, shows, and club events, people often buy tickets in advance, as many do fill up or sell out, especially international offerings.

Go late—really. Otherwise you'll miss out on the atmosphere and find it a bit boring. If necessary, help smooth the adjustment with a *merienda* (a snack of coffee and croissants at around 6 pm) and a "disco siesta."

Find out what's on and where. Scour flyers, websites, ticket agencies, and magazine listings for up-to-date information. There's a lot more going on than you can find out from any single source.

Dress to impress. Porteños like fine clothes, though their style tends to be on the conservative side. So skip the shorts and flip-flops (both social no-nos) in favor of something fashionable. With the exception of one or two scruffy bars in San Telmo, you'll never feel overdressed.

Never imagine you've seen it all. Private parties and last-minute underground events are where it's at. Finding out about them isn't easy, but keep an ear out and tell people you're looking and you might luck out.

Groove. This nightclub, which doubles as a live music venue, may be oddly shaped for spot-on acoustics; however, it attracts plenty of underground and international artists. Weekly parties, metal bands, and European electronic combos form the changing lineup. ⊠ *Santa Fe 4389, Palermo* ☎ *11/5368–0679* ⊕ *www.palermogroove.com* Ⓜ *D to Plaza Italia.*

Luna Park. This indoor stadium at the very top of Corrientes Avenue has been hosting boxing events, ice-skating spectaculars, political rallies, plus rock and pop concerts for more than 80 years. Local acts dominate, but international ones—like Simply Red and Lily Allen—also play here. Tickets normally need to be bought well in advance from the box office or from Ticketportal (⊕ *www.ticketportal.com.ar*). ⊠ *Av. Madero 420, Centro* ☎ *11/5279–5279* ⊕ *www.lunapark.com.ar* ☉ *Box office weekdays 10–7, Sat. 12–7* Ⓜ *B to L. N. Alem.*

ND/Ateneo. This spacious theater and cultural space mainly showcases midlevel local bands, showmen, and comedians, with a few big Argentine names thrown in for good measure. Get tickets at the box office (Monday–Saturday, from noon to 8) or through Ticketek (⊕ *www. ticketek.com.ar*). ⊠ *Paraguay 918, Centro* ☎ *11/4328–2888* ⊕ *www. ndateneo.com.ar* Ⓜ *C to San Martín.*

Ultra. The owners of this dynamic space for art and live music have run an independent record label for more than a decade. On weekends they throw big parties until daybreak, and on most weeknights there's a strong line-up of local bands. ⊠ *San Martin 678, Centro* ☎ *11/4312–5605* ⊕ *www.ultrapop-ar.blogspot.com* Ⓜ *C to Lavalle.*

TANGO
MILONGAS

Confitería Ideal. Soaring columns, tarnished mirrors, and ancient chandeliers are part of Confitería Ideal's crumbling Old World glamour, along with a rather pungent musty smell. The former homewares store that reinvented itself as a tearoom now hosts milongas organized by different groups in its first-floor dance hall every day of the week. Some are held during the afternoon and evening, others late at night. ✉ *Suipacha 384, Plaza de Mayo* ☎ *11/4328–7750* ⊕ *www.confiteriaideal.com* Ⓜ *C to 9 de Julio.*

El Beso. The standard of dancing is usually high at this club, which belongs to La Academia del Tango Milonguero, one of the city's best tango schools. Intermediate dancers can get their footwork up to speed at daily classes before putting themselves to the test at the milongas, run by different organizers Tuesday through Sunday. ✉ *Riobamba 416, Congreso* ☎ *11/3166–4800* ⊕ *www.laacademiatango.com* Ⓜ *B to Callao.*

La Marshall. A refreshing exception to the sometimes suffocatingly macho world of tango, this is *the* gay milonga. The main night is Friday, when a cool set of guys and girls, both gay and straight, look to break with the "he leads, she follows" doctrine. ✉ *Riobamba 416, Congreso* ☎ *11/4300–3487* Ⓜ *B to Callao.*

MUSIC CLUBS

Gran Café Tortoni. Excellent local musicians put on daily performances of tango classics in the downstairs salon of this legendary café, but note that ticket prices can be steeper than average because of the venue's illustrious history. There's jazz sometimes on weekends, too. ✉ *Av. de Mayo 829, Plaza de Mayo* ☎ *11/4342–4328* ⊕ *www.cafetortoni.com.ar* Ⓜ *A to Peru.*

PUERTO MADERO

A business district whose star has risen over the past decade, this formerly dilapidated dockland has adjusted well to its face-lift. Centrally located and home to some of the city's chicest hotels, restaurants, and bars, the Puerto Madero scene keeps getting better and better.

BARS

Asia de Cuba. Once *the* spot to be seen sipping Champagne and eating sushi, Asia de Cuba still draws a smattering of Argentine celebrities, though it's now lost some of its white-hot luster. Candlelight and a red-and-black Asian decor set the mood for an exotic evening—by local standards. Grab a booth to watch and be watched. ✉ *Pierina Dealessi 750, Puerto Madero* ☎ *11/4894–1329* ⊕ *www.asiadecuba.com.ar* Ⓜ *A or D to Catedral.*

TANGO

Madero Tango. Local businesspeople looking to impress international clients invariably choose this showy concept restaurant. A night here may break the bank, but you get varied, highly professional performances sometimes starring Argentinean celebrities. Prices vary depending on

When the Sun Comes Up

Nightlife kicking off so late means that regular cafés are open for a hard-earned *cortado* (coffee cut with a splash of milk) and *medialunas* (croissants) by the time you stumble out of a club at sunrise, but Buenos Aires does offer a couple of crack-of-dawn alternatives. The first is to head to the Costanera for a *choripan* (chorizo sausage and chimichurri sauce on a roll) from the 24-hour stands lining the river. If you're not already near the Costanera, sharing a taxi with friends to get there is part of the fun. The more hard-core option is to keep dancing at one of the many "afters"—clubs that start at 9 am and go until around 3 pm.

how close you are to the stage. ✉ *Alicia Moreau de Justo at Brasil, Puerto Madero* ☎ *11/5239–3009* ⊕ *www.maderotango.com* Ⓜ *C to San Juan.*

Fodor's Choice ★ **Rojo Tango.** Five-star food, musicians, choreography, and glamour: you wouldn't expect anything less from the Faena Hotel. Crimson velvet and gold trim line everything from the walls to the menu at El Cabaret, and tables often hold celebs both local and global. The implausibly good-looking troupe puts on a tango-through-the-ages show, which includes jazz-tango, semi-naked numbers, and even the tango version of Roxanne from *Moulin Rouge*. It's worth raiding the piggy bank for. ✉ *Martha Salotti 445, Puerto Madero* ☎ *11/4952–4111* ⊕ *www. rojotango.com* Ⓜ *D to Catedral.*

SAN TELMO

Originally an immigrant neighborhood, San Telmo continues to be revamped with establishments popping up to cater to the latest wave of visitors to the city—backpackers, expats, and tango hunters. Now home to dozens of trendy bars, the bohemian district is coming into its own again. La Boca to the south, on the other hand, is still best avoided at night.

BARS

Bar Británico. Opened in 1928, this traditional corner bar opposite Parque Lezama is an iconic spot. Day and night it's full of characters who engage in passionate discussions or simply watch the world unfold through the oversized windows. Imbued with nostalgia, Bar Británico has a cinematic appeal—which may explain why it has appeared in movies like *The Motorcycle Diaries* and Francis Ford Coppola's *Tetro*. ✉ *Brasil 399, at Defensa, Barracas* ☎ *11/4300–6894* ⊘ *Mon. 8 am–midnight, Tues.–Sun. 24 hrs* Ⓜ *C to San Juan.*

Breoghan Brew Bar. Two brothers with a passion for craft beer lead this pub, which has become a refreshing alternative to the expat haunt Gibraltar. Ramiro Rodríguez, who also mans the bar, makes all the brews on site; some have even picked up excellence awards in South America. ⊠ *Bolívar 860, San Telmo* ☎ *11/4300–9439* ⊕ *www.breoghanbar.com.ar* Ⓜ *C to Independencia.*

Doppelgänger. With a list of 100 cocktails and an excellent menu to match, this corner bar on the edge of San Telmo is a hidden gem. The fancy glassware and quotations in the menu show that the "double" concept has been thought through down to the finest details. But your focus should be on having a good time as you sip carefully made libations. Happy hour runs from 7 to 9, Tuesday through Friday. ⊠ *Av. Juan de Garay 500, San Telmo* ☎ *11/4300–0201* ⊕ *www.doppelganger.com. ar* Ⓜ *C to San Juan.*

Gibraltar. A traditional British boozer, Gibraltar delivers a taste of London in the heart of San Telmo: ale is poured at the classic wooden bar, and fish-and-chips tops the menu. It also sports a back-room pool table, an outdoor patio, and a standoffish staff. Sink into a leather sofa to watch the big soccer game on the small screen, or take over a wooden booth for an evening. ⊠ *Perú 895, San Telmo* ☎ *11/4362–5310* ⊕ *www. thegibraltarbar.com* Ⓜ *C to Independencia.*

Indie Bar. This modern watering hole—an underrated corner bar on the eastern edge of San Telmo—serves up drinks under mood lighting. A predominantly local crowd is lured in for early-evening cocktails from 6 to 9, with happy-hour prices. ⊠ *Paseo Colón 843, San Telmo* ☎ *11/4307–0997* ⊕ *www.indiebar.com.ar* Ⓜ *C to Independencia.*

Krakow. Owned by a Polish expat, Krakow has one of the lengthiest bars in the neighborhood, plus a great selection of on-tap beers, European-style fare, and a big screen for those all-important soccer matches. It's one of the few bars in the city to offer Wii games. ⊠ *Venezuela 474, San Telmo* ☎ *11/4342–3916* ⊕ *www.krakow-cafe.com.ar* Ⓜ *D to Catedral.*

La Puerta Roja. Pass through the titular scarlet entrance and clamber up the stairs to this trendy yet friendly bar. There's a wide selection of spirits and beers on tap, as well as a pool table, and a sociable mix of local and expat regulars. If you need to nibble, bar snacks here are above average. ⊠ *Chacabuco 733, San Telmo* ☎ *11/4362–5649* ⊕ *www. lapuertaroja.com.ar* Ⓜ *C to Independencia.*

Las del BarCo. Get down with the hipsters who spill out onto the San Telmo sidewalk rain or shine when Las del BarCo gets too full. Pull up a love seat and grab a pint, or check out the ever-changing art exhibitions. Fun and frivolous, this hot spot has already attracted a dedicated following—and not just for its extended happy hour. ⊠ *Bolívar 684, San Telmo* ☎ *11/4331–3004* ⊕ *www.lasdelbarcobar.blogspot.com* Ⓜ *C to Independencia.*

FOLK MUSIC

Originating in the northwestern part of the country, Argentine folk music is heavy on vocal harmonies, drums, and wind instruments. You can hear it in *peñas folkloricas* (informal music halls specifically for folk music). Although most are far from the center and difficult to find, Palermo now has a few of its own, including La Peña del Colorado and Los Cardones.

4

M. You'll recognize M by its one-letter name writ large in ivy near the entrance. Once inside, pull up a red velvet stool at the ground-floor bar for an impeccable cocktail, or reserve your place at the *cava* downstairs for a wine-tasting session. Don't forget to peek at the tunnel which former president Juan Perón used to escape from Government House. M also houses Samsung Studio, San Telmo's latest tiny yet trendy live music venue, round the back. ⊠ *Balcarce 433, San Telmo* ☎ *11/4331–3879* ⊕ *www.mbuenosaires.com.ar* Ⓜ *D to Catedral.*

Makena Cantina Club. A buzzing space that takes music seriously, Makena focuses on funk, soul, and R&B; it also hosts live jams several nights per week. Check out the Afromama night, guaranteed to get you moving then grooving. ⊠ *Fitz Roy 1519, Palermo Hollywood* ☎ *11/4772–8281* ⊕ *www.makenacantinaclub.com.ar* Ⓜ *D to Palermo.*

Oasis Clubhouse. A private members' club and bolthole unexpectedly located in the middle of Palermo Soho, the lush Oasis Clubhouse now opens its doors to nonmembers (subject to guest list approval). Relax around the outdoor swimming pool with a well-prepared cocktail, or lounge in the living space—you'll feel like a VIP regardless. ⊠ *Address supplied on confirmation, Palermo Soho* ☎ *11/4832–5276* ⊕ *clubhouseba.com.*

DANCE CLUBS

Rey Castro. Just because this Cuban restaurant-bar gets a little wild on weekends doesn't mean things get out of hand: the bouncers look like NFL players. It's a popular spot for birthday parties and great mojitos. After the nightly live dance show, DJs crank up the Cuban rhythms; you're likely to learn some sexy new moves. ⊠ *Perú 342, San Telmo* ☎ *11/4342–9998* ⊕ *www.reycastro.com* Ⓜ *A to Perú.*

GAY AND LESBIAN NIGHTLIFE

M.O.D. Variete Club. Mainly attracting men keen for a pick-up, Friday cabaret nights at M.O.D. are buzzing—expect glamour and fun, with plenty of dancing to indie, rock, and '80s music. Slip into the VIP area to get close to the stars of the show. ⊠ *Balcarce 563, San Telmo* ⊕ *www.modclub.com.ar* Ⓜ *D to Catedral.*

LIVE MUSIC
ROCK

La Trastienda. A San Telmo institution, this cabaret-style club is one of Buenos Aires' most popular venues, so grab a table and enjoy an intimate performance for 900. La Trastienda is the place to catch electrotango or new tango groups, although it takes pains to promote other genres as well. Check out national pop and rock legends, as well as local rock, reggae, and funk. ⊠ *Balcarce 460, San Telmo* ☎ *11/4342–7650* ⊕ *www.latrastienda.com* Ⓜ *A to Bolivar.*

TANGO
DINNER SHOWS

Bar Sur. Once a bohemian haunt, this bar went international after serving as a major location for Wong Kar-Wai's cult indie film *Happy Together.* The move to the mainstream has led to glitzier dancing, as well as increasingly bad food and indifferent service. Still, the worn checkered floor and Old World bar make a charming backdrop. ⊠ *Estados*

Unidos 299, San Telmo ☎ *11/4362–6086* ⊕ *www.bar-sur.com.ar* Ⓜ C *to Independencia.*

El Querandí. The polished shows at this classic café trace the history of the tango. The dancing and costumes are great, although the stagy interludes might make you wince. ⊠ *Perú 322, at Moreno, Monserrat* ☎ *11/5199–1770* ⊕ *www.querandi.com.ar.*

El Viejo Almacén. This place was founded by legendary tango singer Edmundo Rivero, but he wouldn't recognize the slick outfit his bar has become. Inside the colonial building lurks a tireless troupe of dancers and musicians who perform showy tango and folk numbers. ⊠ *Balcarce 793--799, at Independencia, San Telmo* ☎ *11/4307–6689* ⊕ *www.viejo-almacen.com.ar* Ⓜ C *to Independencia.*

La Esquina de Homero Manzi. In the heart of the low-key Boedo neighborhood, 30 blocks west of San Telmo, La Esquina was once a traditional café favored by the barrio's old men: in fact, the famous 1948 tango *Sur* begins by mentioning its location on the corner of San Juan and Boedo. After getting the Disney-tango treatment, it's now a kind of 1940s concept bar—though its checkered floor and original bar remain. Performances are showy but reasonably priced. ⊠ *San Juan 3601, Boedo* ☎ *11/4957–8488* ⊕ *www.esquinahomeromanzi.com.ar* Ⓜ E *to Boedo.*

Mansión Dandi Royal. The unashamedly theatrical show at this tango-concept hotel dances you through the history of tango. It's a fascinating look at how the dance evolved, and the hotel's art nouveau architecture is pretty fantastic, too. ⊠ *Piedras 922, San Telmo* ☎ *11/4361–3537* ⊕ *www.mansiondandiroyal.com* Ⓜ C *to Independencia.*

Señor Tango. It doesn't get much glitzier—or much tackier. Performed daily, the unashamedly tourist-oriented shows are so eager to cash in on stereotypes that they even include a number from *Evita* (shock, horror). Still, you can't fault the fishnetted dancers on their footwork. Rather less glam is its location south of San Telmo, in the Barracas neighborhood, which can be sketchy: take a taxi here and back. ⊠ *Vieytes 1655, Barracas* ☎ *11/4303–0231* ⊕ *www.srtango.com* Ⓜ H *to Hospitales.*

MILONGAS

Buenos Ayres Club. Rousing live orchestras keep even nondancers entertained at the nontraditional milongas that are this club's hallmark. La Orquesta Típica el Afronte provides the music for La Maldita (☎ *11/4560–1514*) on Sunday, Monday, and Wednesday, while El Toque Cimarron Salsa (P*11–15/3827–7786)* takes charge on Thursday. Tuesday's Tango Queer (☎ *11–15/3252–6894* ⊕ *www.tangoqueer.com*) draws both gay and straight dancers looking to escape the confines of more conservative dance floors; Friday takes a different turn once again with Latin American music. ⊠ *Perú 571, San Telmo* ☎ *11/4331–1518* ⊕ *www.buenosayresclub.com* Ⓜ D *to Catedral.*

MUSIC CLUBS

Centro Cultural Torquato Tasso. Here classic trios and quartets share the stage with young musicians performing hip tango and folk sets. There are also milongas on weekends. ⊠ *Defensa 1575, San Telmo* ☎ *11/4307–6506* ⊕ *www.torquatotasso.com.ar* Ⓜ C *to San Juan.*

The *Señor Tango* show in San Telmo —photo by laubenthal, Fodors.com member

RECOLETA

Though upscale Recoleta isn't the nightlife spot Palermo and San Telmo are, there's still plenty here and just west in Barrio Norte to warrant exploration. You can find everything from swanky after-office spots to neighborhood watering holes—just avoid the seedier places near Recoleta Cemetery that add a zero to the bill for foreigners.

BARS

Casa Bar. A sports bar rather incongruously housed in a beautiful French mansion, Casa Bar lures in year-abroad students keen for an NFL or European soccer fix, plus an older foreign crew eager to get some spicy chicken–wing action. If balls aren't your bag, perch at the bar for a drink well made with imported liquor. ⊠ *Rodriguez Peña 1150, Recoleta* ☎ *11/4816–2712* ⊕ *www.thecasabar.blogspot.com* Ⓜ *D to Pueyrredón.*

El Alamo Bar. From the outside, it's only the signs asking patrons to leave quietly that suggest this isn't the demure bar it appears to be. The generous drinks promotions (ladies drink free until midnight on Friday) add substantial rowdiness, and it turns into a raucous party zone on weekends. A sports bar at heart, El Alamo also hosts bikini competitions—just so you know. You can also check out its sister branch in Palermo at Córdoba 5267. ⊠ *Uruguay 1177, Recoleta* ☎ *11/4813–7324* ⊗ *24 hrs* Ⓜ *D to Tribunales.*

Gran Bar Danzon. If Carrie Bradshaw lived in Buenos Aires, she'd probably frequent this first-floor hot spot where local business sharks and chic internationals sip cocktails and eat sushi by candlelight. It's extremely

Continued on page 144

The Dance of Buenos Aires

by Victoria Patience

"THE TANGO IS MACHO, THE TANGO IS STRONG. IT SMELLS OF WINE AND TASTES LIKE DEATH."

So goes the famous tango "Why I Sing Like This," whose mix of nostalgia, violence, and sensuality sum up what is truly the dance of Buenos Aires. From its beginnings, tango and its two-four beat marked and reflected the character of Buenos Aires. You may hear strains of tango on the radio while sipping coffee in a café, see high-kicking sequined dancers in a glitzy dinner show, or listen to musicians in a darkened cabaret. But one of the most memorable ways to experience the best of this broody, melancholic, impassioned art form is through dancing it yourself.

DANCING THE TANGO

Many milongas now kick off with group dance classes which usually last an hour or two and cost 15–20 pesos; some lessons are free, though chaotic. These classes are great for getting over nerves and getting you in the mood. However, most *milongueros* (people who dance at *milongas*, or tango dance halls) take tango very seriously and don't look kindly on left-footed beginners crowding the floor. We recommend you take a few private classes first—they can make a huge difference to your technique.

English-speaking private teachers abound in Buenos Aires; classes generally last 1½ hours and prices can range from $20 to $80 a class. Complete beginners should plan on at least three or four classes before hitting a milonga. Many private instructors organize milonga outings with groups of their students (usually for a separate fee). Others even offer a so-called "taxi dance service": you pay for them to dance with you all night. See the end of this feature for a rundown of some of the best options for lessons and milongas.

DANCE STYLES

Tango milonguero, the style danced at milongas and taught in most classes in Buenos Aires, is quite different from the so-called salon or ballroom tango danced in Hollywood movies and in competitions outside Argentina. Ballroom tango is all fixed steps and staccato movements, and dancers' backs arch away from each other in a stiff embrace. Tango milonguero is a highly improvised style built around a variety of typical movements, not fixed steps. Dancers embrace closely, their chests touching. There are other, historical tango styles, but it's

less common to see them on milonga floors. (Confusingly, "milonga" refers both to traditional tango dance halls and to a style of music and dance that predates the tango; though similar to tango, it has a more syncopated beat and faster, simpler steps.)

AT THE MILONGA

Dancers of all ages sit at tables that edge the floor, and men invite women to dance through *cabeceo* (subtle eye contact and head-nodding, a hard art to master. Note that women sitting with male partners won't be asked to the floor by other men.

Dances come in sets of three, four, or five, broken by a *cortina* (obvious divider of non-tango music), and it's common to stay with the same partner for a set. Being discarded in the middle is a sign that your dancing's not up to scratch, but staying for more than two sets with the same partner could be interpreted as a come-on.

To fit in seamlessly, move around the floor counterclockwise without zigzagging, sticking to the inside layers of dancers if you're a beginner. Respect other dancers' space by avoiding collisions and keeping your movements small on crowded floors. Don't spend a long time doing showy moves on the spot: it holds up traffic. Finally, take time to sit some out, catch your breath, and watch the experts.

TANGO TALK

Abrazo: the embrace or stance dancers use; in tango, this varies from hip-touching and loose shoulders to close chests and more fluid hips, depending on style.

Abrazo

Barrida

Barrida: literally, "a sweep"; one partner sweeps the other's foot into a position.

Caminada: a walking step that is the basis of the tango.

Caminada

Canyengue: style of tango dancing with short and restricted steps; from the 1910s and '20s when tight hobble skirts were popular.

Ocho: eight; a criss-crossing walk.

Parada: literally a "stop"; the lead dancer stops the other's foot with his own.

Petitero: measured style of tango developed after the 1955 military coup, when large tango gatherings were banned and the dance rel-egated to small cafés.

MILONGA STYLE

Wearing a fedora hat or fish-net stockings is as good as a neon sign reading "beginner." Forget what on-stage tango dancers wear and follow a few basic rules.

Go for comfortable clothes that allow you to move freely; a sure bet are breathable, natural fabrics with a bit of stretch. Be sure it's something that makes you feel sexy. If in doubt, wear black. Avoid showy outfits: it's your foot-work that should stand out. It's also smart to steer clear of big buckles, studs, stones,

or anything that might catch on your partner. Try not to wear skirts that are too long or too tight. Also a bad idea are jeans or gymwear.

A good example of what to wear for men would be black dress pants and a black shirt; for women, two of many op-tions are a simple halter-neck dress with a loose, calf-length skirt or palazzo pants with a fitted top.

As for your feet: look for dance shoes with flexible leather or suede soles that allow you to glide and pivot. The fit

Parada

should be snug but comfort-able. Note that rubber-soled street shoes or sneakers mark the dance floor and are often forbidden. High heels are a must for women; the most popular style is an open-toed sandal with an ankle strap (which stops them coming off). Black lace-ups are the favorite among men, so leave your two-tone spats at home.

TANGO THROUGH TIME

The tango and modern Buenos Aires were born in the same place: the *conventillos* (tenement houses) of the port neighborhood of La Boca in the late 19th century, where River Plate culture collided with that of European immigrants. The dance eventually swept from the immigrant-quarter brothels and cabarets to the rest of the city; rich playboys took the tango to Paris on their grand tours, and by the 1920s the dance had become respectable enough to fill the salons and drawing rooms of the upper class in Argentina and abroad. In the 1930s, with the advent of singers like Carlos Gardel, tango music became popular in its own right. Accordingly, musical accompaniment started to come from larger bands known as *orquestas típicas*.

Carlos Gardel

By the '40s and '50s, *porteños* (people from Buenos Aires) celebrated tango as the national music of the people, and tango artists lent Evita and Perón their support. The military coup that ousted Perón in 1955 forbade large tango dances, which it saw as potential political gatherings, and (bizarrely) encouraged rock 'n' roll instead. Young people listened, and tango fell out of popular favor.

The '90s saw a huge revival in both traditional *milongas* (dance halls) and a more improvised dance style. Musical offerings now include modern takes on classic tangos and electrotango or *tangofusión*. Even local rock stars are starting to include a tango or two in their repertory. And since 1998, thousands of people from around the world have attended the annual fortnight-long Festival de Tango in Buenos Aires (⊕ *www.tangobuenosaires.gob.ar*), held late winter or spring.

Whether you decide to take in a show or take up dancing yourself, sit down for a classic concert or groove at an electrotango night, there are more ways to experience tango in Buenos Aires than anywhere else on earth.

DID YOU KNOW?

■ Tango so horrified Kaiser Wilhelm and Pope Pius X that they banned the dance.

■ In 1915, before he was famous, Carlos Gardel was injured in a barroom brawl with Ernesto Guevara Lynch, Che's father.

■ One of Gardel's most famous numbers, "Por Una Cabeza," is the tango featured in *Schindler's List, Scent of a Woman,* and *True Lies.*

■ The coup of 1930 prompted composers like Enrique Santos Discépolo to write protest tangos.

■ Finnish tango has been a distinct musical genre since at least mid-century and is still one of the most popular in Finland; there's even an annual *Tangomarkkinat* (tango festival) in Seinäjoki, complete with the crowning of a Tango King and Queen.

4

IN FOCUS

popular during happy hour, but people stick around for dinner and the occasional live jazz shows, too. The wine list and appetizers are superb, as is the flirting. ✉ *Libertad 1161, Recoleta* ☎ *11/4811–1108* ⊕ *www. granbardanzon.com.ar* Ⓜ *C to Retiro.*

Milión. One of the city's most stunning bars is spread across three floors of a perfectly restored French-style mansion. A cool vibe and cooler drinks (try the frozen basil daiquiri) keep this place packed on weekends. When the back garden fills on balmy summer nights, squeeze onto the marble steps with the beautiful people. ✉ *Paraná 1048, Recoleta* ☎ *11/4815–9925* ⊕ *www.milion.com.ar* Ⓜ *D to Callao.*

Pony Line. No expense has been spared at the polo-theme Pony Line, a cool watering hole in the Four Seasons hotel. Creative cocktails, its own line of craft beer, luxury bar snacks, and great tunes have made this a go-to spot for sassy ladies and suave gentlemen. ✉ *Posadas 1086/88, Recoleta* ☎ *11/4321–1728* ⊕ *www.elenaponyline.com* Ⓜ *C to San Martín.*

DANCE CLUBS

The Basement. Owned by an Irish father-and-son duo, this vibrant downstairs nightspot is popular with expats and young upwardly mobile porteño party people. Stop first for a pint at the ground-floor Shamrock pub, where you can yap away in English and easily forget you're in South America; then, following the techno beats, descend to the dance club. Argentina's finest DJs burn up the decks. ✉ *Rodríguez Peña 1220, Recoleta* ☎ *11/4812–3584* Ⓜ *D to Callao.*

GAY AND LESBIAN NIGHTLIFE

Zoom. Half a block from the very cruisey section of Santa Fe, between Avenidas Callao and Coronel Díaz, Zoom offers a lounge bar, a maze, video cabins, and plenty of dark corners. It can get pretty intense, but there's good security. ✉ *Uriburu 1018, Recoleta* ☎ *11/4827–4828* ⊕ *www.zoombuenosaires.com* ⊙ *24 hrs* Ⓜ *D to Pueyrredón.*

LIVE MUSIC

JAZZ

Clásica y Moderna. An older, artsy crowd gathers here for live jazz complemented by dinner, drinks, and a dash of philosophy. Musicians make good use of the vintage venue's grand piano, while singers offer their take on the bossa nova, tango, and bolero. Bibliophiles will also appreciate the on-site bookshop. ✉ *Av. Callao 892, Recoleta* ☎ *11/4812–8707* ⊕ *www.clasicaymoderna.com* Ⓜ *D to Callao.*

Notorious. A jazz bar, restaurant, and record shop rolled into one, Notorious often hosts some of the area's best musicians. Certain nights have a fixed calendar, others are one-off gigs. You can also listen to the club's extensive music collection on the CD players at each table. ✉ *Av. Callao 966, Recoleta* ☎ *11/4813–6888* ⊕ *www.notorious.com.ar* Ⓜ *D to Callao.*

ALMAGRO

As the erstwhile home of Carlos Gardel, this neighborhood is steeped in tango traditions; however, venues like the Ciudad Cultural Konex ensure you'll find cutting edge alternatives in Almagro, too.

GAY AND LESBIAN NIGHTLIFE

Angels. Technically in the otherwise business-oriented barrio of Once (pronounced On-say), adjacent to Almagro, Angels sits just behind the magnificent Palacio de Aguas Corrientes building in easy reach of Recoleta and Centro. It has several dance floors that play electronica, pop, and Latin music. Expect strippers, transvesties, and plenty of gay fun. ⊠ *Viamonte 2168, Once* ☎ *11-15/3139–3431* ⊕ *www.discoangels.com.ar* Ⓜ *D to Facultad de Medicina.*

LIVE MUSIC

Ciudad Cultural Konex. A mixed bag of live music, film screenings, wild parties, and interactive theater make for an interesting line-up at this huge converted factory. The outdoor space morphs into an inner-city beach complete with hammocks in summer; the winter months see DJs and bands hash it out indoors. ⊠ *Sarmiento 3131, Abasto* ☎ *11/4864–3200* ⊕ *www.ciudadculturalkonex.org* Ⓜ *B line to Carlos Gardel.*

TANGO

MILONGAS

La Catedral. This former grain factory has been converted into a hip club where the tango is somehow very rock. There are classes and milongas every evening, although Tuesday is the most popular. It's a cool night out even if you're not planning to dance, as you can watch the pros in action later on. ⊠ *Sarmiento 4006, Almagro* ☎ *11-15/5325–1630* ⊕ *www.lacatedralclub.com* Ⓜ *B to Carlos Gardel.*

MUSIC CLUBS

12 de Octubre. Cobweb-covered bottles line the walls of this tiny venue, with maybe the most authentic tango music in town. It's known by all as "El Boliche de Roberto" after its owner, who presides from behind the heavy wooden bar. When the singing gets going at 2 or 3 am, it's usually so packed there's no room to breathe, but the guitar-and-voice duos manage gritty, emotional versions of tango classics all the same. ⊠ *Bulnes 331, Almagro* ☉ *Thurs.–Sat. after midnight.*

Club Atlético Fernández Fierro (*CAFF*). The creative force behind this laid-back venue is the eponymous Orquesta Típica Fernández Fierro—a scruffy young tango collective known for its rock-like take on the 2/4

4

beat. You can usually catch the orquesta at least one night a week; edgy musicians and the occasional classic quartet perform other nights. ✉ *Sánchez de Bustamante 764, Almagro* ⊕ *www.caff.com.ar* Ⓜ *B to Carlos Gardel.*

PALERMO

Palermo is B.A.'s largest barrio and, befitting its size, offers the broadest range of nightlife. You can sample a veritable buffet of after-dark options here. Milongas and oh-so authentic folk music halls appeal to traditionalists, while wine and jazz fans will both find bars that cater to their tastes. Prefer to amp things up? Opt for an underground speakeasy or go over the top at an all-night dance club.

BARS

878. B.A.'s original speakeasy has spawned a spate of followers over the past few years, but it remains a classic for cocktail lovers: 878 has an extensive drinks list, armchairs to sink into, plus a supercool clientele. Be sure to stick your head around the more private back bar. ✉ *Thames 878, Palermo Viejo* ☎ *11/4773–1098* ⊕ *www.878bar.com. ar* Ⓜ *B to Malabia.*

Acabar. This offbeat bar in the heart of Palermo Hollywood has become a big hit, and the lines to get in are only exacerbated by the abundance of board games inside, including giant Jenga. Those who manage to snag a table are quickly charmed by the easy-going atmosphere. The barstaff whip up some great fresh juices, too. ✉ *Honduras 5733, Palermo Hollywood* ☎ *11/4772–0845* ⊕ *www.acabarnet.com.ar* Ⓜ *D to Palermo.*

Antares. Originating in Mar del Plata in 1999, Antares is now a successful national brewer making seven of its own ales, which you can taste in shot-size glasses. The spacious bar attracts a cosmopolitan group of drinkers who keep it packed from after-office until the small hours. Service is friendly and efficient, the music is feel-good, and the bar snacks are tasty. Also check out the newer outposts in Las Cañitas at Arévalo 2876 and San Telmo at Bolivar 491. ✉ *Armenia 1447, Palermo Soho* ☎ *11/4833–9611* ⊕ *www.cervezaantares.com* Ⓜ *B to Malabia.*

Bangalore. A pub and curry house in Buenos Aires? Well located, the Bangalore has it all—right down to a blazing log fire in winter. There's limited seating both at the bar and in the tiny restaurant upstairs, and the place is often packed from early evening on. Service is friendly, and there's a wide range of draft beers. Revelers spill out onto the street with their pints in the warmer months. ✉ *Humboldt 1416, Palermo Hollywood* ☎ *11/4779–2621* Ⓜ *B to Dorrego.*

Fodor's Choice
★

Bar du Marché. One of the growing number of wine bars in the city, Bar du Marché is getting it exactly right. This cute French-inspired spot has an ample wine selection and some delicious *picadas* for sharing. ✉ *Nicaragua 5946, Palermo Hollywood* ☎ *11/4778–1050* ⊕ *www. bardumarchepalermo.com* Ⓜ *D to Carranza.*

Carnal. Opposite Niceto, Carnal and its buzzing terrace are immensely popular during the warmer months and remain busy all night long.

The name is completely apt; as the rock blasts and the cocktails flow, many customers aren't shy about getting to know each other a bit better—especially behind the curtained-off sections. ⊠ *Niceto Vega 5511, Palermo Hollywood* ☎ *11/4772–7582* ⊕ *www.carnalbar.com.ar* Ⓜ *B to Dorrego.*

Caracas Bar. Catering to hip young things, Caracas has the great selection of rum-based cocktails and the kind of funky vibe you would expect from a Venezuelan night spot. Sample Caribbean bar snacks while sipping on a mojito, listen to the DJ's super-smooth sounds, check out the on-site art exhibits, and take advantage of one of the largest terraces in Palermo. ⊠ *Guatemala 4802, Palermo Soho* ☎ *11/4776–8704* ⊕ *www.caracasbar.com* Ⓜ *D to Plaza Italia.*

Congo. Beautiful people—in faded fitted jeans, hipster sneakers, and leather jackets—frequent this hangout postdinner and preclub. Browse the great cocktail list at Congo's lengthy bar, or head for the large back patio: either way, you'll easily be able to convince new friends to stick around for another drink or three. ⊠ *Honduras 5329, Palermo Soho* ☎ *11/4833–5857* ⊕ *www.barcongo.com.ar* Ⓜ *D to Plaza Italia.*

Finisterra. Ancient coffee machines and 1930s posters give Finisterra a vintage look, but it's the solid mix of '80s hits that puts drinkers in a dancing mood. The crowd arrives early to nibble on a selection of cured meats and cheeses while taking advantage of the *cerveza-o-metro* (a liquid meter of beer). Only the very hardy should give the same length of local tipple Fernet and Coke a go. ⊠ *Honduras 5190, Palermo Viejo* ☎ *11/4832–1240* ⊕ *www.finisterra-bar.com* Ⓜ *D to Plaza Italia.*

Frank's Bar. While other bars of its ilk have gone legit, Frank's takes open pride in its reputation as a speakeasy. Simply knowing the address isn't enough—you also need a number and a password for the phone booth that leads into an understated yet sophisticated two-floor setting, complete with staff dressed the old-school way in suspenders. This bar has picked up a heap of awards in recent years, so you'll be sipping some of the best cocktails in the city. ⊠ *Arévalo 1445, Palermo Hollywood* ☎ *11/4777–6541* ⊕ *www.franks-bar.com* ☾ *Sun.–Wed.* Ⓜ *B to Dorrego.*

The Harrison Speakeasy. Modern-day guys and dolls embrace the *Boardwalk Empire* vibe at Harrison's, one of the finest speakeasies around. Its time-warp cocktails have earned a cluster of awards, so you're in expert hands. Membership is required; alternatively, you can dine at the shop-front sushi restaurant, and then ask "to see the bodega." ⊠ *Malabia 1764 and Costa Rica, Palermo* ⊕ *www.nicky-harrison.com* Ⓜ *D to Scalabrini Ortiz.*

Isabel. Glamour is the name of the game at Isabel, one of Palermo's posher watering holes. You can feel like a star sipping a cocktail under the twinkling ceiling lights, while actually star spotting if you're up to date with your Argentine models and polo players. Hip DJs spin tunes for a bling-y crowd, so booking is essential—as is a bottomless wallet. ⊠ *Uriarte 1664, Palermo Soho* ☎ *11/4834–6969* ⊕ *www.isabelbar.com* Ⓜ *D to Plaza Italia.*

Locos x El Fútbol. Porteños love sports—and sports, for them, means *fútbol* (soccer). Although Argentine teams also excel at basketball, rugby, and especially polo, it's fútbol that evokes the most passion, with fans attending even the smallest scrimmages; most games play on wall-mounted TVs in regular cafés and restaurants. But perhaps it's the ubiquity of soccer that means there aren't the really atmospheric screenings in bars that many visitors hope to find: to get the real buzz, you have to go to the stadium. Your second-best option is definitely Locos x El Futbol. Just try to count the number of TVs here, and you'll realize the extent of the locals' love for the beautiful game—the *x* stands for *por,* which makes this place "crazy for soccer." Key games require a reservation, but otherwise just turn up for big screens and bigger servings of pizza, fries, and beer. ⊠ *Gral Las Heras 2010, Recoleta* ☎ *11/4807–3777* ⊕ *www.locosxelfutbol.com* ✉ *Minimum consumption for big matches* ☽ *Sun.–Thurs. 9–2, Fri. and Sat. 9–4 or 5* Ⓜ *D to Pueyrredón.*

Magdalena's Party. The cool expat kids have taken Magdalena's Party under their wing and rightly so, given that it has all the bases covered: decent cocktail list, weekend brunch offerings, mood lighting. Join the movers and shakers who start their nights here by pulling up a bar stool or a comfy armchair, or follow the party out onto the street. ⊠ *Thames 1795, Palermo Soho* ☎ *11/4833–9127* ⊕ *www.magdalenasparty.com* Ⓜ *D to Plaza Italia.*

Mundo Bizarro. Longevity is a mark of Mundo Bizarro's success—after all, this place has been perfecting cocktails and building a faithful late-night following since 1997. Red lights, kitsch artwork, rock and roll, and even a pole for dancing provide the backdrop; the rest gets improvised afresh every evening. ⊠ *Serrano 1222, Palermo Soho* ☎ *11/4773–1967* ⊕ *www.mundobizarrobar.com* Ⓜ *B to Malabia.*

Pain et Vin. At the aptly named Pain et Vin, a husband-and-wife team bake the bread daily while expertly advising on fermented grape choices. Sip a glass, join a group tasting, or buy a bottle from the boutique winery to take home. ⊠ *Gorriti 5132, Palermo Soho* ☎ *11/4832–5654* Ⓜ *D to Plaza Italia.*

Puro Bistró. One of the very few cigar bars in Buenos Aires, Puro Bistró also has a killer cocktail list. Relax in a comfy armchair and enjoy the relative peace and quiet while gazing out onto the busy street beyond. It's a haven for drinkers and smokers in the heart of Palermo. ⊠ *Thames 1920, Palermo Soho* ☎ *11/4776–8129* ⊕ *www.purobistro.com.ar* Ⓜ *D to Plaza Italia.*

Rey de copas. Part Moroccan boudoir with an impressive brass instrument collection, part cutesy patio with white wrought-iron garden furniture, the kitschy Rey de Copas is an interesting addition to Palermo's drinking scene. Some concoctions come served in metal *yerba maté* gourds. ⊠ *Gorriti 5176, Palermo* ☎ *11/2068–5220* ⊕ *www. reydecopasbar.com* Ⓜ *D to Plaza Italia.*

Río Café. Its impossibly cool atmosphere makes Río Café an obvious favorite with hipsters. Pick a front table to watch the world bustle through to the back patio, or simply pitch up outside. Wednesday rocks, thanks to great cocktails and DJs whipping up '80s mash-ups for a crowd that's ready to party. ✉ *Honduras 4772, Palermo Viejo* ☎ *11/4832–2318* ⊕ *www.riocafe.com.ar* Ⓜ *D to Scalabrini Ortiz.*

The Shanghai Dragon. From the folks who brought Gibraltar and Bangalore to B.A. comes this hat-trick establishment. Less dark and woody and certainly more spacious than its traditional siblings, the Dragon has the air of a modern London pub and serves up draft beer as well as a tasty Chinese menu. ✉ *Aráoz 1199, Palermo* ☎ *11/4778–1053* Ⓜ *B to Malabia.*

Sugar Bar. If cumbia and salsa are becoming a bitter pill to swallow, a trip to Sugar will sweeten up your evening. With an extensive happy hour or three until midnight, this Palermo fixture is run by expats and attracts a fun-loving crowd of Argentines and foreigners looking for good times and big-game matches under the flattering red lighting. ✉ *Costa Rica 4619, Palermo Viejo* ☎ *11/4831–3276* ⊕ *www. sugarbuenosaires.com* Ⓜ *D to Scalabrini Ortiz.*

Verne Club. Themed around Jules Verne's *Twenty Thousand Leagues Under the Sea,* Verne Club runs a tight ship thanks to Fede Cuco—one of Argentina's best-known mixologists. This old-school cocktail bar serves innovative offerings that are often inspired by the eponymous author's characters, including a Phileas Fogg Martini. ✉ *Medrano 1475, Palermo* ☎ *11/4822–0980* ⊕ *www.vernecocktailclub.com* Ⓜ *D to Scalabrini Ortiz.*

Victoria Brown. Steampunk is the name of the game at this Palermo bar named for England's venerable Queen Victoria. Pass through the storefront, enter the cute café of the same name, bang on the secret door, and discover one of 2014's top new hot spots. A vast and sultry space awaits—the décor evokes the Industrial Age, but the elaborate drinks list is definitely up to date. ✉ *Costa Rica 4827, Palermo* ☎ *11/4831– 0831* ⊕ *www.victoriabrownbar.com* Ⓜ *D to Plaza Italia.*

Wherever Bar. A superb whiskey bar close to Plaza Italia, Wherever carries 160-plus brands of scotch, both blends and single malts. Elegant with a touch of British pub, it's a fine place to settle in for a civilized evening. ✉ *Fray Justo Santa Maria de Oro 2476, Palermo Soho* ☎ *11/4777–8029* ⊕ *www.whereverbar.com.ar* Ⓜ *D to Plaza Italia.*

DANCE CLUBS

Club Aráoz. A serious party crowd is found at Club Aráoz. Bump and grind it at Thursday's block-rocking hip-hop night; Friday and Saturday see DJs spinning rock and electronic dance music for a relatively laid-back bunch of Buenos Aires youth. ✉ *Aráoz 2424, Palermo* ☎ *11/4833– 7775* ⊕ *www.lostshake.com.ar* Ⓜ *D to Bulnes.*

Crobar. With frequent visits from "superstar DJs" and a dependable line-up of local party starters, this is the Buenos Aires base of the international Crobar club brand. There's lots of space plus the obligatory VIP lounges, and proximity to the transvestite zone means that leaving the club in the morning can get as interesting as the time spent inside. ✉ *Av. del Libertador 3883, Palermo* ☎ *11/4778–1500* ⊕ *www.crobar. com.ar* ☾ *Fri. and Sat. from midnight* Ⓜ *D to Carranza.*

Kika. Right in the heart of Palermo and next door to Congo, Kika is much bigger than you'd guess from the outside. Thanks to its funky musical orientation, its two dance floors fill up quickly. The back room sometimes hosts live bands while Tuesday is all about Hype, an all-in-one electro, hip-hop, indie, and dubstep night that gets students moving till dawn. ⊠ *Honduras 5339, Palermo Soho* ☎ *11/4833–9171* ⊕ *www.kikaclub.com.ar* Ⓜ *D to Palermo.*

Liv. Attracting electronic music lovers keen on catching big names from out of town, Liv has slowly captured the market that the larger Crobar can't muster. A more relaxed club than some of its Palermo counterparts, Liv also caters to those who want the full VIP booth-and-Champagne treatment. ⊠ *Juan B. Justo 1658, Palermo Soho* ☎ *11/6838–8228* ⊕ *www.liv.com.ar* Ⓜ *D to Palermo.*

Fodor'sChoice **Niceto.** One of the city's best venues features everything from demure
★ indie rock to the outrageous and legendary Club 69 on Thursday (think underdressed cross-dressers). Check out live bands and dancing on the A Side, while something contrasting and chill simultaneously takes place in the back B Side room. ⊠ *Coronel Niceto Vega 5510, Palermo Hollywood* ☎ *11/4779–9396* ⊕ *www.nicetoclub.com* Ⓜ *B to Dorrego.*

Podestá Super Club de Copas. Located slap bang in the middle of Palermo Soho, this place promises a good mix of locals and students. The dark ground-floor bar plays rock and serves stiff drinks (happy hour runs from 9 pm to 1 am). Upstairs in the disco, dance-friendly music is pumped into the psychedelic setting: wear white to be especially eye-catching under the neon lights. ⊠ *Armenia 1740, Palermo Soho* ☎ *11/4832–2776* ⊕ *www.podestafotos.com* Ⓜ *D to Plaza Italia.*

Voodoo Motel. The self-styled club and music warehouse on the cool northern edge of Palermo Hollywood offers up a large dance floor and plenty of European beats, as well as Britpop, indie nights, and digital cumbia. Fresh from a face-lift, Voodoo aims to strike a balance between trendy cocktails and move-inducing music. ⊠ *Dorrego 1735, Palermo Hollywood* ☎ *11/4139–7499* ⊕ *www.voodoomotel.com* Ⓜ *B to Dorrego.*

GAY AND LESBIAN NIGHTLIFE

Amerika. This immense gay disco has three floors of high-energy action and shows. Friday and Saturday are fun and frivolous verging on hectic thanks to its one-fee, all-you-can-drink-entry. Thursday and Sunday are quieter, with greater emphasis on the music. Amerika remains the city's gay club to check out—and be checked out in. ⊠ *Gascon 1040, Palermo* ☎ *11/4865–4416* ⊕ *www.ameri-k.com.ar* Ⓜ *B to Medrano.*

LIVE MUSIC
FOLK

La Peña del Colorado. There's nothing pretentious about this place: laid-back groups gather to enjoy traditional Argentine folk music and hand-held foods like *empanadas* and *tamales*. The exposed-brick walls are adorned with rustic memorabilia, including guitars that you're welcome to play if so inspired. ⊠ *Güemes 3657, Palermo* ☎ *11/4822–1038* ⊕ *www.lapeniadelcolorado.com* Ⓜ *D to Bulnes.*

Los Cardones. Named after the tall cactus plants that typify northwest Argentina, Los Cardones is the place to go for a beer around a big table with strangers you'll get to know by the end of the night. Spontaneous dancing at this peña folklorica isn't unheard of; to prepare, ask ahead about their folk-dancing classes. ✉ *Jorge Luis Borges 2180, Palermo Soho* ☎ *11/4777–1112* ⊕ *www.cardones.com.ar* Ⓜ *D to Plaza Italia.*

JAZZ

Thelonious Club. The best porteño jazz bands (and occasional foreign imports) play at this intimate, upscale spot. Arrive early for a good seat, as it's a long, narrow bar and not all tables have good views; on weekends there are usually two shows per night. ✉ *Salguero 1884, Palermo* ☎ *11/4829–1562* ⊕ *www.theloniousclub.com.ar* Ⓜ *D to Bulnes.*

Virasoro Bar. This is an intimate art deco venue for local jazz maestros and appreciative audiences. It's a great space and you can get up close and personal with musicians, who draw from a deep well of talent and cover a lot of ground, from improv to standards and experimental. ✉ *Guatemala 4328, Palermo* ☎ *11/4831–8918* ⊕ *www.virasorobar. com.ar* Ⓜ *D to Scalabrini Ortíz.*

ROCK

No Avestruz. A barely marked door and a narrow passageway open into a world far removed from the flashy bars and restaurants surrounding this music venue. The eclectic programming includes a wide range of folk, tango, jazz, classical, and improvised music as well as some politically charged theatrical performances. Grab the sofa if you can, for maximum comfort. ✉ *Humboldt 1857, Palermo Hollywood* ☎ *11/4777–6956* ⊕ *www.noavestruz.com.ar* Ⓜ *D to Palermo.*

TANGO

MILONGAS

La Viruta. Milongas Wednesday through Sunday make this the place for a very long weekend. Classes at different levels precede them. The vibe on the floor is friendly and rather chaotic, and dancing standards are low, so it's a good place for beginners to get in some practice. DJs mix tango with rock, salsa, and cumbia. ✉ *Armenia 1366, Palermo Viejo* ☎ *11/4774–6357* ⊕ *www.lavirutatango.com* Ⓜ *B to Malabia.*

Fodor's Choice ★ **Salón Canning.** Several milongas call this large dance hall home. The coolest is Parakultural (☎ *11/5738–3850* ⊕ *www.parakultural.com.ar*), which takes place late on Monday, Tuesday, and Friday. Reservations are essential for the last of these—the dance floor is totally packed by midnight, so get here early. Originally an alternative, "underground" milonga, it now attracts large numbers of locals, including longtime expats. ✉ *Av. Scalabrini Ortíz 1331, Palermo* ☎ *11/4832–6753* ⊕ *www. parakultural.com.ar* Ⓜ *B to Malabia.*

BELGRANO

Belgrano isn't a big destination for nightlife, but its popular park—La Glorieta de Barrancas—hosts our favorite outdoor milongas every Saturday and Sunday.

BARS

Puerta Uno. One block from Chinatown, this speakeasy with an Asian touch personifies modern glamour. Grab a spot at the bar for a piece of the main action or detour to the back-room dance floor, where some of the best DJs in town will get you moving. ⊠ *Juramento 1667, Belgrano* ☎ *11/4706–1522* ⊕ *www.puertauno.com* Ⓜ *D to Juramento.*

TANGO

MILONGAS

La Glorieta de Barrancas de Belgrano. For tango alfresco, drop by the bandstand of this Belgrano park on Saturday and Sunday evenings year-round. Classes run from 4:30 to 6:30, then the milonga proper starts at 7. Expect lots of old-timers dancing low-key steps. The event is canceled only during heavy rain; call ahead if you're unsure. ⊠ *11 de Septiembre at Echeverría, Belgrano* ☎ *11/4674–1026* ⊕ *www.glorietadebelgrano. com.ar* Ⓜ *D to Juramento.*

COSTANERA

Formerly the place to go for upscale dining, this stretch of riverfront found a new lease on life as the home of the country's most famed and fabulous dance clubs. Most are within a mile of each other along the Río de la Plata, underneath the buzz of the nearby metropolitan airport.

DANCE CLUBS

Jet Lounge. When the most beautiful of people feel like dancing with a bottle of Champagne at 4 am, they come here. Things get even more glamorous a few hours later, when the dawn breaks through the river and the yacht club is revealed. International DJs drop by to entertain the super-swanky set. ⊠ *Av. Costanera Rafael Obligado 4801, Costanera* ☎ *11/4782–5599* ⊕ *www.jet.com.ar* Ⓜ *D to Plaza Italia.*

Pachá. Clocking up plenty of years on the electro scene, this multilevel, riverside behemoth pulls in big names and bigger crowds. Total sensory overload is the name of the game. In summer, watch the sun ease its way up over the river from one of the best vantage points in the city. ⊠ *Av. Costanera Rafael Obligado 5151, at La Pampa, Costanera* ☎ *11/4788–4280* ⊕ *www.pachabuenosaires.com* Ⓜ *D to Juramento.*

WHERE TO EAT

Updated by
Dan Perlman

Visitors may flock to Buenos Aires for the steak and malbec, but the food scene goes far beyond those two attractions. Over the last dozen or so years, the city has burst onto the international food scene with gusto.

There's a demand for more and more creative food. Here three things have come together to create a truly modern cuisine: diverse cultural influences, high culinary aspirations, and a relentless devotion to aesthetics, from plate garnishes to room décor. Tradition dictates late dining, and the majority of restaurants don't open until 8 or 9 pm for dinner and don't get busy until after 10. Dinner is a leisurely affair, and the *sobremesa*, or after-dinner chat over coffee or digestifs, is nearly obligatory. Rushing from the table is frowned on—anyway, where would you go? Bars and clubs often don't open until after midnight.

The core of the population is of Italian and Spanish heritage, and pizza, pasta, paella, and *puchero* (beef boil) are as common as the *parrilla* (steakhouse). Argentines have taken the classics and made them their own with different techniques and ingredients, but they're still recognizable to the international traveler. Pizzas and empanadas are the favored local snack food, the former piled high with cheese, the latter typically filled with steak or chicken. And while steak is indisputably king in this town, it's got fierce competition in tender Patagonian lamb, game meats, fish, and shellfish. In contrast to that of much of Latin America, Argentine cuisine is not known for its spice, and *picante* dishes are not common.

Cafés, too, are an important part of the culture, and locals will stop in at their favorite for a *cafecito* at least once a day, not only to knock back a little caffeine, but also to see friends and catch up on the latest news and gossip.

PLANNING

DRESS

Porteños dress to impress. Looking good is as important as feeling good in Buenos Aires. The finest restaurants in the city employ an "elegant sport" rule, but few require men to wear a tie and jacket. A sport coat and slacks will suffice, even in most upscale eateries. Jeans are fine just about anywhere, provided they are paired with a smart shirt or blouse.

RESERVATIONS

Getting a reservation in most Buenos Aires restaurants is easy. Most porteños make dinner reservations a day or two ahead of time instead of weeks in advance.

SMOKING

Smoking is no longer allowed in any indoor public spaces in Buenos Aires. If you're a smoker, be prepared to head outside for a cigarette.

TIPPING

In most restaurants in Buenos Aires a 10% tip is the norm. If the service was superb, 15% is appreciated. In bars you can tip a peso or two per drink, but it's not expected. Bills for parties of six or more sometimes include the tip; look at the check. Many restaurants also charge a *servicio de mesa* (table service) or *cubierto,* which typically runs anywhere from 10 to 50 pesos per person, and covers the cost of "breakage and replacement." It is the source of much local contention—those who don't charge it often make it a selling point. If there is a table charge, many locals tip less, though it should be noted that the cubierto does not go to the waiters but to the restaurant's owner.

WHAT IT COSTS

Credit cards are often accepted, but many restaurants accept cash only. If you plan to use a card, it's a good idea when making reservations to check whether it is accepted.

WHAT IT COSTS IN ARGENTINE PESOS			
	$	$$	$$$	$$$$
RESTAURANTS	65 pesos and under	66 pesos–100 pesos	101 pesos–160 pesos	over 160 pesos

Restaurant prices are the average cost of a main course at dinner or, if dinner is not served, at lunch.

RESTAURANT REVIEWS

Listed alphabetically within neighborhood. Use the coordinate (✢ 2:D2) at the end of each listing to locate a site on the corresponding map.

CENTRO

Centro and the surrounding neighborhoods have something for everyone, from traditional to trendy. At lunchtime, the city's bustling downtown is the place where business deals are negotiated over leisurely

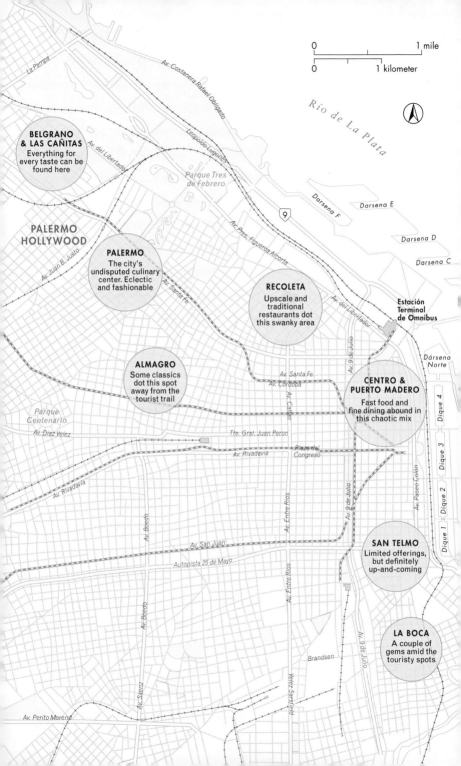

0   1 mile
0   1 kilometer

Río de La Plata

BELGRANO & LAS CAÑITAS
Everything for every taste can be found here

La Pampa

Av. Costanera Rafael Obligado

Leopoldo Lugones

Av. del Libertador

Parque Tres de Febrero

Darsena F

Darsena E

Darsena D

Darsena C

9

PALERMO HOLLYWOOD

Av. Pres. Figueroa Alcorta

PALERMO
The city's undisputed culinary center. Eclectic and fashionable

Av. Juan B. Justo

Av. Santa Fe

RECOLETA
Upscale and traditional restaurants dot this swanky area

Av. del Libertador

Estación Terminal de Omnibus

Dársena Norte

ALMAGRO
Some classics dot this spot away from the tourist trail

Av. Santa Fe.

Av. Córdoba

CENTRO & PUERTO MADERO
Fast food and fine dining abound in this chaotic mix

Dique 4

Parque Centenario

Av. Díaz Velez

Tte. Gral. Juan Peron

Av. Rivadavia

Plaza del Congreso

Av. 9 de Julio

Av. Paseo Colón

Dique 3

Dique 2

Av. Rivadavia

Av. Boedo

Av. Entre Ríos

Av. 9 de Julio

SAN TELMO
Limited offerings, but definitely up-and-coming

Dique 1

Av. San Juan

Autopista 25 de Mayo

Av. Entre Ríos

Av. Saenz

Velez Sarsfield

LA BOCA
A couple of gems amid the touristy spots

Av. Boedo

Brandsen

Av. 9 de Julio

Av. Perito Moreno

BEST BETS FOR BUENOS AIRES DINING

With thousands of restaurants to choose from, how will you decide where to eat? Fodor's writers and editors have selected their favorite restaurants by price, cuisine, and experience in the Best Bets lists below. In the first column, Fodor's Choice properties represent the "best of the best" in every price category. You can also search by neighborhood for excellent eats—just peruse the following pages. Or find specific details about a restaurant in the full reviews, listed alphabetically within neighborhoods.

Fodor's Choice★

Aramburu, p. 164
Astor, p. 182
Bardot, p. 173
Chira, p. 173
El Burladero, p. 168
El Sanjuanino, p. 169
Don Julio, p. 174
La Bourgogne, p. 170
Las Pizarras Bistró, p. 176
Oviedo, p. 171
Pura Tierra, p. 183
Restó, p. 162
Tarquino, p. 171
Trattoria Olivetti, p. 181

Best By Price

$

Club Eros, p. 174

$$

Bangalore, p. 172
El Sanjuanino, p. 169
Filo, p. 160
Trattoria Olivetti, p. 181

$$$

Astor, p. 182
Bardot, p. 173
Bruni, p. 182
Chira, p. 173
Dadá, p. 159
Don Julio, p. 174
El Cuartito, p. 159
Gran Bar Danzón, p. 160
Juana M, p. 169
Las Pizarras Bistró, p. 176
Pura Tierra, p. 183

$$$$

Aramburu, p. 164
Duhau Restaurante & Vinoteca, p. 168
El Burladero, p. 168
Francesco, p. 174
La Bourgogne, p. 170
La Cabrera, p. 176
Osaka, p. 178
Oviedo, p. 171
Tarquino, p. 171
Tegui, p. 181

Best by Cuisine

ARGENTINE

Casa Coupage, p. 173
Duhau Restaurante & Vinoteca, p. 168
El Sanjuanino, p. 169
Pura Tierra, p. 183

FRENCH

Brasserie Petanque, p. 165
La Bourgogne, p. 170

ITALIAN

Bella Italia, p. 173
Bruni, p. 182
La Baita, p. 176

JAPANESE

Osaka, p. 178
Yuki, p. 162

STEAK

Cabaña Las Lilas, p. 163
Don Julio, p. 174
El Estanciero, p. 184
La Cabrera, p. 176

Best by Experience

MOST ROMANTIC

Duhau Restaurante & Vinoteca, p. 168
Pura Tierra, p. 183

HOT SPOTS

Osaka, p. 178
Pura Tierra, p. 183

HOTEL DINING

La Bourgogne, p. 170
Tomo I, p. 162

5

lunches of steak, potatoes, salad, and wine. Recently there's been a surge of quick-and-easy take-out joints popular with local office workers on a short break. In the evening the area can get deserted, except for the pedestrian strip along Avenida Reconquista, which is jammed with bars and restaurants catering to those staying in downtown hotels.

$$$
ECLECTIC   ✕ **Bengal.** Stepping into the wood-panel dining room, with tables draped in white linens and a ceiling tented with a colorful carpet, you may feel like you've entered a British officers' club from the late 1800s. During the day the clientele seem to be mostly embassy employees and foreign-service workers, which just adds to that atmosphere. At night it changes over to a mix of neighbors and tourists enjoying the offbeat menu that's half Italian and half Indian. For those in the mood for spice, a half-dozen reasonably hot curries are on offer (the fish and prawn curries are the stars). For something milder, pasta is the thing, and the excellent lasagnas are the house specialty. The waitstaff is trained to sell and can sometimes seem a little pushy. Ⓢ *Average main: 160 pesos* ✉ *Arenales 837, at Arroyo, Centro* ☎ *11/4314–2926* ◈ *Reservations essential* ⊙ *Closed Sun. No lunch Sat.* Ⓜ *C to San Martín* ✛ *2:D2.*

$$
CAFÉ   ✕ **Café Tortoni.** Filled with Tiffany lamps, towering columns, and marble-top tables, this art nouveau hangout has charm to spare. While you may have to wait in a line outside, depending on the time of day, it'll be worth it to knock back an espresso or sip a *submarino,* the local version of hot chocolate. Nibble on one of the dozens of different sandwiches or fork in one of the exquisite pastries and contemplate that you may well be sitting in the same seat that a former president, a renowned tango singer, or a world-famous artist or writer occupied many a time before. It's a place and time out of the past, and, thankfully, well preserved. Reservations are a must during the dinner-hour tango show. Ⓢ *Average main: 95 pesos* ✉ *Av. de Mayo 825, at Piedras, Centro* ☎ *11/4342–4328* ⊕ *www.cafetortoni.com.ar* Ⓜ *A to Perú* ✛ *2:D4.*

$
CAFÉ   ✕ **Confitería Ideal.** This century-old café is one of the best spots for newcomers to learn some basic tango steps and enjoy a casual bite to eat. Downstairs, a cavernous space with beautiful marble columns is dotted with tables where you can relax with a coffee and pastry (the glazed tea cookies are famed citywide). If you're feeling a little hungrier, dig in to simple local fare like a *milanesa* (breaded veal cutlet), a pizza, or one of a selection of salads and sandwiches. The kitchen closes at 8 pm. Upstairs is the tango hall, where inexpensive lessons can be had two or three times a day. Outside of class hours there's often a tango show, and in the evenings there's always a *milonga,* open to anyone who just wants to show up and dance tango. Ⓢ *Average main: 40 pesos* ✉ *Suipacha*

380, at Av. Corrientes, Centro ☎ *11/4328–7750* ⊕ *www.confiteriaideal. com* ⊟ *No credit cards* Ⓜ *C to C. Pellegrini; D to 9 de Julio* ✛ *2:D4.*

$$$ ✕ **Dadá.** Pop-art posters add some flair to this foodie favorite. With a
ECLECTIC short but creative menu, this spot serves some of the most interesting
food to be found in the district. Don't miss out on the house special-
ties: phyllo-wrapped Morbier cheese salad as a starter and the perfectly
cooked *ojo de bife* (ribeye steak). The kitchen also deftly turns out
perfectly cooked pastas, particularly those incorporating fresh seafood.
Relax, enjoy a glass of wine, read the paper, sit at the bar and chat,
and eat well. Hours can be as eclectic as their food, and they may or
may not open at posted times, though likely they won't be too far off.
Ⓢ *Average main: 120 pesos* ⊠ *San Martín 941, Retiro* ☎ *11/4314–4787*
⊘ *Closed Sun.* Ⓜ *C to San Martín* ✛ *2:D3.*

$ ✕ **Down Town Matías.** On a prominent corner of the downtown business
ARGENTINE district, Down Town Matías is the flagship of a group of Irish-theme
pubs. Drop in at lunchtime for a simple steak with mushroom sauce,
a well-prepared piece of fish, or a simple sandwich. Pints of ale on tap
and plenty of noise, particularly at dinnertime, are the order of the day.
Weekday evenings there's an early happy hour followed by live music,
generally local rock groups, which can make dinner conversation a
challenge. At the other locations outside of downtown, the ambience
is a bit more laid-back, and prices a touch lower. Ⓢ *Average main:
65 pesos* ⊠ *Reconquista 701, at Viamonte, Centro* ☎ *11/4311–0327*
⊕ *www.matiaspub.com.ar* ⊘ *Closed Sun.* Ⓜ *C to San Martín* ✛ *2:D3.*

$$$ ✕ **El Cuartito.** Founded in 1934, this icon of porteño pizza tugs at the
PIZZA heartstrings of locals, who get misty-eyed when they think about the
fresh tomato sauce and the mile-high pile of oozing mozzarella on these
classics. You'll spot the occasional tourist, but the vast majority of seats
will be filled by locals who've been coming here for decades. Every
square inch of wall space is dedicated to posters, photos, and memorabilia of sports legends, musicians, tango dancers, and actors, and every
local has his or her cherished spot in the dining room. The best pizza?
A classic *mitad-mitad,* or half-and-half—one side a straightforward
tomato sauce and cheese, the other swimming with anchovies. Dessert
here is a winner, with the classic flan leading the pack. Ⓢ *Average main:
110 pesos* ⊠ *Talcahuano 937, Centro* ☎ *11/4816–1758* ⊟ *No credit
cards* Ⓜ *D to Tribunales* ✛ *2:C3.*

$$$ ✕ **El Federal.** An homage to the rugged terrain of the Argentine wilds,
MODERN every surface in this downtown eatery seems to be rough wood or
ARGENTINE tanned leather. Chef Paula Comparatore turns out modern twists on
classic regional dishes, often making use of rarely seen ingredients.
Her *tehuelches,* a type of Patagonian empanada named after a near-
extinct southern tribe, are among the best in the city, and her classic
slow braises of lamb, goat, and beef are simply divine. For those with
something lighter in mind, there are indigenous fish preparations and
even a vegetarian dish or two. Ⓢ *Average main: 160 pesos* ⊠ *San Mar-
tín 1015, Retiro* ☎ *11/4313–1324* ⊕ *www.elfederalrestaurante.com*
⊘ *Closed Sun.* Ⓜ *C to San Martín* ✛ *2:D2.*

$$$ ✕ **El Imparcial.** This is the city's oldest restaurant, dating back to the
SPANISH 1860s. The name, which translates as "impartial," was meant to

offer up neutral territory for various Spanish and Basque factions that emigrated to the city during the mid-19th century. The menu is a mix of local Argentine fare and classic Spanish dishes. You're not necessarily going to be wowed by anything, but you're also never going to be disappointed. The paella and other rice dishes, particularly those with seafood, are the way to go. At lunchtime there's a three-course prix-fixe menu that comes in at less than the price of an à la carte appetizer. Don't miss the *natilla madrileña* (custard with caramel) for dessert. $ *Average main: 160 pesos* ✉ *Hipólito Yrigoyen 1201, Centro* ☎ *11/4383–2919* ⊕ *www.elimparcialbsas.com.ar* Ⓜ *C to Av. de Mayo; A to Lima* ✛ *2:C5.*

$$ ✕ **El Palacio de la Papa Frita.** No frills doesn't mean no charm at this long-
ARGENTINE time porteño favorite. Steaks, pastas, and salads are the draw, but don't miss the *papas soufflés,* meaning puffed-up french fries. If you want to go full-tilt local style, order them *à la provençal* and they'll arrive at your table tossed with minced garlic and parsley. After all, this place and the other three branches around town (Palermo, Recoleta, and another in Centro) aren't called "the Palace of the French Fry" for no reason. $ *Average main: 90 pesos* ✉ *Lavalle 735, between Esmeralda and Maipú, Centro* ☎ *11/4393–4849* Ⓜ *C to Lavalle* ✛ *2:B4* $ *Average main: 90 pesos* ✉ *Av. Corrientes 1612, Centro* ☎ *11/4374–8063* Ⓜ *B to Callao* ✛ *2:B4.*

$$ ✕ **Filo.** Crowded and lively, particularly at lunch, Filo is the place for
ITALIAN pizza and pasta in the downtown area. True Neapolitan-style pies with smoky, charred crusts direct from the wood-fired oven are among the best in the city. For a real treat, order the Filo, a wheel of a pizza with each slice a different topping according to the *pizzero's* whims. Pastas are served perfectly al dente—a rarity in town—and come with both classic and creative sauces. If you're dining solo, the bar is a great spot to grab a stool and strike up a conversation. No photos allowed: the management cheekily say some guests "may be dining with someone that they'd prefer their spouse doesn't see." Check out the ever-changing art gallery in the basement. $ *Average main: 100 pesos* ✉ *San Martín 975, between Alvear and Paraguay, Retiro* ☎ *11/4311–1871* ⊕ *www.filo-ristorante.com* Ⓜ *C to San Martín* ✛ *2:D3.*

$$$ ✕ **Gran Bar Danzón.** It's a two-story climb up some steep stairs to the
WINE BAR city's best wine bar. Arrive too early in the evening and this might be your worst nightmare: a dimly lit lounge with hard-drinking business executives. Wait until dinner hour—after 8, at the earliest—and the crowd changes to the local wine-geek set wolfing down some of the best lounge food in town, including great sushi (don't miss the crispy prawn

GRABBING A BITE

Every culture has its version of a "greasy spoon," and in Argentina that's the *pulpería,* a term with as many different definitions as there are scholars to study it. In the beginning these were general stores with a lunch counter of sorts, a place to buy dry goods, beverages, candles, cloth, and other daily necessities, and have a quick bite. Over time they've become casual neighborhood eateries that are often a great place to sample local dishes.

rolls), eclectic appetizers and main courses, and a selection of wines by the glass that can't be beat. The place is not too bad on the wallet, particularly in this neighborhood. Wednesday nights there's live jazz early. $ *Average main: 135 pesos* ⊠ *Libertad 1161, 2nd fl., Retiro* ☎ *11/4811–1108* ⊕ *www.granbardanzon.com.ar* ⌛ *Reservations essential* ☾ *No lunch* Ⓜ *C to San Martín* ✛ *2:C2.*

$$
BASQUE

✕ **Iñaki.** When Iñaki first opened its doors, it was one of the city's more expensive Basque eateries. Over time it's kept the price increases to a minimum, and today it's one of the most reasonable spots to enjoy this spectacular Spanish cuisine. Killer paella and fried calamari—not the usual battered version, but a much more elegant dish dusted in herb and pepper flour and flash-fried—are among the must-try choices. If you want something a little spicier, order *raxo,* a delicious pork dish in a red chili sauce that's paired, strangely enough, with french fries. The service is cheerful and helpful. $ *Average main: 95 pesos* ⊠ *Moreno 1341, at San José, Congreso* ☎ *11/4382–8486* ⊕ *www.xn–iakirestaurante-yqb.com.ar* ☾ *Closed Sun.* ✛ *2:C5*

$$
PIZZA
FAMILY

✕ **Las Cuartetas.** Not known for its décor, this simple spot with tightly packed tables and fluorescent lights is filled with locals who love the coal-fired deep-dish pizza—a style you don't find frequently in this city. It's a great place to go on your own, as solo diners aren't uncommon. Not to be missed is the spinach and white-sauce pizza, a neighborhood favorite. For meat eaters there's the *española* layered with longaniza sausage, the city's answer to pepperoni. It can take awhile to get the staff's attention, and friendliness is not the first order of the day, but the wait and the attitude won't matter once you sink your fork into one of these slices. $ *Average main: 95 pesos* ⊠ *Corrientes 838, between Esmeralda and Suipacha, Centro* ☎ *11/4326–0171* ⊕ *www.lascuartetas.com* ☾ *No lunch Sun.* Ⓜ *B to C. Pellegrini; C to Diagonal Norte; D to 9 de Julio* ✛ *2:D4.*

$$
PIZZA
FAMILY

✕ **Piola.** This old-school pizzeria empire, which now has outposts in a dozen countries, made it big by turning out tasty pizzas, one after another. It's not Argentine-style pizza—the crust is too thin, the sauce too plentiful, and the cheese too sparse—more like an echo of the pizza from the chain's home base in Treviso, Italy. It attracts locals looking for something different and visitors from afar who recognize the name. There's a second branch at Gorriti 5751 in Palermo. $ *Average main: 99 pesos* ⊠ *Libertad 1078, at Av. Santa Fe, Recoleta* ☎ *11/4812–0690* ⊕ *www.piola.it* ☾ *No lunch weekends* Ⓜ *C to San Martín* ✛ *2:C2.*

DOWNTOWN'S BEST CAFÉS

Centro is packed with cafés that are an integral part of Buenos Aires' past and present. Jump into café culture at these top spots:

Café Tortoni (⊠ *Av. de Mayo 829* ✛ *2:D4*) is the most famous Buenos Aires café of all, serving coffee to political, literary, and entertainment legends since 1858.

La Giralda (⊠ *Av. Corrientes 1453* ✛ *2:B4*), a favorite spot for the literary set, is famous for having invented the submarino, BA's answer to hot chocolate, and for its churros.

5

$$$
MODERN
ARGENTINE
Fodor's Choice
★

✕ **Restó.** This place became famous when it was run by founder Maria Barrutia, and on and off it was a popular destination for local foodies over the years. Many people held their breath when she sold the place to Guido Tassi, but we can all breathe a sigh of relief because the cooking is better than ever. The menu is more creative, with bolder flavors and more beautiful presentations. Likewise, the service has been stepped up a notch, as has the wine list. There's now nowhere better in the neighborhood for lunch, nor for dinner on the two nights a week it's open late. The star of the lineup is the roasted, stuffed whole quail, but there's not a misstep on the menu. ⑤ *Average main: 110 pesos* ✉ *Sociedad Central de Arquitectos, Montevideo 938, between M. T. Alvear and Paraguay, Recoleta* ☎ *11/4816–6711* ⚄ *Reservations essential* ▭ *No credit cards* ⊘ *Closed weekends. No dinner Mon.–Wed.* Ⓜ *D to Callao* ✛ *2:B3.*

$$$$
ARGENTINE

✕ **Sabot.** You're likely to be the only newcomer amid scores of older business executives who've been making this landmark a classic for more than 40 years. Day in and day out, this is the spot where behind-the-scenes negotiations take place over French-influenced local fare. The *centolla* (king crab) or *langostino* (prawn) salad is a throwback to another age, but it's perfectly prepared. Tuck into properly prepared pastas and a house specialty, semolina gnocchi, or slice into a delicious steak—the *entrecote* is king here. Add to the food some of the friendliest and most efficient service you'll find in town, and it's a don't-miss downtown lunch. ⑤ *Average main: 160 pesos* ✉ *25 de Mayo 756, between Córdoba and Viamonte, Centro* ☎ *11/4313–6587* ⊘ *Closed weekends. No dinner* Ⓜ *B to L. N. Alem* ✛ *2:E3.*

$$
SPANISH

✕ **Tancat.** The heart of Catalonia beats at this popular tapas bar. Grab a seat at the counter—this one of the few food bars in the city—or snuggle in at one of the cozy, romantic tables. Tancat features Spanish cooking at its best: simple, well-flavored, and expertly cooked. The stars here, besides the array of tapas, are the paella and other stellar seafood dishes. Best yet, this is one of the most reasonably priced Spanish restaurants in the city, especially for the quality. ⑤ *Average main: 100 pesos* ✉ *Paraguay 645, between Maipú and Florida, Retiro* ☎ *11/4312–5442* ⊕ *www.tancatrestaurante.com* ⊘ *Closed Sun.* Ⓜ *C to San Martín* ✛ *2:D3.*

$$$$
ARGENTINE

✕ **Tomo I.** Despite being one of the more sophisticated dining rooms in the city, being a hotel restaurant means that Tomo I will have a mix of couples dressed to the nines and groups of backpackers in T-shirts. Don't let that put you off, as the fare at this bastion of modern French-Argentine cooking is some of the best in the city. The room was renovated a couple of years ago, and now features a full wall of windows looking out over the city's widest avenue. The food tends toward the lighter side, even when considering meat dishes, and truly shines with its updated versions of classic French dishes. ⑤ *Average main: 275 pesos* ✉ *Hotel Panamericano, Carlos Pellegrini 521, Centro* ☎ *11/4326–6695* ⊕ *www.tomo1.com.ar* ⚄ *Reservations essential* ⊘ *Closed Sun. No lunch Sat.* Ⓜ *B to Carlos Pellegrini; D to 9 de Julio* ✛ *2:C3.*

$$$
SUSHI

✕ **Yuki.** Getting in requires a reservation, but once you're through the unmarked facade you'll find yourself in the closest thing the city has to a sushi temple. Japanese business executives are quietly making deals in

CAFÉ LINGO 101

Coffee is taken seriously in Argentina. A morning and evening caffeine jolt is what gets many porteños through their long days and nights. Here's how to order it:

Café: Same as an American espresso

Café con leche: Half coffee and half milk, served in a larger cup

Cortado: A café topped or "cut" with hot foamy milk

Filtro: Brewed coffee

Lágrima: Hot foamy milk with a "drop" of coffee

Ristretto: A small, very strong shot of espresso

Submarino: A tall glass of hot milk served with a chocolate bar submerged into the milk (aka hot chocolate)

Unless you specify otherwise, your café will be served in a short espresso glass. If you want a larger coffee, order a *jarrito*, or medium. If you want an American-size coffee, order a *doble*, or double espresso.

semi-hidden salons lined with tatami mats, while local aficionados are deftly wielding chopsticks around the small tables, or, if they're lucky, seated at the sushi bar in front of sushi-master Kazu-O, whose father opened Yuki some 60 years ago. The fish is pristine and changes daily based on availability, but always goes far beyond the local standard of salmon and cream cheese (the latter thankfully not offered). For a special experience, order either the *omakase* (sushi chef's choice) or *teishoku* (prix-fixe from the kitchen, with or without sushi) menu and let the chef do his thing while you knock back a sake or two from the impressive selection. $ *Average main: 125 pesos* ✉ *Pasco 740, between Independencia and Chile, Congreso* ☎ *11/4942–7510* ⟐ *Reservations essential* ⊘ *Closed Sun. No lunch* Ⓜ *E to Pichincha* ⊹ *2:A6.*

PUERTO MADERO

A magnet for tourists, Puerto Madero's restaurants charge amounts that would make restaurant owners in other parts of the city blush with shame. It's a beautiful area for when you want to stroll along the waterfront or snap a few photos of the expansive views, but unless you're on an expense account, the food is generally far better and far less expensive elsewhere.

$$$$
STEAKHOUSE
✕ **Cabaña Las Lilas.** Probably the best-known steak house in all of Argentina, Cabaña Las Lilas draws most of its clientele from the international travelers that crowd into Puerto Madero. It's not just a tourist trap, as it also draws wealthy porteños intent on showing their disregard for the high prices. The service is impeccable, as is the cooking of various cuts of beef from the owner's own ranch. Particularly noteworthy are the *ojo de bife* and *bife de lomo,* better known to Americans as ribeye and sirloin, respectively. It's by no means the best steakhouse in town, but it is the most expensive, by a significant amount. If you just want to sit and look out over the water and dig into a steak, this is your place.

⑤ *Average main: 275 pesos* ✉ *A. M. de Justo 516, at Corrientes, Puerto Madero* ☎ *11/4313–1336* ⊕ *www. laslilas.com* ⌺ *Reservations essential* ✛ *2:E4.*

$$$$ ✕ **La Rosa Náutica.** Aficionados of
PERUVIAN   Nikkei cuisine know the Nautical Compass, a chain that started on the beach in Lima, Peru, and now has outposts as far away as Abruzzo, Italy. Located in Puerto Madero, the elegant, white-tablecloth dining room has a beautiful view over the water; better yet, sit outside on the covered patio. La Rosa Náutica serves some of the best Peruvian-Japanese fusion food in the city. The stars on the menu are the ceviches, tiraditos and carpaccios, all raw seafood dishes that are impeccable. Service can be a bit slow, but it's worth the wait. ⑤ *Average main: 170 pesos* ✉ *Alicia Moreau de Justo 264, at Lavalle, Puerto Madero* ☎ *11/4311–5560* ⊕ *www.larosanautica.com* ✛ *2:E4.*

> ### FLAVORS OF THE ANDES
>
> We've all been hearing that *Nikkei* cuisine—a blend of Peruvian and Japanese fare—will be the next big thing in the culinary world. The most common style applies Asian techniques to ingredients from the Andes. While there are dozens of eateries offering this type of cuisine, the best include **La Rosa Náutica** (✉ *Av. Alicia M. de Justo 246, Puerto Madero*), **Bardot** (✉ *Av. Honduras 5237, Palermo*) and **Osaka** (✉ *Soler 5608, Palermo*). In an unusual spin-off of the style, **Chira** (✉ *Av. Humboldt 1864, Palermo*) is turning out Peruvian fare that blends traditions of both the Mediterranean and the Caribbean.

SAN TELMO

Home to some of the city's most elaborate mansions, San Telmo was abandoned by the upper classes during the 1871 yellow fever epidemic. These days it has an artsy, bohemian vibe. Although most dining spots are inexpensive, there are some true gems.

$$$$ ✕ **Aramburu.** Hidden away on a gritty, graffiti-covered street is one of
ECLECTIC   the most beautiful, intimate, and romantic restaurants in the city. Night
Fodor's Choice   after night Gonzalo Aramburu turns out his exquisite 12-course tasting
★   menu of seasonal dishes, each reinterpreted through the lens of what here is called *cocina vanguardia*, or cutting-edge cooking. Aramburu is the undisputed star of the nascent local molecular gastronomy scene. If you're going to splurge, go all the way and add in the 320 peso wine pairing put together by star sommelier Agustina de Alba, one of the best in Buenos Aires. For those who want a more wallet-friendly option, Aramburu Bis opened in early 2014 just down the street at Humberto Primo 1207, offering bistro-style dining with those same cutting-edge influences. ⑤ *Average main: 450 pesos* ✉ *Salta 1050, between Carlos Calvo and Humberto Primo, San Telmo* ☎ *11/4305–0439* ⊕ *www. aramvururesto.com.ar* ⌺ *Reservations essential* ⊘ *Closed Sun. and Mon. No lunch* ✛ *2:C6.*

$ ✕ **Bar Plaza Dorrego.** This atmospheric corner building with greenery
CAFÉ   tumbling over wrought-iron balconies has what is unquestionably the best view of Plaza Dorrego. It shouldn't be your first choice for a full

FAVORITE LOCAL DISHES

Even if your Spanish is pretty good, you might not be able to figure out a couple of porteño dishes that you'll find in local eateries.

Revuelta Gramajo is a local classic with a good story behind it to boot. Named after government administrator Artemio Gramajo (friend of then-president Julio Roca), an amateur chef who "designed" a dish of scrambled eggs, fried potatoes, ham, and peas to be served to soldiers in the battlefield.

Milanesa à la Maryland is a breaded veal or chicken cutlet served with creamed corn, fried bananas, peas, ham, and potatoes.

Eating *ñoquis de papas* (potato dumplings) on the 29th of every month is a local tradition, the day that *ñoquis* (slang for civil servants in patronage jobs) pick up their monthly check.

meal, as there are far better options pretty much anywhere, but do stop in for coffee and a pastry or a beer and a dish of peanuts. Then sit back and people-watch. Given the century-old décor and grime, the nose-in-the-air attitude of the waiters is far misplaced. ⑤ *Average main: 60 pesos* ✉ *Defensa 1098, at Humberto I, on Pl. Dorrego, San Telmo* ☎ *11/4361–0141* ✍ *Reservations not accepted* ▭ *No credit cards* Ⓜ *C or E to Independencia* ✛ *2:E6.*

$$$
BRASSERIE
✕**Brasserie Petanque.** One of the few—if not the only—classic French brasseries in Buenos Aires, Petanque is a place to drop in, enjoy hearty French fare, and wash it all down with local wines. The ambience is lively, with marble-top tables so close to each other that you may well find yourself participating in neighboring conversations (and vice versa). The best dishes are the most traditional, often the day's special, which repeat in rotation each day of the week. The sublime *confit de pato*, or duck confit, is not to be missed. The owners have just opened a branch in Santiago, Chile, and have another one coming in Lima, Peru. ⑤ *Average main: 120 pesos* ✉ *Defensa 596, at Mexico, San Telmo* ☎ *11/4342–7930* ⊕ *www.brasseriepetanque.com* ⊘ *Closed Mon.* ✛ *2:D5.*

$$$
MODERN
ARGENTINE
✕**Café San Juan.** When famed "anti-chef" Leandro Cristóbal decided to return to his roots, he dropped his trademark modern cuisine in favor of huge platters of rustic traditional dishes with little creative twists reflecting his own bad-boy personality. That carries over into the décor and setup—the room has a sort of farmhouse-chic feel with the addition of graffiti and tattoo-covered cooks working the open kitchen. Roast partridge with hazelnut stuffing, sweetbread-and-ricotta cannelloni, and tender wine-braised rabbit are among the stars here. A second location is open nearby at Chile 474 focusing more on pastas. ⑤ *Average main: 130 pesos* ✉ *Av. San Juan 450, between Defensa and Bolivár, San Telmo* ☎ *11/4300–1112* ✍ *Reservations essential* ▭ *No credit cards* ⊘ *Closed Mon.* ✛ *2:D6.*

$$
STEAKHOUSE
FAMILY
✕**DesNivel.** Though the name may translate as "uneven," there's nothing remotely so about this classic steakhouse. Don't expect any frills, just great steaks and side dishes (for a real treat order the *papas fritas provençal*, golden french fries tossed in fresh parsley and garlic). Take a

table in the cavernous dining room, or grab something to go—steak sandwiches and empanadas fly out the door as fast as they can make them. The portions are huge and the prices are eminently reasonable. Late night the crowd gets particularly interesting. ⑤ *Average main: 80 pesos* ✉ *Defensa 855, at Giuffra, San Telmo* ☎ *11/4300–9081* ▭ *No credit cards* ⊘ *No lunch Mon.* ✛ *2:D6.*

$$$
BASQUE

✕ **Taberna Baska.** Buenos Aires is home to a large Basque immigrant population, and if there's anywhere in town to turn to for Basque cooking, it's this place. You can expect friendly, efficient service from waiters who know their stuff as they work the antiques-filled dining room. Although the extensive menu may look pricey at first glance, it's really not at all. Most of the plates are big enough to share, and many can be ordered in half-size portions. Top recommendations include the various stews, particularly the spicy *cazuela de mariscos* (seafood casserole). Another don't-miss option is the *gambas al ajillo* (large prawns in garlic and chili sauce). ⑤ *Average main: 110 pesos* ✉ *Chile 980, San Telmo* ☎ *11/4334–0903* ⊘ *Closed Mon. No dinner Sun.; no lunch Fri. and Sat.* Ⓜ *C to Independencia* ✛ *2:C5.*

> ### DRINKING ON DEFENSA
>
> Hitting the countless antiques shops, art galleries, and fashion stores can be tiring work, so go relax in one of many old-school bars. Plaza Dorrego is considered the central point of the neighborhood, and the main drag is Calle Defensa, which is lined with places that offer outdoor seating. Check out the historic **Bar Plaza Dorrego** (✉ *Defensa 1098* ✛ *2:E6*) for prime people-watching on the plaza, or wander up to the end of the lane to Parque Lezama and take a seat at the classic **Bar Británico** (✉ *Defensa and Brasil* ✛ *2:D6*) or **Bar Hipopótamo** (✉ *Defensa and Brasil* ✛ *2:D6*).

LA BOCA

La Boca was the dock and warehouse district, and much of that is still in evidence and much of the area is a bit dicey. At the same time, it is home to Buenos Aires' emblematic picture-postcard tourist site, El Caminito, with its bright-color buildings, street tango demos, and overpriced, poor-quality pasta shops.

$$$
STEAKHOUSE

✕ **El Obrero.** You'll half expect sawdust on the floor and a saloon fight to break out when you walk into this old-time steak house just off the docks of La Boca. While the place is usually filled with locals, it's also a regular stop for touring rock stars who seem to have chosen it as *the* spot to go when in town for a performance. Big, juicy steaks that are perfectly cooked, massive helpings of side dishes, and more ambience than you can shake a stick at make El Obrero a movie director's dream of an Argentine steakhouse. The neighborhood is a little iffy, particularly at night, and it's down a little side street—take a taxi to and from (they'll call one for you). ⑤ *Average main: 120 pesos* ✉ *Augustín R. Caffarena 64, at Don Pedro Mendoza, La Boca* ☎ *11/4362–9912* ▭ *No credit cards* ⊘ *Closed Sun.* ✛ *2:F6.*

'CLOSED-DOOR' RESTAURANTS

One of the most innovative culinary trends to emerge in Buenos Aires is *puertas cerradas,* or "closed door" restaurants. Proprietors fling open the doors of their homes to small groups for intimate meals, often at communal tables where you'll be able to strike up conversations with in-the-know locals or savvy travelers.

In Palermo, the two hot spots for shared-table dining are **NOLA** (✉ www.nolachef.net/restaurant) where Creole, Cajun, and Mexican traditions take the stage for a four-course dinner with wine pairings, and **Adentro Dinner Club** (✉ www.adentrodinnerclub.com), which makes the traditional Argentine *asado,* or backyard grill, accessible to everyone.

Other great in-home dining experiences include **I Latina** (✉ www. ilatinabuenosaires.com), with its modern Colombian fare, and **Casa Coupage** (✉ www.casacoupage. com), featuring creative Argentine cooking smartly paired with fine wines.

5

RECOLETA

Arguably Buenos Aires' poshest neighborhood, Recoleta is the epicenter for high-end shopping, museum-going, and white-tablecloth dining. It's home to most of the swankier hotels, and many of them house excellent restaurants, but it's also home to a good number of classic spots that have been serving up high-quality fare for decades.

The somewhat touristy Village Recoleta area has a mix of old-time cafés like La Biela and Munich nestled side by side with family-friendly steak-and pasta houses. There's also the city's first microbrewery, Buller, and a few nightclubs for those who want a little late night fun.

$$$
AMERICAN
✕ **Buller Brewing Company.** Smack in the middle of the touristy Village Recoleta strip, Buller is the city's first microbrewery. Turning out an impressive seven different styles (don't miss the Oktoberfest or the Porter), the friendly place also offers a sampler of the whole range that's worth a try. Great sandwiches and one of the better burgers in the neighborhood are more reasons to drop in. The service can seem a bit slow, at least until you get your first beer in hand, but it's worth the wait. ⑤ *Average main: 140 pesos* ✉ *R. M. Ortíz 1827, Recoleta* ☎ *11/4808–9061* ⊙ *Closed Sun.* ✛ *2:B1.*

$$$$
ECLECTIC
✕ **Casa SaltShaker.** While *puertas cerradas,* or closed-door restaurants, have been a part of the Buenos Aires dining scene for decades, they were historically a place you discovered by word-of-mouth. In 2006, that all changed when Dan Perlman and Henry Tapia, the *norteamericano* and *peruano* couple behind this 10-seat communal-table home-dining spot, hit the scene. These days scoring a spot to dig in to their Mediterranean-meets-Andean cuisine, five-course menu with paired wines can be hard to do, so book early. You'll meet new friends, swap stories, and enjoy creative home cooking. The exact address is provided with reservation, made via the website only. ⑤ *Average main: 550 pesos* ✉ *Uriburu and Peña, Recoleta* ⊕ *www.casasaltshaker.com* ⬧ *Reservations essential* ⊙ *Closed Sun.–Tues. No lunch.* ✛ *2:A2.*

$$$$
MIDDLE EASTERN

✕ **Club Sirio Libanés.** Dedicated to the cuisines of the Middle East, this sumptuous dining room on the third floor of the Syrian Lebanese Cultural Club serves up one of the city's best all-you-can-eat buffets. For a flat price you get unlimited trips to the cold appetizers bar, unlimited orders of from a palate-pleasing selection of hot dishes, and all the honey-laden pastries you can pack in. Belly dancers entertain on the weekends, when the prices also rise about 20%. If you're in town for an extended stay, Chef Abdala offers a series of classes where he demonstrates how to duplicate his recipes at home. $ *Average main: 190 pesos* ✉ *Syrian Lebanese Cultural Club, Ayacucho 1496, at Pacheco de Melo, Recoleta* ☎ *11/4806–5764* ☉ *Closed Sun. No lunch* ✛ *2:B2.*

$$
MEDITERRANEAN

✕ **Due Resto Café.** This place may resemble a neighborhood coffee shop where folks are just sitting, sipping coffee, and reading the newspaper. But check out the long and narrow dining room at lunchtime, when the kitchen turns out some of the best pasta and fish dishes in the barrio. The menu changes daily, depending on the chef's whims, but you can count on ravioli showing up in a stunning variety of styles. There are also some excellent stir-fried dishes. Don't pass up dessert, which may include a "deconstructed" take on the classic *arroz con leche.* $ *Average main: 80 pesos* ✉ *Juncal 2391, at Pueyrredón, Barrio Norte* ☎ *11/4829–9400* ⊕ *www.duerestocafe.blogspot.com* ☉ *Closed weekends. No dinner.* Ⓜ *D to Pueyreddón* ✛ *1:H6.*

$$$$
MODERN
ARGENTINE

✕ **Duhau Restaurante & Vinoteca.** An oasis of elegance and grace in the heart of Recoleta, the Duhau Restaurante definitely shouldn't be overlooked because it's inside a chain hotel. While French cooking techniques may dominate in the kitchen, the ingredients are pure South America. Particularly favored by the chef are seafood and meats flown in from Patagonia. Standout dishes include butter-soft Angus tenderloin, crispy sweetbreads, and a decadent molten chocolate cake. If the weather is nice, grab a table on the terrace overlooking the courtyard gardens. Don't miss a pre- or postdinner visit to the wine-and-cheese bar with a fantastic array of each, and then take an after-meal stroll through the hotel's underground art gallery. $ *Average main: 270 pesos* ✉ *Park Hyatt Palacio Duhau, Av. Alvear 1661, at Montevideo, Recoleta* ☎ *11/5171–1340* ⊕ *www.buenosaires.park.hyatt.com* ☉ *No lunch weekends* ⌂ *Reservations essential* ✛ *2:C1.*

$$$$
TAPAS
Fodor's Choice
★

✕ **El Burladero.** In a city filled with Spanish and Basque restaurants, there's not much of a tapas bar scene in Buenos Aires. El Burladero provides a mix of bar seating and communal tables, along with a more formal dining room, where you can mix and mingle with other diners. It serves up not only the best tapas selection in town, but also some of the best Spanish food. Don't miss one of the city's most satisfying versions of *chipirones en su tinta* (baby squid in its own ink), or the mouthwatering *conejo en sidra* (rabbit braised in cider). And speaking of cider, the bar pulls pints of the stuff to start off or accompany your meal. At lunch there's a fantastic three-course menu that costs less than a main course off the à la carte selection. $ *Average main: 170 pesos* ✉ *Pres. J. E. Uriburu 1488, at Peña, Recoleta* ☎ *11/4806–9247* ⊕ *www. sottovoce.com.ar* ⌂ *Reservations essential* ☉ *No dinner Sun.* ✛ *2:A2.*

TAKING TEA

Along Avenida Alvear are some of the best-known names of the fashion world—Hermès, Louis Vuitton, Ermenegildo Zegna, Ralph Lauren, Cartier—and it's no surprise that some of the city's finest hotels are located in the same area.

For a true old-world experience, with white-gloved waiters and silver service, find your way to **L'Orangerie** (⊠ *Av. Alvear 1891* ✛ *2:B1*) in the Alvear Palace

Hotel. Wave after wave of finger sandwiches and pastries accompany specially blended teas from Tealosophy, a world-class tea shop in the hotel's lobby.

If your tastes run to something simpler, a chain of great tea shops has opened up in the city. **Tea Connection** (⊠ *Arenales 2102 and Uriburu 1597*) has two locations in Recoleta and another six in other parts of the city.

5

$$ ✕ **El Sanjuanino.** Tourists from the nearby hotels flock to this Northern
ARGENTINE Argentine regional spot, but you'll definitely also see lots of locals, par-
Fodor'sChoice ticularly at lunchtime. It's cramped, crowded, and kitschy, and in hot
★ weather the roaring wood-fired ovens can make the main floor a bit too
toasty (head downstairs, where it's cooler), but it's worth it for great
empanadas, the city's best *locro* (corn, squash, and meat stew), and, if
you're feeling adventurous, one of the iconic game dishes. Don't bother
with the wine list, because the house wine served in pitchers is just as good
at half the price. The waiters have fun with the crowd, and speak at least
basic conversational phrases in a half dozen or more languages. ⓢ *Aver-
age main: 90 pesos* ⊠ *Posadas 1515, at Callao, Recoleta* ☎ *11/4804–
2909* ⊕ *elsanjuanino.co/esp/sucursales.html* ⓧ *Closed Mon.* ✛ *2:C1.*

$$$$ ✕ **Elena Restaurante.** With a new name and a new chef, the Four Seasons
ARGENTINE Hotel's spectacularly renovated dining room serves creative fare that
blends the traditions of Argentina with touches of the sunny Mediter-
ranean. Don't miss the spectacular sweetbread and poached egg appe-
tizer, and for a true taste of what the chef can do off the grill, order
the *parrillada* (a sampler of various cuts of meat) or the *mariscada*, (a
medley of grilled seafood), both in portions big enough for up to four
people to share. If you're in a more casual mood, the Pony Line bar
offers fantastic cocktails, great pizzas, and one of the best burgers in
town. Weekend afternoons you help yourself to a brunch spread that's
unrivaled in the city. A children's menu is available. ⓢ *Average main:
200 pesos* ⊠ *Four Seasons Hotel Buenos Aires, Posadas 1086, at Cer-
rito, Recoleta* ☎ *11/4321–1728* ⊕ *www.elenaponyline.com/elena.html*
ⓧ *No lunch Sat.–Sun.* ⚱ *Reservations essential* ✛ *2:C1.*

$$$ ✕ **Juana M.** It's the salad bar that brings in the crowds—nowhere else
STEAKHOUSE in town will you find one this extensive, or one that offers unlimited
trips. But that isn't the be all and end all of Juana M, where you'll find
perfectly cooked prime cuts of steak, along with pork, chicken, and fish.
There's also a great selection of pasta dishes and local classics. Oh, and
back to that salad bar—it's included in the price of your main course
and is packed with everything from fresh vegetables to bean salads,
piping hot chard croquettes, and cheeses. The place is a cavernous

basement with few windows, so your view tends to be your dining companions and a selection of ever-changing and sometimes questionable artwork. Our only quibble: the wine list isn't nearly as good as everything else in the place. $ *Average main: 130 pesos* ⊠ *Carlos Pellegrini 1535, basement level, Retiro* ☎ *11/4326–0462* ⊕ *www.juanam. com* Ⓜ *C to San Martín* ✛ *2:D2.*

$$$ ✕ **La Biela.** When the weather cooperates, locals and tourists mix and
ARGENTINE mingle at La Biela's outdoor tables—this despite the fact that there's a higher charge for the privilege. That leaves the dining room dominated by a local crowd. A blast from the past, this traditional café is one of the best spots in Recoleta for people-watching and celebrity-spotting. For the most part, it's place to linger over coffee and a pastry, or perhaps a savory sandwich at midday, but there's also a full menu of local specialties, and they're not half bad. $ *Average main: 125 pesos* ⊠ *Quintana 596, at Junín, Recoleta* ☎ *11/4804–0449* ⊕ *www.labiela.com* ✛ *2:B1.*

$$$$ ✕ **La Bourgogne.** You'll be welcomed with a complimentary flute of spar-
FRENCH kling wine and a selection of hors d'oeuvres when you take your table in
Fodor'sChoice this elegant dining room on the side of the famed Alvear Palace Hotel.
★ Chef Jean-Paul Bondeaux (you may meet him as he strolls around the dining room) turns out brilliant French classics updated for modern sensibilities. While not on the menu, the kitchen will happily prepare a completely vegetarian menu. The service is impeccable, and you'll feel exquisitely cared for even as you take your leave, when the staff present you with a breakfast treat for the next morning. The best value is the seven-course tasting menu that includes six wines—it will run you less than a three-course dinner with a bottle of wine. The wine list is extensive, focusing on the finest from France and Argentina. Jackets are recommended, though not required, for men. $ *Average main: 370 pesos* ⊠ *Alvear Palace Hotel, Ayacucho 2027, at Alvear, Recoleta* ☎ *11/4805–3857, 11/4808–2100* ⌧ *Reservations essential* ⊘ *Closed Sun. No lunch* ✛ *2:B1.*

$$$ ✕ **La Parolaccia Trattoria.** Close to the neighborhood's most popular shop-
ITALIAN ping strip, La Parolaccia Trattoria feels like the kind of family-run and
FAMILY family-friendly Italian eateries you could find in any big city. It serves surprisingly excellent pastas made on the premises that are topped with a wide variety of sauces—particularly good are the hand-rolled fusilli. Don't overlook the three-course lunch specials, which can be a great deal. The staff is happy to prepare half portions of pasta dishes for your kids. You'll be greeted at your table with a complimentary cocktail and sent off with a digestif of limoncello at the end of your meal. $ *Average main: 150 pesos* ⊠ *Riobamba 1046, Recoleta* ☎ *11/4812–1053* ⊕ *www. laparolaccia.com* Ⓜ *C to Congreso; B to Callao* ✛ *2:A2.*

$$$ ✕ **Munich Recoleta.** This convivial place looks like a relic of another
ARGENTINE era—located along a strip filled with casual eateries, it has white tablecloths draping the tables, waiters clad in black vests, and managers in tuxes. The décor is old-school, with coats of arms and mounted animal heads hanging over the dining room. The food is classic porteño, prepared with a flair. The sizzling steaks are delicious, though they tend to be close to well done regardless of how they're ordered. At lunch the not-to-be-missed dish is the *revuelto gramajo*, a local classic with ham,

eggs, onions, and fried potatoes elegantly plated like a French omelet. For dessert, don't miss the *panqueque de manzana,* a thin crêpe with caramelized apples and flamed in rum. $ *Average main: 135 pesos* ⊠ *R. M. Ortíz 1871, at Av. Quintana, Recoleta* ☎ *11/4804–3981* ⊕ *www. munich-recoleta.com.ar* ⊗ *Closed Tues.* ✣ *2:B1.*

$$$$ ✕ **Oviedo.** A tranquil ambience, soft lighting, and sea-theme artwork
ARGENTINE   adorning the walls greet you in this elegant Spanish-style establish-
Fodor'sChoice   ment in the heart of Recoleta. In a meat-centric city like Buenos Aires,
★   beautifully cooked seafood is a welcome change, and Oviedo is the best in the city. From classic dishes to modern creations, the kitchen turns out beautifully plated fillets of fish—don't miss the daily catch with pickled baby vegetables. You can't go wrong with any of the pristine shellfish dishes. Top it all off with one of the better wine lists in the area and you're in for a memorable lunch or dinner. $ *Average main: 175 pesos* ⊠ *Beruti 2602, at Ecuador, Recoleta* ☎ *11/4821–3741* ⊕ *www. oviedoresto.com.ar* ⊗ *Closed Sun.* Ⓜ *D to Pueyrredón* ✣ *2:A2.*

$$ ✕ **Tandoor.** A favorite of the local Indian community, Tandoor is a des-
INDIAN   tination for embassy officials who want a food fix from home. It's no surprise that it's also a winner with American expats, many of whom are looking for something a little spicier than the local fare. When the place first opened the chef went full tilt on the picante, but he eventually toned down the spices a bit to appeal to a local clientele. You can always add in more chilies, available on request. The room is chic and sleek, and the service is polished. At lunch there's an inexpensive prix-fixe menu option. $ *Average main: 100 pesos* ⊠ *Laprida 1293, at Charcas, Barrio Norte* ☎ *11/4821–3676* ⊕ *www.tandoor.com.ar* ⊗ *Closed Sun.* ✣ *1:H5.*

$$$$ ✕ **Tarquino.** The city's rock star of molecular gastronomy, Dante Lipo-
MODERN   race, has reappeared in this sophisticated hotel garden setting, where
ARGENTINE   he's adding touches of those cutting-edge techniques to a menu dedi-
Fodor'sChoice   cated to meat in all its forms. This is world-class cooking with flavors
★   guaranteed to please any carnivore. From the moment you sit down and receive your own baguette with a bowl of beef broth to dip it in until the last shred of beef, veal, pork (or, the occasional fish or fowl) enters your mouth, everything is sensational. It comes at a price, as do the six- and 11- course tasting menus (850 and 1,000 pesos, respectively, not counting wine), but every moment is worth it. $ *Average main: 200 pesos* ⊠ *Hub Porteño Hotel, Rodriguez Peña 1967, at Posadas, Reco-leta* ☎ *11/6091–2160* ⊕ *www.tarquinorestaurante.com.ar* ⌕ *Reserva-tions essential* ⊗ *Closed Sun. No lunch Sat.* ✣ *1:C1.*

PALERMO

The city's largest neighborhood, Palermo offers something for every taste, style, and budget. It's the city's undisputed culinary hot spot, with enclaves that have their own distinct style and vibe.

If you want the tastiest, most cutting-edge, most traditional, most eth-nic, most daring, and most fashionable food in Buenos Aires, then you head to Palermo. It's that simple. The sprawling neighborhood is home to the hip areas of Palermo Soho and Hollywood as well as the quieter pockets of Palermo Botánico and Chico.

5

Staying Up with the Porteños

Buenos Aires is a 24-hour city, and you *can* find places that serve food around the clock, but most of these are downtown and tend to fall into the fast-food and pizza categories. Although much is made about porteños' late eating habits, the truth is the ideal and the most popular dining time is 9–9:30 pm (though you can easily show up for dinner at midnight and no one will blink an eye). Most restaurants open at 8 pm for dinner and will serve until 1 or 2 am. You can find more late-night *confiterías* (confectioneries) and cafés in the Centro area; most other neighborhoods have scarce late-night offerings.

You can find breakfast—coffee and pastries—anywhere, at any time. Lunch is served from noon to 4 pm, 1 to 2 pm being the rush hour, especially downtown, which is packed with office workers.

Soho's main landmark is the artsy Plaza Serrano. But steer clear of the restaurants that line the plaza; they uniformly serve bland and overpriced food. Instead, wander a few blocks in any direction, and you're bound to come across a worthwhile dining spot.

Across the train tracks and Avenida Juan B. Justo lies Palermo Hollywood, which does an admirable job of mixing old and new cuisines in a cool setting of TV production houses and studios.

$$$$
ARGENTINE
✕ **Adentro Dinner Club.** Realizing that not every visitor to Buenos Aires has friends or family to invite them to an *asado,* the traditional backyard barbecue, Colorado native Kelly Brenner and *argentino* Gabriel Aguallo decided to take the plunge. They threw open the doors to their charming home, where guests join them on the patio around a massive grill and then adjourn to the farmhouse-style dining area for a family-style steak or seafood fest. Plenty of grilled vegetable dishes, creative salads, and glasses of local wine accompany the meat. More wines are available from the short but well-selected wine list. The exact address is provided when you make a reservation. ⑤ *Average main: 450 pesos* ✉ *Fray Justo Santamaria de Oro and Costa Rica, Palermo Soho* ⊕ *www.adentrodinnerclub.com* ⌂ *Reservations essential* ☉ *No lunch. Hrs vary wkly* ✛ *1:E4.*

$$
VEGETARIAN
✕ **Artemisia.** In a city known for its steak and potatoes, vegetarians generally have to make do with salads, pastas, and pizzas to get by. That's slowly changing thanks to gems like Artemisia, which serves up what is arguably the city's best and most creative meat-free fare, spiced up with Peruvian flavors. It also offers what may be the city's best veggie burger, packed with flavorful lentils. If you're traveling with omnivores, there's always one fish dish on the menu. The service tends to be a bit slow, but it fits the relaxed vibe. There's a sister spot at Cabrera 3877, also in Palermo. ⑤ *Average main: 100 pesos* ✉ *Gorriti 5996, at Arévalo, Palermo* ☎ *11/4776–5484* ☉ *Closed Mon. No dinner Sun.* ✛ *1:D3.*

$$
INDIAN
✕ **The Bangalore Pub & Curry House.** On the southern edge of Palermo, this place serves pints of ale—not too cold, as is British custom—and what are easily the tastiest Indian-style curries in the city. The best part

is that there's no stinting on the *picante,* as is more typical at Indian restaurants in this spice-averse city. These dishes will make you sweat, so you'll definitely need that beer. This place is a hangout for British and American expats, but there are always a few intrepid locals. If you choose to sit upstairs rather than take a seat in the pub, order your food before climbing the steps. The waiters will go up to deliver your plates but not to take your order. ⑤ *Average main: 100 pesos* ✉ *Humboldt 1416, at Niceto Vega, Palermo Hollywood* ☏ *11/4779–2621* ⚐ *Reservations not accepted* ☉ *No lunch* ✛ *1:D4.*

$$$ ✕ **Bardot.** Peruvian fusion cuisine is all the rage these days, but not
PERUVIAN everyone is looking to blend Japanese and Peruvian fare. In Bardot's
Fodor's Choice sizzling lounge atmosphere, chef Germán Cardenas and his staff are
★ bringing flavors of the Amazon basin to the table with exotic fruits like *camu-camu* and the fiery *charapita* chilies. Start off with a cocktail made with one of the dozens of pisco infusions lining the bar, then settle in for some of the best modern Peruvian food in town. Lemony ceviche topped with red onions and cilantro and a truly mouthwatering *paella amazonica* featuring smoked pork and sausage share the list of favorites. ⑤ *Average main: 140 pesos* ✉ *Honduras 5237, at Uriarte, Palermo Soho* ☏ *11/4831–1112* ⊕ *www.restobardot.net* ⚐ *Reservations essential* ☉ *Closed Mon. No lunch weekdays* Ⓜ *D to Palermo* ✛ *1:E4.*

$$$ ✕ **Bella Italia.** One of the first Italian restaurants in Palermo Botánico,
ITALIAN Bella Italia is the cornerstone of what has become the city's quasi-official Little Italy. The Lena family runs its flagship restaurant and a neighboring café (along with branches in Palermo and Belgrano) with grace, warmth, and elegance. The star of the menu is one of the city's few veal chops, a whopping cut of perfectly cooked meat encrusted with salt and rosemary and served over beautifully roasted potatoes. This dish is easily enough for two, especially if you start with one of the kitchen's stellar pastas. The restaurant also features a well-thought-out and fairly priced wine list. ⑤ *Average main: 140 pesos* ✉ *Republica Arabe Siria 3285, at Segui, Palermo Botánico* ☏ *11/4802–4253* ⊕ *www.bellaitalia-gourmet.com.ar* ⚐ *Reservations essential* ☉ *Closed Sun. No lunch* ✛ *1:H3.*

$$$$ ✕ **Casa Coupage.** In the middle of the chaos of Palermo, Casa Coupage
MODERN is an oasis of tranquility. Located in a converted home, the beige-on-
ARGENTINE beige dining area takes up most of the main floor. Décor is simple, mostly wine-related, plus the odd choice of postage stamps glued in a swath around the rooms at eye level. Your best bet is the frequently changing tasting menu that lets you sample the full range of chef Pablo Bolzan's creative take on traditional Argentine cooking. A limited selection of à la carte dishes is always available. Sommelier Santiago Mymicopulo knows his stuff, and his great wine-pairing options are usually a much better value than ordering from the somewhat overpriced wine list. ⑤ *Average main: 450 pesos* ✉ *Soler 5518, at Humboldt, Palermo* ☏ *11/4777–9295* ⊕ *www.casacoupage.com* ⚐ *Reservations essential* ☉ *Closed Sun.–Tues. No lunch* ✛ *1:E3.*

$$$ ✕ **Chira.** While Nikkei cuisine is taking Argentina by storm, some chefs
PERUVIAN have realized that Japanese isn't the only cuisine that pairs with the
Fodor's Choice explosive flavors of Peru. In this understated dining room, chef Renato
★ Ortigas is turning out fascinating modern Andean dishes that combine

elements from the Mediterranean and the Caribbean, to resounding accolades. The name comes from the Quechua word for a chili seed, and there's no question that Ortigas is trying to plant something new. Not to be missed are his *anticuchos de chipirones,* tender baby squid bathed in a smoking red pepper sauce. The service is friendly and faultless, though perhaps over-informative, as the staff seem to have been trained to let you in on every element of the dishes. $ Average main: 140 pesos ✉ Humboldt 1864, between El Salvador and Costa Rica, Palermo Soho ☎ 11/4777–0724 ⊕ www.chiracocinafusion.com.ar ☉ Closed Sun. ✛ 1:E4

$ ✕ **Club Eros.** Known for its no-frills décor, this Palermo Soho stalwart is
ARGENTINE   where generations of locals have been coming to dine. It's located inside a soccer club of the same name and draws its clientele from club members, neighborhood residents, and pretty much anyone who wants honest cooking that doesn't put a dent in their budget. While the menu features three different pastas and a dozen items off the *parrilla* (grill), your waiter will tell you what's actually available for the day. $ Average main: 50 pesos ✉ Uriarte 1609, at Honduras, Palermo Soho ☎ 11/4832–1313 ⌧ Reservations not accepted ▤ No credit cards ✛ 1:E4.

$$$ ✕ **Don Julio.** Behind an unassuming facade, one of Palermo's best steak-
STEAKHOUSE   houses features cowhide tablecloths, wagon-wheel lighting fixtures, and
Fodor'sChoice   rows and rows of empty wine bottles signed by satisfied customers. The
★   place features one of the city's better-curated wine lists—ask for owner Pablo Rivero, who knows the ins and outs of every vintage. Packing the place at lunch and dinner is a mix of locals and expats dining on the fantastic ojo de bife and *cuadril* (rump steak). The chorizo sausages are also great, as is pretty much anything else off a grill. $ Average main: 120 pesos ✉ Guatemala 4691, at Gurruchaga, Palermo Soho ☎ 11/4831–9564 ✛ 1:F4.

$$$ ✕ **El Trapiche.** This eatery's design aesthetic—a bare, unadorned space
ARGENTINE   illuminated with industrial lighting—doesn't translate to the dishes, which, while not fancy, include hearty portions of grilled and fried Argentine dishes and a smattering of Spanish specialties. At lunch it's packed with Palermo office workers, and at dinner there's a mix of locals and tourists, all tucking into the well-seasoned and properly cooked steaks and chops. Don't miss the *boquerones* (marinated anchovies) as an appetizer. The *entraña,* or hanger steak, particularly when accompanied by the excellent *papas a la crema* (creamed potatoes), are a don't-miss main course perfect for sharing. While the menu might look pricey at first glance, most of the steaks easily serve more than one person. There are also inexpensive prix-fixe lunch options. $ Average main: 125 pesos ✉ Paraguay 5099, at Humboldt, Palermo Hollywood ☎ 11/4772–7343 Ⓜ D to Estación Palermo ✛ 1:E3.

$$$$ ✕ **Francesco.** With a privileged view of a quiet residential street in Pal-
PERUVIAN   ermo, Francesco was one of the first high-end Peruvian restaurants in Buenos Aires. While it's still as good as it ever was, these days it faces some stiff competition where the food is just as good or, in a couple of cases, even better. But the ceviches continue to be wonderful, and the chef shows a deft hand with fresh fish. The dining room is elegant, and the service is efficient (if rather formal). The place lacks the bells

and whistles of the newer spots, but it's perfect if you want to avoid a "scene." $ *Average main: 175 pesos* ⊠ *Soler 5598, at Fitz Roy, Palermo Soho* ☎ *11/4774–4011* ⊕ *www.francescorestaurant.com.ar* ☉ *Closed Sun. No lunch Sat.* ✢ *1:E3.*

$$$ ╳ **Green Bamboo.** Covered with more knick-knacks than the space com-
VIETNAMESE fortably allows, the bar at the city's only Vietnamese restaurant looks like someone bought out a souvenir shop. The barstools are irrelevant, because there's no place to set your drink anyway. But that's fine, because you can just grab a table or relax on a sofa in the dining area and enjoy one of the signature cocktails while you peruse the menu of Vietnamese classics. Perennial favorites include the crispy smoked eggplant dumplings, prawns with rice pasta, chicken curry, and five-spice spareribs. Bowing to local custom, there's little heat in any of the dishes, even if you ask for extra chilies, but ask for a bowl of Sriracha hot sauce to be brought to your table. $ *Average main: 145 pesos* ⊠ *Costa Rica 5802, at A. J. Carranza, Palermo Hollywood* ☎ *11/4775–7050* ⊕ *www. green-bamboo.com.ar* ⌦ *Reservations essential* ☉ *No lunch* ✢ *1:D3.*

$$$ ╳ **Hernán Gipponi.** This long, narrow room leading to Fierro Hotel's gar-
ECLECTIC den patio may not seem like a hot spot for creative cooking, but don't let appearances fool you. Using skills he honed while working for years in the top kitchens of Spain, chef Hernán Gipponi turns out some of the most creative food in Palermo, particularly fish dishes. While you can order from the à la carte menu, local foodies gravitate toward the changing seven-course tasting menu for 350 pesos. For lunch there's a three-course prix-fixe for 170 pesos. Backing up the kitchen is one of the better wine lists in the city, managed by a team of top sommeliers, as well as an excellent cocktail selection from the bar. Weekends are known for one of the city's most fabulous brunches. $ *Average main: 120 pesos* ⊠ *Fierro Hotel, Soler 5862, at Ravignani, Palermo Hollywood* ☎ *11/3220–6820* ⊕ *www.fierrohotel.com/restaurant/hernan-gipponi* ☉ *No dinner Sun. and Mon.* ⌦ *Reservations essential* Ⓜ *D to Ministro Carranza* ✢ *1:D3.*

$$$$ ╳ **i Latina.** These charming and handsome Colombian brothers ran a suc-
SOUTH cessful restaurant in Patagonia before moving to Buenos Aires, opening a
AMERICAN new place, and receiving enthusiastic reviews. In an intimate space, Santiago Macias turns out some of the most creative, interesting Colombian-influenced food in the city. The prix-fixe tasting menu changes regularly. Flawless service is provided in the dining room under the direction of Santiago's brother Camilo. For something just a little bit different and off the beaten path, this is a don't-miss experience. Wine pairings are extra (230 pesos). $ *Average main: 540 pesos* ⊠ *Murillo 725, at Acevedo, Villa Crespo* ☎ *11/4857–9095* ⊕ *ilatinabuenosaires.com* ⌦ *Reservations essential* ☉ *Closed Sun. and Mon. No lunch* ✢ *1:C6.*

$$$ ╳ **Kansas.** Located alongside the Hipódromo, the city's hottest horse-
AMERICAN racing track, this eatery has great views. Boisterous definitely defines
FAMILY the ambience as diners tuck into barbecued ribs, chops, steaks, pastas, and salads, all washed down with copious amounts of beer and iced tea. There are plenty of options for children on the menu. This is the top of the heap for diners searching for a U.S.-style chain, and it attracts local business executives during the day and families at night. Reservations

5

recommended, especially for dinner, and there's almost always a wait for a table. $ *Average main: 130 pesos* ⊠ *Av. Libertador 4625, at Matienzo, Palermo* ☎ *11/4776–4100* ⊕ *www.kansasgrillandbar. ar* ✢ *1:E1.*

$$$
ITALIAN

✕ **La Baita.** Sophisticated, elegant, and cozy all at the same time, this cozy corner spot in Palermo Soho offers a combination of classic dishes and modern creations. A favorite of Italophile locals, it's the perfect location for a romantic night out, perhaps with a reenactment of the famous scene from *Lady and the Tramp.* Housemade pastas are the stars here, topped with sauces so vibrant you know they were made the same day. The kitchen sometimes has a heavy hand with salt, so if it's an issue let your server know when you order. Service is friendly and efficient. The wine list, while an excellent selection, is a tad on the pricey side, but you're paying for the atmosphere as well. $ *Average main: 110 pesos* ⊠ *Thames 1603, at Honduras, Palermo Soho* ☎ *11/4832-7234* ⊕ *www.labaita-restaurante.com.ar* ⊗ *No lunch Mon.* ✢ *1:E4.*

$$$$
STEAKHOUSE

✕ **La Cabrera.** Spanish may actually be the least common language spoken at this touristy place, but that doesn't mean it's not a great steakhouse. Generally big enough to share, huge slabs of meat are seasoned, seared, and cooked to perfection and accompanied by a variety of condiments. There's also an array of "side dishes," a touch gimmicky, but tasty, ranging from different vegetable purees and pickles. The service is impeccable—it has to be with the international crowd it attracts. *Provoletas* (gooey, slightly crispy grilled cheese slabs) are a must to start, either the standard cow or the much touted goat versions. The exact same menu is served down the block at La Cabrera Norte, at 5127 Cabrera, a location that was opened just to handle the overflow. While reservations are accepted, they're rarely honored, so expect to stand in line during prime dinner hours. $ *Average main: 200 pesos* ⊠ *Cabrera 5099, at Thames, Palermo Soho* ☎ *11/4832-5754* ⊕ *www. parrillalacabrera.com.ar* ⌲ *Reservations essential* ⊗ *No lunch Tues.–Thurs.* ✢ *1:E5.*

$$$
ECLECTIC
Fodor'sChoice
★

✕ **Las Pizarras Bistró.** Quirky and kitschy, this 40-seat hole-in-the-wall looks like any of hundreds of other neighborhood hangouts throughout the city. But take a look at the chalkboard-covered walls (*las pizarras*) and you'll know instantly this isn't your typical spot for cheap steaks and milanesas. Chef Rodrigo Castilla is one of the most unsung chefs in the city. He turns out a constantly changing, market-driven menu of a dozen plates of some of the most interesting, eclectic food you'll find in the area, making the local food cognoscenti very happy. There's an equally creative wine list. Pricing is civil, portions are huge, and the service can be a trifle slow, but it's worth the wait. $ *Average main: 110 pesos* ⊠ *Thames 2296, at Charcas, Palermo* ☎ *11/4775-0625* ⌲ *Reservations essential* ⊗ *Closed Mon. No lunch.* Ⓜ *D to Plaza Italia* ✢ *1:F4.*

$$$
MEDITERRANEAN

✕ **Lelé de Troya.** "Somewhere Over the Rainbow" seems to be playing in the background as you enter this boldly colored space. Five rooms—four of them decked out in yellow, red, blue, or green, the fifth in an odd combination of cantaloupe and purple—make up the *salas* of this converted home. Every surface, right down to painted speaker covers, screams each room's hue. In the yellow salon you'll find the open kitchen, where a variety of breads is baked daily for the great sandwiches, bruschettas, and other dishes. The theme is "Ring Around the Mediterranean," with dishes reflecting the flavors of coastal Spain, France, Italy, and Greece, as well as the Middle East and North Africa. Delicious pastas are favorites, as are the spicy seafood dishes (if you like heat, don't miss the *papillote del mar*, a fiery shellfish stew in a phyllo pastry nest). $ *Average main: 115 pesos* ⊠ *Costa Rica 4901, at Thames, Palermo Soho* ☎ *11/4832–2726* ⊕ *www.leledetroya. com* ✛ *1:E4.*

$$$ ✕ **María Félix.** The porteño aversion to anything spicy means there's just not a lot of demand for authentic Mexican fare. But María Félix probably comes the closest, serving an array of Mexican dishes with a touch of Tex-Mex. The food is fresh and vibrant and the flavors are remarkably varied, if lacking in that hit of heat. Asking for hot sauce doesn't result in anything much stronger on the table. Still, it makes a nice change from the usual local fare, and when you wash it down with a reasonably good margarita you won't leave with any complaints. Thursday through Saturday evenings there's a wandering mariachi band. $ *Average main: 120 pesos* ⊠ *Guatemala 5200, at Godoy Cruz, Palermo Soho* ☎ *11/4775–0380* ⊕ *www.mariafelix.com.ar* ✛ *1:E4.*

MEXICAN

$$ ✕ **Mark's Deli & Coffee House.** When you hear the term "deli," you may think double-decker sandwiches laden with smoked and cured meats, but this place is more California than New York. Look for huge salads with an array of fresh ingredients, inventive sandwiches on excellent housemade breads, delicious pastries, and just-brewed coffee. Sit on the patio outside and you may as well be in a scene from *The O.C.*, right down to the slow service and snooty attitude. Still, this is a great choice for a casual lunch or brunch. The kitchen stays open until early evening, so if you're looking for a quick, casual bite in Palermo Soho, it's a decent choice. $ *Average main: 80 pesos* ⊠ *El Salvador 4701, at Armenia, Palermo Soho* ☎ *11/4832–6244* ⊕ *www.markspalermo.com. ar* ⌬ *Reservations not accepted* ⊟ *No credit cards* ✛ *1:F5.*

AMERICAN
FAMILY

$ ✕ **Ña Serapia.** One of the city's best known and beloved pulperías, Ña Serapia (local slang that means the "Martyred Lady") is tiny, with only a dozen seats wedged into a space big enough for half as many. Grab some cheap eats, including great empanadas, local stews like locro or lentil, or even small pizzas. $ *Average main: 50 pesos* ⊠ *Av. Las Heras 3357, Palermo* ☎ *11/4801–5307* ⊟ *No credit cards* ✛ *1:H4.*

ARGENTINE

$$$ ✕ **NCF&F.** When you're searching for creative Argentine tapas, look no further than the eclectic selection of dishes off the rambling menu at this longtime favorite. Don't miss the perfectly poached eggs with bacon and grilled cheese, served up in a cocktail glass for dipping, nor the perfectly smoked fresh fish. Formerly Freud & Fahler (the NC stands for "Nueva Casa"), they took over the space vacated by the much-lamented loss of

ECLECTIC

PASS THE MATÉ

The country's unofficial national drink is called maté (pronounced MAH-tay). The bright green herb is packed into a gourd, infused with hot water, and then sucked through a metal straw. Its bitter flavor packs a punch. Drinking maté is a true ritual in Argentina.

La Cupertina, everyone's favorite empanada shop. By turns coffee and pastry shop and evening tapas bar, with a few solid main courses thrown in, as well as a selection of prix-fixe and tasting-menu options, this is not the place you'll remember if you visited the old location. Best bet: a bottle of wine and a selection of tapas from the ever-changing menu. $ *Average main: 140 pesos* ⊠ *Cabrera 5300, at Godoy Cruz, Palermo Soho* ☎ *11/4833–2153* ⊕ *www.freudandfahler.blogspot.com.ar* ⊟ *No credit cards* ⊘ *Closed Sun.* ⊹ *1:E4.*

$$$$ ✕ **NOLA.** New Orleans is where chef Liza Puglia grew up, and she brings
CREOLE her passion for the flavors of her early years to the table at this *puerta cerrada,* one of the city's famous "closed door" eateries. It's the only place in town to find Cajun and Creole cooking. Puglia doesn't stint on the spice, and also likes to add some flavors from Mexico. Using locally sourced ingredients to stand in for those she can't get from home, she turns out delightful, rustic dishes, including a superb *gumbo.* The dining room and its communal table are attended to by partner in life and work, Francisco "Ticol" Terren, who pairs some of his favorite local wines with the four-course menus. $ *Average main: US$70* ⊠ *Gorriti and Julián Alvarez, Palermo* ☎ *15/5348–4509* ⊕ *nolachef. net/restaurant* ⌣ *Reservations essential* ⊹ *1:F5.*

$$$$ ✕ **Osaka.** Behind a bamboo facade is the first modern Japanese fusion
JAPANESE spot in Buenos Aires, this Lima-based chain combines flavors from
FUSION across Asia with plenty of touches from Peru. The sushi and other small plates are excellent, though bordering on outrageously pricey, and the service is spot-on, particularly at the gleaming sushi bar. In the evening the crowd can be a bit loud and pretentious as the bar scene heats up and spills over into the dining area. There's also a location in Puerto Madero in the Faena Arts Center. $ *Average main: 185 pesos* ⊠ *Soler 5608, at Fitz Roy, Palermo* ☎ *11/4775–6964* ⊕ *www.osaka.com.pe* ⌣ *Reservations essential* ⊘ *Closed Sun.* ⊹ *1:E3.*

$$$ ✕ **Quimbombó.** In a beautiful trilevel space overlooking Plaza Armenia,
MODERN ASIAN chef Daniel López Martitegui serves up the most creative food in the area—do your best to get a table beside one of the tall windows. In general, the fare tends toward lighter, healthier options, with a good number of vegetarian dishes. The food is delightfully spiced with blends from China, India, and wherever the chef's mind wanders. Cocktails and teas are tasty, but tend to be made on the sweet side unless you ask for them otherwise. The vegetable carpaccio salad and various wraps are the best dishes on the menu. $ *Average main: 120 pesos* ⊠ *Costa Rica 4562, on Pl. Armenia, Palermo Soho* ☎ *11/4831–5556* ⊕ *www. quimbombo.com.ar* Ⓜ *D to Scalabrini Ortíz* ⊹ *1:F5.*

$$$$ ✕ **Río Alba.** When you want to go old school, you won't find anywhere
STEAKHOUSE in Palermo better than this venerable steakhouse. This longtime favorite has waiters in bowties and vests who maneuver around the green metal columns that define the farmhouse-style dining room. Among the flavorful, tender cuts of meat, don't pass up the entraña or the *matambrito* (pork flank)—the latter is one of the best in Buenos Aires. Although the menu appears fairly pricey, the portions are massive, and they know it: the steaks are set atop small hibachis to keep them hot. Your best bet is to order one steak for two to share and a platter of the *papas rejillas,*

CLOSE UP

All The Cow But The Moo

Argentina is the world's capital of beef, and Buenos Aires the capital of Argentina. So does Buenos Aires have the world's best steak?

It's hard to say no after your first bite into a tender morsel of deeply flavored beef carefully charred by an open fire. Indeed, aside from the *estancias* (ranches) on the *pampas* (grasslands) themselves, Buenos Aires is probably the best place to eat in a *parrilla* (steak house). That said, it can be difficult, upon a first glance at the bewildering menu of a parrilla, to know where to begin. Merely speaking Spanish isn't enough: entire books have been written attempting to pin down which cuts of meat in Argentina correspond to which ones in the United States and Europe. There's much disagreement. The juicy *bife de chorizo*, for example, the king of Argentine steaks, is translated by some as a bone-in sirloin, by others as a rump steak—and it's not as if "sirloin steak" is well defined to begin with.

Don't worry about definitions. If you order a *parrillada*—everything but the kitchen sink—a sizzling platter will be brought to you. Don't be timid about trying the more unfamiliar pieces. The platter will usually include a salty, juicy link or two of *chorizo* (a large, spicy sausage), and a collection of *achuras* (innards), which some first-timers struggle with. King among them is the gently spicy and oozingly delicious *morcilla* (blood sausage—like the British black pudding or the French *boudin noir*); give it a chance. Even more challenging are the chewy *chinchulines* (coils of small intestine), which are best when crisped on the outside, and the strongly flavored *riñones* (kidneys). Although *mollejas* (sweetbreads) aren't usually part

of a parrillada spread (they're more expensive), don't miss their unforgettable taste and fatty, meltingly rich texture, like a meatier version of foie gras. You'll also want to try the rich *provoleta* (grilled provolone cheese sprinkled with olive oil and oregano) and garlic-soaked grilled red peppers.

You can also skip the ready-made parrillada and instead order à la carte, as the locals often do. You might try the *vacio* (flank steak, roughly translated), a common cut that is flavorful but can also be tough, especially if overcooked. You may instead be seduced by the *lomo* (tenderloin or filet mignon), the softest and priciest cut, or the immortal bife de chorizo, always a safe bet. Both of those steaks are better when requested rare ("*vuelta y vuelta*"), or at the least medium-rare ("*jugoso*").

But the true local favorite is the inimitable *asado de tira*, a rack of beef short ribs often cooked on a skewer over an open fire. Done properly, the asado brandishes the meatiest grass-fed flavor of all. For accompaniments, the classics are a mix-and-match salad and/or french fries. And don't forget that delicious Argentine red wine: malbecs and cabernets both pair well with the deeply flavored meat. And though the first time you visit a parrilla the mountain of meat might seem mind-bogglingly high, chances are that by the time you leave you'll be cleaning your plate and gnawing at the bones with the best of them.

—Robin Goldstein

5

thick waffle-cut chips, and dig in to a classic Argentine meal. $ *Average main: 200 pesos* ✉ *Cerviño 4499, at Fray J. S. de Oro, Palermo* ☎ *11/4773–5748* ✛ *1:G3.*

$ ✕ **Sarkis.** Sure, this family-style restaurant can be chaotic, but it's the
MIDDLE EASTERN place to go for great Middle Eastern food. You could easily fill up
FAMILY on several of the small dishes from the expansive selection of *mezes,* which are the restaurant's best work. The lamb *kafta completo* is the most memorable item on the menu, but there are also great options for vegetarians. Be sure to leave room for one of the honey and nut pastries. Most nights there are belly dancers and coffee-ground readers wandering through the dining room. Arrive early or expect to wait for a table. The place is technically in Villa Crespo, but it's only about a block from Palermo Soho, across Avenida Córdoba. $ *Average main: 60 pesos* ✉ *Thames 1101, at Jufré, Palermo* ☎ *11/4772–4911* ▬ *No credit cards* ✛ *1:D5.*

$$ ✕ **Siamo nel Forno.** Every country has its own style of pizza, and in
PIZZA Argentina it's piled high with cheese. After spending a year studying traditional techniques in Naples, *pizzero* Nestor Gattorna took another route. He even imported a wood-burning oven, and brings in specially milled flour and extra-virgin olive oil, all to reproduce the best Neapolitan-style pizza in the heart of Palermo. Italophiles jam into the place for a bite of one of his smoky, perfectly charred pies and equally good calzones. Try a delicious specialty like the potato pizza, and end your meal with a "white pie" filled with Nutella. $ *Average main: 100 pesos* ✉ *Costa Rica 5886, Palermo Hollywood* ☎ *11/5290–9529* ☉ *Closed Mon. No lunch* Ⓜ *D to Ministro Carranza* ✛ *1:D3.*

$$$ ✕ **Social Paraíso.** This Mediterranean-style bistro is wildly popular at
MEDITERRANEAN night, and reservations are recommended if you're intent on sampling the creative fare. At lunch, when most of the same menu items are available, it's far easier to snag a table. Enjoy a risotto or pasta dish from the à la carte menu, or opt for the great value two-course lunch special. You can practically sit inside the open kitchen and watch the young cooks work their magic on a range of dishes, including many vegetarian choices. If you prefer dining alfresco, there's a small garden patio with a couple of tables and sidewalk seating out front. $ *Average main: 120 pesos* ✉ *Honduras 5182, between Thames and Uriarte, Palermo Soho* ☎ *11/4831–4556* ☝ *Reservations essential* ☉ *Closed Mon. No dinner Sun.* ✛ *1:E4.*

$$$ ✕ **Te Mataré, Ramírez.** When you step behind the red velvet curtains you'll
ECLECTIC feel like you've wandered into a carnival, because that's kind of where you are. Part restaurant, part cabaret, part sideshow, this exotic place is designed to distract your attention and separate you and your cash—although it's all in good taste and good fun. Bizarre names for dishes meant to invoke sexual situations are just a smokescreen for creative and interesting-sounding ideas—they don't always live up to the billing. The cabaret shows, a mix of sleight of hand, a teasing level of stripping, and sometimes even puppetry, are fun, but expect a modest charge on your bill. $ *Average main: 145 pesos* ✉ *Gorriti 5054, between Thames and Serrano, Palermo Soho* ☎ *11/4831–9156* ⊕ *www.tematareramirez.*

com ⚑ *Reservations essential* ▭ *No credit cards* ⊘ *No lunch* Ⓜ *D to Plaza Italia* ✛ *1:E4.*

$$$$ ✕ **Tegui.** German Martitegui was among the city's first leaders of the
ECLECTIC *cocina de vanguardia* movement, or what people tend to think of as *gastronomía molecular*. After taking the helm at Casa Cruz and then Ølsen, he hit his stride with the open kitchen at Tegui, which still has both local and international foodies lining up at the door. Whether you order from the regularly changing à la carte menu (with one-, two-, or three-plate options), or go for the full experience with an eight-course tasting menu (which, with all the extras, is more like a 12-course food orgy). Martitegui has a deft hand with fish in particular and is fond of using fruit in his savory dishes. Add an option of paired wines under the direction of sommelier Martín Bruno and you'll have an experience like no other in the city. Ⓢ *Average main: 220 pesos* ⊠ *Costa Rica 5852, between Carranza and Ravignani, Palermo Hollywood* ☎ *11/5291–3333* ⊕ *www.tegui.com.ar* ⚑ *Reservations essential* ⊘ *Closed Sun. and Mon. No lunch* ✛ *1:D3.*

$$ ✕ **Trattoria Olivetti.** In a city so packed with Italian restaurants that you
ITALIAN could spend years visiting all of them, to claim that one or another is
FAMILY the best is presumptuous. But Trattoria Olivetti's casual style, fantastic
Fodor's Choice service and atmosphere, and prime location in Palermo Chico's Little
★ Italy bodes well for the claim that this is the city's top trattoria. For the more adventurous, don't miss Chef Luca Lepri Berluti's "surf and turf" of *gamberi e animelle* (perfectly grilled prawns and sweetbreads), or his *guanciola* (beautifully braised pork cheeks). For those less inclined to stray into that territory, the multilayer house lasagna may just be the finest in Argentina. There's a great wine list, too. Ⓢ *Average main: 95 pesos* ⊠ *República Arabe Siria 3200, at Cerviño, Palermo Botánico* ☎ *11/4802–7321* ⊕ *www.trattoriaolivetti.com* ⊘ *Closed Mon.* ✛ *1:H3.*

$$$ ✕ **Xalapa.** One look at the frozen margarita machines and bags of super-
SOUTHWESTERN market corn chips and you'll know what you're in for at this colorful dining room. But strangely enough, this is where you'll find some of the city's better Mexican food—it's reasonably authentic and comes truly spicy if you request. Don't expect to be wowed, but an ice-cold beer with a plate or two of quesadillas or the delicious *tacos al pastor* (stuffed with sliced pork) may just hit the spot. Ⓢ *Average main: 110 pesos* ⊠ *El Salvador 4800, at Gurruchaga, Palermo Soho* ☎ *11/4833–6102* ▭ *No credit cards* ⊘ *No lunch weekdays* ✛ *1:E5.*

BELGRANO

Belgrano is filled with family-friendly spots and a few gems, while über-cool Las Cañitas rocks seven nights a week with a vast array of culinary options.

Despite its reputation as a snooty upper-class enclave, Belgrano is in fact one of the city's most diverse food neighborhoods. Indeed, there are million-dollar mansions and embassies, but there are also sections filled with Asian immigrants, traditional English- and Irish-style homes and cafés, a big university, and a chaotic shopping street, Avenida Cabildo.

$$$
MODERN
ARGENTINE
Fodor's Choice
★

✕**Astor, Manduque Porteño.** The name—which means, more or less, "the way locals eat"—may be a bit of a misnomer, because this restaurant doesn't serve anything that you'd find in a traditional local restaurant. Chef Antonio Sorano takes those traditional concepts and turns them on their head, creating beautifully plated, perfectly prepared dishes that retain the spirit of the original. The menu changes weekly. A well-curated wine list is under the direction of charming sommelier Pablo Colina. This may not be the way locals have been eating, but they're starting to, and you should, too. ⑤ *Average main: 130 pesos* ✉ *Ciudad de la Paz 353, at Jorge Newbery, Belgrano* ☎ *11/4554–0802* ⊕ *www.astorbistro.com* ⊗ *Closed Sun. No lunch* ✛ *1:D2.*

> **BARRIO CHINO**
>
> Buenos Aires' Barrio Chino, or Chinatown, is a mishmash of Chinese, Korean, and Japanese citizens and cultures. Compared with those of many other big cities, the Barrio Chino is relatively small, occupying just a few blocks on and around Calle Arribeños, near the Belgrano C train station. There you can find a smattering of supermarkets, shops, and restaurants. Among the best are the Taiwanese-style **Lai-Lai** (✉ *Arribeños 2168* ✛ *1:C1*) and the pan-Asian **BuddhaBA** (✉ *Arribenos 2288* ✛ *1:C1*), which has a lovely garden and an art gallery.

$$$
ITALIAN

✕**Bruni.** This elegant corner Italian restaurant features wraparound windows overlooking Parque Paseo de las Americas was one of the first spots to bring some life to "Bajo Belgrano." Now, there are a half dozen restaurants within a block, and this area is a dining destination, not only for local Belgrano residents but for visiting gastronomes from across the city and globe. The duo that owns it—restaurateur Fernando Brucco (also owner of Happening in Puerto Madero) and local rocker Fabián "Zorrito" Quintiero (who also owns Soul Café)—have maintained the standards originally set by consulting chef and local food TV personality Donato deSantis. The stars here, other than the owners, are the pastas, made fresh in-house and topped with creative, delicious sauces—don't miss the "Unico," a whopping raviolo filled with spinach and cheese and topped with mushrooms and truffle sauce. ⑤ *Average main: 125 pesos* ✉ *Sucre 696, at Castañeda, Belgrano* ☎ *11/4783–6267* ⊕ *www.brunirestaurante.com* ⊗ *No lunch* ✛ *1:E1.*

$$$
ASIAN

✕**BuddhaBA.** In the heart of the city's Chinatown, BuddhaBA is part pan-Asian restaurant, part tranquil garden, and part art gallery. The service is understated, but always gracious, and the food is a pleasure to both look at and eat. The tastiest dish on the menu is the *paté imperial,* a unique twist on the classic Vietnamese *banh mi* sandwich, reinterpreted as a pair of long, delicate, crispy spring rolls. The Chinese sweet-and-sour dishes are always delicious, if sometimes erring a trifle on the sweet side. Finish up with a pot of tea, perhaps out in the garden during nice weather. ⑤ *Average main: 120 pesos* ✉ *Arribeños 2288, at Olazabal, Belgrano* ☎ *11/4706–2382* ⊕ *www.buddhaba.com.ar* ⊗ *Closed Mon. No lunch Thurs. and Fri.; no dinner Sun.* Ⓜ *D to Juramento* ✛ *1:C1.*

$
CHINESE
FAMILY

✕**Lai-Lai.** While the city's Chinatown is not all that big, it does have its fair share of notable eateries. Lai-Lai stands out for its varied menu, combining not just the more usual Taiwanese cuisine, but also spicier dishes from the Hunan and Szechuan provinces. Not to be missed are the Szechuan dumplings in broth (*empanaditas chinas picantes*, in Spanish), tofu in a fiery red sauce, and the big-enough-to-share half duck glazed in honey and tea. ⑤ *Average main: 65 pesos ⊠ Arribeños 2168, between Juramento and Mendoza, Belgrano* ☎ *11/4780–4900* ⚏ *Reservations not accepted* ⊟ *No credit cards* ✛ *1:C1.*

$$$$ ✕ **Lotus Neo Thai.** Like the proverbial tortoise, Buenos Aires's first Thai
THAI   restaurant has kept a slow, steady pace and outlasted all its Southeast Asian competitors. Huge glowing flowers dominate the décor, and there's perhaps a bit too much incense filling the air. While the food here won't amaze anyone who knows Thai cooking, it's a great change of pace for locals looking for something different or travelers who are tired of steaks. The options are fresh and tasty, particularly the curries, though if you want any heat, don't forget to ask for your dish to be served *picante*. Portions can be a bit skimpy given the prices, though there are lunch prix-fixe options that are more wallet-friendly. ⑤ *Average main: 165 pesos ⊠ Arribeños 2265, between Mendoza and Olazabal, Belgrano* ☎ *11/4783–7993* ⊕ *www.lotusneothai.com* ⊗ *No lunch Mon.* Ⓜ *D to Juramento* ✛ *1:C1.*

$$$$ ✕ **Pura Tierra.** In a charming and creative space that was once a private
MODERN   residence in Belgrano, chef Martín Molteni's dining room offers up
ARGENTINE a tribute to the lesser-known products of the region. Specializing in
Fodor'sChoice unusual meats—llama, wild boar, rabbit, and quail are regular offer-
★   ings—as well as fresh fish, unusual grains and vegetables, and hand-crafted cheeses, Molteni brings his overseas training in France and Australia to bear on his Argentine heritage. The menu changes completely every two or three months to reflect the freshest seasonal ingredients. While the menu doesn't list vegetarian options, give advance notice when you reserve and the kitchen will turn out equally stunning vegetable plates. A chef's tasting menu is also available. ⑤ *Average main: 200 pesos ⊠ 3 de Febrero 1167, at Federico Lacroze, Belgrano* ☎ *11/4899–2007* ⊕ *www.puratierra.com.ar* ⚏ *Reservations essential* ⊗ *Closed Sun. No lunch* ✛ *1:C1.*

$$$ ✕ **Sucre.** "Cavernous" may be the first word that comes to mind upon
MODERN   entering this multilevel concrete-and-metal space with a backlit bar
ARGENTINE taking up an entire wall, an open kitchen dominating the rear, and a hulking glass wine cave smack in the center of the dining area. Sucre was and is the cutting edge of cuisine in Bajo Belgrano, and though it's off the beaten path, it's well worth the trip. Enjoy the delicious and creative appetizers, but save room for a main course straight off the wood-fired grill: spit-roasted *bondiola* (pork shoulder) and melt-in-your-mouth Patagonian lamb are among the stars, but any meat or fish coming off the parrilla is going to be a winner and be accompanied by something far more creative than the ubiquitous side of fries. Locals and tourists alike fill the room, and with no soft surfaces it can get loud. ⑤ *Average main: 140 pesos ⊠ Sucre 676, between Alcorta and Castañeda, Belgrano* ☎ *11/4782–9082* ⊕ *www.sucrerestaurant.com.ar* ✛ *1:C1.*

HEAVENLY HELADO

Buenos Aires has some of the best ice cream in the world. Porteños take their *helado* (ice cream) seriously, and shops can be found on nearly every other corner around the city. The neighborhood with the most *heladerías* is Belgrano, where fantastic mom-and-pop operations and chain shops abound. At many you'll find an entire section of the menu devoted to caramel-y dulce de leche combinations.

Cabaña Tuyu (✉ *José Hernández 2275* ✛ *1:B1*) for dozens of selections, including the buttery, wine-infused sabayon.

Freddo (✉ *Av. Libertador 5200* ✛ *1:D1*) for its juicy sorbets and refreshing fruit flavors (try banana).

Persicco (✉ *Vuelta de Obligado 2092 and Migueletes 886* ✛ *1:E1*), a local chain, for its delectable dulce de leche combinations.

Un Altra Volta (✉ *Echeverria 2302* ✛ *1:C1*) for its gorgeous chocolates and sculptural ice cream desserts, which taste as good as they look.

LAS CAÑITAS

Until a few years ago a strictly residential neighborhood, Las Cañitas has become the city's "restaurant row," with everything from steak-houses, pizza, and pasta to a new influx of Mexican, North American, Middle Eastern, and German spots. It's particularly popular with the expat community, but there are plenty of locals who frequent the area as well.

$$$

STEAKHOUSE

✕ **El Estanciero.** This steakhouse perfectly captures the vibrancy of Las Cañitas—even on weekdays, when you can see couples and groups heading in the door as late as midnight. They come for the juicy cuts of beef and flavorful achuras, all of which are grilled over an open fire by a professional staff. Grab one of the tables on the open second floor and you'll get an even better view of the parrilla and the action outside. Ask for your favorite steak "vuelta y vuelta" for best results. ⑤ *Average main: 120 pesos* ✉ *Báez 202, at Argüibel, Las Cañitas* ☎ *11/4899–0951* ⊕ *www.elestancieroresto.com.ar* ⊘ *No lunch weekdays* Ⓜ *D to Ministro Carranza* ✛ *1:E2.*

$$

PIZZA

FAMILY

✕ **Morelia.** Long before grilled pizza became commonplace elsewhere, it was already part of the local tradition, where pizza dough was tossed on the grill, cooked quickly like a flatbread, and then topped with fresh, favored ingredients. The best place to sample grilled pizza is Morelia, which has a popular branch on the trendy restaurant row of Calle Báez. Choose your favorite combination of toppings, though a perennial favorite is the *montecattini* with prosciutto and arugula. In nice weather grab a seat on the rooftop terrace, one of the best spots in town to eat pizza. ⑤ *Average main: 80 pesos* ✉ *Báez 260, between Arévalo and Arguibel, Las Cañitas* ☎ *11/4772–0329* ⊘ *No lunch* Ⓜ *D to Ministro Carranza* ✛ *1:E2.*

BUENOS AIRES DINING AND LODGING

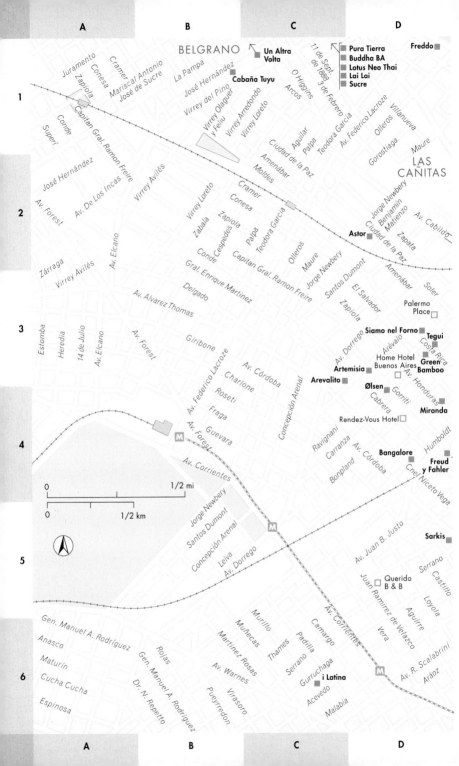

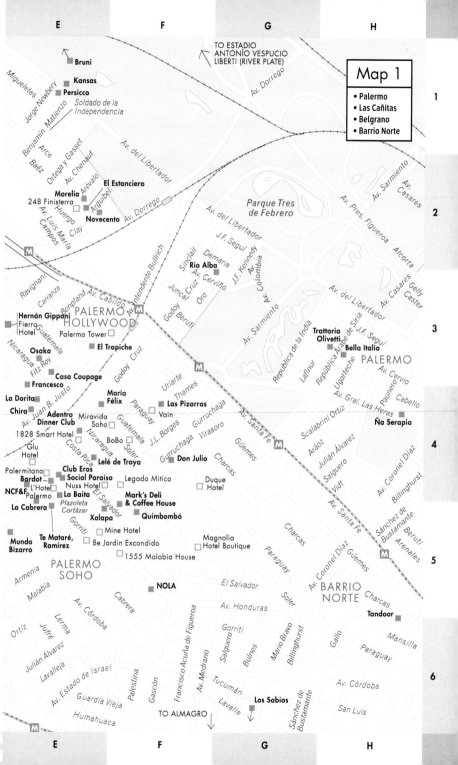

Map 1

- Palermo
- Las Cañitas
- Belgrano
- Barrio Norte

TO ESTADIO
ANTONIO VESPUCIO
LIBERTI (RIVER PLATE)

Bruni
Kansas
Persicco
Soldado de la
Independencia

Miguanezos
Jorge Newbery
Benjamín Arce
Baéz
Ortega y Gasset
Av. Chenaut
Arévalo
Arguibel
El Estanciero
Morelia
248 Finisterra
Novecento
Av. Luis María Campos
Huergo
Clay
Av. Dorrego
Av. del Libertador

Av. Dorrego

Parque Tres
de Febrero

Av. Sarmiento
Av. Casares
Av. Pres. Figueroa Alcorta
Av. Casares
Gelly Castex

Ravignani
Carranza
Bonpland
Av. Cabildo
Av. Intendente Bullrich

PALERMO
HOLLYWOOD
Hernán Gipponi
Fierro
Hotel
Palermo Tower
Palermo Tower

Sinclair
Demaria
Rio Alba
Av. Cerviño
Juncal
Cruz
Oro
Godoy
Berutti
J.F. Seguí
J.F. Kennedy
Av. Colombia
Av. Colombia
Av. del Libertador
J.F. Seguí
Trattoria
Olivetti
Bella Italia
República Árabe de Siria
PALERMO
Av. Cervio
Paunero
Cabello

Nicaragua
Fitz Roy
Osaka
Guatemala
Casa Coupage
Francesco
El Trapiche
Godoy Cruz
Uriarte
Thames
República de la India
Av. Sarmiento
Lafinur
República Árabe de Siria
Ugarteche
Av. Gral. Las Heras
Ña Serapia

La Dorita
Chira
Av. Juan B. Justo
Adentro
Dinner Club
1828 Smart Hotel
Glu
Hotel
María
Félix
Miravida
Soho
Paraguay
Guatemala
Nicaragua
Costa Rica
BoBo
Soler
Las Pizarras
Vain
J.L. Borges
Gurruchaga
Virasoro
Güemes
Av. Santa Fe
Scalabrini Ortíz
Aráoz
Julián Álvarez
Salguero
Vidt
Av. Coronel Díaz
Billinghurst
Sánchez de Bustamante
Beruti
Arenales

Palermitano
Bardot
NCF&F
L'Hotel
Palermo
La Cabrera
Club Eros
Social Paraíso
Nuss Hotel
La Baita
Lelé de Troya
Plazoleta
Cortázar
Gurruchaga
Don Julio
Charcas
Legado Mitico
Duque
Hotel
Mark's Deli
& Coffee House
Xalapa
Quimbombó
Av. Salvador
Gorriti
Av. Santa Fe

Mundo
Bizarro
Te Mataré,
Ramírez
Mine Hotel
Be Jardin Excondido
1555 Malabia House
Magnolia
Hotel Boutique
Charcas
Paraguay
Av. Coronel Díaz
Güemes
PALERMO
SOHO
Armenia
Malabía
Av. Córdoba
Cabrera
NOLA
El Salvador
Av. Honduras
Soler
BARRIO
NORTE
Charcas
Tandoor
Mansilla

Ortíz
Lerma
Jufré
Julián Álvarez
Lavalleja
Av. Estado de Israel
Guardia Vieja
Humahuaca
Palestina
Gascón
Francisco Acuña de Figueroa
Av. Medrano
TO ALMAGRO
Gorriti
Salguero
Bulnes
Tucumán
Lavalle
Los Sabios
Mario Bravo
Billinghurst
Sánchez de Bustamante
Gallo
Paraguay
Av. Córdoba
San Luis

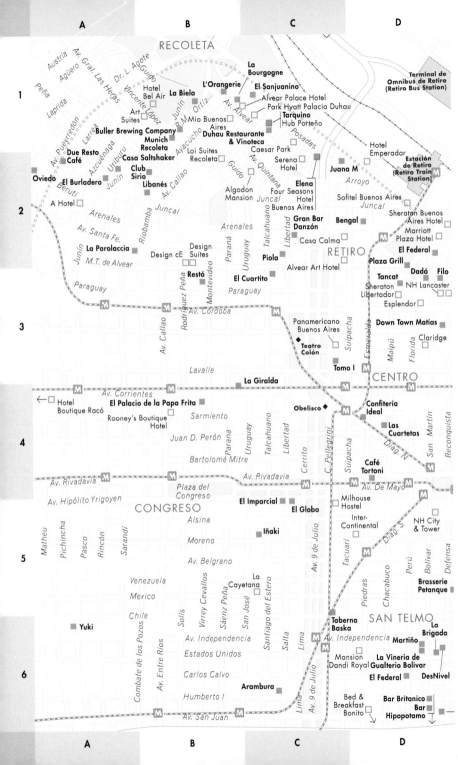

RECOLETA

A · B · C · D

Austria
Av. Gral. Las Heras
Av. Agüero
Dr. L. Agote
Guido
Peña
Laprida
Vincente López
R.M. Ortiz
Junín
Av. Alvear
Posadas

La Bourgogne
L'Orangerie
El Sanjuanino
La Biela
Hotel Bel Air
Alvear Palace Hotel
Park Hyatt Palacio Duhau
Tarquino
Art Suites
Mío Buenos Aires
Hub Porteño
Buller Brewing Company
Duhau Restaurante & Vinoteca
Munich Recoleta
Caesar Park
Due Resto Café
Casa Saltshaker
Serena Hotel
Hotel Emperador
Estación de Retiro (Retiro Train Station)
Terminal de Omnibus de Retiro (Retiro Bus Station)

Oviedo
El Burladero
Club Sirio Libanés
Loi Suites Recoleta
Juana M
Sofitel Buenos Aires

A Hotel
Algodon Mansion
Elena
Four Seasons Buenos Aires
Arroyo
Sheraton Buenos Aires Hotel

Av. Puegredón
Larrea
Azcuénaga
Uriburu
Junín
Av. Callao
Guido
Av. Quintana
Juncal
Arenales
Beruti
Riobamba
Juncal

Arenales
Av. Santa Fe.
Junín
M.T. de Alvear
Av. Santa Fe.
Paraná
Uruguay
Talcahuano
Libertad
Arenales
Gran Bar Danzón
Bengal
Marriott Plaza Hotel

La Parolaccia
Design cE
Design Suites
Piola
Casa Calma
El Federal
Plaza Grill

Restó
El Cuartito
Alvear Art Hotel
RETIRO
Tancat
Dadá
Filo
Sheraton Libertador
NH Lancaster

Paraguay
Montevideo
Rodríguez Peña
Paraná
Paraguay
Esplendor

Av. Córdoba
Panamericano Buenos Aires
Suipacha
Down Town Matías
Claridge

Av. Callao
Teatro Colón
Maipú
Florida

Lavalle
La Giralda
Tomo I
CENTRO

Av. Corrientes
Hotel Boutique Racó
El Palacio de la Papa Frita
Obelisco
Confitería Ideal

Rooney's Boutique Hotel
Sarmiento
Talcahuano
Libertad
Cerrito
C. Pellegrini
Suipacha
Las Cuartetas
San Martín
Reconquista

Juan D. Perón
Parana
Uruguay
Diag. N

Bartolomé Mitre
Café Tortoni

Av. Rivadavia
Av. Rivadavia
Av. De Mayo

Av. Hipólito Yrigoyen
Plaza del Congreso
Milhouse Hostel
Inter-Continental
NH City & Tower

CONGRESO
El Imparcial
El Globo
Diag. S
Perú
Bolívar
Defensa

Matheu
Pichincha
Pasco
Rincón
Sarandí
Alsina
Moreno
Iñaki
Av. Belgrano

Venezuela
México
Chile
La Cayetana
Virrey Cevallos
Sáenz Peña
San José
Santiago del Estero
Salta
Lima
Tacuarí
Piedras
Chacabuco
Brasserie Petanque

Yuki
Solis
Taberna Baska
SAN TELMO
La Brigada

Av. Independencia
Av. Independencia
Martiño

Estados Unidos
Mansion Dandi Royal
La Vineria de Gualterio Bolivar
DesNivel

Carlos Calvo
El Federal

Arambura
Humberto I
Bed & Breakfast Bonito
Bar Britanico
Bar Hipopotamo

Av. San Juan
Combate de los Pozos
Av. Entre Ríos
Lima
Av. 9 de Julio

A · B · C · D

E F G H

Av. Ant. Argentina
Av. Ramon S. Castillo
Av. Tomás Edison

Dársena B

Dársena A

Map 2

- Recoleta
- Centro
- San Telmo
- Puerto Madero
- Retiro
- Congreso

1

0   1,000 M

0   1,000 ft

2

Dársena Norte

Antepuerto

Melia Buenos Aires
NH Florida

Av. Córdoba

Sabot

3

Dique 4

Av. Costanera Carlos Noel

N. Alem
NH Jousten

La Rosa Nautica
Cabana Las Lilas

Hilton Buenos Aires

25 de Mayo
Av. Leandro N.
Rosales
Av. Eduardo Madero
Av. Dávila

Macacha Guemes

4

Juana Manso

Plaza de Mayo
◆ **Casa Rosada**

Reserva Ecologica

PLAZA DE MAYO

Dique 3

Moreno Hotel

PUERTO MADERO

Balcarce
Av. Paseo Colón
Azopardo
Av. Ing. Huerza
Av. Dávila

Azucena Villaflor

5

Dique 2

Faena Hotel

Hotel Babel
Balcarce

Vera Peñaloza

Hotel Madero

6

Bar Plaza Dorrego

Dique 1

Cafe San Juan

El Obrero

E F G H

WHERE TO STAY

By Karina
Martinez-Carter

In Buenos Aires, European elegance collides with Latin American energy and style to create a certain *no sé que*—the Argentine version of the French *je ne sais quoi*—that makes the city unlike any place in the world. Even within the city, neighborhoods have their own distinct personality and spirit, and hotels tend to both reflect and enhance the identity of their neighborhood.

The lodging options in Buenos Aires rival those of any international, cosmopolitan locale. From jaw-dropping luxury hotels to intimate boutique hotels injected with local flair, one thing is certain: you're bound to encounter far more appealing lodging options than days you'll have in the city. Hotels are constantly opening, renovating, and amplifying their offerings. Despite climbing prices in recent years, Buenos Aires is still affordable for international visitors on the dollar, euro, and real, and its irresistible pull remains strong. Many visitors, having discovered the intoxicating energy of the city, return again and again. Hotel owners and their staffs, eager to share their city and culture, often play a key role in Buenos Aires winning people over and encouraging them to return.

Downtown in the Centro as well as nearby Puerto Madero you'll find sleek, soaring hotel properties; inch toward Recoleta and you have your pick from the ritziest hotels in town, particularly on and around Avenida Alvear. One-of-a-kind boutique hotels, usually small and always thoughtfully run, are where the city really shines, and while these inviting properties are found across the city, they are concentrated in vast, lively Palermo, particularly the Soho and Hollywood neighborhoods. San Telmo, with cobblestone streets lined with gracious mansions, is one of the city's most historic neighborhoods. Working-class Almagro and up-and-coming Villa Crapo are culturally vibrant in their own ways, and a stay in one gives you a chance to dive into everyday porteño life. In the end, every neighborhood offers visitors the chance to experience one side of the buzzing, beguiling city of Buenos Aires.

PLANNING

Buenos Aires has chain hotels, boutique hotels, apart-hotels (short-term rental apartments), bed-and-breakfasts—you name it. World-class facilities include the majestic Alvear Palace Hotel and the ultrahip Faena Hotel—both of them celebrity favorites. High season includes the summer months of mid-December through February and the winter holidays that fall in July. (Keep in mind that seasons in the Southern Hemisphere are opposite those in the Northern Hemisphere.) Most hotels have at least one English-speaking employee on call at a given time.

RESERVATIONS

Buenos Aires has steadily climbed as a popular tourist destination in the past decade, a trend that shows little signs of slowing. As a result, many hotels are at full capacity year-round, not just in the October to March high season. It is always best to make a reservation as early as possible. Most hotels in the city have websites equipped with online reservation services. Some require a credit card.

FACILITIES

The majority of hotels offer Wi-Fi, though some charge guests extra for the service. High-definition television is a near certainty in your room, and many favorite U.S. television programs play around the clock in Argentina, though they may be dubbed into Spanish. English-language news channels will be harder to find, though.

CHECK-IN/OUT

As a rule, check-in is after 3 pm, and checkout is before noon; smaller hotels tend to be more flexible.

MEAL PLANS

Most hotel rates include breakfast, although with the exception of the most expensive hotels this generally means a Continental breakfast with Argentine fare, such as coffee, pastries, fruit, meats, cheese, and perhaps eggs. If you are looking for a heartier breakfast, be sure to inquire what breakfast includes when making a reservation. Remember, though, that most Argentineans eat small, simple breakfasts. Still, some properties take the extra step to shine in the morning and offer a more varied spread.

FAMILY TRAVEL

International chain hotels are always the most family-friendly, often ready with booster seats, changing tables, roll-away beds, or other family lodging necessities. Most smaller, trendy boutique hotels do not often accommodate families with children, though some are more than prepared and happy to do so. It is best to ask ahead exactly what your stay may be like with children in tow.

USING THE MAPS

Throughout the chapter, you'll see mapping symbols and coordinates (✛ 2:D5) after property reviews. To locate the property on the map, turn to the Buenos Aires Dining and Lodging Atlas at the end of the Where to Eat chapter. The first number after the ✛ symbol indicates the map number. Following that is the property's coordinate on the map.

PARKING

Driving in Buenos Aires is more trouble than it's worth for a tourist. The city streets are clogged and chaotic, and parking is scarce. Renting a car for your stay will prove to be a hassle, especially considering that the public transportation system (buses and the *subte*) and taxis can get you anywhere you want to go. Most hotels can also arrange private transport, if you prefer. If you do have a car, some hotels provide parking, but it is usually off site, and they will probably charge a fee.

PRICES

Though some small Argentinean-owned hotels advertise their rates in pesos, most places cite them in dollars. That said, always confirm which currency is being quoted. The lodging tax is 21%; this may or may not be included in a rate, so always ask about it up front. *Hotel reviews have been shortened. For full information, visit Fodors.com.*

WHAT IT COSTS IN ARGENTINE PESOS			
$	$$	$$$	$$$$
HOTELS	under $115	$115–$175	$176–$250	over $250

Hotel prices are the lowest cost of a standard double room in high season.

HOTEL REVIEWS

Listed alphabetically within neighborhood. Use the coordinate (✛ 2:D2) at the end of each listing to locate a site on the corresponding map.

CENTRO

You'll find the majority of the city's big-name hotels occupying lofty buildings in the Centro. These massive structures, it should be noted, afford some of the best views of the city. Tucked between the towers, though, are some unique boutique properties. This location puts you close to the Casa Rosado and other historic attractions.

$$$$
HOTEL
Alvear Art Hotel. The newest property from the country's most respected lodging chain, the sleek Alvear Art Hotel is set back behind some trees on a pedestrian-only street in the heart of the city's business district. **Pros:** gorgeous views from the sky-high pool; well-appointed gym; quiet location. **Cons:** pool and gym areas open only until 9 pm. ⑤ *Rooms from: US$295* ✉ *Suipacha 1086, Centro* ☎ *11/4114–3400* ⊕ *www.alvearart.com* ⇆ *139 rooms, 2 suites* ❤️⊙︎ *No meals* ✛ *2:D2.*

$$$
HOTEL
Fodor'sChoice
★
Casa Calma. This "wellness hotel" in the heart of downtown Buenos Aires has taken the concept of in-house spa to a new level, equipping each of its 17 rooms with jetted tubs—six deluxe rooms also have saunas where you can relax after a day of exploring the city. **Pros:** gorgeous design; serene atmosphere. **Cons:** on a chaotic city street. ⑤ *Rooms from: US$235* ✉ *Suipacha 1015, Centro* ☎ *11/4312–5000* ⊕ *www.casacalmahotel.com* ⇆ *17 rooms* ❤️⊙︎ *No meals* ✛ *2:C2.*

$$
HOTEL
Claridge Hotel. Tall white columns and stately bow windows flank the entrance of the Claridge Hotel, beyond which you'll find the

WHERE SHOULD I STAY?

NEIGHBORHOOD	VIBE	PROS	CONS
CENTRO and PUERTO MADERO	The center of it all; you have a little bit of everything here, from history (Retiro and Congreso) to modernity (Puerto Madero). It buzzes by day but is quiet at night.	Close to all major city sights; good transportation options to other parts of the city. If you're only in town briefly, this is your place.	Certain areas are loud, chaotic, dirty, and deserted at night, which can make them dangerous. Don't walk around alone.
SAN TELMO and LA BOCA	The oldest barrios in the city; you can get a real feel of how Buenos Aires has operated for the past 100-plus years.	Old-world charm: cobblestone streets, corner cafés, tango music. You're sure to meet some interesting characters in this area.	Streets are dark and not well policed. Limited public transportation options. Locals have been known to target tourists.
RECOLETA	The most upscale area of the city, home to Argentina's high society. Certain enclaves will convince you you're in Paris.	Proximity to sights in Centro. It's safe, friendly, and chic. Great eating options; high-end stores and art galleries abound.	Prices are sometimes inflated for foreigners. Streets and sights are often crowded with tourists.
PALERMO	The biggest neighborhood in the city; it's a mix of old family homes, soaring new towers, and renovated warehouses.	It's the undisputed hot spot of Buenos Aires' gastronomic scene. The city's biggest park, polo field, horse track, and casino are also here.	The übercool attitude of some locals can be a turnoff. Quality-of-life issues like clean sidewalks and quiet streets have been ignored in recent property developments.
ALMAGRO/BELGRANO/LAS CAÑITAS	Quiet, leafy, family neighborhoods home to schools, and universities. Las Cañitas is more of a Palermo vibe, whereas Belgrano and Almagro are more no-frills, working-class.	Fantastic restaurants and bars in Las Cañitas. Stately, unique homes in Belgrano. In certain areas it's easy to forget you're in a megametropolis.	In other areas, the main thoroughfares are packed with noisy city buses and reckless messengers on motorcycles. You're far from downtown action.

high-ceilinged lobby and a traditional British café and piano bar that draws a steady stream of politicians and businessmen. **Pros:** just blocks from shopping on Florida Street; lobby bar serves up superb cocktails; spacious gym. **Cons:** bathrooms are small. $ *Rooms from: US$150* ✉ *Tucumán 535, Centro* ☎ *11/4314–7700, 800/223–5652 in U.S.* ⊕ *www.claridge.com.ar* ✈ *146 rooms, 6 suites* ⏲ *Breakfast* Ⓜ *C to San Martín* ✚ *2:D3.*

$$ 🖼 **Design cE.** With spacious rooms like TriBeCa lofts, the Design cE has HOTEL rotating flat-screen TVs that let you watch from bed or from one of the leather recliners. **Pros:** supermodern suites; great location; breakfast is served 24 hours a day. **Cons:** common areas are on the small side. $ *Rooms from: US$140* ✉ *Marcelo T. Alvear 1695, Centro*

BEST BETS FOR
FOR BUENOS AIRES LODGING

Fodor's offers a selective listing of quality lodging experiences at every price range, from the city's best budget stay to its most sophisticated luxury hotel. Here we've compiled our top recommendations by price and experience. The very best properties—in other words, those that provide a particularly remarkable experience in their price range—are designated in the listings with the Fodor's Choice logo.

Fodor's Choice ★

Alvear Palace Hotel, p. 201
Casa Calma, p. 194
Faena Hotel, p. 199
Fierro Hotel, p. 204
The Glu Hotel, p. 204
Hotel Boutique Racó de Buenos Aires, p. 202
Magnolia Hotel Boutique, p. 204
Miravida Soho Hotel & Wine Bar, p. 205
Palacio Duhau Park Hyatt, p. 202

BY PRICE

$

Art Suites, p. 201
Bed & Breakfast Bonito, p. 199

$$

BoBo, p. 203
L'Hôtel Palermo, p. 204

Querido B&B, p. 205
Rooney's Boutique Hotel, p. 198

$$$

Legado Mítico, p. 204

$$$$

Algodon Mansion, p. 201
Alvear Art Hotel, p. 194
Faena Hotel, p. 199
Four Seasons Buenos Aires, p. 201
Sofitel Buenos Aires, p. 198

BY EXPERIENCE

BEST RESTAURANT

BoBo, p. 203
Fierro Hotel, Hernán Gipponi, p. 204
Four Seasons, Elena and Nuestro Secreto, p. 201

Moreno, Aldo's Vinoteca y Restorán, p. 200

BEST VIEWS

Alvear Art Hotel, p. 194
Panamericano Buenos Aires, p. 198
Sheraton Buenos Aires, p. 198

BEST TO FEEL LIKE A LOCAL

1555 Malabia House, p. 203
Bed & Breakfast Bonito, p. 199
Hotel Boutique Racó de Buenos Aires, p. 202
Magnolia Hotel Boutique, p. 204

BEST SCENE

Faena Hotel, p. 199
Fierro Hotel, p. 204
Miravida Soho Hotel & Wine Bar, p. 205

BEST DESIGN

Faena Hotel, p. 199
Legado Mítico, p. 204
Mio Buenos Aires, p. 202
Serena Hotel, p. 202

BEST FOR ROMANCE

Algodon Mansion, p. 201
Duque Hotel Boutique & Spa, p. 203
The Glu Hotel, p. 204
L'Hôtel Palermo, p. 204
Rooney's Boutique Hotel, p. 198

☞ 11/5237–3100 ⊕ www.designce.com ↘ 20 rooms, 8 suites ⦿ Breakfast Ⓜ D to Callao ⊕ 2:B2.

$$ ⛨ **Design Suites.** This futuristic hotel has a glass-covered lobby that
HOTEL grooves to chilled-out electronic music and a slender swimming pool
that's often used for photo shoots. **Pros:** cool, clean, and classy vibe;
a lobby art gallery showcases works by up-and-coming local painters.
Cons: the gym is several blocks away; city buses linger out front during
rush hour. Ⓢ *Rooms from: US$150* ✉ *M. T. de Alvear 1683, Centro*
☞ 11/4814–8700 ⊕ www.designsuites.com ↘ 58 rooms ⦿ Breakfast
Ⓜ D to Callao ⊕ 2:B2.

$$$ ⛨ **Esplendor Buenos Aires.** Argentine icons—Eva Perón, Che Guevara,
HOTEL Jorge Luis Borges, among others—remind you just where you are when
you stay at downtown's brashest hotel; their enormous portraits line
the walls of the sleek lobby and art gallery. **Pros:** roomy suites have
comfy chaise lounges; steps from Galerías Pacífico shopping mall.
Cons: open-air hallways have a corporate feel; weekday traffic nearby
is disconcerting. Ⓢ *Rooms from: US$179* ✉ *San Martin 780, Centro*
☞ 11/5256–8814 ⊕ www.esplendorbuenosaires.com ↘ 23 rooms, 28
suites ⦿ No meals Ⓜ C to San Martin ⊕ 2:D3.

$$$ ⛨ **Hotel Emperador.** The first thing that strikes you upon entering the
HOTEL Hotel Emperador is its magnificently ornate lobby, replete with beautiful marble floors, plush sofas, and gurgling fountains. **Pros:** fantastic
location; huge accommodations; business services. **Cons:** common areas
can be chaotic. Ⓢ *Rooms from: US$250* ✉ *Av. del Libertador 420, Centro* ☞ 11/4131–4000 ⊕ www.hotel-emperador.com.ar ↘ 214 rooms, 51
suites ⦿ No meals ⊕ 2:D2.

$$$ ⛨ **InterContinental Buenos Aires.** This lovely hotel has so much going for
HOTEL it—a historic setting, a pair of fine restaurants, a fitness room, and
sophisticated rooms, for starters. **Pros:** modern, spacious rooms; good
bar; smart staff know how to handle expectations of foreign visitors. **Cons:** lower floors have limited views; surrounding area can be
dangerous at night. Ⓢ *Rooms from: US$190* ✉ *Moreno 809, Centro*
☞ 800/444–0022 ⊕ www.icbuenosaires.com.ar ↘ 309 rooms, 10 suites
⦿ Breakfast Ⓜ E to Belgrano ⊕ 2:D5.

$$ ⛨ **Hotel NH City & Tower.** Topped with an eye-catching rooftop pool and
HOTEL patio, this enormous art deco showplace is a reminder of an earlier
era. **Pros:** central location; amazing views from the roof; transports
you back to another era. **Cons:** feels isolated from other attractions;
area can be sketchy at night. Ⓢ *Rooms from: US$170* ✉ *Bolívar 160,
Centro* ☞ 11/4121–6464 ⊕ www.nh-hotels.com/nh/en/hotels/argentina/
buenos-aires.html ↘ 327 rooms, 42 suites ⦿ Breakfast Ⓜ A to Perú;
E to Bolívar ⊕ 2:D5.

$$ ⛨ **Hotel NH Jousten.** Over the years this landmark has hosted some of the
HOTEL country's biggest movers and shakers, including Juan and Eva Perón—
no surprise, since it has a presidential suite that occupies an entire floor.
Pros: classic charm and service make this a great choice for history
buffs; central location. **Cons:** some of the spaces were sized for another
era. Ⓢ *Rooms from: US$120* ✉ *Corrientes 280, Centro* ☞ 11/4321–
6750 ⊕ www.nh-hoteles.com ↘ 84 rooms, 5 suites ⦿ Breakfast Ⓜ B
to L. N. Alem ⊕ 2:E4.

6

$$ **Hotel NH Lancaster.** This historic hotel was treated to a facelift when
HOTEL it was purchased by NH Hotels, but the Spanish chain made certain
to respect the Lancaster's proud past. **Pros:** close to the financial dis-
trict. **Cons:** Avenida Córdoba is crowded and loud around the clock.
⑤ *Rooms from: US$155* ⊠ *Av. Córdoba 405, Centro* ☎ *11/4131–6464*
⊕ *www.nh-hotels.com/nh/en/hotels/argentina/buenos-aires.html* ⇗ *115
rooms, 20 suites* ⑩ *Breakfast* Ⓜ *C to San Martín* ✛ *2:D3.*

$$ **Meliá Buenos Aires.** On a pedestrian-only thoroughfare, this Spanish-
HOTEL owned hotel in the heart of the financial district is a good option for
business travelers and cruise-ship passengers. **Pros:** plenty of amenities;
efficient staff; nearby pubs are hopping at night. **Cons:** area can attract
partiers who've had one too many. ⑤ *Rooms from: US$160* ⊠ *Recon-
quista 945, Centro* ☎ *11/4891–3800* ⊕ *www.melia.com* ⇗ *187 rooms,
22 suites* ⑩ *No meals* ✛ *2:E3.*

$$$ **Panamericano Buenos Aires.** Near the famed Teatro Colón and the
HOTEL landmark Obelisco, the upscale Panamericano Buenos Aires has a lobby
FAMILY with a checkerboard marble floor that leads to large salons, a snazzy
café, and conference rooms that are popular with local politicians. **Pros:**
in the heart of the downtown action; amazing views of the city; spacious
rooms. **Cons:** located on a busy avenue. ⑤ *Rooms from: US$189* ⊠ *Car-
los Pellegrini 551, Centro* ☎ *11/4348–5000* ⊕ *www.panamericano.us*
⇗ *267 rooms, 95 suites* ⑩ *No meals* Ⓜ *B to C. Pellegrini* ✛ *2:C3.*

$$$ **Plaza Hotel.** Originally built in 1909, this Buenos Aires landmark
HOTEL brims with old-school style—the elegant lobby, crystal chandeliers, and
swanky bar evoke Argentina's opulent, if distant, past. **Pros:** elegant
lobby; brimming with history; a fascinating view of the city. **Cons:**
check-in can be a lengthy process; could use an update. ⑤ *Rooms from:
US$250* ⊠ *Florida 1005, Centro* ☎ *11/4318–3000, 800/228–9290 in
U.S.* ⊕ *www.marriott.com/hotels/hotel-photos/buear-plaza-hotel-
buenos-aires* ⇗ *270 rooms, 48 suites* ⑩ *No meals* Ⓜ *C to San Martín*
✛ *2:D2.*

$$ **Rooney's Boutique Hotel.** On the third floor of a century-old building,
B&B/INN this hotel exudes such French elegance that you might expect to find
Marie Antoinette herself lolling about in one of the guest rooms filled
with lovingly restored antiques. **Pros:** complimentary tango lessons
three nights per week; lovely rooms and common areas. **Cons:** location
in the Centro is far from relaxed. ⑤ *Rooms from: US$115* ⊠ *Sarmiento
1775, 3rd fl., Centro* ☎ *11/5252–5060* ⊕ *www.rooneysboutiquehotel.
com* ⇗ *14 rooms* ⑩ *Breakfast* Ⓜ *B to Callao* ✛ *2:B4.*

$$ **Sheraton Buenos Aires Hotel & Convention Center.** What it lacks in
HOTEL intimate charm, it makes up for in practicality, professionalism, and
FAMILY energy. **Pros:** all the creature comforts you expect at home; good location; affordably priced. **Cons:** for some, perhaps overwhelmingly big;
rooms could use sprucing up. ⑤ *Rooms from: US$150* ⊠ *San Martín
1225/1275, Centro* ☎ *11/4318–9000, 800/325–3535 in U.S.* ⊕ *www.
sheraton.com/buenosaires* ⇗ *711 rooms, 29 suites* ⑩ *Breakfast* Ⓜ *C
to Retiro* ✛ *2:D2.*

$$$$ **Sofitel Buenos Aires.** Built in 1929 by a Yugoslavian shipping magnate,
HOTEL this was the city's tallest building for many years; it might have lost its
lofty title, but it's still considered one of the classiest hotels in Buenos

Aires, known for its understated elegance. **Pros:** on a swanky street lined with art galleries; long list of amenities. **Cons:** the lobby can get crowded and noisy. $ *Rooms from: US$345* ⊠ *Arroyo 841, Centro* ☎ *11/4131–0000* ⊕ *www.sofitel.com/gb/hotel-3253-sofitel-buenos-aires/index.shtml* ↪ *115 rooms, 29 suites* ♔ *No meals* Ⓜ *C to San Martin* ✛ *2:D2.*

PUERTO MADERO

Not too long ago, Puerto Madero was vast tracts of undeveloped land. The hotels in this waterfront neighborhood often push the limits of architecture and interior design, and are just about as impressive as you can get. Near the Centro, this neighborhood is especially popular with cruise ship passengers.

$$$$
HOTEL
Fodor'sChoice
★

🛏 **Faena Hotel.** Argentine fashion impresario Alan Faena and famed French architect Philippe Starck set out to create a "universe" unto itself with this hotel, and they succeeded: rooms are Feng Shui perfect, with rich reds and crisp whites, sporting velvet curtains and blinds opening electronically to river and city views. **Pros:** quite simply, one of the most dramatic hotels on the planet; luxury abounds; celebrity magnet. **Cons:** an "are you cool enough?" vibe is everpresent. $ *Rooms from: US$550* ⊠ *Martha Salotti 445, Puerto Madero* ☎ *11/4010–9000* ⊕ *www.faena.com* ↪ *110 rooms, 16 suites* ♔ *Breakfast* ✛ *2:G5.*

$$$
HOTEL
FAMILY

🛏 **Hilton Buenos Aires.** This massive glass-and-steel structure puts you close to downtown *and* the seafood restaurants and fresh air of Puerto Madero. **Pros:** fairly priced; central location; great staff. **Cons:** popular for conventions, which often means lots of people try to check in and out at the same time; no subway service nearby. $ *Rooms from: US$220* ⊠ *Macacha Güemes 351, Puerto Madero* ☎ *11/4891–0000, 800/774–1500 in U.S.* ⊕ *www.hilton.com* ↪ *418 rooms, 13 suites* ♔ *Breakfast* ✛ *2:F4.*

$$$
HOTEL

🛏 **Hotel Madero.** A favorite for visiting British rock stars, television personalities, and fashion photographers, this slick hotel is within walking distance of downtown as well as the riverside ecological reserve. **Pros:** the lobby bar attracts a cool after-office crowd; see-and-be-seen clientele; central location. **Cons:** the gym and pool are in cramped quarters; no subway service nearby. $ *Rooms from: US$190* ⊠ *Rosario Vera Peñaloza 360, Puerto Madero* ☎ *11/5776–7777* ⊕ *www.hotelmadero.com* ↪ *169 rooms, 28 suites* ♔ *Breakfast* ✛ *2:F6.*

SAN TELMO

Though it's unlikely that the city's upper crust had housing tourists in mind when constructing their elegant mansions in Sam Telmo, today these properties make wonderfully atmospheric lodgings. These intimate stays also afford a peek at the city's proud past.

$
B&B/INN

🛏 **Bed & Breakfast Bonito.** Behind the wrought-iron doors and up the marble staircase of this art nouveau mansion is a beautifully restored 19th-century home with wooden floors, French windows, and décor décor that smartly blends the past with the present. **Pros:** rooftop garden offers a wonderful view; lovingly renovated rooms. **Cons:** the metal spiral staircase (there is no elevator) can cause vertigo. $ *Rooms from: US$90* ⊠ *Av. Juan de Garay 458, San Telmo* ☏ *11/4362–8451* ⊕ *www.bonitobuenosaires.com* ↘ *7 rooms* ❙○❙ *Breakfast* Ⓜ *C to San Juan* ✛ *2:D6.*

$ **Hotel Babel.** A 15-minute walk from the Casa Rosada, this 200-year-
B&B/INN   old former home of late Argentine president Juan Manuel de Rosas sits on one of the city's most historic streets in the heart of San Telmo. **Pros:** beautiful and welcoming lobby; guests are greeted with a complimentary glass of Argentine wine upon arrival; local artists display their works throughout the hotel and hold monthly openings. **Cons:** it's an old house: rooms are close together and the open-air patio can mean noise—and sometimes rainwater—outside your door. $ *Rooms from: US$100* ⊠ *Balcarce 946, San Telmo* ☏ *11/4300–8300* ⊕ *www. hotelbabel.com.ar* ↘ *9 rooms* ❙○❙ *Breakfast* ✛ *2:E6.*

$ **La Cayetana Hotel Boutique.** This reformed *casa chorizo*—named such
B&B/INN   because the connected rooms resemble the links of a chorizo sausage—dates back to 1820, a fact that won't escape you as you enter the long, open-air entrance with plants and fountains on the left and rooms on the right. **Pros:** a cozy common area and well-stocked library are perfect for relaxing and reading; a *parrilla* (grill) is available if you feel like trying your hand at an Argentine *asado* (barbecue). **Cons:** a bit off the beaten path; the neighborhood can be dodgy at night, so take a taxi. $ *Rooms from: US$100* ⊠ *México 1330, Montserrat* ☏ *11/4383–2230* ⊕ *www.lacayetanahotel.com.ar* ↘ *11 rooms* ❙○❙ *Breakfast* ✛ *2:C5.*

$ **Mansión Dandi Royal.** For a glimpse of early-20th-century high society,
B&B/INN   look no further than this hotel, where exquisite rooms are decorated with classic wood furnishings and period murals. **Pros:** a tango junkie's heaven; stunning interiors. **Cons:** the surrounding streets are often populated with unsavory characters. $ *Rooms from: US$90* ⊠ *Piedras 922, San Telmo* ☏ *11/4361–3537* ⊕ *www.mansiondandiroyal.com* ↘ *26 rooms, 4 suites* ❙○❙ *Breakfast* Ⓜ *C to San Juan* ✛ *2:D6.*

$ **Moreno Hotel.** When they were reviving this art deco masterpiece, the
HOTEL   architects ably met the challenge of restoring the 1929 building without disturbing its original elements, like mosaic tiling and stained-glassed windows. **Pros:** designed to the max; plenty of charm; great views. **Cons:** some rooms are just steps away from the main lobby and elevator. $ *Rooms from: US$90* ⊠ *Moreno 376, San Telmo* ☏ *11/6091–2000* ⊕ *www.morenobuenosaires.com* ↘ *39 rooms* ❙○❙ *Breakfast* Ⓜ *A to Plaza de Mayo* ✛ *2:E5.*

RECOLETA

Posh hotels, both big and small, are truly what give Recoleta its unique character. Many of them, especially those that occupy landmark buildings, are must-see sights in their own rights.

$ **A Hotel.** This lodging has an impressive ground-floor gallery where
B&B/INN   exhibits of paintings, photographs, and sculptures by acclaimed Argentine artists change monthly—you might even run into some fabulous art aficionados sipping wine and admiring the creations. **Pros:** its bohemian

vibe will make you feel like you've joined an artists' colony. **Cons:** rooms are somewhat antiquated. $ *Rooms from: US$109* ✉ *Azcuénaga 1268, Recoleta* ☎ *11/4821–4744* ⊕ *www.ahotel.com.ar* ⤵ *34 rooms* ⑩ *Breakfast* Ⓜ *D to Pueyrredón* ✛ *2:A2.*

$$$$
HOTEL
🛏 **Algodon Mansion.** Every detail of this hotel, one of the ritziest properties in the city, makes it clear that your comfort is of the utmost importance. **Pros:** unparalleled service; luxe location; each room comes with a complimentary bottle of wine. **Cons:** the hotel's bars, restaurant, and rooftop draw a crowd. $ *Rooms from: US$480* ✉ *Montevideo 1647, Recoleta* ☎ *11/3530–7777* ⊕ *www.algodonmansion.com* ⤵ *10 suites* ⑩ *Breakfast* Ⓜ *D to Callao* ✛ *2:C2.*

$$$$
HOTEL
Fodor's Choice
★
🛏 **Alvear Palace Hotel.** The standard-bearer for upscale sophistication since 1932, the Alvear Palace is undoubtedly the shining star of the city's hotel scene: scores of dignitaries, celebrities, and VIPs have passed through its doors over the years, and they keep coming back for the world-class service and refined atmosphere. **Pros:** gorgeously appointed rooms; top-notch service; beautiful spa features a sauna and steam rooms. **Cons:** bathrooms are on the small side; one of the country's most expensive hotels. $ *Rooms from: US$510* ✉ *Av. Alvear 1891, Recoleta* ☎ *11/4808–2100, 800/448–8355 in U.S.* ⊕ *www.alvearpalace. com* ⤵ *91 rooms, 100 suites* ⑩ *No meals* ✛ *2:C1.*

$
HOTEL
FAMILY
🛏 **Art Suites.** Perfect for business travelers on extended stays, couples looking for some stretching room, or families in need of some privacy, this apartment-style hotel's accommodations are bright, roomy, and pleasant. **Pros:** fantastic price; friendly service; plenty of elbow room. **Cons:** Wi-Fi can be unreliable. $ *Rooms from: US$110* ✉ *Azcuenaga 1465, Recoleta* ☎ *11/4821–6800* ⊕ *www.artsuites.com.ar* ⤵ *15 suites* ⑩ *Breakfast* Ⓜ *D to Pueyrredón* ✛ *2:B1.*

$$$
HOTEL
🛏 **Caesar Park.** In a prime location for those in town for business or pleasure, this Recoleta hotel caters equally well to both types of travelers. **Pros:** lovely garden; solicitous staff; good location. **Cons:** it can be easy to forget you're in Buenos Aires. $ *Rooms from: US$250* ✉ *Posadas 1232, Recoleta* ☎ *11/4819–1100* ⊕ *www.accorhotels.com* ⤵ *158 rooms, 17 suites* ⑩ *Breakfast* ✛ *2:C1.*

$$$$
HOTEL
🛏 **Four Seasons Hotel Buenos Aires.** A $49 million renovation in 2013 rendered this hotel even grander than before—quite a feat for what was already one of the city's swankiest lodgings. **Pros:** all the class you'd expect; wonderful eateries; swanky bar. **Cons:** the pool is outdoors, making it ideal for sunny spring and summer days but unusable in winter. $ *Rooms from: US$565* ✉ *Posadas 1086, Recoleta* ☎ *11/4321–1200* ⊕ *www.fourseasons.com/buenosaires* ⤵ *116 rooms, 49 suites* ⑩ *No meals* ✛ *2:C2.*

$$$
HOTEL
🛏 **Hotel Bel Air.** Given the frilly French-style facade, you could mistake the Bel Air for a neighborhood hotel somewhere in Paris. **Pros:** great location on one of the city's poshest streets. **Cons:** the staff is easily distracted; hallways and common areas are cramped. $ *Rooms from: US$180* ✉ *Arenales 1462, Recoleta* ☎ *11/4021–4000* ⊕ *www. hotelbelair.com.ar* ⤵ *77 rooms* ⑩ *Breakfast* Ⓜ *D to Tribunales* ✛ *2:B1.*

$$$
HOTEL
FAMILY
🛏 **Loi Suites Recoleta Hotel.** At this urban oasis, a white-marble lobby leads to a palm-fringed garden where you can enjoy a poolside breakfast

or an afternoon cocktail. **Pros:** in the heart of swanky Recoleta; close to historic sites; lots of nearby restaurants. **Cons:** the place seems a bit dated. ⑤ *Rooms from: US$210* ⊠ *Vicente López 1955, Recoleta* ☎ *11/5777–8950* ⊕ *www.loisuites.com.ar/es/recoleta-hotel-buenos-aires/alojamiento-recoleta* ⤳ *88 rooms, 24 suites* ⦿ *Breakfast* ✥ *2:B2.*

$$$$ ⊞ **Mio Buenos Aires.** The Catena family owns this luxurious boutique
HOTEL hotel, so all the rooms come stocked with wines straight from their own Mendoza vineyards. **Pros:** on one of the most picturesque streets in Recoleta; mixes rustic and modern elements; open and airy feel. **Cons:** the ground-floor common areas feel elegant but somewhat somber. ⑤ *Rooms from: US$320* ⊠ *Av. Pres. Manuel Quintana 465, Recoleta* ☎ *11/5295–8500* ⊕ *www.miobuenosaires.com/en/hotel* ⤳ *30 rooms* ⦿ *Breakfast* Ⓜ *D to Callao* ✥ *2:B1.*

$$$$ ⊞ **Palacio Duhau Park Hyatt Buenos Aires.** This landmark hotel ups the
HOTEL ante for elegance in Buenos Aires—its two buildings, a restored 1930s-
Fodor'sChoice era mansion and a 17-story tower, are connected by an underground
★ art gallery and an expansive, leafy garden that's among the city's most attractive outdoor area. **Pros:** understated splendor; great restaurant; has the city's largest indoor pool. **Cons:** a long walk from one side of the hotel to the other. ⑤ *Rooms from: US$510* ⊠ *Av. Alvear 1661, Recoleta* ☎ *11/5171–1234* ⊕ *www.buenosaires.park.hyatt.com* ⤳ *126 rooms, 39 suites* ⦿ *No meals* ✥ *2:C1.*

$$$ ⊞ **Serena Hotel.** The name of this design hotel conjures up a feeling
HOTEL of serenity, and the fountains in the lobby, the outdoor patio ringed with greenery, and the sizable indoor swimming pool take it to the next level. **Pros:** the downstairs relaxation area and outdoor patio are ideal for whiling away hours; smart design; wonderful location. **Cons:** the gym is sparse. ⑤ *Rooms from: US$210* ⊠ *Libertad 1617, Recoleta* ☎ *11/4813–3226* ⊕ *www.serenahoteles.com/en-buenos-aires.html* ⤳ *34 rooms* ⦿ *Breakfast* ✥ *2:C2.*

ALMAGRO

Well removed from the hotel hubs of Palermo and the Centro, the true porteño energy of the city is discernible in the streets of this historically working-class neighborhood.

$ ⊞ **Hotel Boutique Racó de Buenos Aires.** Resembling the old-money man-
B&B/INN sions of San Telmo, this hotel's rooms open onto a central patio where
Fodor'sChoice many guests choose to take their breakfast. **Pros:** A short distance from
★ many attractions; interesting neighborhood; plenty of charm. **Cons:** the downstairs common area feels somewhat hodgepodge. ⑤ *Rooms from: US$80* ⊠ *Yapeyú 271, Almagro* ☎ *11/3530–6075* ⊕ *www.racodebuenosaires.com.ar* ⤳ *13 rooms* ⦿ *Breakfast* Ⓜ *A to Castro Barros* ✥ *2:A4.*

PALERMO

Palermo is the city's largest barrio and is sectioned into sub-neighborhoods, each with a distinct personality. Palermo Soho, populated with cafés and designer stores, is ideal for exploring on foot. Palermo Hollywood gains its name from the number of media, film, and production studios in the area, and draws the night crowds to its blocks of restaurants and bars.

$$
B&B/INN **1555 Malabia House.** Behind the unassuming white facade of this century-old townhouse and convent is what the proprietors have dubbed Argentina's "first designer B&B." **Pros:** you can walk to shopping by day and bars by night; sleek décor; comfortably furnished rooms. **Cons:** can be a bit noisy. $ *Rooms from: US$160 ⊠ Malabia 1555, Palermo Soho ☎ 11/4833–2410 ⊕ www.malabiahouse.com.ar ⇗ 11 rooms, 4 suites ⊖ Breakfast Ⓜ D to Scalabrini Ortíz ✛ 1:F5.*

$$$ HOTEL **1828 Smart Hotel.** Technology is front and center at the 1828 Smart Hotel, where you're lent a tablet computer when you check in that lets you control everything in your room from the curtains to the fragrance, request room service, and order a taxi. **Pros:** impressive amenities for such a small hotel; gorgeous swimming pool; trendy neighborhood. **Cons:** the flashy design isn't for everyone; standard rooms are pricey for their size. $ *Rooms from: US$220 ⊠ Fray Justo Santamaría de Oro 1828, Palermo Soho ☎ 11/2060–9011 ⊕ www.1828smarthotel.com ⇗ 12 rooms, 2 suites Ⓜ D to Palermo ✛ 1:E4.*

$$$$ B&B/INN **Be Jardín Escondido by Coppola.** This is the personal home of director Francis Ford Coppola, who lived here while filming *Tetro* and still visits regularly. **Pros:** 24-hour concierge service; on-call sommelier; plenty of privacy. **Cons:** can feel a bit too Hollywood for some tastes. $ *Rooms from: US$420 ⊠ Gorriti 4746, Palermo ☎ 11/4834–6166 ⊕ www.bebourbon.com ⇗ 7 rooms ⊖ Breakfast ✛ 1:E5.*

$$ B&B/INN **BoBo.** Quirky BoBo shrewdly combines the bourgeois with the bohemian—in fact, the hotel's name subtly references David Brooks's thought-provoking book *Bobos in Paradise,* about the blurred lines between these two concepts. **Pros:** unique design; handy location; friendly staff goes out of its way to help you. **Cons:** some rooms are on the small side. $ *Rooms from: US$125 ⊠ Guatemala 4870, Palermo Soho ☎ 11/4774–0505 ⊕ www.bobohotel.com ⇗ 15 rooms ⊖ Breakfast Ⓜ D to Plaza Italia ✛ 1:F4.*

$$ B&B/INN **Duque Hotel Boutique & Spa.** As the name suggests, this 1920s French-style hotel is fit for a duke—or even a president, as the mansion once served as an Argentine president's private residence. **Pros:** gorgeous entrance; spacious and inviting common areas; an enclosed patio means many guests use rooms only for sleeping. **Cons:** some rooms are on the small side. $ *Rooms from: US$160 ⊠ Guatemala 4364, Palermo Soho ☎ 11/4832–0312 ⊕ www.duquehotel.com ⇗ 14 rooms ⊖ Breakfast ✛ 1:F4.*

$$ 🏨 **Fierro Hotel.** Often called "the hotel for the gourmand"—the restaurant's chef Hernan Gipponi is a driving force behind the Buenos Aires foodie scene—the Fierro is a choice lodging for travelers looking for a five-star stay in a boutique package. **Pros:** among the city's best dining and drinking; rooftop pool with skyline views; sleek décor. **Cons:** common areas are small. ⑤ *Rooms from: US$160* ⊠ *Soler 5862, Palermo* ☎ *11/3220–6800* ⊕ *www.fierrohotel.com* ⤳ *22 rooms, 5 suites* ⑩ *Breakfast* ✛ *1:E3.*

HOTEL
Fodor'sChoice
★

$$$ 🏨 **The Glu Hotel.** Run with great attention to detail by the Glusman Family, this boutique hotel has 11 spacious rooms, all stylishly modern and minimalist and equipped with low-slung furnishings, bright wooden floors, and small bar areas. **Pros:** sought-after location; sleek interior décor; tip-top concierges provide highly personalized and attentive service. **Cons:** its location on a happening street means constant traffic, though rooms are soundproofed. ⑤ *Rooms from: US$210* ⊠ *Godoy Cruz 1733, Palermo* ☎ *11/4831–4646* ⊕ *www.thegluhotel.com* ⤳ *11 rooms* ✛ *1:E4.*

HOTEL
Fodor'sChoice
★

$$ 🏨 **Home Hotel Buenos Aires.** Run by Argentinean Patricia O'Shea and her British husband Tom Rixton, Home Hotel oozes coolness and class. **Pros:** impossibly hip and fun; always interesting people staying here; great pool area. **Cons:** lots of nonguests come here to hang out. ⑤ *Rooms from: US$165* ⊠ *Honduras 5860, Palermo Hollywood* ☎ *11/4778–1008* ⊕ *www.homebuenosaires.com* ⤳ *14 rooms, 4 suites, 2 apartments* ⑩ *Breakfast* Ⓜ *D to Ministro Carranza* ✛ *1:D3.*

B&B/INN

$$ 🏨 **L'Hôtel Palermo.** A cobblestone walkway with a canopy of vines leads to the heart and soul of this rustically elegant property: a verdant back garden with colorful blooms, wrought-iron chairs, and a pleasant pool. **Pros:** attractive outdoor areas; breezy rooftop terrace; homey rooms. **Cons:** standard rooms are small. ⑤ *Rooms from: US$130* ⊠ *Thames 1562, Palermo Soho* ☎ *11/4831–7198* ⊕ *www.lhotelpalermo.com* ⤳ *21 rooms, 2 suites* ⑩ *Breakfast* Ⓜ *D to Plaza Italia* ✛ *1:E4.*

B&B/INN

$$$ 🏨 **Legado Mítico.** Blessed with city's most gorgeous sitting room, the Legado Mítico also has an enormous library with plush leather couches, antique furnishings, a fireplace, and bookshelves stocked with English- and Spanish-language classics. **Pros:** exquisitely decorated rooms; welcoming vibe; an authentic and unique Argentine experience. **Cons:** common areas and hallways are very dark; the upstairs terrace disappoints for a property of this quality. ⑤ *Rooms from: US$250* ⊠ *Gurruchaga 1848, Palermo* ☎ *11/4833–1300* ⊕ *www.legadomitico.com* ⤳ *11 rooms* ⑩ *Breakfast* ✛ *1:F4.*

B&B/INN

$$$ 🏨 **Magnolia Hotel Boutique.** This boutique lodging feels like home—if home were a high-ceiling, lavishly decorated Palermo townhouse dating from the 1890s. **Pros:** top-floor terrace is the perfect urban escape; lots of cozy common areas; homemade baked goods at breakfast. **Cons:** some rooms require walking outdoors. ⑤ *Rooms from: US$210* ⊠ *Julián Alvarez 1746, Palermo Soho* ☎ *11/4867–4900* ⊕ *www.magnoliahotelboutique.com* ⤳ *8 rooms* ⑩ *Breakfast* ✛ *1:F5.*

B&B/INN
Fodor'sChoice
★

$$$ 🏨 **Mine Hotel.** A modernist and minimalist property built of concrete and exposed stone, this boutique hotel comes complete with cool common areas, a full bar and restaurant, and a youthful staff. **Pros:** handy

HOTEL

location in Palermo; on-site bar and restaurant; the pool is the perfect spot to laze away the day or usher in the night. **Cons:** rooms are on the small side; pricey compared with similar properties. $ *Rooms from: US$205* ✉ *Gorriti 4770, Palermo* ☎ *11/4832–1100* ⊕ *www.minehotel. com* ⤚ *20 rooms* ⏐◯⏐ *Breakfast* ✛ *1:E5.*

$$
B&B/INN
Fodor's Choice
★

🛏 **Miravida Soho Hotel & Wine Bar.** This enchanting boutique hotel is owned and operated by two German expats who personally see to it that you receive the most thoughtful and personalized service starting the minute you walk in the door. **Pros:** charm to spare; breakfast options like homemade granola will have you eager to start the day; end the day with a delicious tipple by the ground-floor bar. **Cons:** if street noise is a concern, request a room in the back. $ *Rooms from: US$160* ✉ *Dar-regueyra 2050, Palermo* ☎ *11/4774–6433* ⊕ *www.miravidasoho.com* ⤚ *6 rooms* ⏐◯⏐ *Breakfast* Ⓜ *D to Palermo* ✛ *1:F4.*

$$$
HOTEL

🛏 **Nuss Hotel.** Housed in a former convent on one of Palermo's most happening corners, the Nuss is a great option for those who want to be in the heart of the barrio's action. **Pros:** rooftop pool area is a winner; sunny lobby bar perfect for afternoon cocktails; small gym and spa just right for working up a sweat. **Cons:** small bathrooms. $ *Rooms from: US$250* ✉ *El Salvador 4916, Palermo Soho* ☎ *11/4833–8100* ⊕ *www. nusshotel.com* ⤚ *22 rooms* ✛ *1:E4.*

$$
HOTEL

🛏 **Palermitano Hotel.** This lodging occupies a spot on one of the chicest strips in Palermo Soho, more than holding its own against neighboring see-and-be-seen establishments. **Pros:** spacious outdoor areas; great décor; close to some of the best spots in Palermo Soho. **Cons:** virtually no indoor common space; rooms near the street hear after-dark traffic. $ *Rooms from: US$120* ✉ *Uriarte 1648, Palermo Soho* ☎ *11/4897–2100* ⊕ *www.palermitano.biz* ⤚ *14 rooms, 2 suites* ⏐◯⏐ *Breakfast* Ⓜ *D to Plaza Italia* ✛ *1:E4.*

$$$
HOTEL

🛏 **Palermo Place.** Slippers are already waiting by your bed when you check into the Palermo Place, making the spacious, studio-style rooms especially inviting. **Pros:** ample kitchens, an amenity that few hotels in the city can claim. **Cons:** bathrooms are a tight squeeze; spotty Wi-Fi access; dark halls. $ *Rooms from: US$250* ✉ *Nicaragua 5865, Palermo Hollywood* ☎ *11/3220–9600* ⊕ *www.palermoplace.com* ⤚ *26 rooms* Ⓜ *D to Ministro Carranza* ✛ *1:D3.*

$$$$
HOTEL

🛏 **Palermo Tower.** If you need some elbow room, the Palermo Tower has some of the biggest rooms you'll find in Buenos Aires, all of them featuring sitting areas with comfy couches and nicely outfitted kitchenettes. **Pros:** plenty of space to spread out; two terraces for lounging: one by the pool, another near the breakfast area. **Cons:** nearby thoroughfare is noisy at all hours; pricey compared with similar properties. $ *Rooms from: US$320* ✉ *Charcas 4955, Palermo Hollywood* ☎ *11/3220–1100* ⊕ *www.palermotower.com* ⤚ *23 rooms* ⏐◯⏐ *Breakfast* Ⓜ *D to Palermo.* ✛ *1:F3.*

$$
B&B/INN

🛏 **Querido B&B.** The biggest draw at this sunny B&B is the location in the up-and-coming neighborhood of Villa Crespo, a 10-minute walk from Palermo. **Pros:** modern design is easy on the eye; desirable neighborhood; discounts for paying in cash. **Cons:** televisions are small; walls surrounding the patio make it feel confining. $ *Rooms from: US$130* ✉ *Juan Ramírez del Velazco 934, Villa Crespo* ☎ *11/4854–6297*

⊕ *www.queridobuenosaires.com* ↰ *8 rooms* ⦿| *Breakfast* Ⓜ *B to Malabia* ✛ *1:D5.*

$$ 🏨 **Rendez-Vous Hotel.** The fresh exterior of this French Petit Hotel pops
B&B/INN   on the streets of Palermo Hollywood, while the warm oranges, creams, and dark browns decorating the ground floor lure guests inside. **Pros:** an inviting ground-floor setup for breakfast, drinks, and reading; relaxing atmosphere. **Cons:** nearby nightlife can mean street noise. Ⓢ *Rooms from: US$135* ✉ *Bonpland 1484, Palermo Hollywood* ☎ *11/3964–5222* ⊕ *www.rendezvoushotel.com.ar* ↰ *11 rooms* ⦿| *Breakfast* Ⓜ *D to Ministro Carranza* ✛ *1:D4.*

$$ 🏨 **Vain Boutique Hotel.** Built from two carefully restored private homes,
B&B/INN   this Palermo Soho hot spot's crisply decorated rooms have high ceilings, hardwood floors, and enormous beds topped with luxe linens. **Pros:** eye-catching design; décor is warm and welcoming; great location near scores of fantastic restaurants. **Cons:** can be noisy: buses pass right in front, and a nearby school means the sounds of kids every afternoon. Ⓢ *Rooms from: US$160* ✉ *Thames 2226, Palermo Soho* ☎ *11/4776–8246* ⊕ *www.vainuniverse.com* ↰ *15 rooms* ⦿| *Breakfast* Ⓜ *D to Plaza Italia* ✛ *1:F4.*

LAS CAÑITAS

This pocket bordering Belgrano and Palermo has a see-and-be-seen vibe and attracts an elite crowd.

$$ 🏨 **248 Finisterra.** A mix of cutting-edge and vintage designs character-
B&B/INN   izes this boutique hotel, located on the main drag of trendy Las Cañitas. **Pros:** close to restaurants and bars; pleasant garden and terrace; comfy common areas. **Cons:** tiny bathrooms and even tinier showers. Ⓢ *Rooms from: US$170* ✉ *Báez 248, Las Cañitas* ☎ *11/4773–0901* ⊕ *www.248finisterra.com* ↰ *10 rooms, 1 suite* ⦿| *Breakfast* Ⓜ *D to Ministro Carranza* ✛ *1:E2.*

SIDE TRIPS

Buenos Aires Province and Iguazú Falls

WELCOME TO BUENOS AIRES SIDE TRIPS

TOP REASONS TO GO

★ **Wall of Water:**
Nothing can prepare you for the roaring, thunderous Cataratas del Iguazú (Iguazú Falls). We think you'll agree.

★ **Cowboy Culture:**
No visit to the *pampas* (grasslands) is complete without a stay at an *estancia,* a stately ranch house, like those around San Antonio de Areco. Sleep in an old-fashioned bedroom and share meals with the owners for a true taste of the lifestyle.

★ **Delta Dreaming:**
Speeding through the Paraná River Delta's thousands of kilometers of rivers and streams, we'll forgive you for humming "Ride of the Valkyries"—it does feel very Mekong.

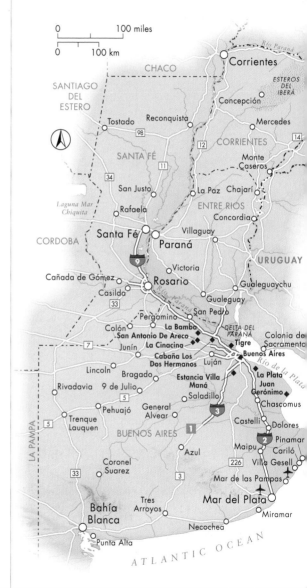

GETTING ORIENTED

Argentina's famous pampas begin in Buenos Aires Province—an unending sea of crops and cattle-studded grass that occupies nearly one-quarter of the country's landscapes. Here are the region's most traditional towns, including San Antonio de Areco. Suburban trains connect Buenos Aires to Tigre, close to the labyrinthine waterways of the Paraná Delta, explorable only by boat. On Argentina's northeastern tip, readily accessible by plane, are the jaw-dropping Cataratas del Iguazú.

1 Buenos Aires Province. An hour's drive from Buenos Aires leads to varied sights. The gaucho town of San Antonio de Areco lies northwest of other sites, such as the semitropical delta of the Paraná River, near the town of Tigre, and the provincial capital La Plata.

2 Iguazú Falls (Cataratas del Iguazú). The grandeur of this vast sheet of white water cascading in constant cymbal-banging cacophony makes Niagara Falls and Victoria Falls seem sedate. Allow at least two full days to take in this magnificent sight.

Updated by Allan Kelin

To hear *porteños* (inhabitants of Buenos Aires) talk of their city, you'd think Argentina stops where Buenos Aires ends. Not far beyond it, however, the skies open up and the *pampas*—Argentina's huge flat grasslands—begin. Pampean traditions are alive and well in farming communities that still dot the plains that make up Buenos Aires Province.

The best known is San Antonio de Areco, a well-preserved provincial town that's making a name for itself as gaucho central. You can ride across the pampas and get a taste of country life (and lots of grass-fed beef) by visiting—or staying at—a traditional *estancia* (ranch).

Ranchland gives way to watery wonders. The quiet suburban town of Tigre is the gateway to the network of rivers and tributaries that form the delta of the Paraná River, lined with luscious tropical vegetation. Low wooden launches speed along its waterways to the houses, restaurants, and lodges built on stilts along the riverbanks.

If you like your natural wonders supersized, take a short flight or a long bus ride to Iguazú Falls, northeast of Buenos Aires in semitropical Misiones Province. Here, straddling the border between Argentina and Brazil, two natural parks contain and protect hundreds of roaring falls and a delicate jungle ecosystem. The spectacle caused Eleanor Roosevelt to exclaim "Poor Niagara!" but most people are simply left speechless by the sheer size and force of the Garganta del Diablo, the grandest falls of them all.

PLANNING

WHEN TO GO
Temperatures in Buenos Aires Province rarely reach extremes. Note that some hotels and restaurants in areas popular with local tourists open *only* on weekends outside of peak season—this coincides with school holidays in summer (January and February), winter (July), and the Easter weekend. You'll get great discounts at those that open midweek in winter.

Early November's a good time to visit San Antonio de Areco, which holds its annual gaucho festival then. Like Buenos Aires, it feels curiously empty in January, when everyone decamps to the coast.

Though Iguazú Falls is thrilling year-round, seasonal rainfall and upstream Brazilian *barrages* (minidams) can affect the amount of water. If you visit between November and March, booking a hotel with air-conditioning and a swimming pool is as essential as taking mosquito repellent.

BORDER CROSSINGS

Crossing into Brazil from Argentina can be a thorny issue. By law, all U.S. citizens need a visa to enter Brazil. Visas can sometimes be issued in as little as three hours from the Brazilian consulate in Puerto Iguazú (as opposed to the three days they take in Buenos Aires) but can take up to two days. So it's best to secure your visa, which costs $160, well before you expect to cross. The Buenos Aires consulate also has a reputation for refusing visas to travelers who don't have onward tickets from Brazil.

If you stay in Foz do Iguaçu, travel on to other Brazilian cities, or do a day trip to Brazil by public bus or through an Argentine company, you'll need a visa. There have been reports of getting around this by using a Brazilian travel agent or by using local taxis (both Argentine and Brazilian) that have "arrangements" with border control. Though the practice is well established (most hotels and travel agents in Puerto Iguazú have deals with Brazilian companies and can arrange a visa-less visit), it *is* illegal. Enforcement of the law is generally lax, but sudden crackdowns and on-the-spot fines of hundreds of dollars have been reported.

CAR TRAVEL

Argentina has one of the world's worst records for traffic accidents, and the busy highways of Buenos Aires Province are often where they happen. January and February are the worst times, when drivers anxious to get to and from their holiday destination speed, tailgate, and exercise illegal maneuvers even more alarmingly than usual. If you're driving, do so very defensively and avoid traveling on Friday and Sunday, when traffic is worst.

Expressways and interprovincial routes tend to be atrociously signposted, so take a map. Getting a GPS-equipped rental car costs an extra 35 pesos or so per day: devices usually work well in cities, but the calibration is often a couple of hundred yards off in rural areas. Major routes are usually privately owned, which means frequent tolls. There are sometimes alternative roads to use, but they're generally smaller, slower, and in poor condition. On main roads the speed limit is 80 kph (50 mph), while on highways it's 130 kph (80 mph), though Argentinean drivers rarely pay heed to this.

SAFETY

Provincial towns like San Antonio de Areco are usually extremely safe, and the areas visited by tourists are well patrolled. Puerto Iguazú is fairly quiet in itself, but mugging and theft are common in nearby Foz do Iguaçu in Brazil, especially at night, when its streets are deserted.

WHAT IT COSTS IN ARGENTINE PESOS				
	$	$$	$$$	$$$$
Restaurants	under 30 pesos	30–50 pesos	51–75 pesos	over 75 pesos
Hotels	under 300 pesos	301–500 pesos	501–800 pesos	over 800 pesos

Restaurant prices are per person for a main course at dinner. Hotel prices are for a standard double room in high season.

BUENOS AIRES PROVINCE

Plains fan out where the city of Buenos Aires ends: this is the beginning of the pampas, which derive their name from the native Quechua word for "flat field." All over this fertile earth are signs of active ranch life, from the grazing cattle to the modern-day gauchos. The region is also noted for its crops, although these days the traditional alfalfa, sunflowers, wheat, and corn have largely been replaced by soy.

While Argentina was still a Spanish colony, settlers gradually began to force indigenous tribes away from the pampas near Buenos Aires, making extensive agriculture and cattle breeding possible. (In 1880, during the bloody Campaign of the Desert, the southern pampas were also "cleared" of indigenous tribes.) By the latter half of the 19th century the region had become known as the grain supplier for the world. From 1850 to 1950 more than 400 important estancias were built in Buenos Aires Province alone. Some of these have been modified for use as guest ranches and provide the best glimpse of the fabled pampean lifestyle.

TIGRE AND THE PARANÁ DELTA

30 km (19 miles) northwest of Buenos Aires on the Ruta Panamericana, 35 km (22 miles) northwest of Buenos Aires on Avenida Libertador.

A coastal train ride or a drive through the shady riverside suburbs of Buenos Aires takes you to the riverport town of Tigre, the embarkation point for boats that ply the Delta del Paraná. A couple of hours is plenty of time to visit the town itself from Buenos Aires; allow a whole day if you also plan to explore the delta—a vast maze of canals, tributaries, and river expanding out like the veins of a leaf. Heavy vegetation and rich birdlife (as well as clouds of mosquitoes) make the network of rivers feel tropical. The delta's many islands hide peaceful luxury getaways and cozy riverside restaurants accessible only by boat.

The waterways and close-packed islands that stretch northwest of Tigre are the most accessible part of the 14,000 square km (5,400 square miles) that make up the delta, where roads are replaced by rivers. Churning brown waters and heavy vegetation are vaguely reminiscent of Southeast Asia, though the chic houses and manicured gardens that line the rivers of the Primera Sección (closest to Tigre) are a far cry from Mekong River settlements.

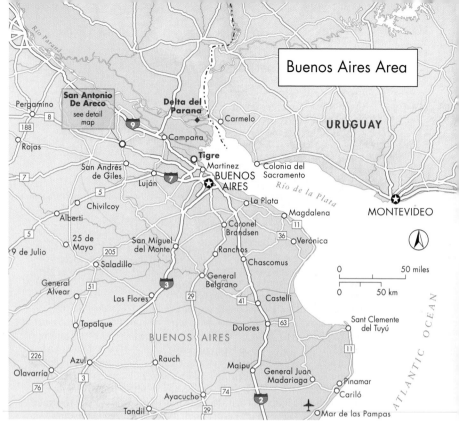

If you want to take in more of the delta than a short boat trip allows, do as porteños do and combine it with a day's wining and dining at an island restaurant or a weekend at one of the hotels or luxury lodges a little farther afield. Many offer private transportation. The delta gets very hot and humid in summer, and the mosquitoes are ferocious, so bring insect repellent.

GETTING HERE AND AROUND

The cheapest way to get to Tigre by train is on the suburban commuter train from Estación Retiro to the central Estación Tigre. There are about four departures an hour on the Ramal Tigre (Tigre Branch) of the Línea Mitre; round-trip tickets cost 2.70 pesos. Alternatively, take the slick, tourist-oriented Tren de la Costa. It meanders through some of Buenos Aires' most fashionable northern suburbs and along the riverbank, stopping at nine stations before arriving at Estación Delta, near the Río Luján and Puerto de Frutos market. It starts halfway between Buenos Aires and Tigre, so you'll have to first take Línea Mitre, Ramal Mitre from Retiro to Estación Bartolomé Mitre, where you can change to the Tren de la Costa's Maipú Station. Round-trip fare is 40 pesos. The center of Tigre is small enough to walk around easily, but there are also taxis outside both train stations.

The most comfortable—and the most touristy—way to travel the delta's waterways is aboard the two-story catamarans that leave from docks on the Luján River, inside the Puerto de Frutos market. Rio Tur catamarans meander through 14 miles of waterways in about 90 minutes. They're a great way to glimpse delta life, and you'll see houses on stilts and boats piled high with provisions for towns upriver. ■TIP→ **The last boat of the day usually catches the sunset.**

The low-slung wooden *lanchas colectivas* (boat buses) are the cheaper and more authentic way to explore the waterways; locals use them to get around the delta. These leave from the Estación Fluvial (Boat Station), on the other side of the round-about from Estación Tigre, the main train station. The main transport company for the delta is Interisleña, which serves all of the closest islands to the Tigre. Round-trip tickets start at 56 pesos. Líneas Delta Argentino uses similar boats but also runs one-hour tourism-oriented trips every couple of hours on weekends and holidays, which cost 60 pesos. Buy tickets from Booth 6, opposite the jetty. Touts offering private boat trips loiter outside the Tigre tourist board offices at the train and boat stations, but it's best to stick with recognized companies. As the boats leave the delta, they pass the magnificent turn-of-the-20th-century buildings of Tigre's heyday and colorfully painted houses built on stilts to protect them from floods.

ESSENTIALS

Boat Contacts Interisleña. Located within the Estación Fluvial, Interisleña runs a fleet of lanchas colectivas. Tell the ticket agent where you're visiting on the delta, and he'll tell you which boat will take you. Round-trip fares start at 56 pesos. ⊠ *Estación Fluvial, Mitre 345, Tigre* 🕾 *11/4749–0900.* **Líneas Delta Argentino.** This lanchas colectivas company runs transportation to various islands on the delta but also offers one-hour excursions on weekends and holidays. It's well worth the 60 pesos to get an idea of this aquatic community. ⊠ *Estación Fluvial, Mitre 345, Tigre* 🕾 *11/4731–1236* ⊕ *www.lineasdelta.com.ar.*

Train Contacts Línea Mitre 🕾 *11/3220–6300* ⊕ *www.mininterior.gov.ar/sofse.* **Tren de la Costa** 🕾 *11/4002–6000* ⊕ *www.omnilineas.com.ar/buenos-aires/colectivo/linea-tren-de-la-costa.*

Visitor and Tour Info Rio Tur ⊠ *Sarmiento and Buenos Aires, on the Río Luján, Tigre* 🕾 *11/4731–0280* ⊕ *www.rioturcatamaranes.com.ar* 💷 *100 pesos* 🕙 *Weekdays noon–4, weekends 11–6.* **Tigre Tourist Board** ⊠ *Estación Fluvial, Bartolome Mitre 305, Tigre* 🕾 *11/4512–4497* ⊕ *www.vivitigre.gov.ar* 🕙 *Daily 8–6.*

EXPLORING

TOP ATTRACTIONS

Museo de Arte de Tigre. An arcade of Doric columns leads from the Luján River to this ornate building, built in 1909 to house a social club and casino. It contains a modest collection of Argentine paintings by artists like Quirós, Castagnino, Soldi, and Quinquela Martín, as well as works portraying life in the delta. The real showstopper, however, is the beautifully restored architecture: a sweeping marble staircase, stained-glass windows, gilt-inlaid columns, and soaring ceilings conspire to form a microcosm of the fin-de-siècle European style adored by the porteño elite. A trim sculpture garden and flower-filled park surround the museum, which is best reached by walking along Paseo Victorica. ✉ *Paseo Victorica 972, Tigre* ☎ *11/4512–4528* ⊕ *www.mat. gov.ar* 🎫 *20 pesos* ⊙ *Wed.–Fri. 9–7, weekends noon–7.*

Museo Del Mate. Maté drinking in Argentina is even more deeply culturally rooted than coffee in the U.S. or even tea in the U.K. The maté gourd and the accompanying flask of hot water is ubiquitous throughout all social classes and age groups, whether one is sipping alone or sharing with a group of friends. The Museo del Mate is a great place to learn about the history of yerba maté—the shrub the bitter tea is made from—and the sometimes very stylish matés it's drunk from. Many of the matés, both antique and modern, are made from beautifully crafted porcelain or metal. Tours are available in English. ✉ *Lavalle 289, Tigre* ☎ *11/4506–9594* ⊕ *www.elmuseodelmate.com* 🎫 *20 pesos* ⊙ *Wed.– Sun. and holidays 11–6.*

Museo Naval de la Nación. Although most of its visitors are into naval, military, or nautical history, this museum's collection will fascinate even those whose interests point elsewhere. The interior of the building, which looks like a hangar-size Victorian barn, is filled with paintings, statues, uniforms, and beautifully crafted model ships. On the grounds are long-retired planes from Argentina's aviation history, including a great example of a North American AT-6 "Texan" from 1939. ✉ *Av. Victorica 602, Tigre* ☎ *011/4749–0608* 🎫 *10 pesos* ⊙ *Tues.–Fri. 8:30– 5:30, weekends and holidays 10:30–6:30.*

Puerto de Frutos. The center of the action at Tigre is its picturesque market. Hundreds of stalls selling furniture, handicrafts, and reasonably priced souvenirs fill the area around the docks along the Río Luján. It's particularly busy on weekends (indeed, many stalls are closed midweek). Grab a quick lunch from stands selling steak and chorizo sandwiches. ✉ *Sarmiento at Buenos Aires, Tigre* ⊕ *www.puertodefrutos-arg. com.ar* ⊙ *Weekdays 10–6, weekends 10–7.*

WORTH NOTING

FAMILY **Parque de la Costa.** This is Argentina's largest and most modern amusement park. Its main attractions are the two side-by-side roller coasters, El Boomerang and El Desafío. There's also a splashy river ride, swinging inverter ship, and a host of milder thrills, including a petting zoo. Admission is often heavily discounted in winter. ✉ *Vivanco 1509, Tigre* ☎ *11/4002–6000* ⊕ *www.parquedelacosta.com.ar* 🎫 *101 pesos* ⊙ *Jan. and Feb., Tues.–Sun. 11–8; Mar.–Nov., weekends and holidays 11–7.*

Paseo Victorica. Italianate mansions, museums, restaurants, and several rowing clubs dot this paved walkway and waterside park that curves alongside the Río Luján for about 10 blocks. To reach it, cross the bridge next to the roundabout immediately north of Estación Tigre, then turn right and walk five blocks along Avenida Lavalle, which runs along the Río Tigre. ✉ *Along Río Luján between Río Tigre and Río Reconquista, Tigre.*

WORD OF MOUTH

"My brother-in-law had heard such great things about Tigre that he made us go there. It was a really good choice. After a surprisingly easy train ride out, we took a day-long boat tour. It was a beautiful day, and the islands were peaceful and nice to look at." —Messifan

WHERE TO EAT

$$$$ MODERN ARGENTINE ✕ **Almacén de Flores.** Just about 100 yards west of the Estación Fluvial, this cozy eatery is seemingly miles away from the automobile and boat traffic. In a quiet quarter among a scattering of shops and cafés with bohemian flair, it's a great place to get away from the weekend crowds and enjoy a freshly made salad or sandwich. Aside from the tasty food and friendly staff, you're sure to enjoy being surrounded by freshly cut flowers, as the place is also a florist. $ *Average main: 120 pesos* ✉ *Blvd. Saenz Peña 1336, Tigre* ☎ *11/5197–4009* ⊙ *Closed Mon. and Tues.*

$$$$ ARGENTINE ✕ **Il Novo María del Luján.** An expansive terrace overlooking the river is the appropriate backdrop for Tigre's best fish dishes. The kitchen favors elaborate preparations: some are so packed with unlikely ingredients that the fish gets lost; others, such as the sole in lemon-infused cream, are spot-on. Land-based offerings like pork belly braised in beer are equally well executed. Both the terrace and the sunny, peach-colored inside room fill up on weekends, when harried waitstaff often take a long time to bring your orders or even the check. $ *Average main: 200 pesos* ✉ *Paseo Victorica 611, Tigre* ☎ *11/4731–9613* ⊕ *www.ilnovomariadellujan.com* ✍ *Reservations essential.*

WHERE TO STAY

The city of Tigre is so close to Buenos Aires that there's little reason to stay overnight there. However, a night or two in the Paraná Delta is a rewarding experience.

$$$$ B&B/INN ALL-INCLUSIVE **Bonanza Deltaventura.** Thick vegetation surrounds the tomato-red 19th-century country house that's the center of the eco-action at Bonanza Deltaventura. **Pros:** very back-to-nature; great home cooking; lots of sports. **Cons:** rooms get hot in summer; no pool; minimal luxury. $ *Rooms from: 1175 pesos* ✉ *Arroyo Rama Negra, Tigre* ☎ *11/5603–7176* ⊕ *www.deltaventura.com* *4 rooms, 3 guesthouses* *No credit cards* *All-inclusive.*

$$$$ RESORT ALL-INCLUSIVE **La Becasina Delta Lodge.** Wooden walkways connect the luxurious bungalows—each with a private riverside deck. **Pros:** total peace and quiet; lots of creature comforts; wild delta surroundings. **Cons:** expensive rates; there's nothing else nearby; lots of mosquitoes. $ *Rooms*

from: 2400 pesos ✉ *Arroyo las Cañas, San Fernando* ☎ *11/4328–2687* ⊕ *www.labecasina.com* ⌁ *15 bungalows* ▭ *No credit cards* ¶⊙¶ *All-inclusive.*

SAN ANTONIO DE ARECO

110 km (68 miles) west of Buenos Aires.

There's no better place to experience traditional provincial life in the pampas than this well-to-do farming town. Grand estancias dot the land in and around San Antonio. Many of the families that own them, which form a sort of local aristocracy, mix lucrative soy farming with estancia tourism. The gauchos who were once ranch hands now cook up huge *asados* (barbecues) and lead horseback expeditions for the ever-growing numbers of foreign tourists. You can visit one for a day—*un día de campo*—or immerse yourself with an overnight visit.

Porteño visitors tend to base themselves in the town itself, which is becoming known for its B&Bs. The fiercely conservative inhabitants have done a good job of preserving the turn-of-the-20th-century Italianate buildings that fill the sleepy *casco histórico* (historic center). Many contain bars and general stores, which maintain their original fittings; others are the workshops of some of the best craftspeople in the country.

In summer the banks of the Río Areco (Areco River), which runs through town, are teeming with picnickers—especially near the center of town, at the Puente Viejo (Old Bridge), which is overlooked by the open-air riverside tables of various riverside parrillas. Nearby is the Museo Gauchesco y Parque Criollo Ricardo Güiraldes, which celebrates historical gaucho life. During the week surrounding November 10, the Día de la Tradición (Day of Tradition) celebrates the gaucho with shows, community barbecues, riding competitions, and a huge crafts fair. It's more fun to visit San Antonio on weekends, as many restaurants are closed Monday to Thursday.

GETTING HERE AND AROUND

To drive to San Antonio de Areco, leave Buenos Aires on RN9, crossing to RN8 when it intersects at Km 35 (total tolls of 15.60 pesos). There are more than 20 buses daily from Buenos Aires' Retiro Station to San Antonio; most are run by Nueva Chevallier, and some by Pullman General Belgrano. Each company operates from its own bus stop in San Antonio. Once you've arrived, the best way to get around is on foot, but you'll need a *remis* (radio taxi) to get to most estancias, though some have their own shuttle service.

ESSENTIALS

Bus Contacts Chevallier ☎ *11/4000–5255* ⊕ *www.nuevachevallier.com.* **Pullman General Belgrano** ☎ *11/4018–0010* ⊕ *www.gralbelgrano.com.ar.* **Terminal de Ómnibus Retiro** ☎ *11/4310–0700* ⊕ *www.tebasa.com.ar.*

Taxi Contacts Remis Centro ☎ *2326/456–225.*

Visitor Info San Antonio de Areco Tourist Board ✉ *Blvd. Zerboni at Arellano, San Antonio de Areco* ☎ *2326/453–165* ⊕ *www.sanantoniodeareco.com* ⊙ *Weekdays 8–7, weekends 8–8.*

San Antonio
de Areco

KEY

1 *Exploring sights*
① *Hotels & Restaurants*

EXPLORING
TOP ATTRACTIONS

Museo Gauchesco y Parque Criollo Ricardo Güiraldes. Gaucho life of the past is celebrated—and idealized—at this quiet museum on a small estate just outside town. Start at the 150-year-old *pulpería* (the gaucho version of the saloon), complete with dressed-up wax figures ready for a drink. Then head for the museum proper, an early-20th-century replica of a stately 18th-century *casco de estancia* (estancia house). Polished wooden cases contain a collection of traditional gaucho gear: elaborately decorated knives, colorful ponchos, and all manner of elaborate saddlery and bridlery. The museum is named for local writer Ricardo Güiraldes (1886–1927), whose romantic gaucho novels captured the imagination of the Argentinean people. Several rooms document his life in San Antonio de Areco and the real-life gauchos who inspired his work. ✉ *Camino Ricardo Güiraldes, San Antonio de Areco* ☎ *2326/455–839* ⊕ *www.museoguiraldes.com.ar* ✆ *Free* ⊙ *Weekdays 10–5.*

Museo Las Lilas de Areco. Although iconic Argentinean painter Florencio Molina Campos was not from San Antonio de Areco, his humorous paintings depict traditional pampas life. The works usually show red-nose, pigeon-toe gauchos astride comical steeds, staggering drunkenly outside taverns, engaged in cockfighting or folk dancing, and taming bucking broncos. The collection is fun and beautifully arranged, and your ticket includes coffee and croissants in the jarringly modern café, which also does great empanadas and sandwiches. Behind its curtained walls lie huge theme park–style re-creations of three paintings. The lively and insightful voiceover explaining them is in Spanish only. ⊠ *Moreno 279, San Antonio de Areco* ☎ *2326/456–425* ⊕ *www.museolaslilas.org* 🎟 *65 pesos* ⊗ *June–Sept., Thurs.–Sun. 10–6; Oct.–May, Thurs.–Sun. 10–8.*

WORTH NOTING

Museo Taller Draghi. San Antonio is famed for its silversmiths, and the late Juan José Draghi was the best in town. This small museum adjoining his workshop showcases the emergence and evolution of the Argentine silver-work style known as *platería criolla*. The pieces are mostly ornate takes on gaucho-related items: spurs, belt buckles, knives, stirrups, and the ubiquitous matés, some dating from the 18th century. Also on display is the incredibly ornate work of Juan José Draghi himself; you can buy original pieces in the shop. His son and a host of disciples keep the family business alive—they're often at work shaping new pieces at the back of the museum. ⊠ *Lavalle 387, San Antonio de Areco* ☎ *2326/454–219* ⊕ *www.draghiplaterosorfebres.com* ⊗ *Daily 9–1 and 4–8.*

WHERE TO EAT

$$$$
ARGENTINE
✕ **Almacén de Ramos Generales.** Airy and charming, this eatery's classic Argentine fare is consistently good. You can snack on cheeses, olives, prosciutto, salami, and eggplant *en escabeche* (pickled). The *bife de chorizo* (sirloin steak), meanwhile, is perfectly juicy, tender, and flavorful, all the more so when accompanied by wondrous french fries with basil. The country-store-meets-elegant-restaurant atmosphere is just right. No wonder locals and visiting porteños alike vie for tables—on weekends, reservations are essential. ⑤ *Average main: 120 pesos* ⊠ *Zapiola 143, between Lavalle and Sdo. Sombra, San Antonio de Areco* ☎ *2326/456–376* ⊕ *www.ramosgeneralesareco.com.ar* ⊗ *Open daily for lunch and dinner.*

$$$$
MODERN
ARGENTINE
✕ **Café de las Artes.** The charismatic owner of this intimate restaurant clearly gets a kick out of breaking the rules. Instead of the country-style décor favored by most San Antonio eateries, the walls here are painted bordello red and are cluttered with artworks, photos, and souvenirs from all over the world. Pasta dishes are the specialty: expect unusual combinations like duck ravioli in a saffron and walnut sauce or tenderloin and carrot ravioli in spiced tomato. Only the wine list comes up short—literally so—though the few options are very reasonably priced, as is the food. ⑤ *Average main: 140 pesos* ⊠ *Bolívar 70, San Antonio de Areco* ☎ *2326/456–398* ⊟ *No credit cards* ⊗ *Closed Mon.–Thurs. No lunch Fri.*

$$$$
ARGENTINE
✕ **Puesto la Lechuza.** Your first difficult decision at this waterfront eatery is where to sit: one of the breezy outside tables overlooking the river, or in the rustic yellow-painted interior hung with historic pictures of gauchos. Let gaucho-diet principles guide your order—go for the beef asado or *vacío* (on or off the bone, respectively), slow-cooked over hot coals. The little stage where folky guitar players perform in the evenings

Continued on page 227

7

THE COWBOYS at WORLD'S END

by Victoria Patience

Along a country road, you may come across riders herding cattle. Dressed in baggy pants and shirts, a knife stuck in the back of their belts, these are the descendants of the gauchos, Argentina's cowboys. These men of few words symbolize honor, honesty, and courage— so much so that a favor or good deed is known locally as a *gauchada*.

WHAT'S IN A NAME?

No one can agree on where the word "gaucho" comes from. Some say it's derived from the native Quechua-language word *guachu*, meaning "orphan" or "outcast"; others attribute similar meanings to the French word *gauche*, another suggested source. Yet another theory traces it (via Andalusian Spanish) to the Arabic word *chaouche*, a kind of whip for herding cattle.

Gauchos were the cattle-herding settlers of the pampas (grasslands), renowned for their prowess as horsemen. Most were criollos (Argentina-born descendants of Spanish immigrants) or mestizos (of mixed Spanish and native Argentine descent). They lived in villages but spent much of their time riding the plains, much like North American cowboys.

With the establishment of big estancias (ranches) in the early- and mid-19th century, landowners began taking on gauchos as hired hands. The sheer size of these ranches meant that the gaucho's nomadic lifestyle remained largely unchanged, however.

In the 1860s Argentina's president Domingo Faustino Sarmiento encouraged massive settlement of the pampas, and branded gauchos as barbaric, potentially criminal elements. (Despite being of humble origins, Sarmiento as a snob about anything he saw as uncivilized.) Laws requiring travelers to carry passes ended the gaucho's right to roam. Many more than ever signed on as permanent ranch hands; others were drafted into military service, at times becoming deserters and outlaws.

Vindication came in the late-19th and early-20th century, when a wave of literary works like José Hernández's Martín Fierro and Ricardo Güiraldes's Don Segundo Sombra captured the national imagination with their dramatic, romantic descriptions of gauchos and their nomadic lifestyle. The gaucho—proud, brave, and melancholy—has been a national icon ever since.

Gaucho on an estancia near
El Calafate, Patagonia, Argentina

GAUCHO GEAR

SOMBRERO
Although a sombrero (flat-crowned, wide-brimmed hat) is the most typical style, conical felt hats (shown), berets, flat caps, and even top hats are also worn.

CAMISA
Traditionally smocked shirt with baggy sleeves. Modern gauchos wear regular long-sleeved cotton shirts.

BOMBACHA
Baggy pants cinched at the ankle; the story goes that after the Crimean War, surplus Turkish-style army pants were sold to Argentina by Britain and France. The fashion caught on: no gaucho is seen without these.

BOTAS
Early gauchos wore rough, rawhide boots with open toes or a flip-flop-style thong. Today, gauchos in colder parts of Argentina wear flat-soled, tapered boots, usually with a baggy pirate-style leg.

PAÑUELO
Large, brightly colored kerchief, worn knotted around the neck; some gauchos drape them under their hats to protect their necks from the sun or cold.

CHAQUETA
Jacket; often kept for special occasions, and usually worn short and unbuttoned, to better display the shirt and waistcoat underneath.

CHIRIPÁ
Before bombachas arrived, gauchos used to wind a large swathe of woven fabric (like an oversize loincloth) over thin, long underpants.

FAJA
A long strip of colorful woven fabric once worn to hold the pants up, now mainly decorative and often replaced by a leather belt. Either way, gauchos stick their knives in the back.

ESPUELAS
Spurs; most gauchos favor those with spiked wheel-like designs.

Gaucho traditionally dressed

SUPER GAUCHOS

REBENQUE
A short rawhide crop, often with a decorative metal handle.

PONCHO
Woven from sheep's or llama's wool, usually long and often vertically striped. Some colors denote certain provinces.

ALPARGATAS
Spanish immigrants in the 18th century popularized flat, rope-soled espadrilles in warmer parts of Argentina. Today, rubber-soled versions are more common.

BOLEADORAS
Gauchos adopted this native Argentinian device for catching animals. It's made of two or three stones wrapped in cowhide and mounted at the end of a cowhide cord. You whirl the boleadora then release it at the animal's legs.

LAZO
A braided rawhide lasso used for roping cattle.

CUCHILLO OR FACÓN
No gaucho leaves home without his knife. Indeed, most Argentine men have one to use at barbecues (early gauchos used theirs for fighting, too). Handles are made of wood or horn, blades are triangular.

Unsigned mural of Gauchito Gil, a saint-like character in popular Argentine belief (supposedly a Robin Hood-type outlaw called Antonio Mamerto Gil Núñez).

EL GAUCHITO GIL: legend has it that this gaucho from Corrientes Province was hunted down by a sheriff over a woman. He was hung by his feet from a tree but, just before his throat was cut, he predicted that the sheriff would find his son at home mortally ill and only able to recover if the sheriff prayed to Gil. The prediction came true, and the repentant sheriff spread the word. Today, roadsides all over Argentina are dotted with red-painted shrines to this folk saint. Superstitious locals leave offerings, hoping for help with their problems.

MARTÍN FIERRO: the fictional hero of an eponymous 19th-century epic poem written by José Hernández. Fierro is a poor but noble gaucho who's drafted into the army. He deserts and becomes an outlaw. His pride, independence, and love of the land embody the national ideal of what a man should be. Writer Jorge Luis Borges so loved the poem that he started a literary magazine with the same name.

JUAN MOREIRA: a real-life gaucho who married the daughter of a wealthy landowner, provoking the wrath of a jealous local judge. Wrongly accused of various crimes, Moreira became a fugitive and a famed knife-fighter, killing 16 men before eventually dying in a police ambush in 1874 in the town of Lobos in Buenos Aires Province. A 1973 biographical film by arty local director Leonardo Favio was a box-office smash.

7

IN FOCUS THE COWBOYS AT WORLD'S END

UN DIA DE CAMPO

Gaucho on an estancia near El Calafate, Patagonia, Argentina

In the late 19th century, well-to-do European families bought huge blocks of pampas land on which to build estancias, often with luxurious houses reminiscent of the old country. The advent of industrial agriculture has led many estancias to turn to tourism for income; others combine tourism with small-scale farming.

The gauchos who once herded cows now have a new sideline shepherding visitors, putting on riding shows or preparing large-scale *asados* (barbecues). You can visit an estancia for a *día de campo* (day in the country) or to stay overnight or for a weekend. There are estancias for most budgets: some are ultraluxurious bed-and-breakfasts, others are homey, family-run farms.

A day at an estancia typically involves a late breakfast; horseback riding or a long walk; a full-blown asado accompanied by Argentine red wine; and afternoon tea. Longer stays at upscale establishments might also include golf or other sports; at working farms you can feed animals or help with the milking. Estancia accommodation generally includes all meals, and although some estancias are close to towns, it's rare to leave the grounds during a stay.

HORSEMANSHIP

During a visit to an estancia, you may see gauchos demonstrating traditional skills and games such as:

Zapateo Criollo: a complicated, rhythmic, foot-stomping dance.

Jineteada or Doma: rodeo, gaucho-style.

La Carrera de Sortija: riders gallop under a bar from which metal rings are hung, trying to spear a ring on a stick as they pass.

Carrera Cuadrera: a short horseback sprint that riders start from a standstill.

Boleadas and Pialadas: catching an animal using boleadoras or a lasso, respectively.

La Maroma: participants hang from a bar or rope and jump onto a horse that gallops beneath them.

GAUCHO GRUB

When gauchos were out on the pampas for weeks, even months, at a time, their diet revolved around one food—beef—and one drink—mate (a type of tea). Times may have changed, but most Argentinians still consume a lot of both.

MAKING THE MOST OF AN ASADO

Whether you're just at someone's home or out on an estancia, a traditional Argentinian asado is a drawn-out affair. All sorts of meats go on the grill initially, including chorizo sausage, black pudding, and sweetbreads. These are grilled and served before the larger cuts. You'll probably also be served a picada (cheese, salami, and other snacks). Follow the local example and go easy on these starters: there's lots more to come.

The main event is, of course, the beef. Huge, grass-fed chunks of it, roasted for at least two hours over hot coals and flavored with little more than salt. While the asador (barbecuer) does his stuff, it's traditional to admire his or her skills; interfering (criticism, touching the meat, or the like) is not part of this tradition. The first meat to be served is often thick-cut ribs, accompanied simply by a mixed salad and bread. Then there will be a pause for digestion, and the asador will serve the choicest cuts: flank or tenderloin, usually. All this is washed down with a robust red wine and, not surprisingly, followed by a siesta.

Gaucho *asado* (barbecue), Argentina

MATE FOR BEGINNERS

Mate (mah-tay) is a strong tea made from the dried leaves of *Ilex paraguariensis*, known as yerba. It's drunk from a gourd (also called a mate) through a metal straw with a filter on the end (the *bombilla*).

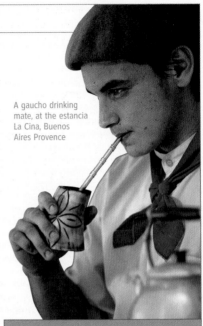

A gaucho drinking mate, at the estancia La Cina, Buenos Aires Provence

Mate has long been a traditional drink for the Guaraní people native to Argentina's northeast. They introduced it to Jesuit missionaries, who learned to cultivate it, and today, most yerba mate is still grown in Misiones and Corrientes provinces. The drink eventually became popular throughout Argentina, Uruguay, and southern Brazil.

Much like tea in England, mate serves as the basis of social interaction: people drink it at any hour of the day. Several drinkers share the same gourd, which is refilled and passed round the group. It's often extended to strangers as a welcoming gesture. If you're shown this hospitality be sure to wait your turn, drink all the mate in the gourd fairly quickly, and hand the gourd directly back to the *cebador* (server). Don't pour yourself a mate if someone else is the cebador, and avoid wiping or wiggling the straw around. Also, you don't say "gracias" until you've had your fill.

WHAT'S IN A MATE?

Caffeine: 30 mg per 8-oz serving (versus 47 mg in tea and 100 mg in coffee)

Vitamins:
A, C, E, B1, B2, B3, B5, B complex

Minerals:
Calcium, manganese, iron, selenium, potassium, magnesium, phosphorus, zinc

Antioxidant properties:
similar to green tea

SERVING MATE

1) Heat a kettle of water to just before boiling (176°F/80°C)—boiling water ruins yerba.

2) Fill ⅔ of the gourd with yerba.

3) Without the bombilla in place, cover the gourd with your hand, and turn it quickly upside down (to get rid of any fine yerba dust that can block the bombilla).

4) For some reason, yerba never sits flat in the gourd; pour some hot water in the empty space left by the slightly slanting yerba leaves. Let the yerba swell a little, cover the top of the bombilla with your thumb, and drive it firmly into the leaves.

5) Finish filling the gourd with water, pouring it in slowly near the bombilla's base. (Some people also add sugar at this point.)

6) Drink all the mate in the gourd (the cebador traditionally drinks first, so the mate isn't so bitter when brewed for others) and repeat Step 5, passing the gourd to the next drinker—and so on—until the yerba mate loses its flavor.

might look touristy, but locals love the singsong here as much as visitors. Weekend reservations are essential. $ *Average main: 125 pesos* ✉ *Victorino Althaparro 423, San Antonio de Areco* ☎ *2326/1540–5745* ▭ *No credit cards.*

WHERE TO STAY

$$$ **Antigua Casona.** The brass bedsteads, antique wardrobes, and embroi-
B&B/INN dered linens of this small B&B make you feel like you're staying in a Merchant-Ivory film. **Pros:** vintage furnishings; sunny patio; two blocks from the main square. **Cons:** high ceilings make some rooms drafty in winter; getting to the bathroom of one room involves crossing the (admittedly pretty) kitchen. $ *Rooms from: 700 pesos* ✉ *Segundo Sombra 495, at Bolívar, San Antonio de Areco* ☎ *2326/453–148* ⊕ *www. antiguacasona.com* ⤳ *6 rooms* ▭ *No credit cards* ⦿ *Breakfast.*

$$$$ **La Bamba de Areco.** Dating from the 1830s, the venerable La Bamba
B&B/INN de Areco was once an important stop along the road from Buenos Aires to the northern reaches of Argentina. **Pros:** plenty of peace and quiet; gorgeous décor; great for outdoors lovers. **Cons:** might be too isolated for some. $ *Rooms from: US$700* ✉ *Ruta 31, San Antonio de Areco* ☎ *2326/454–895* ⊕ *www.labambadeareco.com* ⤳ *11 rooms* ⦿ *All meals.*

$$$$ **Patio de Moreno.** Being in the pampas doesn't mean you have to forget
HOTEL about slick design: this 1910 town house has been transformed into the coolest hotel around. **Pros:** two blocks from main street; beautifully designed rooms and lobby; spacious bathrooms. **Cons:** rooms overlooking street can be noisy; families might be uncomfortable with very adult vibe; service is professional but impersonal. $ *Rooms from: 1200 pesos* ✉ *Moreno 251, at San Martín, San Antonio de Areco* ☎ *2326/455–197* ⊕ *www.patiodemoreno.com* ⤳ *11 rooms* ⦿ *Breakfast.*

NIGHTLIFE

"Pulpería", "almacén" (general store), and "despacho de bebidas" (drinks counter) are some of the labels you might find on San Antonio's many traditional bars. Some genuinely haven't changed in 50 years (neither have their clientele), and others are well-intentioned re-creations; all provide truly atmospheric surroundings for a coffee or a drink.

La Cervecería. Silver and leather aren't the only hand-crafted products in San Antonio. Seven varieties of artisanal beer, brewed on site, have made a name for La Cervecería. The amber-color Scottish ale packs a punch in winter; the paler pilsner's ideal for cooling off in summer. Pizzas, sandwiches, and other snacks accompany them. ✉ *Zapiola 76, San Antonio de Areco* ☎ *15/5163–6764.*

La Esquina de Mertí. Candy jars, old bottles, and a gleaming antique cash register sit atop the decades-old zinc-top bar of La Esquina de Mertí, a gorgeous old café on Plaza Arellano. The owners seem more preoccupied with the charm of the building than that of the waitstaff, so stick with drinks—mugs of icy beer or Cinzano and soda are the local favorites. ✉ *Arellano 149, at Segundo Sombra, San Antonio de Areco* ☎ *2326/456–705.*

SHOPPING

San Antonio de Areco is an excellent place to pick up high-quality hand-icrafts and gifts, especially traditional silverware and leather goods. Workshops that double as stores fill the old houses lining Calle Alsina and other streets leading off Plaza Arellano, the main square.

Cristina Giordano. The handwoven belts and ponchos Cristina Giordano creates in soft, naturally dyed fibers are fit to hang on the wall as art, and have justifiably made her San Antonio's best-known exponent of the traditional craft of weaving. ⊠ *Sarmiento 112, San Antonio de Areco* ☎ *2326/452–829* ⊕ *www.telarcriolloypampa.com.ar.*

Gustavo Stagnaro. Gustavo Stagnaro is a big name in San Antonio silversmithing. His majestic corner store sells gaucho knives, no-nonsense silver jewelry, and maté paraphernalia. ⊠ *Arellano at Matheu, San Antonio de Areco* ☎ *2326/454–801* ⊕ *www.stagnaro.com.ar.*

La Olla de Cobre. All of the mouthwatering chocolates and *alfajores* (dulce de leche sandwiched between two cookies) at La Olla de Cobre are handmade on the premises. Best of all, you can sample at leisure before you buy. ⊠ *Matheu 433, San Antonio de Areco* ☎ *2326/453–105* ⊕ *www.laolladecobre.com.ar* ☉ *Closed Tues.*

Platería de Campo. All the gaucho accessories you can think of—including knives, belt buckles, and kerchief rings—are exquisitely made in silver at Platería del Campo. ⊠ *Alsina 86, San Antonio de Areco* ☎ *2326/456–825* ⊕ *www.plateriadecampo.com.ar* ☉ *Closed Sun.*

IGUAZÚ FALLS

1,358 km (843 miles) north of Buenos Aires; 637 km (396 miles) west of Curitiba; 544 (338 miles) west of Vila Velha.

Iguazú consists of some 275 separate waterfalls—in the rainy season there are as many as 350—that plunge more than 200 feet onto the rocks below. They cascade in a deafening roar at a bend in the Iguazú River (Río Iguazú in Spanish, Rio Iguaçu in Portuguese) where the borders of Argentina, Brazil, and Paraguay meet. Dense, lush jungle surrounds the falls: here the tropical sun and the omnipresent moisture produce a towering pine tree in two decades instead of the seven it takes in, say, Scandinavia. By the falls and along the roadside, rainbows and butterflies are set off against vast walls of red earth, which is so ubiquitous that eventually even paper currency in the area turns red from exposure to the stuff.

The falls and the lands around them are protected by Argentina's Parque Nacional Iguazú (where the falls are referred to by their Spanish name, the Cataratas de Iguazú) and by Brazil's Parque Nacional do Iguaçu (where the falls go by the Portuguese name of Cataratas do Iguaçu).

To visit the falls, you can base yourself in the Argentine town of Puerto Iguazú, or its sprawling Brazilian counterpart, the city of Foz do Iguaçu. The two cities are 18 km (11 miles) and 25 km (15 miles) northwest

of the falls, respectively, and are connected by an international bridge, the Puente Presidente Tancredo Neves.

PUERTO IGUAZÚ, ARGENTINA

Originally a port for shipping wood from the region, Puerto Iguazú now revolves around tourism. This was made possible in the early 20th century when Victoria Aguirre, a wealthy visitor from Buenos Aires, funded the building of a road to the falls. Despite the constant stream of visitors from Argentina and abroad, Puerto Iguazú remains small and sleepy. Many of its secondary roads still aren't paved.

Many travelers to the falls—including those from Brazil—opt to stay on the Argentine side of the border because it's less expensive than the Brazilian side. The town is also a good place to wind down after a day or two of high-energy adventure before heading back to Buenos Aires. So spare some time to experience being surrounded by hummingbirds in a garden, or just grab some *helado* (ice cream) and meander to el Hito Tres Fronteras.

GETTING HERE AND AROUND

Aerolíneas Argentinas flies four to five times daily between Aeroparque Jorge Newbery in Buenos Aires and the Aeropuerto Internacional de Puerto Iguazú, which is about 20 km (12 miles) southeast of Puerto Iguazú; the trip takes 1¾ hours. LAN does the same trip two or three times daily. Normal rates start at about 800 pesos each way. Four Tourist Travel runs shuttle buses from the airport to hotels in Puerto Iguazú. They leave after every flight lands and cost 25 pesos. Taxis to Puerto Iguazú cost 100 pesos.

Vía Bariloche operates several daily buses between the Retiro bus station in Buenos Aires and the Puerto Iguazú Terminal de Omnibus in the center of town. The trip takes 16–18 hours, so it's worth paying the little extra for *coche cama* (sleeper) or *cama ejecutivo* (deluxe sleeper) services, which cost about 903 pesos one-way (regular semi-cama services cost around 410 pesos). You can travel direct to Rio de Janeiro (22 hours) and São Paolo (15 hours) with Crucero del Norte; the trips cost 1,035 and 904 pesos, respectively.

From Puerto Iguazú to the falls or the hotels along RN12, take El Práctico from the terminal or along Avenida Victoria Aguirre. Buses leave every 15 minutes from 7 to 7 and cost 20 pesos round-trip.

There's little point in renting a car around Puerto Iguazú: daily rentals start at 260 to 300 pesos, more than twice what you pay for a taxi between the town and the falls.

Crucero del Norte runs an hourly cross-border public bus service (60 pesos) between the bus stations of Puerto Iguazú and Foz do Iguaçu. Locals don't have to get on and off for immigration, but be sure you do so. To reach the Argentine falls, change to local minibus service El Práctico at the intersection with RN12 on the Argentine side. For the Brazilian park, change to a local bus at the Avenida Cataratas roundabout.

Argentinean travel agency Sol Iguazú Turismo organizes door-to-door transport to both sides of the falls, and can reserve places on the Iguazú Jungle Explorer trips.

Bus Contacts Crucero del Norte ☎ *11/4315–1652 in Buenos Aires, 3757/421–916 in Puerto Iguazú* ⊕ *www.crucerodelnorte.com.ar.* **Four Tourist Travel** ☎ *3757/420–681.* **Vía Bariloche** ☎ *0810/333–7575 in Buenos Aires, 3757/420–854 in Puerto Iguazú* ⊕ *www.viabariloche.com.ar.*

Visitor Info Cataratas del Iguazú Visitors Center ✉ *Off Ruta Nacional 101, Puerto Iguazú* ☎ *3757/491–469* ⊕ *www.iguazuargentina.com* ☉ *Mar.–Aug., daily 8–6; Sept.–Feb., daily 8–8.* **Iguazú Tourist Information** ☎ *3757/491–469* ⊕ *www. iguazuargentina.com.* **Puerto Iguazú Tourist Office** ✉ *Av. Victoria Aguirre 311, Puerto Iguazú* ☎ *3757/420–800* ⊕ *www.iguazuturismo.gov.ar* ☉ *Daily 7–1 and 2–9.* **Sol Iguazú Turismo** ☎ *3757/421–008* ⊕ *www.soliguazu.com.ar.*

EXPLORING

The falls are not the only sites to see in these parts, though few people actually have time (or make time) to go see others.

TOP ATTRACTIONS

Güira Oga. Although Iguazú Falls is home to around 450 bird species, the parks are so busy these days that you'd be lucky to see so much as a feather. It's another story at Güira Oga, which means "House of the Birds" in Guaraní. Birds that were injured, displaced by deforestation, or confiscated from traffickers are brought here for treatment. The large cages also contain many species you rarely see in the area, including the fearsome harpy eagle and the gorgeous red macaw. The sanctuary is in a forested plot just off RN12, halfway between Puerto Iguazú and the falls. The entrance price includes a 90-minute guided visit (in English and Spanish). ⊠ *RN12, Km 5, Puerto Iguazú* ☎ *3757/423–980* ⊕ *www.guiraoga.com.ar* 🖂 *75 pesos* ☉ *Daily 8:30–5.*

WORTH NOTING

Jardín de los Picaflores. With more than 400 species of birds in the national parks surrounding Iguazú Falls, bird-watchers will be kept happily busy. After trekking in the forest for a day or two, the sight of scores of hummingbirds in a more intimate setting might be a birder's dream. This tiny garden north of Puerto Iguazú serves as more of a feeding station than a refuge, but it's busy with the little powerhouses zipping about. ⊠ *Fray Luis Beltran 150, Puerto Iguazú* ☎ *3757/424–081* 🖂 *30 pesos* ☉ *Daily 8:30–6.*

Hito Tres Fronteras. This viewpoint west of the town center stands high above the turbulent reddish-brown confluence of the Iguazú and Paraná rivers, which also form the Triple Frontera, or Triple Border. A mini pale-blue-and-white obelisk reminds you you're in Argentina; across the Iguazú River is Brazil's green-and-yellow equivalent; farther away, across the Paraná, is Paraguay's, painted red, white, and blue. A row of overpriced souvenir stalls stands alongside it. ⊠ *Av. Tres Fronteras, Puerto Iguazú.*

La Aripuca. It looks like a cross between a log cabin and the Pentagon, but this massive wooden structure—which weighs 551 tons—is a large-scale replica of a Guaraní bird trap. La Aripuca officially showcases different local woods, supposedly for conservation purposes—ironic, given the huge trunks used to build it and the overpriced wooden furniture that fills the gift shop. ⊠ *RN12, Km 5, Puerto Iguazú* ☎ *3757/423–488* ⊕ *www.aripuca.com.ar* 🖂 *30 pesos* ☉ *Daily 9–6.*

WHERE TO EAT

$$$$
MODERN
ARGENTINE

✕ **Aqva.** Locals are thrilled: finally, a date-night restaurant in Puerto Iguazú. Although the high-ceiling split-level cabin seats too many to be truly intimate, the owners make up for it with well-spaced tables, discreet service, and low lighting. Softly gleaming timber from different local trees lines the walls, roof, and floor. Local river fish like *surubí* and *dorado* are the specialty: have them panfried, or, more unusually, as pasta fillings. Forget being romantic at dessert time: the chef's signature dessert, fresh mango and pineapple with a torrontés sabayon, is definitely worth keeping to yourself. Reservations are essential on weekends. ⑤ *Average main: 220 pesos* ⊠ *Av. Córdoba at Carlos Thays, Puerto Iguazú* ☎ *3757/422–064* ⊕ *www.aqvarestaurant.com.*

$$$$
ARGENTINE

✕ **La Rueda.** This parrilla is so popular that it starts serving dinner as early as 7:30 pm—teatime by Argentine custom. The local beef isn't quite up to Buenos Aires standards, but La Rueda's perfectly cooked bife de chorizo is one of the best in town. Locally caught surubí is another house specialty, but skip the traditional Roquefort sauce, which overwhelms the fish's flavor. The surroundings stay true to the restaurant's rustic roots: hefty tree trunks hold up the bamboo-lined roof, and the walls are adorned by a curious wooden frieze carved by a local artist. $ *Average main: 200 pesos* ⊠ *Av. Córdoba 28, Puerto Iguazú* ☎ *3757/422–531* ⊕ *www.larueda1975.com.ar* ⌣ *Reservations essential* ☾ *No lunch Mon. and Tues.*

WHERE TO STAY

$$$$
HOTEL

⊡ **Panoramic Hotel Iguazú.** The falls aren't the only good views in Iguazú: half the rooms of this chic hotel look onto the churning, jungle-framed waters of the Iguazú and Paraná rivers. **Pros:** river views; great attention to detail; the gorgeous pool. **Cons:** the in-house casino makes the lobby noisy; staff can seem indifferent; in-house transportation is overpriced. $ *Rooms from: 1627 pesos* ⊠ *Paraguay 372, Puerto Iguazú* ☎ *3757/498–100, 3757/498–050* ⊕ *www.panoramic-hoteliguazu.com* ↝ *91 rooms* ⍵⊙⍵ *Breakfast.*

$$$
B&B/INN

⊡ **Posada 21 Oranges.** Friendly owners Rémy and Romina give you a warm welcome at this rootsy B&B, which is surrounded by a lush garden. **Pros:** wonderfully helpful and attentive owners; peaceful surroundings; abundant homemade breakfasts served on a terrace in the garden. **Cons:** too far from the town center to walk to; low on luxury. $ *Rooms from: 692 pesos* ⊠ *Montecarlo s/n, near RN12, Km 5, Puerto Iguazú* ☎ *3757/494–014* ⊕ *www.21oranges.com* ↝ *10 rooms* ▭ *No credit cards* ⍵⊙⍵ *Breakfast.*

$$$$
B&B/INN

⊡ **Secret Garden Iguazú.** Dense tropical vegetation overhangs the wooden walkway that leads to this tiny guesthouse's three rooms, tucked away in a pale-blue clapboard house. **Pros:** wood deck overlooking the back-to-nature garden; owner's charm and expert mixology; home-away-from-home vibe. **Cons:** the three rooms book up fast; no pool; comfortable but not luxurious. $ *Rooms from: 936 pesos* ⊠ *Los Lapachos 623, Puerto Iguazú* ☎ *3757/423–099* ⊕ *www.secretgardeniguazu.com* ↝ *3 rooms* ▭ *No credit cards* ⍵⊙⍵ *Breakfast.*

$$$$
HOTEL

⊡ **Sheraton International Iguazú.** That thundering you hear in the distance lets you know how close this hotel is to the falls—the lobby opens right onto the park trails, and half the rooms have big balconies with fabulous falls views. **Pros:** the falls are on your doorstep; great buffet breakfasts; well-designed spa. **Cons:** rooms are in need of a complete makeover; mediocre food and service at dinner; other restaurants are an expensive taxi ride away. $ *Rooms from: 3132 pesos* ⊠ *Within Parque Nacional Iguazú, off RN101, Puerto Iguazú* ☎ *3757/491–800* ⊕ *www.sheraton.com* ↝ *176 rooms, 4 suites* ⍵⊙⍵ *Breakfast.*

Continued on page 240

By Victoria Patience

IGUAZÚ FALLS

Big water. That's what *y-guasu*—the name given to the falls by the indigenous Guaraní people—means. As you approach, a thundering fills the air and steam rises above the trees. Then the jungle parts. Spray-soaked and speechless, you face the Devil's Throat, and it's clear that "big" doesn't come close to describing this wall of water.

Taller than Niagara, wider than Victoria, Iguazú's raging, monumental beauty is one of nature's most awe-inspiring sights. The Iguazú River, on the border between Argentina and Brazil, plummets 200 feet to form the Cataratas de Iguazú (as the falls are known in Spanish) or Foz do Iguaçu (their Portuguese name). Considered to be one waterfall, Iguazú is actually made up of around 275 individual drops, that stretch along 2.7 km (1.7 mi) of cliff-face. Ranging from picturesque cascades to immense cataracts, this incredible variety is what makes Iguazú so special. National parks in Brazil and Argentina protect the falls and the flora and fauna that surround them. Exploring their jungle-fringed trails can take two or three days: you get right alongside some falls, gaze down dizzily into others, and can take in the whole spectacle from afar. You're sure to come across lizards, emerald- and sapphire-colored hummingbirds, clouds of butterflies, and scavenging raccoonlike coatis. You'll also glimpse monkeys and toucans, if you're lucky.

GEOLOGY 101

Over 100 million years ago, lava surged up through cracks in the earth's crust near Iguazú. It spread out over the surrounding area, forming three layers of basalt (a dark, fine-grained rock) tens of meters high. The Iguazú River, which starts 1,200 km (745 mi) east, flowed over this. Later, the movement of tectonic plates raised parts of the surface, which became stepped. As the river flowed over these steps it eroded the rock surface it fell on even more, and over the next few million years, the waters carved out what are now the falls.

WHEN TO GO

Time of year	Advantages	Disadvantages
Nov.—Feb.	High rainfall in December and January, so expect lots of water.	Hot and sticky. December and January are popular with local visitors. High water levels stop Zodiac rides.
Mar.—Jun.	Increasingly cooler weather. Fewer local tourists. Water levels are usually good.	Too cold for some people, especially when you get wet. Occasional freak water shortages.
Jul.—Oct.	Cool weather.	Low rainfall in July and August—water levels can be low. July is peak season for local visitors.

WHERE TO GO: ARGENTINA VS. BRAZIL

Argentines and Brazilians can fight all day about who has the best angle on the falls. But the two sides are so different that comparisons are academic. To really say you've done Iguazú (or Iguaçu), you need to visit both. If you twist our arm, we'll say the Argentine side is a better experience with lots more to do, but (and this is a big "but") the Brazilian side gives you a tick in the box and the best been-there-done-that photos. It's also got more non-falls-related activities (but you have to pay extra for them).

	ARGENTINA	BRAZIL
Park Name	Parque Nacional Iguazú	Parque Nacional do Iguaçu
The experience	Up close and personal (you're going to get wet).	What a view!
The falls	Two-thirds are in Argentina including Garganta del Diablo, the star attraction.	The fabulous panoramic perspective of the Garganta do Diablo is what people really come for.
Timing	One day to blitz the main attractions. Two days to explore fully.	Half a day to see the falls; all day if you do other activities.
Other activities	Extensive self-guided hiking and Zodiac rides.	Organized hikes, Zodiac rides, boat rides, helicopter rides, rafting, abseiling.
Park size	67,620 hectares (167,092 acres)	182,262 hectares (450,379 acres)
Animal species	80 mammals/450 birds	50 mammals/200 birds

VITAL STATISTICS

Number of falls: 160—275*	Total length: 2.7 km (1.7 mi)	Average Flow: 396,258 gallons per second Peak Flow: 1,717,118 gallons per second
Major falls: 19	Height of Garganta del Diablo: 82 m (270 feet)	Age: 120—150 million years

*Depending on water levels

IGUAZÚ ITINERARIES

LIGHTNING VISIT. If you only have one day, limit your visit to the Argentine park. Arrive when it opens, and get your first look at the falls aboard one of Iguazú Jungle Explorer's Zodiacs. The rides finish at the Circuito Inferior: take a couple of hours to explore this. (Longer summer opening hours give you time to squeeze in the **Isla San Martín**.) Grab a quick lunch at the Dos Hermanas snack bar, then blitz the shorter Circuito Superior. You've kept the best

Tren Ecologico de la Selva

for last: catch the train from **Estación Cataratas** to **Estación Garganta del Diablo**, where the trail to the viewing platform starts (allow at least two hours for this).

BEST OF BOTH SIDES. Two days gives you enough time to see both sides of the falls. Visit the Brazilian park on your second day to get the panoramic take on what you've experienced up-close in Argentina. If you arrive at 9 AM, you've got time to walk the entire trail, take photos, have lunch in the Porto Canoas service area, and be back at the park entrance by 1 PM. You could spend the afternoon doing excursions and activities from Macuco Safari and Ma-

KEY

♿	Wheelchair-accessible
🍴	Restaurant
🔱	Scenic Viewpoint
---	Walking/Hiking Trails
🚡	Ferry Lines
├┼┤	Rail Lines

Estación Garganta del Diablo

Garganta del Diablo

Garganta del Diablo

ARGENTINA

Parque Nacional do Iguaçu

BRAZIL

Isla San Martín

Río Iguazú

cuco EcoAventura, or visiting the Itaipú dam. Alternatively, you could keep the visit to Brazil for the afternoon of the second day, and start off with a lightning return visit to the Argentine park and see the **Garganta del Diablo** (left) with the sun rising behind it.

SEE IT ALL. With three days you can explore both parks at a leisurely pace. Follow the one-day itinerary, then return to the Argentine park on your second day. Make a beeline for the Gar-

ganta del Diablo, which looks different in the mornings, then spend the afternoon exploring the **Sendero Macuco** (and Isla San Martín, if you didn't have time on the first day). You'll also have time to visit Güira Oga bird sanctuary or La Aripuca (both on RN 12) afterwards. You could spend all of your third day in the Brazilian park, or just the morning, giving you time to catch an afternoon flight or bus.

Walkway view at
Garganta del Diablo

Estación
Central

Estación
Cataratas

Circuito
Superior

Parque Nacional
Iguazú

Circuito
Inferior

Dos Hermanas

VISITING THE PARKS

Visitors gaze at the falls in Parque Nacional Iguazú.

Argentina's side of the falls is in the **Parque Nacional Iguazú,** which was founded in 1934 and declared a World Heritage Site in 1984. The park is divided into two areas, each of which is organized around a train station: Estación Cataratas or the Estación Garganta del Diablo. (A third, Estación Central, is near the park entrance.)

Paved walkways lead from the main entrance past the **Visitor Center,** called *Yvyrá Retá*—"country of the trees" in Guaraní (☏ 3757/49-1469 ⊕ www.iguazuargentina. com ✉ 170 pesos ☉ Mar.–Aug. 8–6; Sept.– Feb. 8–8). Colorful visual displays provide a good explanation of the region's ecology and human history. To reach the park proper, you cross through a small plaza containing a food court, gift shops, and ATM. From the nearby Estación Central, the gas-propelled Tren de la Selva (Jungle Train) departs every 20 minutes.

In Brazil, the falls can be seen from the **Parque Nacional Foz do Iguaçu** (☏ 45/3521–4400 ⊕ www.cataratasdoiguacu.com.br ✉ R$40 ☉ Apr.–Sep 9–5; Oct.–Mar. 9–6). Much of the park is protected rain forest—off-limits to visitors and home to the last viable populations of panthers as well as rare flora. Buses and taxis drop you off at a vast, plaza alongside the park entrance building. As well as ticket booths, there's an ATM, a snack bar, gift shop, and information and currency exchange. Next to the entrance turnstiles is the small **Visitor Center,** where helpful geological models explain how the falls were formed. Double-decker buses run every 15 minutes between the entrance and the trailhead to the falls, 11 km (7 mi) away; the buses stop at the entrances to excursions run by private operators Macuco Safari and Macuco Ecoaventura (these aren't included in your ticket). The trail ends in the **Porto Canoas** service area. There's a posh linen-service restaurant with river views, and two fast-food counters the with tables overlooking the rapids leading to the falls.

VISAS

U.S. citizens don't need a visa to visit Argentina as tourists, but the situation is more complicated in Brazil. ⇨ See the planning section at the beginning of the chapter.

EXCURSIONS IN AND AROUND THE PARKS

A Zodiac trip to the falls.

Iguazú Jungle (☎ 3757/42–1696 ⊕ www. iguazujungle.com) runs trips within the Argentine park. Their standard trip, the Gran Aventura, costs 450 pesos and includes a truck ride through the forest and a Zodiac ride to San Martín, Bossetti, and the Salto Tres Mosqueteros (be ready to get soaked). The truck carries so many people that most animals are scared away: you're better off buying the 75-peso boat trip—Aventura Nautica—separately.

You can take to the water on the Brazilian side with **Macuco Safari** (☎ 045/3574–4244 ⊕ www.macucosafari.com.br). Their signature trip is a Zodiac ride around (and under) the Salto Tres Mosqueteros for R$170. You get a more sedate ride on the Iguaçu Explorer, a 3½ hour trip up the river.

It's all about adrenaline with **Iguazú Forest** (☎ 3757/42–1140 ⊕ www.iguazuforest.com). Their full day expedition involves kayaking, abseiling, waterfall-climbing, mountain-biking, and canopying all within the Argentine park.

In Brazil, **Cânion Iguaçu** (☎ 045/3529–6040 ⊕ www.campodedesafios.com.br) offers rafting and canopying, as well as abseiling over

the river from the Salto San Martín. They also offer wheelchair-compatible equipment.

Argentine park ranger Daniel Somay organizes two-hour Jeep tours with an ecological focus through his Puerto Iguazú–based **Explorador Expediciones** (☎ 3757/49–1469 ⊕ www. rainforest.iguazuargentina.com). The tours cost 260 pesos and include detailed explanations of the Iguazú ecosystem and lots of photo ops. A specialist leads the birdwatching trips, which cost 320 pesos and include the use of binoculars.

Macuco Ecoaventura (☎ 045/3529–9665 ⊕ www.macucoecoaventura.com.br) is one of the official tour operators within the Brazilian park. Their Trilha do Pozo Negro combines a 9-km guided hike or bike ride with a scary boat trip along the upper river (the bit before the falls for R$135). The aptly-named Floating trip is more leisurely; shorter jungle hikes are also offered.

ON THE CATWALK

You spend most of your visit to the falls walking the many trails and catwalks, so be sure to wear comfortable shoes.

FOZ DO IGUAÇU, BRAZIL

The construction of the Itaipú Dam (now the world's second largest) in 1975 transformed Foz do Iguaçu into a bustling city with seven times more people than nearby Puerto Iguazú. It's precisely because of the city's size that many visitors to the falls arrange accommodations in or near Foz do Iguaçu. After daytime adventures in the national park, the city's nightlife extends the fun. Aside from pubs, clubs, and all kinds of live music, there's even a samba show.

GETTING HERE AND AROUND

There are direct flights between Foz do Iguaçu and São Paulo (1½ hours; $230), Rio de Janeiro (2 hours; $260), and Curitiba (1 hour; $280) on TAM, which also has connecting flights to Salvador, Recife, Brasilia, other Brazilian cities, and Buenos Aires. Low-cost airline GOL operates slightly cheaper direct flights on the same three routes.

The Aeroporto Internacional Foz do Iguaçu is 13 km (8 miles) southeast of downtown Foz. The 20-minute taxi ride should cost R$40 to R$50; the 45-minute regular bus ride about R$2.60. Note that several major hotels are on the highway to downtown, so a cab ride from the airport to these may be less than R$30. A cab ride from downtown hotels directly to the Parque Nacional in Brazil costs about R$70.

Via bus, the trip between São Paolo and Foz do Iguaçu takes 15 hours (R$153). The Terminal Rodoviário in Foz do Iguaçu is 5 km (3 miles) northeast of downtown. There are regular buses into town; they stop at the Terminal de Transportes Urbano (local bus station, often shortened to TTU) at Avenida Juscelino Kubitschek and Rua Mem de Sá. From platform 2, Bus No. 120 (labeled "Parque Nacional") also departs every 15 minutes (from 7 to 7) to the visitor center at the park entrance; the fare is R$2.60. The buses run along Avenida Juscelino Kubitschek and Avenida Jorge Schimmelpfeng, where you can also flag them down.

There's no real reason to rent a car in Foz do Iguaçu, as you can't cross the border in a rental car. There are *pontos de taxi* (taxi stands) at intersections all over town. Hotels and restaurants can call you a cab, but you can also hail them on the street.

Bus Contacts Pluma ☎ *045/3522–2988 in Foz do Iguaçu* ⊕ *www.pluma.com.br.*

Visitor Info Foz do Iguaçu Tourist Office ✉ *Praça Getúlio Vargas 69* ☎ *45/3521–1455* ⊕ *www.iguassu.tur.br* ⊙ *8–6.*

EXPLORING

TOP ATTRACTIONS

Itaipú Dam and Hydroelectric Power Plant. It took more than 30,000 workers eight years to build this 8-km (5-mile) dam, voted one of the Seven Wonders of the Modern World by the American Society of Civil Engineers. The monumental structure, which produces 25% of Brazil's electricity and 78% of Paraguay's, was the largest hydroelectric power plant in the world until China's Three Gorges Dam was completed.

You get plenty of insight into how proud this makes the Brazilian government—and some idea of how the dam was built—during the 30-minute video that precedes the hour-long guided panoramic bus tours of

KEY

1 *Exploring sights*

① *Hotels & Restaurants*

Foz do Iguaçu

the complex. Although commentaries are humdrum, the sheer size of the dam is an impressive sight. To see more than a view over the spillways, consider the special tours, which take you inside the cavernous structure and into the control room. Night tours—which include a light-and-sound show—begin at 8 on Friday and Saturday, 9 during the summer months (reserve ahead). ⊠ *Av. Tancredo Neves 6702, Foz do Iguaçu* ☎ *0800/645–4645* ⊕ *www.turismoitaipu.com.br* ☑ *Panoramic tour R\$24, special tour R\$64* ☉ *Regular tours daily 8–4 (on the hr). Special tours daily at 8, 8:30, 10, 10:30, 1:30, 2, 3:30, and 4*

Parque das Aves (*Bird Park*). Flamingos, parrots, and macaws are some of the more colorful inhabitants of this privately run park. Right outside the Parque Nacional Foz do Iguaçu, it's an interesting complement to a visit to the falls. A winding path leads you through untouched tropical forest and walk-through aviaries containing hundreds of species of birds. One of the amazing experiences is the toucan enclosure, where they are so close you could touch them. Iguanas, alligators, and other nonfeathered friends have their own pens. ⊠ *Rodovia das Cataratas, Km 17.1, Foz do Iguaçu* ☎ *045/3529–8282* ⊕ *www.parquedasaves. com.br* ☑ *R\$28* ☉ *Daily 8:30–5.*

WORTH NOTING

Ecomuseu de Itaipú (*Itaipú Eco-Museum*). At the Ecomuseu de Itaipú you can learn about the geology, archaeology, and efforts to preserve the flora and fauna of the area since the Itaipú Dam was built. This museum is funded by the dam's operator, Itaipú Binacional, so the information isn't necessarily objective. ⊠ *Av. Tancredo Neves 6731, Foz do Iguaçu* ☏ *045/3529–2892* ⊕ *www.turismoitaipu.com.br* ⊠ *R$10* ⊙ *Tues.–Sun 8–4:30.*

WHERE TO EAT

$$$$
BRAZILIAN

✕ **Búfalo Branco.** The city's finest and largest churrascaria does a killer *rodizio* (all-you-can-eat meat buffet). The *picanha* (beef rump cap) stands out among the dozens of meat choices, but pork, lamb, chicken, and even bull testicles find their way onto the metal skewers they use to grill the meat. Never fear, vegetarians—the salad bar is also well stocked. The dining room is bright and cheerful, and bow-tied waiters serve your food. ⑤ *Average main: R$90* ⊠ *Av. Rebouças 530, Foz do Iguaçu* ☏ *45/3523–9744* ⊕ *www.bufalobranco.com.br* ⊙ *Daily noon–11.*

$$$$
BRAZILIAN

✕ **Tempero da Bahia.** If you're not traveling as far as Salvador and the state of Bahia, you can at least check out its flavors at this busy restaurant. It specializes in northeastern fare like *moquecas* (a rich seafood stew made with coconut milk and palm oil). The version here is unusual for mixing prawns with local river fish. Spicy panfried sole and salmon are lighter options. The flavors aren't quite so subtle at the all-you-can-eat seafood buffets served several times a week. At R$40, it certainly pulls in crowds. ⑤ *Average main: R$80* ⊠ *Rua Marechal Deodoro 1228, Foz do Iguaçu* ☏ *45/3025–1144* ⊕ *www.restaurantetemperodabahia.com* ⊙ *Mon.–Sat. open from 6, Sun. from noon.*

$$$
SPANISH

✕ **Zaragoza.** On a tree-lined street in a quiet neighborhood, this traditional restaurant's Spanish owner is an expert at matching Iguaçu's fresh river fish to authentic Spanish seafood recipes. Brazilian ingredients sneak into some dishes—the surubí à Goya (catfish in a tomato and coconut-milk sauce) definitely merits a try. ⑤ *Average main: R$50* ⊠ *Rua Quintino Bocaiúva 882, Foz do Iguaçu* ☏ *045/3028–8084* ⊕ *www.restaurantezaragoza.com.br* ⊙ *Daily 11:30–3 and 7–midnight.*

WHERE TO STAY

$$$$
RESORT
Fodor's Choice
★

⊡ **Hotel das Cataratas.** Not only is this stately hotel *in* the national park, with views of the smaller falls from the frontside suites, but it also provides the traditional comforts of a colonial-style establishment: large rooms, terraces, vintage furniture, and hammocks. **Pros:** right inside the park, a short walk from the falls; serious colonial-style charm; friendly, helpful staff. **Cons:** rooms aren't as luxurious as the price promises; far from Foz do Iguaçu so you're limited to the on-site restaurants; only the most expensive suites have views of the falls. ⑤ *Rooms from: R$960* ⊠ *Rodovia das Cataratas, Km 28, Foz do Iguaçu* ☏ *045/2102–7000, 0800/726–4545* ⊕ *www.hoteldascataratas.com.br* ⤴ *198 rooms, 5 suites* ⦿ *Breakfast.*

SIDE TRIPS TO
URUGUAY

WELCOME TO SIDE TRIPS TO URUGUAY

TOP REASONS TO GO

★ **Bask in colonial splendor:** There's little that could be called old in this modern, progressive country—except for the once-walled 1680 Portuguese settlement of Colonia del Sacramento. Flowers spill over balconies, balladeers serenade their sweethearts, and lanterns illuminate the streets of this well-preserved colonial city.

★ **Frolic with the rich and famous:** One visit to Uruguay's tony Punta del Este, and Brazil's beaches will forever seem a tad too déclassé. From December through February, fun-in-the-sun crowds flock here.

★ **Ride 'em, cowboy:** The *gaucho* embodies the country's spirit, and these rugged cowboys still mount their trusty horses to round up livestock on vast ranges. If your time is limited, you don't even need to leave urban Montevideo to see the spectacle: the capital's El Prado district is the site of the best rodeos.

1 Montevideo. True to developing-country patterns, all roads, literal and figurative, lead to Montevideo. Uruguay's friendly capital strings for miles along the southern coast with an odd positioning that means you can walk south, north, or west from the center city to reach the water.

2 Colonia del Sacramento. It's hard not to fall in love with Colonia. The picturesque town has a six-by-six-block old city with wonderfully preserved architecture, rough cobblestone streets, and a sleepy grace. Tranquility reigns here—bicycles and golf carts outnumber cars.

3 Punta del Este. One of the world's trendiest beach communities, Punta del Este is a glitzy destination that doesn't sleep in peak season. Every summer, families and the celebrity jet-set flock to its shore for sun, good food, and luxury.

GETTING ORIENTED

Uruguay is one of South America's smallest countries, both in area (it's roughly the size of England) and population. Montevideo anchors the coast, and most of the population and action hugs the water line. Vast ranches and farms fill the hilly, sparsely developed interior. Uruguay's elite beach destination Punta del Este attracts beachgoers from across South America and beyond while historic Colonia del Sacramento offers a quiet getaway for many Buenos Aires residents who take a quick ferry ride across the Río de la Plata. Ferries also reach Montevideo from Buenos Aires in a couple hours, making Uruguay a favorite and easy trip from Argentina's capital.

8

Updated by Karina Martinez-Carter

It used to be that Uruguay missed out on the touristic attention it deserved, dwarfed by its larger neighbors Argentina and Brazil. That has changed dramatically in the past years, though, as many around the world have turned their attention to this serene, welcoming country. The government has mounted concerted efforts to advertise Uruguay and its offerings to international travelers, and there is plenty to show: Colonia del Sacramento, one of South America's most historic cities; tony resort town Punta del Este; and the coastal capital city Montevideo. Many travelers come away impressed and inspired with Uruguay's tranquil beauty and laid-back vibe.

On a continent with a turbulent past, Uruguayans have parlayed their human and natural resources into a history of success. A strong middle class, a high standard of living, relative prosperity, and a long tradition of peace, good government, and democracy have defined Uruguay (although that last feature did disappear for a dozen years in the last century). The country has enacted landmark legislation that made it the first in South America to sever relations between church and state, to grant women the right to vote, to permit same-sex civil unions, to legalize cannabis, and to enact a generous social-welfare system. The *Economist* even named Uruguay its "country of the year in 2013" for its landmark legislation.

Today about half the country's population lives in Uruguay's capital city. The country takes pride in the number of famous artists it produces, and Uruguayans like to claim their country as the birthplace of the internationally renowned tango singer Carlos Gardel, although the Argentineans and French also vie for this honor. As in Argentina, the legendary *gaucho* is Uruguay's most potent cultural fixture, and it's difficult to pass a day without some reference to these cowboys who once roamed the country singing their melancholy ballads or, of course, to drive without seeing grazing cows or horses. You can still see remnants of the gaucho lifestyle on active ranches throughout the country.

PLANNING

WHEN TO GO

Between October and March the temperatures are pleasant—it's warm and the country is in bloom. Unless you're prepared to tangle with the multitude of tourists that overwhelm Punta del Este in January and February, late spring (November–December) and late winter (March) are the most appealing months to lounge on the beach.

Uruguay's climate has four distinct seasons. Summer (January–March) can be hot and humid, with temperatures as high as 90°F. Fall (April–June) is marked by warm days and evenings cool enough for a light sweater. Winter (July–September) is cold and rainy, with average temperatures generally below 50°F. Although it seldom reaches freezing, the wind off the water can give you quite a chill. Spring (October–December) is much like the fall, except that the trees will be sprouting, rather than dropping, their leaves.

GETTING HERE AND AROUND

AIR TRAVEL

Most international flights land at Montevideo's Aeropuerto Internacional de Carrasco, about 24 km (15 miles) east of downtown. Nearly all Montevideo-bound flights are routed through Buenos Aires. Aerolíneas Argentinas, LAN, GOL, TAM, and Avianca run regular flights to Latin American metropolises like Buenos Aires and São Paulo, and there also is a nonstop American Airlines flight from Miami as well as direct flights to Paris and Madrid.

If you fly a strictly Argentina–Uruguay itinerary, you'll likely depart from Buenos Aires' domestic airport, the Aeroparque Jorge Newbery. Through flights on American Airlines use the capital's international airport at Ezeiza.

Service to the Aeropuerto Internacional de Punta del Este is frequent from many South American cities during the resort's December–March high season, but almost nonexistent the rest of the year.

BOAT TRAVEL

Ferries cross the Río de la Plata between Argentina and Uruguay several times daily. They travel to Montevideo or Colonia, where you can get a bus to Montevideo and Punta del Este. The best companies are Aliscafos, Buquebus, Ferrylíneas Argentina, and Ferry Tur.

BUS TRAVEL

You can go almost anywhere in Uruguay by bus. Some are quite luxurious, with air-conditioning, movies, and snack service. Departures are frequent and fares low. Most companies are based in Montevideo and depart from its state-of-the-art Terminal Tres Cruces. The station's

8

website (⊕ *www.trescruces.com.uy*) lists all bus schedules to and from Montevideo.

CAR TRAVEL

From Argentina you can transport your car across the Río de la Plata by ferry. Alternatively, you can cross the Argentina–Uruguay border in three places: Puerto Unzue-Fray Bentos, Colón-Paysandu, or Concordia-Salto.

Roads between Montevideo and Punta del Este or Colonia del Sacramento are quite good, as are the handful of major highways. In the countryside, roads are usually surfaced with gravel. If you want to leave the main roads, it's best to speak with locals about current conditions before setting off. Trips will often take longer than expected, so budget extra time. On the upside, country roads often have little traffic and spectacular scenery.

Car-rental rates are often higher in Uruguay than in the United States because of the value-added tax. For an economy-size car, expect to pay around US$55 per day. Uruguayans tend to drive carefully, but visitors from Argentina have the reputation of driving with wild abandon. Since almost all roads have only two lanes, keep an eye out for passing vehicles.

HEALTH AND SAFETY

It's a good idea to avoid tap water, as pipes in many older buildings are made of lead. Almost everyone drinks locally bottled *agua mineral* (mineral water), which is available *con gas* or *sin gas* (with or without carbonation).

Uruguay would win most "Safest South American Country" competitions, but standard travel precautions apply. Keep an eye on your purse or wallet, avoid unnecessary displays of wealth, and avoid wandering back streets of Montevideo at night.

RESTAURANTS

Argentina may leap to mind when discussing South American beef, but some 12 million cattle, primarily Hereford and Angus, graze Uruguay's open, vast grasslands—this in a nation of roughly 3 million people. Beef is the staple of the Uruguayan diet. It's quality, cheap, abundant, and often grilled in a style borrowed from the gauchos, and known as *parrillada*. A meal in a Uruguayan steakhouse should be on your agenda. Beef is also made into sausages, such as *chorizo* and *salchicha*, or is combined with ham, cheese, bacon, and peppers to make *matambre*.

Seafood is also popular here—and it's fresh and delicious, especially the *lenguado* (flounder), *merluza* (hake), and *calamar* (squid). Try the *raya a la manteca negra* (ray in blackened butter). If you are not up to a full meal, order what is often considered the national sandwich, *chivito*, a steak sandwich with thin strips of beef.

Uruguayan wines under the Bouza, Santa Rosa, and Calvinor labels are available in most restaurants. As Uruguayan wines also have raised their profile in the past decade, a vineyard visit or wine tasting is highly recommended. *Clericó* is a mixture of white wine and fruit juice, while *medio y medio* is part sparkling wine, part white wine.

Lunch is served between noon and 3; restaurants begin to fill around 12:30 and are packed by 1:30. Many restaurants do not open for dinner until 8 pm, and often don't start to get crowded until 9:30. Most pubs and *confiterías* (cafés) are open all day. Formal dress is rarely required. Smart sportswear is acceptable at even the fanciest establishments.

HOTELS

Hotels here are generally comfortable and good value for your money. Most include breakfast in their rates. All but the most basic hotels have air-conditioning—you'll appreciate it during the hot summers. *Hosterías* are country inns that not only offer modest rooms but are open for dinner as well. Menus tend to be limited, though the food served is unfailingly hearty.

Lodging at the beach requires reservations no matter what the time of year. Rooms fill up quickly (and prices increase dramatically) during the December–February high season. Rates go down during the shoulder months of November and March, but you can still count on good weather. Many hotels close for a few weeks between Easter and late May and/or in September. *Hotel reviews have been shortened. For full information, visit Fodors.com.*

WHAT IT COSTS IN URUGUAYAN PESOS				
	$	$$	$$$	$$$$
RESTAURANTS	Under 301	301–450	451–600	over 600
HOTELS	Under 1,501	1,501–3,000	3,001–4,500	over 4,500

Restaurant prices are the average cost of a main course at dinner or, if dinner is not served, at lunch. Hotel prices are the lowest cost of a standard double room in high season.

VISITOR INFORMATION

Contact Ministry of Tourism and Sport ✉ *Rambla 25 de Agosto 1825, Ciudad Vieja, Montevideo* ☎ *2/1885* ⊕ *www.uruguaynatural.com.*

MONTEVIDEO

Uruguay's capital city hugs the eastern bank of the Río de la Plata. A massive coastal promenade (*malecón*) that passes fine beaches, restaurants, and numerous parks recalls the sunny sophistications of the Mediterranean and is always dotted with Montevideans strolling, exercising, and lounging along the water. Montevideo has its share of glitzy shopping avenues and modern office buildings, balanced with its historic old city and sumptuous colonial architecture, as well as numerous leafy plazas and parks. It is hard not to draw comparisons to its sister city Buenos Aires across the river, and indeed Montevideo strikes many as a calmer, more manageable incarnation of Argentina's capital.

When the weather's good, La Rambla, a 22-km (14-mile) waterfront avenue that links the Old City with the eastern suburbs and changes names about a dozen times, gets packed with fishermen, ice-cream vendors, and joggers. Around sunset, volleyball and soccer games wind down as couples begin to appear for evening strolls. Polls consistently rate Montevideo as having the highest quality of life of any city in Latin America. After one visit here, especially on a lovely summer evening, you probably will agree.

GETTING HERE AND AROUND

BY AIR

Uruguay's principal airport, Aeropuerto Internacional de Carrasco (MVD), is 24 km (15 miles) east of Montevideo. A taxi to downtown costs about 550 pesos; plan on 620 pesos to reach the Ciudad Vieja. A city bus (marked Ciudadela) is cheap—about 26 pesos—but the drawback is that it takes an hour to get downtown.

BY BOAT AND FERRY

Buquebus operates ferry service between Buenos Aires and the ports at Montevideo and Colonia. The trip takes less than three hours to Montevideo and less than four hours to Colonia. A round-trip ticket between Buenos Aires and Montevideo costs about 3,000 pesos. A package that includes a round-trip ticket between Buenos Aires and Colonia and a shuttle bus to or from Montevideo costs about 2,000 pesos.

BY BUS

Montevideo's public buses are a great alternative to taxis, which can be difficult to find during peak hours. Buses crisscross the entire city 24 hours a day. You don't need exact change, and the price for any trip within Montevideo is only 213 pesos.

Colonia is serviced by several regional bus lines, including Cot and TURIL. The three-hour ride costs less than 400 pesos.

BY CAR

Because La Rambla, Montevideo's riverside thoroughfare, extends for dozens of miles, driving is a good way to see the city. Roads are well maintained and drivers obey the traffic laws—a rarity in South America. It's easy to rent a car, both downtown and at the airport. In Montevideo you can rent from several major international companies, including Avis, Budget, and Dollar, and from smaller companies such as Inter Car and Multicar.

BY TAXI

All cabs have meters that count *fichas*, or pulses, each 1/10 km (1/20 mile). When you arrive at your destination, the driver will take out an official chart that calculates the fare from the number of fichas elapsed. You can hail taxis on the street with ease, or call one to pick you up at your hotel. A ride to the airport from the Old City costs about 500 pesos.

SAFETY AND PRECAUTIONS

Although Montevideo doesn't have the problems with crime that larger cities in South America do, it's best to watch your wallet in crowded markets and to avoid walking down deserted streets at night. Most of Montevideo's residents stay up late, so the streets are usually full of people until 1 am. The city bus authority discourages boarding empty buses at night. Look for the helpful tourist police decked out in blue berets and yellow vests that say *policía turística*. They patrol Avenida

18 de Julio, the Ciudad Vieja, and the Mercado del Puerto.

ESSENTIALS

Air Contacts Aerolíneas Argentinas ☎ 0810/222-86527 ⊕ www.aerolineas. com.ar. **Aeropuerto Internacional de Carrasco** ⊠ Ruta 101, Km 19.950, Ciudad de la Costa, Canelones ☎ 2604-0329 ⊕ www.aeropuertodecarrasco. com.uy. **American Airlines** ☎ 800/437-300 ⊕ www.aa.com.

Boat Contacts Buquebus ☎ 4316-6500 ⊕ www.buquebus.com.

Bus Contacts COT ☎ 2409-4949 in Montevideo ⊕ www.cot.com.uy. **Terminal Tres Cruces** ⊠ Bulevar General Artigas 1825, Centro ☎ 2401-8998 ⊕ www. trescruces.com.uy. **Turil** ☎ 477-1990 in Montevideo ⊕ www.turil.com.uy.

Car-Rental Contacts Avis ☎ 5982-1700 ⊕ www.avis.com.uy. **Dollar** ☎ 2682-8350 at Aeropuerto de Carrasco ⊕ www.dollar.com.uy.

Taxi Contacts Taxi Aeropuerto Internacional de Carrasco ☎ 2604-0323 ⊕ www.taxisaeropuerto.com.

Visitor Information Ministry of Tourism and Sport ⊠ Rambla 25 de Agosto 1825, Ciudad Vieja ☎ 2/1885 ⊕ www.uruguaynatural.com. **Ministerio de Turismo** ⊠ Rambla 25 de Agosto 1825, Ciudad Vieja ☎ 2900-1078 ⊕ www. uruguaynatural.com.

EXPLORING

Modern Montevideo expanded outward from the peninsular Ciudad Vieja, the Old City, still noted for its narrow streets and mix of elegant colonial and art deco architecture. El Prado, an exclusive enclave a few miles north of the city center, is peppered with lavish mansions and grand parks. When you remember that these mansions were once summer homes for aristocratic Uruguayans who spent most of the year elsewhere, you'll get some idea of the wealth this small country once enjoyed.

CIUDAD VIEJA

Ciudad Vieja is fairly compact, and you could walk from one end to the other in about 15 minutes. Take care at night, when the area is fairly deserted.

TOP ATTRACTIONS

Fodor's Choice ★ **Mercado del Puerto.** For Montevideo's quintessential lunch experience, head to the old port market, a restored 1868 building of vaulted iron beams and colored glass, and a terrific example of urban renewal at its best. The market shields 14 stalls and eateries where, over large fires, the best *asado* (barbecue) in the city is cooked. It's a mix of casual lunch-counter places and sit-down restaurants. The traditional drink here is a bottle of medio y medio. Many other eateries congregate outside

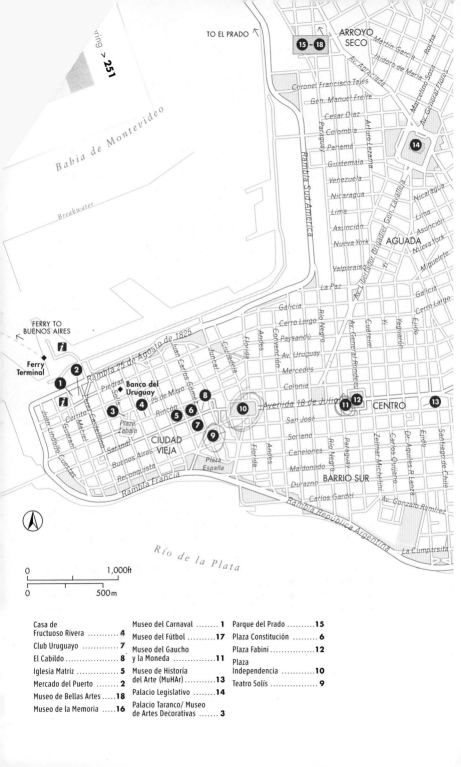

Bahía de Montevideo

Breakwater

ARROYO SECO

AGUADA

CENTRO

BARRIO SUR

CIUDAD VIEJA

FERRY TO BUENOS AIRES

Ferry Terminal

TO EL PRADO

Banco del Uruguay

Plaza Zabala

Plaza España

Plaza Independencia

Río de la Plata

| 0 | | 1,000ft |
| 0 | | 500m |

around the perimeter of the building and are open for dinner as well as lunch. ✉ *Rambla 25 de Agosto, between Av. Maciel and Av. Pérez Castellano, across from port, Piedras 237, Ciudad Vieja* ⊕ *www. mercadodelpuerto.com.uy* ◷ *Daily 11–6.*

Museo del Carnaval. Move over, Rio. Montevideo's annual Carnaval celebration may be more low-key than that of its northern neighbor,

CRIOLLAS

Also known as *jineteadas,* the Uruguayan-style rodeos called *criollas* are held all over the country, but the most spectacular one takes place in Montevideo's El Prado neighborhood every Easter. Gauchos from all over the country come to display their skill in riding wild horses.

but it lasts for a full 40 days. This museum next to the Mercado del Puerto celebrates and honors the pre-Lenten festivities year-round with displays featuring the elaborate costumes and photos of processions. Guided tours are available. ✉ *Rambla 25 de Agosto 1825, Ciudad Vieja* ☎ *2915–0807* ⊕ *www. museodelcarnaval.org* 💲 *80 pesos* ◷ *Tues.–Sun. 11–5.*

Fodor'sChoice
★
Plaza Independencia. Connecting Cuidad Vieja and the Centro, Independence Square is the heart of Montevideo. All that remains of the original walls of the Spanish fort is the Puerta de la Ciudadela, the triumphal gate to the Old City. In the center stands a 30-ton statue of General José Gervasio Artigas, the father of Uruguay and the founder of its 19th-century independence movement. At the base of the monument, polished granite stairs lead to an underground mausoleum that holds Artigas's remains. The mausoleum is a moving memorial: bold graphics chiseled in the walls of this giant space detail the feats of Artigas's life. Two uniformed guards dressed in period uniforms stand at solemn attention beside the urn in this uncanny vault. There's a changing of the guard every Friday at noon.

Towering over the north side of the plaza, the 26-story **Palacio Salvo** was the tallest building in South America when it inaugurated in 1928 (it's still one of the tallest buildings in Uruguay). Today this emblematic art deco edifice is simply an office building. It was here where the palace now stands that Gerardo Matos Rodríguez composed *La Cumparsita,* a famous tango that transformed into a Uruguayan cultural hymn. You can still hear strains playing around the building twice a day.

WORTH NOTING

Casa de Fructuoso Rivera. Once the home of General Fructuso Rivera, Uruguay's first president, this neoclassical Rivera House from the early 1800s was acquired by the government in 1942 and opened as a national history museum. Exhibits inside this pale yellow colonial house with an octagonal cupola document the development of Uruguay and showcase daily life in Montevideo of the 1900s. ✉ *Calle Rincón 437, Ciudad Vieja* ☎ *2915–1051* ⊕ *www.museohistorico.gub.uy* 💲 *Free* ◷ *Tues.–Fri. 11–4.*

Club Uruguay. Uruguay's most prestigious private social club, founded in 1888, is headquartered in this eclectic, three-story neoclassical national monument on the south side of Plaza Matriz. The club was formed

The Plaza Independencia is the heart of Montevideo, a great place for history lovers and people-watchers.

for high society of European descent, but today is open to the public. Friendly, English-speaking guides happily bring visitors up the marble staircases so that they can marvel at the elegant salons. The club also hosts cultural events, including music performances and art shows, throughout the year. Nonmembers are welcome at the on-site bar and restaurant, but full access to the club's luxe facilities, including a library and billiards room, is reserved exclusively for its members. ⊠ *Calle Sarandí 584, Ciudad Vieja* 🕾 *2915–7820* ⊕ *www.cluburuguay.com.uy* 🖃 *Free* ☉ *Weekdays 9–8.*

El Cabildo. The original City Hall is where the Uruguayan constitution was signed in 1830. This two-story colonial edifice houses an impressive collection of paintings, antiques, costumes, and rotating history exhibits. Fountains and statuary line the interior patios. English-speaking guides are available. ⊠ *Calle Juan Carlos Gómez at Calle Sarandí, Ciudad Vieja* 🕾 *2915–9685* ⊕ *www.cabildo.montevideo.gub.uy* 🖃 *Free* ☉ *Wed.–Fri. noon–5:45, Sat. 11–4.*

Iglesia Matriz. It's officially the Cathedral of the Immaculate Conception and St. Phillip and St. James, but it is known to Montevideans as the Matriz ("head") Church, as well as the Catedral Metropolitana de Montevideo. The cathedral is the oldest public building in Montevideo, with a distinctive pair of dome-cap bell towers that stand guard over the plaza below. Besides its rich marble interior, colorful floor tiling, stained glass, and dome, the Matriz Church is notable as the final resting place of many of Uruguay's most important political and military figures. ⊠ *Calle Ituzaingó 1373, at Calle Sarandí, Ciudad Vieja* 🕾 *2915–7018* ⊕ *www.arquidiocesis.net* ☉ *Daily 9–7; mass Sat. at 5, Sun. at 11 and 5.*

Palacio Taranco/Museo de Artes Decorativas. Built in 1907, the ornate Taranco Palace in the Ciudad Vieja is representative of the French-inspired architecture favored in fin-de-siècle Montevideo. Even the marble for the floors was imported from France. Today you can survey that bygone glory in the palace's new incarnation as the Museo de Artes Decorativas (Museum of Decorative Arts). Its rooms are filled with period furniture, statuary, draperies, clocks, and portrait paintings. A cultural center within has a calendar of performances and live music. ⊠ *Calle 25 de Mayo 376, Ciudad Vieja* ☎ *2915–6060* ⊕ *www.mec.gub. uy/museoartesdecorativas* ☜ *Free* ☉ *Weekdays 12:30–5:40.*

Plaza Constitución. This plaza, also known as Plaza Matriz, is the heart of Montevideo's Ciudad Vieja. An ornate cantilever fountain in the center of this tree-filled square was installed in 1871 to commemorate the construction of the city's first water system.

Fodor's Choice ★ **Teatro Solís.** Named in honor of the discoverer of the Río de la Plata, Juan Díaz de Solís, the 1856 Solís Theater is famed for its fine acoustics. Informative guided tours of the building are offered in Spanish; call ahead to arrange one in English for a small extra cost. (The afternoon tours are occasionally canceled if the theater is in use for rehearsals.) The theater maintains an active calendar of concerts, dance, and plays, all in Spanish, and all for prices much lower than you'd pay for a comparable evening back home. ⊠ *Reconquista at Bartolomé Mitre, Ciudad Vieja* ☎ *1950–3323* ⊕ *www.teatrosolis.org.uy* ☜ *Tours 20 pesos (free Wed.)* ☉ *Tours Tues. and Thurs. at 4, Wed., Fri., and Sun. at 11, noon, and 4, Sat. at 11, noon, 1, and 4.*

CENTRO

Montevideo's main street, the Avenida 18 de Julio, runs through the heart of the city's center. You'll find everything here—shops and museums, cafés and plazas, bustling traditional markets, chrome-and-steel office towers, and places to change money. The avenue runs east from Plaza Independencia, away from the Ciudad Vieja, passing through bustling Plaza Fabini and tree-lined Plaza Cagancha.

It's a 20-minute walk from Plaza Independencia to the Palacio Municipal. If shopping is your main interest, you may want to devote an entire afternoon to browsing and buying along the avenue.

TOP ATTRACTIONS

Fodor's Choice ★ **Museo del Gaucho y la Moneda** (*Cowboy and Coin Museum*). This museum is in a rococo 19th-century mansion near Calle Julio Herrera y Obes, four blocks east of Plaza Independencia. Here you'll find articles from the everyday life of the gauchos, from traditional garb to the detailed silver work on the cups used for maté (an indigenous herb from which tea is brewed). Ancient South American and European coins are on the first floor. Tours in English are available with a couple days' notice. ⊠ *Av. 18 de Julio 998, Centro* ☎ *2900–8764* ☜ *Free* ☉ *Weekdays 10–4.*

Museo de Historia del Arte (MuHAr). In the Palacio Municipal (an ambitious name for this unremarkable brick city hall) you'll find the Museum of Art History, which has the country's best collection of pre-Columbian and colonial artifacts. You'll also find Greek, Roman, and Middle

Eastern art, including ceramics and other antiquities. On the street level is the **Biblioteca de Historia del Arte** (Library of Art History), worth a stop if you're a student of the subject matter. ⊠ *Calle Ejido 1326, Centro* ☎ *1950–2191* ⊕ *www.muhar.montevideo.gub.uy* 🖺 *Free* ☉ *Museum Tues.–Sun. noon–5:30. Library weekdays 9:30–4:30.*

WORTH NOTING

Plaza Fabini. In the center of this lovely, manicured square is the Monumento del Entrevero, a large sculpture depicting a whirlwind of gauchos, *criollos* (mixed-blood settlers who are half native, half European), and native Uruguayans in battle. It's one of the last works by sculptor José Belloni (1882–1965). An open-air market takes place here every morning. ⊠ *Bounded by Av. 18 de Julio and Calles Río Negro, Colonia, and Julio Herrera y Obes, Centro.*

EL PRADO

The district known as El Prado lies roughly 6 km (4 miles) north of Plaza Independencia. You could make the long uphill walk along the busy Avenida Agraciada, but it's a lot easier in a taxi. It is pleasant to walk along Avenida Buschental in fall and spring when the trees are in full color. The Jardín Botánico (Botanical Garden) inside the Parque del Prado is a worthwhile stop, where you can admire thousands of plant species, many of which were brought to Uruguay in the 19th century by Charles Racine.

TOP ATTRACTIONS

Museo de Bellas Artes (*Museum of Fine Arts*). Known locally as the Blanes Museum, the Museum of Fine Arts is housed in an elegant colonial mansion that once belonged to Uruguay's foremost 19th-century painter, Juan Manuel Blanes. He was entirely self-taught, and did not begin painting until he was in his fifties. His realistic portrayals of gauchos and the Uruguayan countryside compose the core of the museum's collection. ⊠ *Av. Millán 4015, El Prado* ☎ *2336–2248* ⊕ *blanes. montevideo.gub.uy* 🖺 *Free* ☉ *Tues.–Sun. 12:15–5:45.*

Palacio Legislativo. Almost 50 different types of native marble were used in the construction of the Legislative Palace, the seat of Uruguay's bicameral legislature. Free Spanish- and English-language tours are available when the congress is in session; passes are available inside at the information desk. ⊠ *Av. Agraciada at Av. Flores, El Prado* ☎ *2200–1334* 🖺 *US$3 for foreigners* ☉ *Weekdays 9–6; tours at 10:30 and 3:30.*

Parque del Prado. The oldest of the city's parks is also one of the most popular. Locals come to see El Rosedal, the rose garden with more than 800 different varieties, and the fine botanical garden. Also in the 262-acre park you'll find the statue called *La Diligencia*, by sculptor José Belloni. ⊠ *Av. Carlos Brussa, El Prado* ☉ *Daily 7–7.*

WORTH NOTING

Museo del Fútbol. "Other countries have their history," Helenio Herrera, Uruguay's most famous soccer coach once said. "We have our fútbol." Indeed, *fútbol*—that's "soccer" to U.S. readers—is played anywhere there's space, by kids of all ages. Uruguay both hosted and won the first World Cup competition in 1930 here at the Estadio Centenario. In the pits of the stadium is this museum dedicated to the country's soccer heritage. It's worth a detour if you're a big fan of the sport. ✉ *Av. Ricaldoni s/n, El Prado* ☏ *2480–1259* ⊕ *www.auf.org.uy* 🖃 *100 pesos* ⊙ *Weekdays 10–5.*

Museo de la Memoria. The question still pains Uruguayans who remember the era: How did South America's strongest democracy dissolve into 12 years of brutal military dictatorship? This museum documents the history of the 1973–85 period that people here call simply the *dictadura*, during which an astounding 2% of the population experienced arrest for "political crimes" at some time or other. (The government did not begin investigating abuses by the military government until 2011.) The museum won't be a stop on most visitors' Montevideo itineraries, but if you're a student of Latin American history and politics, it's worth a look. ✉ *Av. Las Instrucciones 1057, El Prado* ☏ *2355–5891* ⊕ *mume. montevideo.gub.uy* 🖃 *Free* ⊙ *Mon.–Sat. noon–6 (1–7 in summer).*

GREATER MONTEVIDEO

FAMILY
Fodor'sChoice
★

Playa de los Pocitos. This stretch of sand is the city's most attractive beach, and surprisingly tranquil. Throughout the day you'll see locals running, biking, strolling, and rollerblading along the *rambla* (boardwalk) here. Snap a picture with the sculpture spelling out "Montevideo" for a classic tourist shot. **Amenities:** food and drink; lifeguards; showers; toilets. **Best for:** solitude; sunrise; sunset; swimming; walking. ✉ *Rambla Perú at Gabriel A. Pereira, Pocitos.*

OFF THE
BEATEN
PATH

Bodega Bouza. Argentina and Chile grab all the attention in discussions of South American wines, but Uruguay has a number of impressive wineries of its own. It's worth stopping by the Bodega Bouza outside of Montevideo for a tour and sampling; it's one of the few wineries open for daily visits. For a real treat (US$80), reserve the works: a tour, tasting, and extravagant lunch with, of course, wines to accompany each course. It's worth visiting the winery for its standout restaurant alone. ✉ *Camino de la Redención 7658* ☏ *2323–7491* ⊕ *www.bodegabouza. com* 🖃 *Tours US$20, with sampling US$38* ⊙ *Tours weekdays at 11, 1:30, and 4, weekends at 11 and 4.*

8

WHERE TO EAT

Montevideo was not long ago a city that almost exclusively subsisted on steak and potatoes and pastas, but the city's restaurant scene has experienced a slow-but-sure emergence the past decade. You still can find all the tasty steak you want, but offerings have diversified with an increasing number of international and fusion restaurants. From fine dining to quality chivito joints, you'll have your share of memorable meals in Montevideo.

CIUDAD VIEJO

$
SOUTH
AMERICAN

✕ **Café Bacacay.** This small and smartly designed restaurant facing Teatro Solís inhabits a building that dates to 1844 and attracts a young, hip crowd. The owner takes special care in preparing the excellent salads, such as the Bacacay (spinach, raisins, carrots, nuts, grilled eggplant) or the Sarandí (celery, chicken, apples, carrots). ⑤ *Average main: 120 pesos*

✉ *Bacacay 1306, at Calle Buenos Aires, Ciudad Vieja* ☎ *2916–6074* ⊕ *www.bacacay.com.uy* ☽ *Closed Sun.*

$$
SOUTH
AMERICAN

✕ **Jacinto.** The smell of fresh-baked bread wafts through this pleasant, sunny spot off Plaza Zabala. Plates are fresh, inspired, and expertly prepared, from the soup of the day to desserts like panna cotta with red grapes and a sweet orange sauce. Jacinto is a favorite among the city's foodie crowd and stylish set. ⑤ *Average main: 400 pesos* ✉ *Sarandí 349, Ciudad Vieja* ☎ *2915–2731* ⊕ *www.jacinto.com.uy* ☽ *Closed Sun. No dinner.*

$$$$
EUROPEAN

✕ **Rara Avis.** Located in the Teatro Solís theater building, Rara Avis is one of Montevideo's best restaurants. Both the food—such as a black-oyster risotto with smoked salmon or duck magret in baby greens with a pepper sauce—and the setting are sophisticated. It's a great option for the pre- and posttheater crowds. ⑤ *Average main: 700 pesos* ✉ *Buenos Aires 652, Ciudad Vieja* ☎ *2915–0330* ⊕ *www.raraavis.com.uy* ☽ *Closed Sun. No lunch Sat.*

CENTRO

$$
SOUTH
AMERICAN

✕ **Corchos Bistro y Boutique de Vinos.** Uruguay's wines take center stage at this unpretentious restaurant located near Plaza Independencia. Wine is even incorporated into most dishes, including a salad with wine-soaked pears and white wine–infused chorizo. The fixed-price lunch menu is a hit with professionals who work nearby, and the prices won't hold you back from ordering another glass (or flight) of wine either. Corchos' staff also can arrange tastings and tours upon request. ⑤ *Average main: 400 pesos* ✉ *25 de Mayo 651, Centro* ☎ *2917–2051* ⊕ *www.corchos. com.uy* ☽ *Closed weekends. No dinner Mon.–Thurs.*

GREATER MONTEVIDEO

$$
SOUTH
AMERICAN

✕ **Expreso Pocitos.** This classic and beloved diner-style establishment has been around for more than a century, and it is clear that some of the customers have been frequenting it for almost as long. Many congregate here for a coffee or beer, and the chivito, which is made with fresh, fluffy bread, is considered one of the best in town. ⑤ *Average main: 350 pesos* ✉ *Benito Blanco at Av. Brasil, Pocitos* ☎ *2708–1828.*

$$$$
SOUTH
AMERICAN
Fodor'sChoice
★

✕ **La Casa Violeta.** Meats are the specialty at this beautiful restaurant facing Puerto del Buceo, one of the prettiest spots in the city. You can opt for a steak tasting menu that is served in the method called *espeto corrido*, with meat brought to your table on a long skewer. There's also a salad bar, which not many restaurants of this type can claim. There's a big deck shaded with umbrellas and with attractive views of the port and surrounding homes. ⑤ *Average main: 900 pesos* ✉ *Rambla Armenia 3667, corner of 26 de Marzo, Puerto del Buceo, Pocitos* ☎ *2628–7626* ⊕ *www.lacasavioleta.com.*

$$$$
MEDITERRANEAN

✕ **Restaurant Francis.** This bright, upscale restaurant is a local favorite and always filled, yet the efficient, friendly staff manages to keep up. The menu is gourmet and extensive, ranging from sushi to paella to cuts of meat on the grill. Everything is high quality and innovative, but the seafood dishes in particular stand out, like the *chipirones* (baby cuttlefish) in a garlic and parsley sauce with grilled onions. ⑤ *Average* *main: 700 pesos* ✉ *Luis de la Torre 502, Punta Carretas* ☎ *2711–8603* ⊕ *www.francis.com.uy.*

$$$ ✕ **Tandory.** With Tandory, French-Uruguayan chef and owner Gabriel
INTERNATIONAL Coquel has created an intimate yet convivial restaurant with top-level
Fodor'sChoice service. Fusion dishes harmoniously blend Asian, Latin American,
★ and European flavors, and the eclectic décor includes heirlooms and
souvenirs from his travels around the world. Diplomats, tourists, and
well-traveled Uruguayans seeking cuisine more inspired than steak and
potatoes fill the tables here. The menu changes daily based on what's
fresh and in season, and don't worry if you can't decide what to order.
Coquel frequently pops by diners' tables to offer suggestions. ⑤ *Average
main: 600 pesos* ✉ *Ramon Masini at Libertad, Pocitos* ☎ *2709–6616*
⊕ *www.tandory.com.uy* ☽ *Closed Sun.*

WHERE TO STAY

Many downtown hotels are grouped around the big three squares:
Plaza Independencia, Plaza Fabini, and Plaza Cagancha. In the weeks
before and after Carnaval in February, rooms become hard to come by.
Otherwise, rooms are plentiful in summer, when beach-bound residents
desert the city.

CENTRO

$$ ⛳ **Oxford Hotel.** Glass walls, broad windows, and mirrors give the small
HOTEL lobby an open but intimate feel, much like that of the hotel itself. **Pros:**
central location; attentive staff. **Cons:** some oddly configured rooms;
small bathrooms. ⑤ *Rooms from: 1840 pesos* ✉ *Calle Paraguay
1286, Centro* ☎ *2902–0046* ⊕ *www.hoteloxford.com.uy* ↘ *66 rooms*
|⊙| *Breakfast.*

$$$ ⛳ **Radisson Montevideo Victoria Plaza.** This luxurious glass-and-brick
HOTEL structure overlooks Plaza Independencia and blends harmoniously with
the surrounding architecture. **Pros:** great location for sightseeing; attentive staff; many amenities. **Cons:** some reports of window frames that
rattle with temperature changes. ⑤ *Rooms from: 4000 pesos* ✉ *Plaza
Independencia 759, Centro* ☎ *2902–0111* ⊕ *www.radisson.com.uy*
↘ *190 rooms, 64 suites* |⊙| *Breakfast.*

$$$$ ⛳ **Sheraton Montevideo.** One of the city's biggest hotels is removed from
HOTEL the Old City, and, decidedly modern, feels a world away. **Pros:** attentive
staff; many amenities; shopping nearby. **Cons:** distant from downtown
and sights. ⑤ *Rooms from: 6000 pesos* ✉ *Victor Soliño 349, Punta
Carretas* ☎ *2710–2121* ⊕ *www.starwoodhotels.com/sheraton* ↘ *197
rooms, 10 suites* |⊙| *No meals.*

GREATER MONTEVIDEO

$$ ⛳ **Armon Suites.** This hotel in a quiet neighborhood east of downtown
HOTEL is an all-suites hotel, and the spaces are huge. **Pros:** good value; ample-
size suites. **Cons:** far from sights. ⑤ *Rooms from: 2760 pesos* ✉ *21
de Setiembre 2885, Pocitos* ☎ *2712–4120* ⊕ *www.armonsuites.com.
uy* ↘ *40 rooms* |⊙| *Breakfast.*

$$ ⛳ **Hotel Ermitage Montevideo.** The Ermitage is in an unprepossessing,
HOTEL sandstone-front building overlooking the lovely Plaza Tomás Gomen-
soro, and is a good, affordable choice if you want to be near the shore.

8

Where to Eat and
Stay in Montevideo

TO EL PRADO

ARROYO
SECO

AGUADA

Palacio
Legislativo

CENTRO

CIUDAD
VIEJA

BARRIO
SUR

FERRY TO
BUENOS AIRES

Ferry
Terminal

Bahia de Montevideo

Breakwater

Banco del
Uruguay

Plaza
Independencia

Plaza
Zabala

Plaza
España

Río de la Plata

0   1,000ft
0   500m

7 - 14

Pros: great location in attractive Pocitos; wonderful historic building; good value. **Cons:** far from sights. ⑤ *Rooms from: 2000 pesos* ✉ *Calle Juan Benito Blanco 783, Pocitos* ☎ *2710–4021, 2711–7447* ⊕ *www.ermitagemontevideo.com* ➲ *100 rooms* ﹫ *Breakfast.*

$$$$
HOTEL
Fodor'sChoice
★

☷ **Sofitel Montevideo Casino Carrasco & Spa.** Originally opened in 1921 as a summer escape for the Uruguayan elite, this stunning Belle Époque waterfront building, known as the "palace on the sand," underwent an intensive restoration process and reopened in splendor as part of the Sofitel chain. **Pros:** attractive casino, restaurant, and bar on site; inspired spa treatments. **Cons:** a lengthy taxi ride to the sights of Montevideo. ⑤ *Rooms from: 6560 pesos* ✉ *Rambla República de México 6451, Montevideo* ☎ *598/2604–6060* ⊕ *www.sofitel.com* ➲ *93 rooms, 23 suites* ﹫ *No meals.*

SMOKE-FREE URUGUAY

Lighting up is prohibited in enclosed public places, including stores, offices, transportation terminals, restaurants, bars, and casinos. Ubiquitous black-red-and-white signs in Spanish, English, and Portuguese remind patrons of the law. Heavy fines both to noncomplying smokers and to the locale where they're caught mean nearly perfect compliance.

NIGHTLIFE

Montevideo's nightlife scene is a smattering of pubs, bars, clubs, and tango and folk music venues. With few exceptions, bars and clubs come to life around 1 am and don't close until it's time for breakfast. Still, "after office" outings are popular, which is essentially happy hour with groups hitting the bars on an earlier-than-usual schedule.

BARS AND PUBS

La Pasiva. For an ice-cold beer, this popular beer house is a late-night favorite. The specialties are frankfurters, chivitos, and other bar food. In good weather you can socialize at the outdoor tables in Plaza Matriz. This Montevideo staple has franchises throughout the city, including a prominent location on Plaza Fabini. ✉ *Calle Sarandí at Calle J. C. Gómez, Ciudad Vieja* ☎ *2915–7988* ➪ *Reservations not accepted* ▭ *No credit cards.*

Shannon Irish Pub. This pub in the Old City is a classic Montevideo nightlife spot with good rock music and an unpretentious vibe. ✉ *Mitre 1318, Ciudad Vieja* ☎ *2916–9585* ⊕ *www.theshannon.com.uy.*

Volvé Mi Negra. Lines form frequently outside this nightlife spot on weekends, where locals come for generous-sized drinks. While it's technically a pub complete with wood paneling, bar stools, and pool tables, live DJs get people dancing and give it a club vibe. ✉ *Francisco Muñoz 3177, Pocitos* ☎ *9708–7922* ⊕ *www.volveminegra.com.*

DANCE CLUBS

2 am. If you're itching to indulge in a full night out in Montevideo, make this *boliche* (club) your destination. Appropriately named, 2 am opens its doors at that hour to the city's young and stylish set, who dance into the morning to the beats of cumbia and Top 40. ⊠ *Rambla Wilson at Requena y Garcia, Punta Carretas* ⊙ *Closed Sun.–Thurs.*

Fodor'sChoice ★   **Lotus Club.** Located in Montevideo's World Trade Center, this club for years has been considered one of Montevideo's best. The red-and-black color scheme gives the place an upscale feel, and Montevideans dance until the wee hours under shimmering disco balls. Get your night out started early on Wednesday at the "after-office" party. ⊠ *Lecuender at Bonavita, Pocitos* ☎ *2628–1379* ⊕ *www.lotus.com.uy* ⊙ *Closed Sun.–Tues.*

TANGO SHOWS

Joventango. If you're itching to try out your dance steps, Joventango is the best place in the city to learn tango. Shows are frequent; call or check the website for times. ⊠ *Calle San José 1314, Centro* ☎ *2908–1550* ⊕ *www.joventango.org.*

SHOPPING

Let's face it: Montevideans head to Buenos Aires when they want to go on an extra-special shopping excursion. But quality and selection are decent here, and prices often are lower than in Argentina. Stores in Centro, along Avenida 18 de Julio, offer the standard selection of urban merchandise. The truly fun shopping experience is to be found in the city's markets, which are vibrant and numerous.

ANTIQUES

Calle Tristán Narvaja north of Avenida 18 de Julio is packed with antiques shops. In the Old City, the streets north of Plaza Constitución are also lined with such stores.

Louvre. This antiques store is the only source for handmade and painted trinket boxes—the perfect *recuerdos* (souvenirs). It also offers an impressive selection of jewelry and silver. ⊠ *Calle Sarandí 652, Ciudad Vieja* ☎ *2916–2686* ⊕ *www.louvreantiguedades.com.uy.*

HANDICRAFTS

Fodor'sChoice ★   **Manos del Uruguay.** With six locations total in Montevideo, Punta del Este, and Colonia del Sacramento, Manos del Uruguay stock a wide selection of woolen wear and locally produced ceramics crafted by women's artisan cooperatives around the country. ⊠ *Punta Carretas Shopping, José Ellauri 350, Centro* ☎ *2710–6108* ⊕ *www.manos.com.uy.*

JEWELRY

Giamen. Giamen carries amethyst and topaz jewelry, agate slices, and elaborate objects made of precious gems. ⊠ *Av. 18 de Julio 948, Centro* ☎ *2902–2572.*

LEATHER

Montevideo is a good source for inexpensive leather. Shops near Plaza Independencia specialize in hand-tailored coats and jackets made out of nutria (fur from a large semiaquatic rodent).

Casa Mario. Casa Mario has a particularly good selection of leather clothes. As a bonus, they offer free transportation, which your hotel can arrange. ⊠ *Calle Piedras 641, Centro* ☎ *2916–2356* ⊕ *www. casamarioleather.com.*

MARKETS

Weekend ferias (open-air markets) are the best place for leisurely browsing among a warren of crafts stalls. Government regulations dictate that all ferias must close in the early afternoon, so make sure to arrive by 10 am.

El Mercado de la Abundancia. Dating back to 1836, El Mercado de la Abundancia is a fun indoor market in Centro, a few blocks from the Palacio Municipal. Inside are a tango dance center, a handful of good choices for a lunchtime parrillada, and a crafts fair. ⊠ *Aquiles Lanza 1312, Centro.*

Fodor'sChoice **Feria Tristán Narvaja.** Started in the early 1900s by Italian immigrants,
★ Feria Tristán Narvaja is Montevideo's top attraction on Sunday and one of the city's largest and most popular fairs. (It operates only on Sunday, a day when all other markets, and much of the city, are closed. Hours run about 9–4.) The fair, a 5- to 10-minute walk from the Old City and in the Centro district, is plentifully stocked with secondhand goods and antiques. ⊠ *Dr. Tristán Narvaja at Av. Uruguay, Centro.*

Plaza Cagancha. Between Avenida 18 de Julio and Calle Rondeau in Centro, Plaza Cagancha regularly has vendors set up in the area selling trinkets and crafts. ⊠ *Av. 18 de Julio between Av. Gral Rondeau and Pasaje de los Derechos Humanos.*

SHOPPING CENTERS

Fodor'sChoice **Punta Carretas Shopping.** Housed in a former prison, Punta Carretas
★ Shopping is the city's largest and most upscale mall, measuring in at around 200 stores mixing local and international brands. It's in a pleasant residential area near the Sheraton Montevideo, a 10-minute cab ride from the Old City. ⊠ *Calles Ellauri and Solano, Punta Carretas* ☎ *2711–6940* ⊕ *www.puntacarretasshopping.com.uy.*

COLONIA DEL SACRAMENTO

The peaceful cobbled streets of Colonia are just over the Río de la Plata from Buenos Aires, but they seem a world away. Charm might be an overused descriptor, but Colonia, with its old-world architecture, serenity, and water lapping at sandy shores is a place that redefines it.

The best activity in Colonia is walking through its peaceful Barrio Histórico (Old Town), a UNESCO World Heritage Site. Porteños come to Colonia for romantic getaways or for a break from the city. If you like to keep busy on your travels, a late-morning arrival and early-evening departure give you plenty of time to see the sights and wander at will. To really see the city at its own pace, spend the night in one of its many colonial-style bed-and-breakfasts: This offsets travel costs and time and makes a visit here far more rewarding.

GETTING HERE AND AROUND

Hydrofoils and ferries cross the Río de la Plata between Buenos Aires and Uruguay several times a day. Boats often sell out, particularly on summer weekends, so book tickets at least a few days ahead. The two competing companies that operate services—Buquebus and Colonia Express—often wage a reduced-rates war in the low season.

Buquebus provides two kinds of service for passengers and cars: the quickest crossing takes an hour by hydrofoil and the slower ferry takes around three hours. The Buquebus terminal in Buenos Aires is at the northern end of Puerto Madero at the intersection of Avenida Alicia M. de Justo and Avenida Córdoba (which changes its name here to Bulevar Cecilia Grierson). It's accessible by taxi or by walking seven blocks from L. N. Alem subte station along Trinidad Guevara.

Colonia Express operates the cheapest and fastest services to Colonia but has only four daily services in each direction. There often are huge discounts on the 50-minute catamaran trip if you buy tickets in advance. The Colonia Express terminal in Buenos Aires is south of Puerto Madero on Avenida Pedro de Mendoza, the extension of Avenida Huergo. It's best reached by taxi, but Bus No. 130 from Avenidas Libertador and L. N. Alem also stops outside it.

The shortest way to the Barrio Histórico is to turn left out of the port parking lot onto Florida—it's a six-block walk. Walking is the perfect way to get around this part of town; equally practical—and lots of fun—are golf carts and sand buggies that you can rent from Thrifty.

ESSENTIALS

Ferry Contacts Buquebus ⊠ *Av. Antartida Argentina 821, Puerto Madero, Buenos Aires* ☎ *11/4316–6500* ⊕ *www.buquebus.com* ⊠ *Av. Córdoba 867, Centro, Buenos Aires.* **Colonia Express** ⊠ *Av. Pedro de Mendoza 330, La Boca, Buenos Aires* ☎ *11/4317–4100 in Buenos Aires* ⊕ *www.coloniaexpress.com* ⊠ *Av. Córdoba 753, Centro, Buenos Aires.*

Rental Cars Thrifty ⊠ *Av. Gral. Flores 172* ☎ *4522–2939* ⊕ *www.thrifty.com.uy.*

Taxi Contact Taxis Colonia ☎ *598/4522–2920.*

Visitor Information Colonia del Sacramento Tourism Office ⊠ *Manuel Lobo, between Ituzaingó and Paseo San Antonio* ☎ *4522–6886* ⊕ *www. coloniaturismo.com.*

EXPLORING

Begin your tour at the reconstructed Portón de Campo or city gate, where remnants of the old bastion walls lead to the river. A block farther is Calle de los Suspiros, the aptly named Street of Sighs, a cobblestone stretch of one-story colonials that can rival any street in Latin America for sheer romantic effect. It runs between a lookout point on the river, called the Bastión de San Miguel, and the Plaza Mayor, a lovely square filled with Spanish moss, palms, and spiky, flowering *palo borracho* trees. The many cafés around the square are ideal places to take it all in. Clusters of bougainvillea flow over the walls here and in the other

Cobblestones abound in the Old Town section of Colonia del Sacramento, Uruguay.

quiet streets of the Barrio Histórico, many of which are lined with art galleries and antiques shops.

Another great place to watch daily life is the Plaza de Armas Manoel Lobo, where you can find the Iglesia Matriz, the oldest church in Uruguay. The square itself is crisscrossed with wooden catwalks over the ruins of a house dating to the founding of the town. The tables from the square's small eateries spill from the sidewalk right onto the cobblestones: they're all rather touristy, but give you an excellent view of the drum-toting *candombe* (a style of music from Uruguay) squads that beat their way around the Old Town each afternoon.

You can visit all of Colonia's museums with the same ticket, which you buy from the Museo Portugués or the Museo Municipal for about $2.50. Most take only a few minutes to visit, but you can use the ticket on two consecutive days.

TOP ATTRACTIONS

Faro (*Lighthouse*). Towering above the Plaza Mayor is the lighthouse, which was built in 1857 on top of a tower that was part of the ruined San Xavier convent. The whole structure was engulfed in flames in 1873 after a lighthouse keeper had an accident with the oil used in the lamp at the time. Your reward for climbing it are great views over the Barrio Histórico and the River Plate. ⊠ *Pl. Mayor* ☉ *Weekdays 1–sunset, weekends 11 am–sunset.*

Museo Portugués. The museum that's most worth a visit is this one, which documents the city's ties to Portugal. It's most notable for its collection of old map reproductions based on Portuguese naval expeditions. A small selection of period furnishings, clothes, and jewelry from

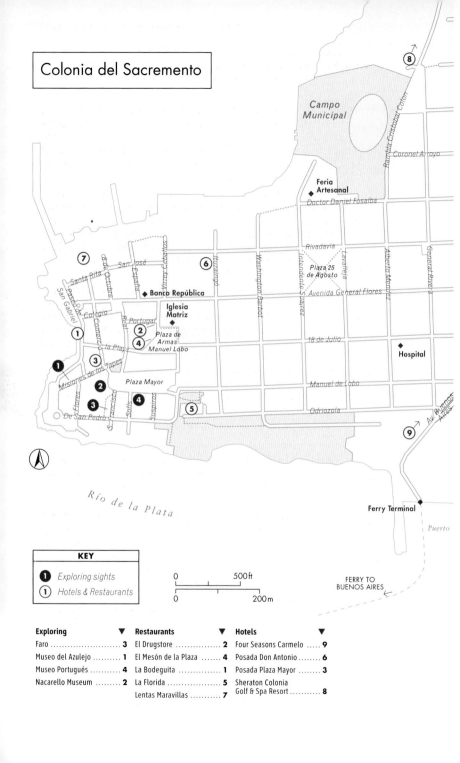

Colonia del Sacremento

Campo Municipal

Rampla Cristobal Colon

Coronet Arraya

Feria Artesanal

Doctor Daniel Fosalba

Rivadavia

Lavalleja

Alberto Mendez

General Rivera

Plaza 25 de Agosto

Avenida General Flores

Washington Barbot

Intendente Suarez

Tirzango

⑥

de 8 Octubre

San José

Santa Rita

Espana

Virrey Cebellas

Portugal

Banco República

Iglesia Matriz

Plaza de Armas Manuel Lobo

Comercio

Real

18 de Julio

Hospital

Calego

❶

②

④

de la Playa

San Gabriel

Paseo del

③

❶

Misiones de los Tapes

Plaza Mayor

❷

④

Manuel de Lobo

⑦

Flores

Solis

Suspiros

❸

⑤

Odriozola

Av. Buenos Aires

⑨

De San Pedro

Río de la Plata

Ferry Terminal

Puerto

KEY

❶ Exploring sights
① Hotels & Restaurants

0   500 ft
0   200 m

FERRY TO
BUENOS AIRES

Colonia's days as a Portuguese colony complete the offerings. Exhibits are well labeled, but in Spanish only. ⊠ *Pl. Mayor between Calle de los Suspiros and De Solís* ⊙ *Thurs.–Tues. 11:15–4:45.*

WORTH NOTING

Museo del Azulejo. A small collection of the beautiful handmade French majolica tiles that adorn fountains all over Colonia are on display at the tile museum, housed in a small 18th-century building near the river. The 50-peso entry fee is good for all Colonia's museums. ⊠ *Misiones de los Tapies 104, at Paseo San Gabriel* 🕾 *4522–1056* ⊕ *www.museoscolonia. com.uy* ⊙ *Sat.–Wed. 11:15–4:45.*

Nacarello Museum. A colonial Portuguese residence has been lovingly re-created inside this 17th-century structure. The simple bedroom and kitchen furnishings are period pieces, but the real attraction is the house itself, with its thick, whitewashed walls and low ceilings. For 50 pesos you gain access to all Colonia's museums, including this one. ⊠ *Pl. Mayor at Henríquez de la Peña* ⊕ *www.museoscolonia.com.uy* ⊙ *Wed.– Thurs. and Sat.–Mon. 11:15–4:45.*

OFF THE BEATEN PATH

Narbona Wine Lodge. For an upscale, indulgent Uruguayan wine experience, Narbona Wine Lodge is your place. The peaceful property includes a vineyard, a restaurant with exposed-brick walls that serves Italian-influenced dishes featuring the wines and products like cheeses made on site, and a luxurious tasting room. If you understandably find yourself unable to leave at the end of the day, book a stay at one of property's five sophisticated, bright, and homey rustic rooms named after varietals. Your stay includes a vineyard tour, mountain bikes for borrowing, and access to Narbona's private beach. ⊠ *Ruta 21, Km 268, Carmelo* ⊕ *www.narbona.com.uy.*

8

WHERE TO EAT

In Colonia, both dollars and Uruguayan pesos are accepted. Uruguayan food is as beef-based as Argentine fare, and also has a notable Italian influence. Here, enticing cafés and restaurants with plaza and riverfront views are numerous.

$$
SOUTH
AMERICAN

✕ **El Drugstore.** The colorful, eclectic decor has turned this restaurant into a notorious spot in tranquil Colonia. You'll find Uruguayan standby dishes like pastas and chivito on the menu, all of which come in generous portions. People are drawn to this restaurant for its relaxed, funky ambience, which the open kitchen and frequent live musicians enhance. Outdoor tables on the plaza are prime real estate. ⑤ *Average main: 450 pesos* ⊠ *Portugal 174* 🕾 *4522–5241.*

$$
MEDITERRANEAN

✕ **El Mesón de la Plaza.** Simple dishes—many steak-based—made with good-quality ingredients have made this traditional restaurant a favorite with porteño visitors to Colonia. The comprehensive wine list showcases Uruguayan vineyards hard to sample anywhere outside the country. Try to get one of the outside tables that sit right on the peaceful Plaza de Armas. Guitar-strumming musicians regularly play for diners, adding to the ambience. ⑤ *Average main: 400 pesos* ⊠ *Vasconcellos 153* 🕾 *598/4522–4807* ⊙ *No dinner Mon.*

$ ✕ **La Bodeguita.** This hip restaurant serves delicious, crispy pizza, sliced
SOUTH into bite-size rectangles. The backyard tables overlook the river, and
AMERICAN inside is cozy, with warm walls. The terrace is a great spot for a bite
and beer when it's warm. $ *Average main: 150 pesos* ⊠ *Calle del Com-*
ercio 167 ☎ *598/4522–5329* ⊕ *www.labodeguita.net* ▭ *No credit cards*
⊘ *Closed Mon. in winter. No lunch Tues.–Fri.*

$$$$ ✕ **La Florida.** The black-and-white photos, lace tablecloths, and quaint
LATIN AMERICAN knickknacks that clutter this long, low house belie the fact that it was
Fodor'sChoice once a brothel. It still has private rooms, but it's dining that politicians
★ and the occasional celeb rent them for these days. You, too, can ask
to be seated in one, but consider the airy back dining room, which has
views over the river. It's hard to say if it's the flamboyant French-Argen-
tinean owner's tall tales that keep regulars returning or his excellent
cooking. Specialties include kingfish, sole, and salmon cooked to order.
You can suggest sauces of your own or go with house suggestions like
orange-infused cream. $ *Average main: 800 pesos* ⊠ *Odriozola 215*
☎ *598/094 293–036* ⊕ *www.restoranlaflorida.com* ▭ *No credit cards*
⊘ *Closed Wed. Dinner by reservation only Apr.–Nov.*

$ ✕ **Lentes Maravillas.** There's no spot more perfect in Colonia to while
CAFÉ away an afternoon with a leisurely lunch or tea than this café nestled
Fodor'sChoice along the water. The baked goods are not to be missed—the *redon-*
★ *dos* (rich, round cheesecakes) are particularly heavenly. Lounge in the
lush, enclosed yard, or cozy into the main dining room, which feels
like a friend's welcoming living room, complete with a bookshelf for
borrowing and perusing. $ *Average main: 250 pesos* ⊠ *Santa Rita 61*
☎ *4522–0636* ▭ *No credit cards* ⊘ *Closed Wed. No dinner.*

WHERE TO STAY

Since Colonia is the consummate day trip from Montevideo or Buenos
Aires, few visitors actually spend the night here. Consider breaking that
mold; there's no shortage of homey lodgings to choose from, and an
overnight stay really gives you the opportunity to unwind and adopt
the relaxed Colonia pace.

$$$$ ⌷ **Four Seasons Carmelo.** Serenity pervades this harmoniously deco-
RESORT rated resort an hour west of Colonia del Sacramento, reachable by
Fodor'sChoice car, boat, or a 25-minute flight from Buenos Aires. **Pros:** all rooms are
★ spacious bungalows; fabulous, personalized service; on-site activities
compensate for distance to sights and restaurants. **Cons:** despite copi-
ous netting and bug spray, the mosquitoes can get out of hand; food
quality is erratic; noisy families can infringe on romantic getaways.
$ *Rooms from: 11500 pesos* ⊠ *Ruta 21, Km 262, Carmelo* ☎ *4542–*
9000 ⊕ *www.fourseasons.com/carmelo* ⬐ *20 bungalows, 24 duplex*
suites ⍾⌷ *Breakfast.*

$$ ⌷ **Posada Don Antonio.** Long galleries of rooms overlook an enormous
HOTEL split-level courtyard at Posada Don Antonio, the latest incarnation of
a large, elegant building that has housed one hotel or another for close
to a century. **Pros:** sparkling turquoise pool, surrounded by loungers;
two blocks from the Barrio Histórico; rates are low, but there are proper
hotel perks like poolside snacks. **Cons:** ill-fitting doors let in courtyard

noise; some rooms open onto the street. ⑤ *Rooms from: 2500 pesos* ✉ *Ituzaingó 232* ☎ *598/4522–5344* ⊕ *www.posadadonantonio.com* ⮐ *38 rooms* ⦿ *Breakfast.*

$$ ⌂ **Posada Plaza Mayor.** A faint scent of jasmine fills the air at this lovely
B&B/INN   old hotel, where all the rooms open onto a large, plant-filled court-yard complete with a bubbling fountain. **Pros:** beautiful green spaces; on a quiet street of the Barrio Histórico; cheerful, accommodating staff. **Cons:** cramped bathrooms; the three cheapest rooms are small. ⑤ *Rooms from: 2865 pesos* ✉ *Calle del Comercio 111* ☎ *598/4522–3193* ⊕ *www.posadaplazamayor.com* ⮐ *17 rooms* ⦿ *Breakfast.*

$$$ ⌂ **Sheraton Colonia Golf & Spa Resort.** This riverside hotel and spa is a
RESORT   favorite with porteños on weekend escapes. **Pros:** peaceful location with river views from many rooms; great spa; rooms are often discounted midweek. **Cons:** it's a 10-minute drive or taxi ride north of the Barrio Histórico; can be noisy on weekends. ⑤ *Rooms from: 3900 pesos* ✉ *Continuación Rambla de las Américas s/n* ☎ *4522–9000* ⊕ *www.sheraton.com* ⮐ *96 rooms, 8 suites* ⦿ *Breakfast.*

PUNTA DEL ESTE

Fodor'sChoice   *134 km (83 miles) east of Montevideo.*
★

Often likened to the Hamptons or St-Tropez, Punta del Este is a flashy destination where parties run nonstop in peak season. But it is also a destination that draws a range of beachgoers to its shores, from summering families to the celebrity jet-set. There's a bustling city on the beach downtown, as well as quiet countryside populated solely with upscale ranches called *chacras* or *estancias*, and creative, buzzing hamlets like La Barra and José Ignacio. Though it's pricey and at times a logistical challenge to get around, everyone finds something about Punta to love.

The resort takes its name from the "east point" marking the division of the Río de la Plata on the west from the Atlantic Ocean to the east. It also lends its name to the broader region encompassing the nearby communities of Punta Ballena and La Barra de Maldonado. These days even José Ignacio, some 20 miles away, is grouped in. It's usually a given that Argentina's upper class spends at least part of the summer in Punta, soaking in the ample rays.

GETTING HERE AND AROUND

Most visitors headed to the beach fly into Montevideo's Aeropuerto Internacional de Carrasco (MVD). Flights arrive from many South American cities, in high season only, directly to the Aeropuerto Internacional de Punta del Este (PDP), about 24 km (15 miles) east of town.

Many bus lines travel daily between Montevideo's Terminal Tres Cruces and Punta del Este's Terminal Playa Brava. Two companies that serve the entire region are Copsa and Cot. Buquebus also offers flights, and ferries with a bus connection to Punta.

To get to Punta del Este from Montevideo, follow Ruta 1 east to the Ruta 93 turnoff. The road is well maintained and marked, and the trip

8

takes about 1½ hours. Rental agencies, such as Avis, Budget, and Dollar, are in downtown Punta del Este.

SAFETY AND PRECAUTIONS

For such a touristy locale, Punta maintains a reassuring level of security. Nevertheless, it pays to watch your things. Swimming is not safe at several of the beaches, especially those on the Atlantic side of the point. Never swim alone, and gauge your abilities carefully.

ESSENTIALS

Airport Contact Aeropuerto Internacional de Punta del Este ✉ *Ruta 93, Km 113* ☎ *4255–9777* ⊕ *www.puntadeleste.aero.*

Bus Contacts COT ☎ *2409–4949 in Montevideo* ⊕ *www.cot.com.uy.* **Copsa** ☎ *2902–1818* ⊕ *www.copsa.com.uy.* **Terminal de Omnibus** ✉ *Rambla Artigas and Calle 32.*

Visitor and Tour Information Maldonado Tourist Office ✉ *Parada 1, Calles 31 and 18* ☎ *4222–1921.* **Punta del Este Tourist Office** ✉ *Av. Gorlero* ☎ *4244–8685* ⊕ *www.turismo.gub.uy.*

EXPLORING

TOP ATTRACTIONS

Avenida Gorlero. Punta del Este is circled by the Rambla Artigas, the main coastal road that leads past residential neighborhoods and pristine stretches of beach. You can find everything on Avenida Gorlero, Punta's main commercial strip. The thoroughfare runs northeast–southwest through the heart of the peninsula and is fronted with cafés, restaurants, boutiques, and casinos.

Casapueblo. A hotel and museum at the tip of a rocky point with tremendous views of the Río de la Plata is the main draw in Punta Ballena, east of Punta del Este. Uruguayan abstract artist Carlos Páez Vilaró created his work as a "habitable sculpture" and it defies architectural categorization. With allusions to Arab minarets and domes, cathedral vaulting, Grecian whitewash, and continuous sculptural flourishes that recall the traceries of a Miró canvas, this curvaceous 13-floor surrealist complex climbs up a hill and looks like nothing else in South America—or anywhere much else.

The spaces include an excellent series of galleries dedicated to the artist's work. Here you can see photos of him with friends like Picasso and peruse copies of his books. One book tells the true story of his son Carlos Miguel, who survived a plane crash in the Andes, which was made into the 1993 film *Alive.* ✉ *Punta Ballena* ☎ *4257–8611* ⊕ *www.clubhotelcasapueblo.com* 🖾 *180 pesos* ☉ *Daily 10–dusk.*

Isla de Lobos. This island is a government-protected natural reserve and national park home to one of the world's largest colonies of sea lions. You can view them from tour boats that leave regularly from the marina. Its 1907 lighthouse stands nearly 190 feet tall.

Restaurants ▼

Hotels ▼

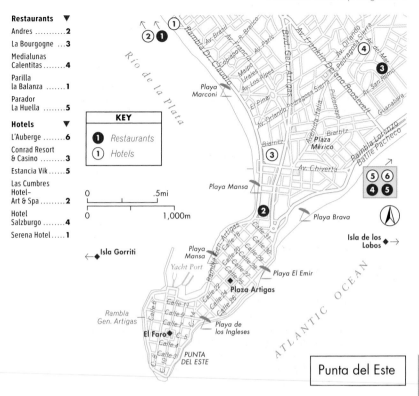

Punta del Este

8

WORTH NOTING

Arboretum Lussich. Naturally perfumed with the scent of eucalyptus, this huge arboretum is one of the most important botanical gardens in the world. Its creation was the labor of love of Croatian-Uruguayan botanist Antonio Lussich (1848–1928). The approximate 474 acres contain more than 350 species of trees from outside Uruguay as well as 70 domestic species. Guided tours are in Spanish only. ⊠ *Av. Antonio Lussich* ☎ *4257-8077* ☒ *Free* ☉ *Jan. and Feb., daily 8–8; Mar.–Dec., daily 9–6.*

Isla Gorriti. Once the site of a prison, Isla Gorriti now attracts a different type of exclusive crowd. High-end residents with their own boats often set Gorriti as their destination to play and party for the day. You can catch a ferry ride from the marina, though, and make a day trip of it. Note that the island is reachable only by boat, (The *parador,* or beach club, has a good restaurant.)

Punta del Este Port. Punta's sunsets seem even more spectacular when witnessed over its port, with sails and boats dotting the bay. Stop for a drink at any one of the many restaurants lining the street, or make it your destination for a leisurely walk or scenic run. ⊠ *2 de Febrero at Mareantes.*

BEACHES

This stretch of coast has a dozen or so beaches, each with its own high-season personality. All bets are off on activity levels the rest of the year, and remember: what's hot one season may be so "last year" the next. Punta is that kind of place. Locals frequently shorthand things to the *mansa* (calm) side fronting the Río de la Plata—many sections are fine for swimming—and the *brava* (rough) side lining the Atlantic Ocean—its waves draw surfers but should make you think twice about going into the water. By law, all beaches in Uruguay are public.

RÍO DE LA PLATA SIDE

Playa Chihuahua. Uruguay's only sanctioned nude beach—look for the *playa naturista* ("naturalist beach") sign—sits out near the airport west of Punta Ballena and divides into a straight and a gay section. Be cool about it if you go: no cameras, no binoculars, no gawking. **Amenities:** none. **Best for:** nudists.

Playa El Chiringo. This beach, just east of Punta Ballena, can be a bit rough, with gritty sand and deep water. Chiringo catches full sun at midmorning, but shadows descend as the afternoon progresses, and the sun sets behind Punta Ballena. The wind and waves make swimming risky here. **Amenities:** lifeguards. **Best for:** solitude; sunrise.

FAMILY
Fodor'sChoice
★
Playa Mansa. The waters are calm at Punta's longest beach and one of its most popular. Good sand, shallow water, many food stands, and proximity to the center of town make it the area's most family-oriented stretch of coast. Catch good sunset views here, and take in one of the late-afternoon beach aerobics classes, too. **Amenities:** food and drink; lifeguards; parking; showers; toilets; water sports. **Best for:** sunset; swimming; walking.

Playa Solanas. The famous Casapueblo museum and hotel sit above this calm beach, also called Portezuelo, at Punta Ballena. Its shallow water shielded from the wind makes it a favorite of families with small children. Great sunset views are a plus here, too. **Amenities:** lifeguards; showers; toilets. **Best for:** sunrise; sunset; swimming; walking.

ATLANTIC SIDE

Fodor'sChoice
★
La Barra. The La Barra hamlet is both artistic and trendy, with a number of popular boutiques, restaurants, and nightlife spots. A mostly locally patronized beach sits here, too, where the Río Maldonado spills into the ocean. Keep in mind that swimming is risky. **Amenities:** food and drink; lifeguards; parking; toilets. **Best for:** partiers; sunrise; sunset; surfing; walking.

In high season, people come to see and be seen at Punta del Este's glamorous beaches.

Fodor's Choice
★ **José Ignacio.** This hamlet with a vibrant art community and some of the most jaw-dropping properties for miles is the choice beach for Punta's most well-heeled and stylish. José Ignacio sits on a miniature peninsula and has beaches with both calm and rough waters. Because it's just enough outside the downtown Punta orbit, visiting is a day trip for most. **Amenities:** food and drink; lifeguards; toilets. **Best for:** partiers; sunrise; sunset; surfing; swimming; walking; windsurfing.

SUNRISE, SUNSET

How many beach resorts let you enjoy spectacular sunrises *and* sunsets over the water? Punta's orientation on a narrow north–south peninsula allows you to take in both.

Playa de los Ingleses. While this beach has fine sand, the wind and waves are strong here. Venture into the water at your own risk. You're still close to the center of Punta, meaning this beach sees many nonswimming visitors. Restaurants lining this so-called "Englishmen's Beach" were the spots for afternoon tea in a bygone era. **Amenities:** none. **Best for:** walking.

Playa El Emir. This beach is named for an eccentric Middle Eastern emir who vacationed here and built a house near this stretch of sand. High waves make this beach popular with surfers but somewhat dangerous for swimmers. **Amenities:** food and drink; lifeguards; showers; toilets. **Best for:** surfing; walking.

Playa Brava. The golden sand and numerous food stands here draw a young crowd that mostly stays on the beach rather than braving the rough water. Brava is one of the most frequented beaches—largely thanks to *La Mano de Punta,* a giant sculpture with the fingers of an enormous hand appearing to reach out of the sand—where many visitors will surely be snapping photos. This work by Chilean artist Mario Irarrázabal gives the beach its colloquial name, Playa de los Dedos (Beach of the Fingers). **Amenities:** food and drink; lifeguards; showers; toilets. **Best for:** sunrise; sunset; walking.

Playa Montoya. Just east of La Barra beach (but still belonging to La Barra) is this stretch of sand, where a young, attractive crowd mostly stays dry but always seems to have a volleyball or soccer game going. Montoya also is the site of a number of surf competitions. **Amenities:** lifeguards; showers; toilets. **Best for:** partiers; sunset; surfing; swimming; walking,

Fodor'sChoice **Playa Manantiales.** Locals have dubbed this trendy stretch of sand Bikini
★ Beach. The swimwear skews a tad more daring here, where people come to see and be seen, as well as swim or play volleyball. During peak season DJs often spin through sunset. If you're looking for a party beach, this is where you want to be. **Amenities:** food and drinks; lifeguards; parking; showers; toilets. **Best for:** partiers; sunrise; sunset; surfing; swimming; windsurfing.

WHERE TO EAT

$$$ ✕ **Andres.** Still bearing the name of its founder, this small restaurant
EUROPEAN on the Rambla Artigas, the oceanside promenade, offers fine dining at moderate prices—its successful recipe for attracting clientele for more than 40 years. You can't beat the view, and in the summer you can appreciate the excellent service while also enjoying the sea breeze. They are famous for their spinach and cheese soufflés, and their grilled meats and fish also are exquisite. ⑤ *Average main: 500 pesos ⊠ Parada 1, Edificio Vaguardia* ☎ *4248–1804* ⊕ *www.restaurantandres.com.uy/en* ⊙ *Closed Mon.–Thurs. Mar.–Nov.*

$$$$ ✕ **La Bourgogne.** A shaded terra-cotta terrace gives way to a breezeway
FRENCH with arched windows at this restaurant, considered one of the best in
Fodor'sChoice Latin America, and opens onto a large split-level dining room with
★ antique sideboards. French chef Jean Paul Bondoux is at the helm, and the food, served by impeccably clad waiters who go about their business with cordial authority, is prepared with only the finest and freshest of ingredients. The breads are baked on the premises (an adjoining bakery sells them by the loaf), and the herbs and berries are grown in the backyard garden. The desserts are sublime—the sampler is a good way to try them all. ⑤ *Average main: 2500 pesos ⊠ Av. del Mar at Calle Pedragosa Sierra* ☎ *4248–2007* ⌫ *Reservations essential* ⊙ *Closed Mon.–Thurs. May–Nov.*

$ ✕ **Medialunas Calentitas.** People flock to this classic Punta spot at all
CAFÉ hours for their piping-hot *medialunas,* which are crescent moon–
Fodor'sChoice shaped pastries that taste like fluffy croissants and come brushed with
★ a sweet syrup. In fact, many patrons profess they're the best medialunas to be found anywhere. You can sit down or grab your medialunas (and other food, such as chivitos) to go. ⑤ *Average main: 200 pesos*

✉ *Ruta 10 at Camino del Cerro Eguzquiza* ☎*4277–2347* ⊕*www. medialunascalentitas.com.*

$$$
SOUTH
AMERICAN
Fodor'sChoice
★

✕**Parador La Huella.** *Huella* means footprint, and this now-legendary restaurant certainly has left its mark. Built right on the sand, La Huella takes beach dining to an unrivaled level with exquisite grilled seafood and meats—the octopus is not to be missed—as well as fresh sushi, pastas, and pizzas. The restaurant epitomizes the best of beach culture and spirit, and while celebrity sightings are common, everyone seems to be relaxed and easygoing. Because the place is wildly popular, reservations in peak seasons are necessary. ⑤ *Average main: 550 pesos* ✉ *Calle de los Cisnes, Brava Beach* ☎*4486–2779* ⊕ *www.paradorlahuella.com* 🍴 *Reservations essential* ⊘ *Closed Apr.–Nov., Mon.–Thurs. No dinner Sun.*

$$
SOUTH
AMERICAN

✕**Parrilla la Balanza.** It's a bit hard to believe a place as low-key and affordable as this traditional Uruguayan steakhouse exists in chic Punta del Este, but it does—and that's precisely why locals love it. Your best bet is to stick to steak and sides to share, including the platter of mini *provoleta* (baked, seasoned cheese) with a bottle of wine to wash it all down. Expect to wait for a table at prime mealtimes, but the friendly and fast waitstaff will have you feasting in no time. ⑤ *Average main: 450 pesos* ✉ *25 de Mayo y Santa Teresa* ☎*4225–3909* ⊕ *www. parrillalabalanza.com.*

WHERE TO STAY

Punta hotels operate on a multitier rate system. Prices go through the roof during Christmas and Easter weeks. Standard high-season rates apply in January and go slightly lower in February. March and December see prices a bit lower still, and then November creeps down a bit more, with some real bargains to be found the rest of the year. On the "rest of the year" topic, lodgings may close for a few weeks in the off-season. Always check ahead. Renting also is popular for long-term stays, and listings are available on sites like ⊕ *www.apuntavamos.com.*

$$$$
HOTEL

🏨 **L'Auberge.** At this hotel in the heart of Parque del Golf, one of Punta's chicest neighborhoods, a stone water tower, which now contains guest rooms, rises from a double-wing chalet and affords spectacular Punta panoramas. **Pros:** secluded neighborhood; great restaurant; friendly staff. **Cons:** not on beach. ⑤ *Rooms from: 6870 pesos* ✉ *Parada 19 Brava. Carnoustie y Av. del Agua* ☎*4888–8888* ⊕ *www.laubergehotel. com* 🛏 *34 rooms, 2 suites* ꭥ *Breakfast.*

$$$$
HOTEL

🏨 **Conrad Resort & Casino.** Spectacularly lit fountains and gardens, an abundant use of marble, and stunning artwork make this an extraordinary resort. **Pros:** always something going on; friendly staff; phenomenal shows. **Cons:** not a good choice if you crave intimate surroundings; rooms have started to show some wear. ⑤ *Rooms from: 9500 pesos* ✉ *Rambla Claudio Williman at Parada 4, Playa Mansa* ☎*4249–1111* ⊕ *www.conrad.com.uy* 🛏 *253 rooms, 41 suites* ꭥ *Breakfast.*

$$$$
HOTEL

🏨 **Estancia Vik.** This luxe yet bohemian 12-suite ranch property set on 4,000 acres in José Ignacio offers guests the best of both a countryside and beach retreat. **Pros:** tranquil; impressive amenities. **Cons:** one-mile walk to the beach. ⑤ *Rooms from: 25000 pesos* ✉ *Camino Eugenio Saiz Martinez, Km 8* ☎ *9460–5212, 9460–5314* ⊕ *www.vikhotels.com* ⬯ *12 suites* ❑ *Breakfast.*

$$$$ ⌧ **Las Cumbres Hotel–Art & Spa.** At this alluring, un-Punta-like lodging
HOTEL   up a 160-meter (520-foot) hill north of Punta Ballena, you can expect great views and a wooded, away-from-it-all vibe. **Pros:** quiet location; attentive staff; cooler temperatures than in town. **Cons:** far from Punta; need car to stay here; open weekends only during off-season. ⑤ *Rooms from: 5400 pesos* ✉ *Ruta 12, Km 3.5, Laguna del Sauce* ☎ *4257–8689* ⊕ *www.cumbres.com.uy* ⬯ *18 rooms, 10 suites* ⊙ *Closed Mon.–Thurs. Apr.–Nov.* ❑ *Breakfast.*

$$ ⌧ **Hotel Salzburgo.** This delightful hotel occupies a white-stucco,
HOTEL   three-story chalet with polished slate floors and exposed beams. **Pros:** friendly owner; secluded neighborhood. **Cons:** removed from the beach. ⑤ *Rooms from: 2000 pesos* ✉ *Calle Pedragosa Sierra at El Havre* ☎ *4248–8851* ⊕ *www.hotelsalzburgo.com* ⬯ *36 rooms* ❑ *Breakfast.*

$$$$ ⌧ **Serena Hotel.** While few Punta hotels actually sit on the beach, this
HOTEL   is the rare exception: a stay here puts you steps from tranquil Playa Mansa and all its amenities. **Pros:** right on beach. **Cons:** not an option for families with young children. ⑤ *Rooms from: 6800 pesos* ✉ *Rambla Williman Parada 24* ☎ *4223–3441* ⊕ *www.serenahotel.com.uy* ⬯ *26 rooms, 6 suites* ❑ *Breakfast.*

NIGHTLIFE

Nightlife and tastes change capriciously from season to season. Expect fast-paced evenings in bars and nightclubs that might open as late as 1 am and reach a fever pitch around sunrise. Many places are open only in high season and have steep covers.

BARS AND PUBS

Moby Dick. Punta del Este's most classic and popular pub sits right across from the city's port. While most other establishments close or slow in low season, Moby Dick keeps whistles wet year-round. ✉ *Rambla de Artigas 650* ☎ *4244–1230* ⊕ *www.mobydick.com.uy.*

Negroni. During peak season the sunset party at nearby Bikini Beach invariably migrates to Negroni, anchoring the Manantiales strip along Punta's main artery, Ruta 10. Bartenders serve up top-notch cocktails while DJs spin. ✉ *Ruta 10, Km 163.5* ☎ *4277–5451* ⊙ *Closed Mar.–Nov.*

DANCE CLUBS

Tequila. This luxe Buenos Aires–based club opens in Punta del Este (La Barra, specifically) during peak summer season and is the place to see and be seen at night. Dress your best and expect to share the dance floor with South America's celebrities and well-heeled. ✉ *Av. Eduardo Víctor Haedo at Las Espumas* ⊙ *Mid-Mar.–Nov.*

LIVE ENTERTAINMENT

Conrad Resort & Casino. For many visitors, the Conrad Resort & Casino defines nightlife in Punta with its casino and a year-round slate of Las Vegas–style shows by some of the biggest stars in Latin entertainment.

Even if you don't recognize the names, taking in a performance at the area's largest hotel is de rigueur. The hotel also has one of the city's best clubs on its premises, Ovo, which attracts top international DJs. ⊠ *Rambla Claudio Williman at Parada 4* ☎ *4249–1111.*

SPORTS AND THE OUTDOORS

Not everyone is in Punta for beach bumming—many spend their time in the water. Surfing is popular on the brava side, as is swimming on the mansa side.

GOLF

Cantegril Country Club. This country club has welcomed visitors to its golf course since 1947. At its main location on Salt Lake and Avenida Mauricio Litman, it offers tennis, and at Honorato de Balzac y Calderón de la Barca, it has rugby and soccer fields and tennis courts. ⊠ *Av. San Pablo s/n* ☎ *4222–3211* ⊕ *www.cantegrilcountryclub.com.uy* ✉ *$150 in high season; $50 in low season* ⚐ *18 holes, 6412 yds, par 71.*

Club del Lago Golf. You can play a round of golf at the challenging Club del Lago Golf, the only green in Punta del Este with 20 holes. As the course is popular in peak season, reservations are recommended, as well as confirming hours off-season. ⊠ *Ruta Interbalnearia, Km 116.5* ☎ *4257–8423* ⊕ *www.lagogolf.com* ✉ *$100* ⚐ *20 holes, 6823 yds, par 82.*

HORSEBACK RIDING

Estancias Gauchas. Montevideo-based Estancias Gauchas offers various trips to nearby estancias, where you can ride horses and take part in the gaucho life. There are English-, French-, German-, and Portuguese-speaking guides. ⊠ *Bacacay 1334, Montevideo* ☎ *2916–3011* ⊕ *www. estanciasgauchas.com.*

SHOPPING

Feria Artesanal. An essential part of visiting Punta is exploring the colorful Feria Artesanal on the town's central Plaza Artigas. It's open weekend evenings all year; between Christmas and Easter it's open weekday evenings as well. Popular items include gourds for sipping maté and leather and silver crafts. ⊠ *Pl. Artigas.*

8

UNDERSTANDING
BUENOS AIRES

SPANISH VOCABULARY

MENU GUIDE

SPANISH VOCABULARY

	ENGLISH	SPANISH	PRONUNCIATION

BASICS

	ENGLISH	SPANISH	PRONUNCIATION
	Yes/no	Sí/no	see/noh
	Please	Por favor	por fah-vor
	Thank you (very much)	(Muchas) gracias	(**moo**-chas) **grah**-see-ass
	You're welcome	De nada	deh **nah**-da
	Excuse me	Con permiso	con pehr-**mee**-so
	Pardon me	¿Perdón?	pehr-**don**
	Could you tell me . . . ?	¿Podría decirme . . . ?	po-**dree**-ah deh-**seer**-me
	I'm sorry	Lo siento/Perdón	lo see-**en**-to/pehr-**don**
	Hello!/Hi!	¡Hola!	**o**-la
	Good morning!	¡Buen día!	bwen **dee**-a
	Good afternoon!	¡Buenas tardes!	**bwen**-as **tar**-des
	Good evening/Good night!	¡Buenas noches!	**bwen**-as **no**-ches
	Goodbye!	¡Chau!/¡Adiós!	chow/a-dee-**os**

NUMBERS

	ENGLISH	SPANISH	PRONUNCIATION
	0	Cero	seh-ro
	1	Un, uno	oon, **oo**-no
	2	Dos	doss
	3	Tres	tress
	4	Cuatro	**kwah**-troh
	5	Cinco	**sin**-koh
	6	Seis	**say**-iss
	7	Siete	see-**yet**-eh
	8	Ocho	och-oh
	9	Nueve	nweh-veh
	10	Diez	dee-**ess**

DAYS OF THE WEEK

	ENGLISH	SPANISH	PRONUNCIATION
	Sunday	domingo	doh-**ming**-oh
	Monday	lunes	**loo**-ness

ENGLISH	SPANISH	PRONUNCIATION
Tuesday	martes	**mar**-tess
Wednesday	miércoles	mee-**er**-koh-less
Thursday	jueves	**hweh**-vess
Friday	viernes	vee-**er**-ness
Saturday	sábado	**sah**-bad-oh

USEFUL PHRASES

Do you speak English?	¿Habla usted inglés? / ¿Hablás inglés?	**ab**-la oo-**sted** ing-**less** / **ab**-las ing-**less**
I don't speak Spanish	No hablo castellano	No **ab**-loh cas-**teh**-sha-no
I don't understand	No entiendo	No en-tee-**en**-doh
I understand	Entiendo	en-tee-**en**-doh
I don't know	No sé	No seh
What's your name?	¿Cómo se llama usted? / ¿Cómo te llamás?	ko-mo seh **shah**-mah oo-**sted** / ko-mo teh **shah**-mass
My name is . . .	Me llamo . . .	meh **shah**-moh . . .
What time is it?	¿Qué hora es?	keh **o**-rah ess
It's one o'clock	Es la una	ess la **oo**-na
It's two/three/four . . . o'clock	Son las dos/tres/cuatro	son lass doss/tress/ **kwah**-troh
Yes, please/	Si, gracias.	see, **grah**-see-ass
No, thank you	No, gracias.	noh, **grah**-see-ass
How?	¿Cómo?	**ko**-mo
When?	¿Cuándo?	kwan-doh
Tonight	Esta noche	**ess**-tah **noch**-eh
What?	¿Qué?	Keh
What is this?	¿Qué es esto?	keh ess **ess**-toh
Why?	¿Por qué?	por keh
Who?	¿Quién?	kee-**yen**
Telephone	teléfono	tel-**eff**-on-oh
I am ill	Estoy enfermo(a)	ess-**toy** en-**fer**-moh(mah)

ENGLISH	SPANISH	PRONUNCIATION
Please call a doctor	Por favor, llame a un médico	Por fah-**vor**, **shah**-meh a oon **meh**-dik-oh
Help!	¡Auxilio!	owk-**see**-lee-oh
Fire!	¡Incendio!	in-**sen**-dee-oh
Look out!	¡Cuidado!	kwee-**dah**-doh

OUT AND ABOUT

Where is . . . ?	¿Dónde está . . . ?	**don**-deh ess-**tah** . . .
the train station	la estación de tren	la ess-tah-see-**on** deh tren
the subway station	la estación de subte	la ess-tah-see-**on** deh **soob**-teh
the bus stop	la parada del colectivo	la pah-**rah**-dah del col-ek-**tee**-voh
the post office	el correo	el cor-**reh**-yoh
the bank	el banco	el **ban**-koh
the hotel	el hotel	el oh-**tel**
the museum	el museo	el moo-**seh**-yoh
the hospital	el hospital	el oss-pee-**tal**
the elevator	el ascensor	el ass-**en**-sor
the bathroom	el baño	el **ban**-yoh
Left/right	izquierda/derecha	iss-kee-**er**-dah/ deh-**rech**-ah
Straight ahead	derecho	deh-**rech**-oh
Avenue	avenida	av-en-**ee**-dah
City street	calle	**cah**-sheh
Highway	carretera/ruta	cah-ret-**eh**-rah
Restaurant	restaurante/restorán	rest-ow-**ran**-teh/ rest-oh-**ran**
Main square	plaza principal	**plass**-ah prin-see-**pal**
Market	mercado	mer-**kah**-do
Neighborhood	barrio	**bah**-ree-oh

MENU GUIDE

With so much meat on the menu, you'll need to know how to order it: *jugoso* (juicy) means medium rare, *vuelta y vuelta* (flipped back and forth) means rare, and *vivo por adentro* (alive inside) is barely warm in the middle. Argentineans like their meat *bien cocido* (well cooked).

aceite de olivo: olive oil

alfajores: Argentine cookies, usually made with dulce de leche and often covered with chocolate, though there are hundreds of varieties

arroz: rice

bife de lomo: filet mignon

bife de chorizo: like a New York strip steak, but double the size (not to be confused with *chorizo*, which is a type of sausage)

budín de pan: Argentine version of bread pudding

cabrito: roasted kid

cafecito: espresso

café con leche: coffee with milk

centolla: King crab, a Patagonian specialty

chimichurri: a sauce of oil, garlic, and salt, served with meat

chinchulines: small intestines

chorizo: thick, spicy pork-and-beef sausages, usually served with bread (*choripan*)

churros: baton-shaped donuts for dipping in hot chocolate

ciervo: venison

chivito: kid

cordero: lamb

cortado: coffee "cut" with a drop of milk

dulce de leche: a sweet caramel concoction made from milk and served on pancakes, in pastries, on cookies, and on ice cream

empanadas: pockets stuffed with meat—usually beef—chicken, or cheese

ensalada de fruta: fruit salad (sometimes fresh, sometimes canned)

estofado: beef stew

facturas: small pastries

huevos: eggs

humitas: steamed cornhusks wrapped around cornmeal and cheese

jamón: ham

lechón: roast suckling pig

lengua: tongue

licuado: milk shake

locro: local stew, usually made with hominy and beans, that's cooked slowly with meat and vegetables; common in northern Argentina

medialuna: croissant

mejillones: mussels

merluza: hake

milanesa: breaded meat cutlet, usually veal, pounded thin and fried; served as a main course or in a sandwich with lettuce, tomato, ham, cheese, and egg

milanesa a la napolitana: a breaded veal cutlet with melted mozzarella cheese and tomato sauce

mollejas: sweetbreads; the thymus glands, usually of the cow but also can be of the lamb or the goat

morcilla: blood sausage

pejerrey: a kind of mackerel

pollo: chicken

provoleta: grilled provolone cheese sprinkled with olive oil and oregano

puchero: boiled meat and vegetables; like pot-au-feu

queso: cheese

salchichas: long, thin sausages

sambayon: an alcohol-infused custard

tamales: ground corn stuffed with meat, cheese, or other fillings and tied up in a corn husk

tenedor libre: all-you-can-eat meat and salad bar

tinto: red wine

trucha: trout

TRAVEL SMART
BUENOS AIRES

GETTING HERE AND AROUND

Argentina extends approximately 3,650 km (2,268 miles) from tip to tail, and many of its attractions are hundreds of miles apart. So you can save a lot in terms of both time and money by carefully plotting your course.

Buenos Aires—the national capital—lies about two-thirds of the way up Argentina's eastern side, on the banks of the Río de la Plata. Three of the country's main draws are about 1,000 km (621 miles) away as the crow flies: Puerto Iguazú, the base for exploring Iguazú Falls, in northeastern Misiones Province; Salta, the gateway to the Andean Northwest; and Mendoza, in the wine region, near the Chilean border. Slightly farther, this time southwest of Buenos Aires, is Bariloche, the hub for northern Patagonia's Lakes District. El Calafate, the hub for southern Patagonia and the launch pad for the Perito Moreno glacier, is a whopping 2,068 km (1,285 miles) from the city.

TRAVEL TIMES FROM BUENOS AIRES		
	BY AIR	BY BUS
San Antonio de Areco	n/a	2 hours
Atlantic Coast	1 hour	5–6 hours
Córdoba	1¼ hours	9–11 hours
Mendoza	1¾ hours	12–14 hours
Puerto Iguazú	1¾ hours	16–19 hours
Salta	2¼ hours	18–21 hours
Bariloche	2¼ hours	21–23 hours
El Calafate	3¼ hours	40 hours

Most domestic flights operate from Buenos Aires, so to fly from the extreme south of the country to the extreme north you often have to change planes here. Flying within Argentina makes sense given these huge distances. That said, domestic flights are expensive, so many visitors opt for overnight sleeper buses for longer trips. A well-developed network of long-distance buses connects Buenos Aires with cities nationwide; buses also operate between many urban centers without passing through the capital.

▮ AIR TRAVEL

TO ARGENTINA

There are direct daily flights between Buenos Aires and several North American cities, with New York and Miami being the primary departure points. Many airlines also serve Buenos Aires via Santiago de Chile or São Paulo in Brazil, which adds only a little to your trip time.

Aerolíneas Argentinas, the flagship airline, operates direct flights between Buenos Aires and JFK once a day and Miami twice a day. Since being renationalized in 2008, its reputation for chronic delays has improved considerably.

Chilean airline LAN is Aerolíneas's biggest local competition. It flies direct from Buenos Aires to Miami, and via Santiago de Chile, São Paulo, or Lima to JFK, Dallas, San Francisco, and Los Angeles. LAN also allows you to bypass Buenos Aires on routes into Mendoza and Córdoba from JFK and Miami, via Santiago de Chile.

U.S carriers serve Buenos Aires, too. There are direct flights from Atlanta on Delta and from Houston on United; American Airlines fly nonstop from JFK, Miami, and Dallas. Flying times to Buenos Aires are: 11–12 hours from New York, 10½ hours from Atlanta, Dallas or Houston, and 9 hours from Miami.

WITHIN ARGENTINA

Aerolíneas Argentinas and its subsidiary Austral link Buenos Aires to more Argentine cities than any other airline, with flights running to Puerto Iguazú, Salta, Mendoza, Córdoba, Bariloche, Ushuaia, and El Calafate at least once a day. LAN also flies to these cities. Andes Líneas Aéreas operates between Buenos Aires, Salta, and Puerto Madryn, and sometimes provides direct service between Puerto Iguazú and Salta and Córdoba.

AIR PASSES

Aerolíneas Argentinas has two coupon-based air passes, which must be purchased before you arrive: the South American Pass and the Visit Argentina Pass. Although you don't need to fly in and out of the continent with Aerolíneas to take advantage of these, prices are cheaper if you do. Each allows you to travel to between three and 12 destinations, using one coupon per flight; coupons from the two passes may also be combined.

The South American Pass includes all countries the carrier serves within the region: Brazil, Chile, Colombia, Paraguay, Peru, Uruguay, and Venezuela. All routes operate from Buenos Aires except for Rio de Janeiro to Puerto Iguazú and Santiago de Chile to Mendoza. Coupons cost between $90 and $250. The Visit Argentina Pass is valid for domestic flights. Coupons cost $180 each except for ones covering Patagonia, which cost $220 (prices are reduced to $150 and $200, respectively, if you fly to Argentina on Aerolíneas). The downside with these passes is that each connection you make through Buenos Aires counts as a flight and, therefore, requires a coupon. For example, if you want to see Buenos Aires, El Calafate, and Iguazú using the Visit Argentina Pass, you would need to buy four coupons.

If you plan to take at least three flights within Argentina or South America in general, you might save money with the Visit South America pass offered by the OneWorld Alliance, of which LAN is a member. Flights are categorized by mileage; segments (both domestic and international) start at $160.

Airline Security Issues Transportation Security Administration ⊕ *www.tsa.gov.*

Air Passes South American Pass
☎ *800/333–0276 for Aerolíneas Argentinas*
⊕ *www.aerolineas.com.ar/en-us/cheap_flights/ south_american_pass.* **Visit Argentina Pass**

☎ *800/333–0276 for Aerolíneas Argentinas*
⊕ *www.aerolineas.com.ar/en-us/cheap_flights/ visit_argentina.* **Visit South America Pass**
☎ *866/435–9526 for LAN* ⊕ *www.lan.com/ en_us/sitio_personas/southamericanairpass/ index.html.*

AIRPORTS

Buenos Aires' Aeropuerto Internacional de Ezeiza Ministro Pistarini (EZE)—known simply as Ezeiza—is 35 km (22 miles) southwest of the city center. It is the base for international flights operated by Aerolíneas Argentinas and its partner Austral; both airlines run a limited number of domestic flights to Puerto Iguazú, El Calafate, Bariloche, Trelew, Córdoba, Ushuaia, and Rosario from here as well. All of these depart from Ezeiza's newest terminal, C; inbound international flights on Aerolíneas, however, arrive at Terminal A. Other major international carriers also use Terminal A, a pleasant glass-sided building. SkyTeam-member airlines (including Delta) are the notable exception: they operate entirely out of Terminal C. At this writing, Terminal B is under renovation.

A covered walkway connects all three terminals. Both A and C have a few small snack bars, a small range of shops (including a pharmacy), a public phone center with Internet services, and a visitor information booth. The ATM, 24-hour luggage storage, and car-rental agencies are in Terminal A. ■TIP→ **By far the best currency exchange rates are at the small Banco de la Nación in the Terminal A arrivals area; it's open around the clock.**

Most domestic flights operate out of Aeroparque Jorge Newbery (AEP). It's next to the Río de la Plata in northeast Palermo, about 8 km (5 miles) north of the city center.

Security at Argentine airports isn't as stringent as it is in the States—computers stay in cases, shoes stay on your feet, and there are no random searches. Air travel is expensive for Argentineans, so airports are more likely to be crowded with foreigners than locals.

Airport Information Aeroparque Jorge Newbery ☏ *11/5480–6111* ⊕ *www.aa2000. com.ar.* **Aeropuerto Internacional de Ezeiza Ministro Pistarini** ☏ *11/5480–2500* ⊕ *www. aa2000.com.ar.*

GROUND TRANSPORTATION

From Ezeiza, the quickest way of getting into town is by taxi. The cheapest and safest option is to use a fixed-rate service such as Taxi Ezeiza. These can be booked on arrival at the airport or in advance, either online or by phone; the trip costs 200 to 250 pesos and takes 45 to 60 minutes. Avoid the black-and-yellow city taxis available at booths or on the curb outside the terminals. Their metered price tends to be much higher, and overcharging (either by rigging the meter or by taking circuitous routes) is commonplace.

Manuel Tienda León operates private shuttle buses that are nearly as fast as taxis and considerably cheaper if you're traveling alone. Buses to and from its terminal in the Retiro district leave roughly every half hour; tickets, which can be purchased at booths in the arrivals halls or in the walkway between terminals A and B, cost 100 pesos.

The only public transport that connects Buenos Aires and Ezeiza is Bus No. 8, *recorrido* (branch) A. It leaves from a shelter in the parking area opposite the Aeropuertos Argentinos 2000 building (turn left out of Terminal B). You need change for the 9-peso ticket and patience for the two to three hours it takes to reach San Telmo and Plaza de Mayo (it runs along Avenida Paseo Colón).

The highway connecting Ezeiza with the city is the Autopista Ricchieri, which is best reached by taking Autopista 25 de Mayo out of the city. ■TIP→ Note that most flights to the United States depart from Buenos Aires in the evening, so plan to offset afternoon traffic snarls by allowing at least an hour of travel time to Ezeiza.

Aeroparque Jorge Newbery is actually inside Buenos Aires, on the Costanera Norte in northeast Palermo. There are several routes to Aeroparque from downtown—the easiest is to take Avenida Libertador north to Avenida Sarmiento, and then take a right and follow it until Costanera Rafael Obligado. Traffic is usually heavy between 5 and 8 pm.

A taxi to Microcentro or San Telmo costs 60 to 80 pesos and takes 15 to 45 minutes, depending on the time of day. Manuel Tienda León operates shuttle buses to and from its terminal and downtown hotels; a ticket costs 40 pesos.

Several city buses run along Avenida Rafael Obligado, outside the airport: No. 160 goes to Plaza Italia, as does No. 37, which continues to Microcentro. Numbers 33 and 45 go to Retiro, Microcentro, and San Telmo; all cost 5 pesos (2.50 pesos if you pay with a SUBE rechargeable swipe card).

TRANSFERS BETWEEN AIRPORTS

Taxi Ezeiza operates between Ezeiza and Aeroparque; the cab ride costs 230 to 250 pesos—including tolls and luggage—and takes an hour in normal traffic. Manuel Tienda León shuttles make the same trip for 110 pesos per person; there are usually one or two departures per hour in each direction.

Taxis and Shuttles Manuel Tienda León ☏ *11/4314–3636, 810/888–5366* ⊕ *www. tiendaleon.com.ar.* **Taxi Ezeiza** ☏ *11-15/6128– 8301* ⊕ *www.taxiezeiza2000.com.ar.*

▐ BOAT TRAVEL

Ferries run frequently across the Río de la Plata between Buenos Aires and the Uruguayan cities of Colonia and Montevideo. Seacat or Colonia Express catamarans, which take an hour or less to Colonia and three hours to Montevideo, offer the best value. Full-price round-trip tickets cost around 1,000 and 1,250 pesos, respectively, but they often drop as low as 650 and 770 pesos if you book online (same-day return tickets are sometimes even less). Buquebus offers similar services on high-speed ferries, with round-trip tickets costing 1,350 pesos to Colonia and 1,550 pesos to Montevideo.

All three companies also sell packages that include bus tickets to Montevideo and Punta del Este direct from Colonia's ferry terminal. You can order tickets by phone or online.

Buquebus and Seacat leave from terminals at the northern end of Puerto Madero. The Colonia Express terminal is south of Puerto Madero on Avenida Pedro de Mendoza (the extension of Avenida Huergo) at 20 de Septiembre. It's best reached by taxi.

Contacts Buquebus ☎ *11/4316–6500* ⊕ *www.buquebus.com.* **Colonia Express** ☎ *11/4317–4100 English operator* ⊕ *www. coloniaexpress.com.* **Seacat** ☎ *11/4314–5100* ⊕ *www.seacatcolonia.com.*

▌ BUS TRAVEL

TO AND FROM BUENOS AIRES

A range of frequent, comfortable, and dependable long-distance buses connect Buenos Aires with cities all over Argentina as well as neighboring countries. Because traveling by road is substantially cheaper than traveling by air, both locals and visitors often choose overnight sleeper buses for longer trips.

CLASSES

All long-distance buses have toilets, air-conditioning, videos, and snacks like sandwiches or cookies. The most basic service is *semi-cama,* which has minimally reclinable seats and often takes a little longer than more luxurious services. It's worth paying the little extra for *coche cama,* sometimes called *ejecutivo,* where you get large, business-class-style seats and, sometimes, pillows and blankets.

The best rides of all are on the fully reclinable seats of *cama suite* or *suite premium* services, which are often contained in their own little booth. Bus attendants

and free drinks are other perks. The more expensive the service, the cleaner and newer the bus.

TERMINAL

Most long-distance buses depart from the Terminal de Omnibus de Retiro, which is often referred to as the Terminal de Retiro or simply Retiro. Ramps and stairs from the street lead to a huge concourse where buses leave from more than 60 numbered platforms. There are restrooms, restaurants, phone and Internet centers, lockers, news kiosks, and a tourism office on this floor.

You buy tickets from the *boleterías* (ticket offices) on the upper level, where there are two ATMs. Each company has its own booth; they're arranged in zones according to the destinations served, which makes price comparisons easy.

The bus terminal's comprehensive website (in Spanish) lists bus companies by destination, including their telephone number and ticket-booth location.

TICKETS

Most major companies have online timetables; some allow you to buy tickets online or over the phone. Websites also list alternative *puntos de venta* (sales offices)—in many cases you can buy tickets from booths in shopping malls or subway stations, though outside peak season you can usually buy them at the terminal right up until departure time.

Arrive early to get a ticket, and be prepared to pay cash. During January, February, and July, buy your ticket as far in advance as possible—a week or more, at least—and arrive at the terminal extra early.

Contacts Terminal de Ómnibus Retiro ✉ *Av. Antártida Argentina at Av. Ramos Mejía, Retiro* ☎ *11/4310–0700* ⊕ *www.tebasa.com.ar.*

WITHIN BUENOS AIRES

City buses, called *colectivos,* connect the barrios and greater Buenos Aires. Stops are roughly every two to three blocks (approximately 650–1,000 feet apart).

Some are at proper shelters with large numbered signposts; others are marked by small, easy-to-miss metal disks or stickers stuck on nearby walls, posts, or even trees. Buses are generally safe and run 24 hours a day, although service is less frequent at night.

A few routes have smaller, faster *diferencial* buses (indicated by a sign on the front) as well as regular ones; they run less frequently, but you usually get a seat on them.

An incipient rapid transit system called Metrobus is being set up in busy parts of town. On Avenida 9 de Julio between avenidas Santa Fe and Independencia, for example, both regular buses and special bi-articulated ones run in lanes down the center of the street, stopping only at intersections with avenidas (every four or five blocks). The clean, well-lighted Metrobus shelters have free Wi-Fi and displays announcing incoming services.

TICKETS

Standard fare prices are available only if you pay using SUBE (Sistema Único de Boleto Electrónico), a rechargeable swipe-card system that works on both buses and the subway. Cards are available for 15 pesos from branches of Correo Argentino (the post office) as well as from many convenience stores and telephone centers. Bus fares are double if you pay cash—exact change isn't necessary, but coins are. This can be a problem because Buenos Aires suffers from a severe coin shortage. Fares within the city are 2.50 pesos with SUBE (5 pesos with cash) for up to 3 km (2 miles), or 2.70 pesos (5.40 pesos with cash) for up to 6 km (4 miles). Hail your bus and tell the driver the value of the ticket you want as you board. Fares outside the city are 3.90 pesos to 4.50 pesos (8 or 9 pesos with cash). There are no daily or weekly discount passes.

Once on board, head for the back, which is where you exit. A small button on the grab bar lets you signal for a stop. Don't depend on drivers for much assistance;

they're busy navigating traffic. Note that routes follow different streets in each direction—these are detailed in the *Guía T*, an essential route guide that you can purchase at any news kiosk.

If you have even a rudimentary grasp of Spanish, you can also rely on the city's Cómo Llego website: it has route and timetable information for all forms of public transportation.

Information Buenos Aires Bus ☎ 11/5238–4600 ⊕ www.buenosairesbus.com ⊗ Nov.–Apr., daily 8:40–7; May–Oct., daily 9–5.**Cómo Llego** ⊕ comollego.ba.gob.ar. **SUBE** ☎ 800/777–7823 ⊕ www.sube.gob.ar.

▮ CAR TRAVEL

Having a car in Buenos Aires is really more trouble than it's worth. After all, there are ample taxis and public transportation options within the city; and if you're eager to take a day's tour of the suburbs, hiring a car and driver through your hotel or travel agent is more convenient than driving yourself. However, a car can be useful for longer excursions to the Atlantic Coast or interior towns of Buenos Aires Province.

Avenida General Paz is Buenos Aires' ring road. If you're driving into the city, you'll know you're in Buenos Aires proper once you cross it. If you're entering from the north, chances are you'll be on the Ruta Panamericana, which has wide lanes and good lighting, but many accidents. The quickest way from downtown to Ezeiza Airport is Autopista 25 de Mayo to Autopista Ricchieri. Ruta 2 takes you to the Atlantic beach resorts in and around Mar del Plata. Microcentro—the bustling commercial district bounded by Carlos Pellegrini, Avenida Córdoba, Avenida Leandro Alem, and Avenida de Mayo—is off-limits to all but specially authorized vehicles on weekdays.

HAZARDS

Porteño driving styles range from erratic to downright psychotic, and the road mortality rate is shockingly high. Drive defensively.

City streets are notorious for potholes, uneven surfaces, and poorly marked lanes and turnoffs.

Rush-hour traffic affects the roads into Buenos Aires between 8 and 10 am, and roads out between 6 and 9 pm; the General Paz ring road and the Panamericana are particularly problematic.

PARKING

On-street parking is limited. Some neighborhoods, such as San Telmo and Recoleta, have meters: you pay with coins, then display the ticket you receive on your dashboard (at this writing, the rate is 1.50 pesos per hour for up to four hours, although there are plans to double it). In meter-free areas, parking is usually only allowed on the right side of the street. Never park where there's a yellow line on the curb, alongside a bus stop, or on the left side of the street unless signs specifically say you can.

In popular areas there's often a self-appointed caretaker who guides you into your spot and watches your car: you pay anything from 2 to 5 pesos when you leave. Car theft is fairly common, so many rental agencies insist you park in a guarded lot—Buenos Aires is full of them. Look for a circular blue sign with a white "E" for *estacionamiento* (parking). Downtown, expect to pay 25–30 pesos per hour, or 70–120 pesos for 12 hours. Illegally parked cars are towed from Microcentro and San Telmo. Getting your car back is a bureaucratic nightmare and costs around 450 pesos. Most malls have lots, which sometimes give you a reduced rate with a purchase.

RULES OF THE ROAD

Buenos Aires has a one-way system in which parallel streets run in opposite directions: never going the wrong way along a street is one of the few rules that Argentines abide by. Where there are no traffic lights at an intersection, you give way to drivers coming from the right, and have priority over those coming from the left.

Most driving rules in the United States theoretically apply here (although locals flout them shamelessly). However, keep in mind that right turns on red are not allowed, and turning left on two-way avenues is prohibited unless there's a left-turn signal or light.

The legal blood-alcohol limit is 500 mg of alcohol per liter of blood, and breathalyzing is becoming more common within the city.

In Buenos Aires a 40-kph (25-mph) speed limit applies on streets, and a 60-kph (37-mph) limit is in effect on avenues. *Porteños* take speed-limit signs, the ban on driving with cell phones, and drinking and driving lightly, so drive very defensively.

Local police tend to be forgiving of foreigners' driving faults and often waive tickets and fines when they see your passport or driver's license. If you do get a traffic ticket, don't argue. Most aren't payable on the spot, but some police officers offer "reduced" on-the-spot fines in lieu of a ticket: it's out-and-out bribery, and you'd do best to avoid it by insisting on receiving the proper ticket.

CAR RENTALS

Daily rental rates range from 430 to 550 pesos, depending on the type of car you choose and the distance you intend to travel. This typically includes tax and 200 free km (125 miles) daily. If you plan to do a lot of driving, consider renting with Hertz, the only local agency that offers unlimited mileage. Note that nearly all rental cars in Argentina have manual transmissions; if you need an automatic, request it in advance.

Reputable firms don't rent to drivers under 21, and renters under 23 often have to pay a daily surcharge. In general, you cannot cross the border in a rental car. Children's car seats aren't compulsory but are available for 35 to 50 pesos per day. Some agencies charge a 10% surcharge for picking up a car from the airport.

Rental deals usually include roadside assistance. Argentina's automobile association, the Automóvil Club Argentina, also offers free roadside service to members of North American automobile associations. If you call for assistance, though, bear in mind that most operators will speak only Spanish.

INSURANCE

Collision damage waiver (CDW) is mandatory in Argentina and is included in standard rental prices. However, you may still be responsible for a deductible fee (known locally as a *franquicia* or *deducible*)—a maximum amount that you'll have to pay if damage occurs. The amount ranges from 3,000 to 6,000 pesos for a car and can be much higher for a four-wheel-drive vehicle. You can reduce the figure substantially or altogether by paying an insurance premium (anywhere from 40 to 1,000 pesos per day, depending on the company and type of vehicle).

Some companies include loss damage waiver (LDW) in the CDW fee, others charge a premium for it (usually 30–50 pesos per day).

Many rental companies don't insure you for driving on unpaved roads, so discuss your itinerary carefully with the agent to be certain you're always covered.

Major international agencies with branches in Buenos Aires include Avis, Budget, Hertz, Alamo, and Dollar. You can rent cars at both airports and through many hotels. If the agency has a branch in another town—and you're prepared to pay a hefty fee—arrangements can usually be made for a one-way drop-off.

Automobile Association Automóvil Club Argentina *(ACA)*. ☎ *11/4808–4000* ⊕ *www. aca.org.ar.*

CAR WITH DRIVER RENTALS

An alternative to renting a car is to hire a *remis*, a car with a driver, especially for day outings. Hotels and travel agents can make arrangements for you. You'll have to pay cash, but you'll often spend less than you would on a rental car or cab for a whole day. Remis service costs about 150–300 pesos per hour, depending on the type of car. There is usually a three-hour minimum and an additional charge per km (½ miles) if you drive over a certain distance or go outside the city limits. If your driver is helpful and friendly, a 10% tip is appropriate.

Remises Abbey Rent-A-Car ☎ *11/4924–1984* ⊕ *www.abbeyrentacar.com.ar.* **Annie Millet Transfers** ☎ *11/6777-7777* ⊕ *www. amillet.com.ar.* **Remises Universal** ☎ *11/4105–5555* ⊕ *www.remisesuniversal. com.* **Vía Remis** ☎ *11/4777-8888.*

▌ SUBWAY TRAVEL

The *subte* (subway) is one of the quickest ways to get around. Packed trains mean it's not always the most comfortable, though it's generally fairly safe. Most stations are reasonably well patrolled by police, and many are decorated with artworks. You'll likely hear musicians and see actors performing on trains and in the stations.

Monday through Saturday, the subte opens at 5 am and shuts down sometime between 10:30 and 11 pm, depending on the line; on Sunday, trains start at 8 am and stop between 10 and 10:30 pm. Single-ride tickets to anywhere in the city cost 5 pesos; you can buy passes in stations for 1, 2, 5, or 10 trips or use a rechargeable SUBE card.

Línea A travels beneath Avenida Rivadavía from Plaza de Mayo to San Pedrito in Flores.

Línea B begins at Leandro Alem Station, in the financial district, and runs under Avenida Corrientes to Juan Manuel de Rosas Station in Villa Urquiza.

Línea C, under Avenida 9 de Julio, connects the two major train stations, Retiro and Constitución, making stops along the way in Centro and San Telmo.

Línea D runs from Catedral Station on Plaza de Mayo to Congreso de Tucumán in Belgrano.

Línea E takes you from Bolívar Station on Plaza de Mayo to Plaza de los Virreyes in Flores.

Linéa H, the subte's newest line, is only partially open. It runs from Corrientes through Plaza Miserere in Once to Hospitales Station in Parque Patricios, crossing lines A and E; eventually it will extend north to Retiro, crossing lines B and D.

Information Subte ⊕ www.buenosaires.gob. ar/subte.

▌ TAXI TRAVEL

Taxis in Buenos Aires are relatively cheap and plentiful. All are black with yellow tops. An unoccupied one will have a small red "Libre" sign in its windshield.

Local wisdom has it that the safest taxis to hail on the street are those with a light on the roof that says "radio taxi"; they belong to licensed fleets and are in constant contact with dispatchers. If you phone for a taxi, you'll have to wait a few minutes, but you can be sure where it's come from and that it is safe.

Legally, all taxis are supposed to have working seat belts in the front and back seats, but this isn't always the case.

Meters start at 11.80 pesos and charge 1.10 pesos per 200 meters (650 feet) from 6 am to 10 pm; the rates jump to 13.20 pesos and 1.32 pesos, respectively, from 10 pm to 6 am; you'll also end up paying for standing time spent at a light or in a traffic jam. From downtown it will cost you around 30 pesos to Recoleta, 20 pesos to San Telmo, 40–50 pesos to Palermo, and 75–85 pesos to Belgrano. Drivers don't expect tips; rounding up to the next peso is sufficient.

Taxi Companies Del Plata ☎ 11/4505–1111 ⊕ www.delplataradiotaxi.com. **Pídalo** ☎ 11/4956–1200 ⊕ www.radiotaxipidalo. com.ar. **Premium** ☎ 11/4374–6666 ⊕ www. taxipremium.com. **Radio Taxi Ciudad** ☎ 11/4923–7007 ⊕ www.radiotaxiciudad.com. ar.

294 < **Travel Smart Buenos Aires**

ESSENTIALS

▌ COMMUNICATIONS

INTERNET

Inexpensive Internet access is widely available in Buenos Aires. Top-tier hotels tend to have high-speed in-room data ports and Wi-Fi, which may incur a charge, while most lower-budget establishments (including hostels) have free Wi-Fi. Many bars and restaurants also have free Wi-Fi—look for stickers on their windows. In general, these are open networks and you don't need to ask for a password to use them. Wider coverage comes courtesy of BA WiFi, a free service provided by the city government in many subte stations, Metrobus shelters, public libraries, museums, cultural centers, and even major streets and squares. The BA WiFi website lists an ever-growing number of hotspots.

If you're traveling without a laptop or smartphone, many hotels have a PC in the lobby for guests to use. Otherwise, look for a *locutorio* (telephone and Internet center), where you'll pay between 6 and 10 pesos per hour to surf the Web.

Contact BA Wi-Fi ⊕ *www.buenosaires.gob.ar/ modernizacion/wi-fi-gratis.*

PHONES

The country code for Argentina is 54. To call landlines in Argentina from the United States, dial the international access code (011) followed by the country code (54), the two- to four-digit area code without the initial 0, then the six- to eight-digit phone number. For example, to call the Buenos Aires number (011) 4123–4567, you would dial 011–54–11–4123–4567.

Any number that is prefixed by a 15 is a cell-phone number. To call cell phones from the United States, dial the international access code (011) followed by the country code (54), Argentina's cell-phone code (9), the area code without the initial 0, then the seven- or eight-digit cell phone number without the initial 15. For example, to call the Buenos Aires cell phone (011) 15 5123–4567, you would dial 011–54–9–11–5123–4567.

CALLING WITHIN ARGENTINA

Argentina's phone service is run by the duopoly of Telecom and Telefónica. Telecom covers the northern half of Argentina (including the northern half of the city of Buenos Aires) and Telefónica covers the south. However, both companies operate public phones and phone centers, called *locutorios* or *telecentros,* throughout the city.

Service is generally efficient, and direct dialing—both long distance and international—is universal. You can make local and long-distance calls from your hotel (usually with a surcharge) and from any public phone or locutorio. Public phones aren't particularly abundant and are often broken. All accept coins; some have slots for phone cards.

Locutorios are useful if you need to make lots of calls or don't have coins on you. Ask the receptionist for *una cabina* (a booth), make as many local, long-distance, or international calls as you like (a small LCD display tracks how much you've spent), then pay as you leave. There's no charge if you don't get through.

All of Argentina's area codes are prefixed with a 0, which you need to include when dialing another area within Argentina. You don't need to dial the area code to call a local number. Confusingly, area codes and phone numbers don't all have the same number of digits. The area code for Buenos Aires is 011, and phone numbers have eight digits. Area codes for the rest of the country have three or four digits, and start with 02 (the southern provinces, including Buenos Aires Province) or 03 (the northern provinces); phone numbers have six or seven digits.

For local directory assistance (in Spanish), dial 110.

Local calls cost 23centavos for two minutes at peak periods (weekdays 8–8 and Saturday 8–1) or four minutes the rest of the time. Long-distance calls cost 57centavos per *ficha* (unit)—the farther the distance, the shorter each unit. For example, 57centavos lasts about two minutes to places less than 55 km (34 miles) away, but only half a minute to somewhere more than 250 km (155 miles) away.

To make international calls from Argentina, dial 00, then the country code, area code, and number. The country code for the United States is 1.

CALLING CARDS
You can use prepaid calling cards (*tarjetas prepagas*) to make local and international calls from public phones, but not locutorios. All cards come with a scratch-off panel, which reveals a PIN. You dial a free access number, the PIN, and the number you wish to call.

Most *kioscos* and small supermarkets sell prepaid cards from different companies: specify it's for *llamadas internacionales* (international calls), and compare each card's per-minute rates to the country you want to call. Many cost as little as 9¢ per minute for calls to the United States.

Telecom and Telefónica also sell prepaid 5-, 10-, and 20-peso calling cards from kioscos and locutorios. They're called Tarjeta Ciudades and Geo Destinos, respectively. Calls to the United States cost 19¢ per minute using both.

Calling card information Telecom ☎ *800/888-0110* ⊕ *www.telecom.com. ar.* **Telefónica** ☎ *800/333-4004* ⊕ *www. telefonica.com.ar.*

MOBILE PHONES
Mobile phones are immensely popular; all are GSM 850/1900 Mhz. Before leaving home you can buy a country-compatible GSM phone through Mobal; rental models are available through Cellular Abroad and PlanetFone. But if you have an unlocked dual-band GSM phone from North America and intend to call local numbers, it makes more sense to bring

that and buy a prepaid Argentine SIM card on arrival—rates will be cheaper than using your U.S. network or renting a phone. Alternatively, you can buy a basic pay-as-you-go handset and SIM card for around 400 pesos.

All cell-phone numbers here use a local area code, then the cell-phone prefix (15), then a seven- or eight-digit number. To call a cell phone in the same area as you, dial 15 and the number. To call a cell phone in a different area, dial the area code including the initial 0, then 15, then the number.

Local charges for calling a cell phone from a landline vary depending on factors like the company and time of day, but most cost between 50¢ and 1.50 pesos per minute. You pay only for outgoing calls from cell phones, which cost around 3 pesos a minute. Calls from pay-as-you-go phones are the most expensive and calls to phones from the same company as yours are usually cheaper.

There are three mobile phone companies in Argentina: Movistar (owned by Telefónica), Claro, and Personal. Although they are similar, Claro is said to have the best rates, while Movistar has the best coverage and Personal has the best service. All three companies have offices and sales stands all over the country.

You can buy a SIM card (*tarjeta SIM*) from any of the companies' outlets for 15 to 20 pesos. Top up credit by purchasing pay-as-you-go cards (*tarjetas de celular*) at kioscos, locutorios, supermarkets, and gas stations, or by *carga virtual* (virtual top-ups) at locutorios, where sales clerks can add credit to your line directly. Adding 30 pesos or more often gives you extra credit.

Contacts Cellular Abroad ☎ *800/287-5072* ⊕ *www.cellularabroad.com.* **Claro** ☎ *800/1232-5276* ⊕ *www.claro.com.ar.* **Mobal** ☎ *888/888-9162* ⊕ *www.mobalrental.com.* **Movistar** ☎ *11/5321-1111* ⊕ *www.movistar. com.ar.* **Personal** ☎ *800/444-0800* ⊕ *www.*

personal.com.ar. PlanetFone ☎ 888/988–4777 ⊕ *www.planetfone.com.*

■ CUSTOMS AND DUTIES

Customs uses a random inspection system that requires you to push a button at the inspection bay—if a green light comes on, you walk through; if a red light appears, your bags are X-rayed and very occasionally opened. In practice, many officials wave foreigners through without close inspection.

Officially, you can bring up to 2 liters of alcoholic beverages, 400 cigarettes, and 50 cigars into the country duty-free. However, Argentina's international airports have duty-free shops after you land, and customs officials never take alcohol and tobacco purchased there into account. Personal clothing and effects are admitted duty-free (provided they have been used), as are personal jewelry and professional equipment including laptops. Fishing gear and skis present no problems.

Argentina has strict regulations designed to prevent illicit trafficking in antiques, fossils, and other items of cultural and historical importance. For more information, contact the Dirección Nacional de Patrimonio y Museos (National Heritage and Museums Board).

Information in Argentina Dirección Nacional de Patrimonio y Museos ☎ *11/4381–6656* ⊕ *www.cultura.gov.ar.*

U.S. Information U.S. Customs and Border Protection ⊕ *www.cbp.gov.*

■ ELECTRICITY

The electrical current is 220 volts, 50 cycles alternating current (AC), so most North American appliances can't be used without a converter. Older wall outlets take continental-type plugs, with two round prongs, whereas newer buildings take plugs with three flat, angled prongs or two flat prongs set at a "V" angle.

Electricity is a hit-and-miss thing in Argentina. Brief power outages (and surges when the power comes back) are fairly regular, so it's a good idea to unplug your laptop when leaving your hotel for the day.

■ EMERGENCIES

In a medical emergency, taking a taxi to the nearest hospital—taxi drivers usually know where to go—can sometimes be quicker than waiting for an ambulance. If you do call for an ambulance, it will take you to the nearest hospital—possibly a public one that may well look run-down; don't worry, though, as the medical attention will be excellent. Alternatively, you can call a private hospital directly.

For theft, wallet loss, small road accidents, and minor emergencies, contact the nearest police station. Expect all dealings with the police to be a lengthy, bureaucratic business—it's probably only worth bothering if you need the report for insurance claims.

American Embassy American Embassy ✉ *Av. Colombia 4300, Palermo* ☎ *11/5777–4354 for emergency assistance, 11/5777–4873 for emergencies after business hours* ⊕ *argentina.usembassy.gov* Ⓜ *D to Plaza Italia (10 blocks from station).*

General Emergency Contacts Ambulance & Medical Emergencies ☎ *107.* **Fire** ☎ *100.* **Police** ☎ *101, 911.*

■ HEALTH

No specific vaccinations are required for travel to Argentina, but the Centers for Disease Control and Prevention recommend vaccinations against hepatitis A and B and typhoid for all travelers. Yellow fever is also advisable if you're traveling to the Iguazú area. Children traveling to Argentina should have current inoculations against measles, mumps, rubella, and polio.

People in Buenos Aires drink tap water and eat uncooked fruits and vegetables. However, if you're prone to tummy trouble, stick to bottled water.

You wouldn't know it from locals' intense love of sunbathing, but the sun is a significant health hazard in Argentina. Stay out of the sun at midday and, regardless of whether you normally burn, wear plenty of good-quality sunblock. A limited selection is available in most supermarkets and pharmacies, but if you use high SPF factors or have sensitive skin, bring your favorite brands with you. A hat and decent sunglasses are also essential.

Contacts Centers for Disease Control and Prevention (*CDC*). ☎ *800/232–4636* ⊕ *wwwnc.cdc.gov/travel.* **World Health Organization** (*WHO*). ⊕ *www.who.int/en.*

HEALTH CARE

Argentina has free national health care that also provides foreigners with free outpatient care. Although medical practitioners working at Buenos Aires' *hospitales públicos* (public hospitals) are usually first-rate, the institutions themselves are often underfunded: bed space and basic supplies are at a minimum. Except in emergencies, consider leaving these resources for those who really need them.

Private consultations and treatment at Buenos Aires' best private hospitals are reasonably priced compared with those in the U.S. (so much so that medical tourism is booming). All the same, it's a good idea to have some kind of medical insurance. Doctors at the Hospital Británico and Hospital Alemán generally speak English; indeed, so do staff at many private hospitals.

Hospitals Hospital Británico (*British Hospital*). ✉ *Perdriel 74, Barracas* ☎ *11/4309–6633* ⊕ *www.hospitalbritanico.org.ar* Ⓜ *H to Caseros (10 blocks from station).* **Hospital Alemán** (*German Hospital*). ✉ *Av. Pueyrredón 1640, Recoleta* ☎ *11/4827–7000* ⊕ *www.hospitalaleman.org.ar* Ⓜ *D to Pueyrredón.*

INSURANCE

You might want to consider buying trip insurance with medical-only coverage. Neither Medicare nor some private insurers cover medical expenses anywhere outside the United States. Medical-only policies typically reimburse you for medical care (excluding that related to pre-existing conditions) and hospitalization abroad and provide for evacuation. You still have to pay the bills and await reimbursement from the insurer, though.

Medical-Only Insurers International Medical Group ☎ *800/628–4664* ⊕ *www. imglobal.com.* **International SOS** ☎ *800/523–8662* ⊕ *www.internationalsos.com.* **Wallach & Company** ☎ *800/237–6615, 540/687–3166* ⊕ *www.wallach.com.*

MEDICAL EVACUATION

Membership in a medical-evacuation assistance company gets you doctor referrals, emergency evacuation or repatriation, 24-hour hotlines for medical consultation, and other assistance. International SOS *(listed above, under "Insurance")* and AirMed International provide evacuation services and medical referrals. MedjetAssist offers medical evacuation.

Medical Assistance Companies AirMed International ☎ *800/356–2161* ⊕ *www. airmed.com.* **MedjetAssist** ☎ *800/527–7478* ⊕ *www.medjetassist.com.*

OVER-THE-COUNTER REMEDIES

Farmacias (pharmacies) carry painkillers, first-aid supplies, contraceptives, diarrhea treatments, and a range of other over-the-counter treatments, including some drugs that would require a prescription in the United States (antibiotics, for example).

Note that acetaminophen—or Tylenol—is known as "paracetamol" in Spanish. If you think you'll need to have prescriptions filled while you're in Argentina, be sure to have your doctor write down the generic name of the drug, not just the brand name.

Farmacity is a supermarket-style drugstore chain with branches all over town;

many of them are open 24 hours and offer a delivery service.

Pharmacies Farmacity ☏ *11/4322–7777* ⊕ *www.farmacity.com.ar.*

▌ HOLIDAYS

January through March is the summer holiday season in Argentina. Winter holidays fall toward the end of July and beginning of August. Most public holidays are celebrated on their actual date, except August 17, October 12, and November 20, which move to the following Monday. When public holidays fall on a Thursday or Tuesday, the following Friday or preceding Monday, respectively, is also declared a holiday, creating a four-day weekend known as a *feriado puente.*

Año Nuevo (New Year's Day), January 1. **Carnaval** (Carnival), Monday and Tuesday six weeks before Easter. **Día Nacional de la Memoria por la Verdad y la Justicia** (National Memory Day for Truth and Justice; commemoration of the start of the 1976–83 dictatorship), March 24. **Día del Veterano y de los Caídos en la Guerra de Malvinas** (Malvinas Veterans' Day), April 2. **Viernes Santo** (Good Friday), March or April. **Día del Trabajador** (Labor Day), May 1. **Día de la Revolución de Mayo** (Anniversary of the 1810 Revolution), May 25. **Día de la Bandera** (Flag Day), June 20. **Día de la Independencia** (Independence Day), July 9. **Paso a la Inmortalidad del General José de San Martín** (Anniversary of General José de San Martín's Death), August 17. **Día del Respeto a la Diversidad Cultural** (Day of Respect for Cultural Diversity), October 12. **Día de la Soberanía Nacional** (National Sovereignty Day; Anniversary of the Battle of Vuelta de Obligado), November 20. **Inmaculada Concepción de María** (Immaculate Conception), December 8. **Christmas,** December 25.

▌ HOURS OF OPERATION

Banks in Buenos Aires are open weekdays from 10 to 3; government offices are usually open to the public on weekdays from 7:30 to noon or 1; post offices are open weekdays from 9 to 5 or 6 and Saturday from 9 to 1. All are closed on public holidays.

Private businesses are typically open weekdays from 9 to 7. Malls, major chain stores, and souvenir shops tend to be open daily from 10 to 8 or 9, supermarkets from 8:30 in the morning to 9 or 10 at night; these generally close only on Christmas Day, New Year's Day, and Labor Day (May 1). Other stores frequently close on Saturday afternoon and Sunday, except in Palermo Viejo, where Monday is the preferred day off.

Telephone centers are generally open daily 8 to 8 or later. Most gas stations are open 24 hours. Museums usually close one day a week (Tuesday is common), and often shut their doors for a whole month in summer. Most restaurants don't open for dinner until 8:30 or 9 pm but stay open until midnight or 1 am. Most bars don't get going until midnight, and many remain open right through the night; there's no official last call.

▌ MAIL

Correo Argentino, Argentina's postal service, has an office in most neighborhoods; some locutorios also serve as collection points and sell stamps. Mailboxes are two-tone blue, and most are found either inside or directly outside post offices.

Mail delivery is far from dependable: it can take six to 21 days for standard letters and postcards to get to the United States. Regular airmail letters cost 19 pesos for up to 20 grams. If you want to be sure something will arrive, send it by *correo certificado* (registered mail), which costs 52 pesos for international letters up to 20 grams. Valuable items are best sent with private express services such as DHL,

UPS, or FedEx—delivery within one to two days for a 5-kilogram package starts at about 2,000 pesos. A similar package would cost 670 pesos to send with Correo Argentino and would take up to a week to arrive.

The national post-code system is based on a four-digit code. Each province is assigned a letter (the city of Buenos Aires is "C," for instance), which goes before the number code, and each city block is identified by three letters afterward (such as ABD). In practice, however, only very big cities use these complete postal codes (which look like C1234ABC), whereas the rest of Argentina uses the basic number code (1234, for example).

Contacts Correo Argentino ⊠ *Av. Córdoba 663, Microcentro* ☎ *11/4891–9191* ⊕ *www. correoargentino.com.ar.* **DHL** ⊠ *Av. Córdoba 783, Microcentro* ☎ *810/1223–345* ⊕ *www.dhl. com.ar* Ⓜ *C to Lavalle or San Martín.* **Federal Express** ⊠ *25 de Mayo 386, Microcentro* ☎ *810/333–3339* ⊕ *www.fedex.com* Ⓜ *B to L. N. Alem.* **UPS** ⊠ *Pte. Luis Saenz Peña 1351, Constitución* ☎ *800/2222-2877* ⊕ *www.ups. com* Ⓜ *E to San José.*

▌ MONEY

Although prices in Argentina have been steadily rising, the number of pesos you get for your dollar has been rising as well. So Buenos Aires is still a reasonable value if you're traveling from a country with a strong currency. Eating out is afford-able, as are mid-range hotels. Room rates at first-class hotels approach those in the United States, however.

You can plan your trip around ATMs—cash is king for day-to-day dealings. U.S. dollars can be changed at any bank and are widely accepted as payment. ⚠ There's a perennial shortage of small change in Buenos Aires—so much so that small shops may refuse a sale if you don't have near-correct change. Follow the locals' example and hoard your coins.

Hundred-peso bills can be hard to get rid of, so ask for some 50s when you change money. Traveler's checks are useful only as a reserve.

You can usually pay by credit card in top-end restaurants, hotels, and stores. Some establishments accept credit cards only for purchases over 100 pesos. Outside big cit-ies, plastic is less widely accepted.

Visa is the most widely accepted credit card, followed closely by MasterCard. American Express is also accepted in hotels and restaurants, but Diners Club and Discover might not even be recog-nized. If possible, bring more than one credit card, as some establishments accept a single type. You usually have to produce photo ID—preferably a passport, but oth-erwise a driver's license—when making credit-card purchases.

Nonchain stores often display two prices for goods: *precio de lista* (the standard price, valid if you pay by credit card) and a discounted price if you pay in *efectivo* (cash). Many travel services and even some hotels also offer cash discounts—it's always worth asking about.

ITEM	AVERAGE COST
Cup of Coffee and Three Medialunas (croissants)	25–35 pesos
Glass of Wine	25–30 pesos
Liter Bottle of Local Beer	40–50 pesos
Steak and Fries in a Cheap Restaurant	60–90 pesos
Taxi Ride per Metered Mile	8.85–10.60 pesos
Museum Admission	Free–50 pesos

Prices throughout this guide are given for adults. Substantially reduced fees are often available for children, students, and senior citizens.

ATMS AND BANKS

There are ATMs, called *cajeros automáticos*, all over Buenos Aires. Most are inside bank lobbies or small cubicles that you have to swipe your card to get into. It's safer to make withdrawals from ATMs during daylight hours.

There are two main systems. Banelco, indicated by a burgundy-color sign with white lettering, is used by BBVA Banco Francés, HSBC, Banco Galicia, Banco Santander Río, and Banco Patagonia, among others. Link, recognizable by a green-and-yellow sign, is used by Banco Provincia and Banco de la Nación, among others. Cards on the Cirrus and Plus networks can be used on both systems.

Many banks have daily withdrawal limits of 2,000 pesos or less (calculated by a 24-hour period, not from one day to the next). ■TIP→ Sometimes ATMs will impose unexpectedly low withdrawal limits (say, 600 pesos) on international cards. You can get around this by requesting a further transaction before the machine returns your card. But first check whether your bank back home charges high per-withdrawal fees. Breaking large bills can be tricky, so try to withdraw odd amounts (490 pesos, for example, rather than 500).

ATM Locations Banelco ⊕ *www.banelco.com. ar.* **Link** ⊕ *www.redlink.com.ar.*

CURRENCY AND EXCHANGE

Argentina's currency is the peso, which equals 100 centavos (100¢). Bills come in denominations of 100 (violet), 50 (navy blue), 20 (red), 10 (ocher), 5 (green), and 2 (light blue) pesos. Coins are in denominations of 1 peso (a heavy bimetallic coin); and 50, 25, and 10 centavos.

U.S. dollars are widely accepted in big-city stores and supermarkets, and at hotels and restaurants (usually at a slightly worse exchange rate than you'd get at a bank; exchange rates are usually clearly displayed). You always receive change in pesos, even when you pay with U.S. dollars. Taxi drivers may accept dollars, but it's not the norm.

Following a series of devaluations, the exchange rate at this writing is 8 pesos to the U.S. dollar. You can change dollars at the official rate at most banks (between 10 am and 3 pm), at a *casa de cambio* (money changer), or at your hotel. All currency exchange involves fees, but as a rule, banks charge the least and hotels the most. You need to show your passport to complete the transaction.

Heavy restrictions on residents buying U.S. dollars has led to a parallel (i.e. black market) exchange rate, known locally as the "*dolar blue,*" usually about 20% above the official rate. Although technically illegal, the dolar blue is so well established that major newspapers publish it alongside the official exchange rate. Many establishments are keen to take your dollars off you for this rate; along busy streets (like Calle Florida) you will likely be propositioned by touts from small shops, referred to locally as "*cuevas,*" or caves. Most are safe, but try to change relatively small amounts regularly to minimize any possible trouble.

Exchange-Rate Information XE.com
⊕ *www.xe.com.*

■ PASSPORTS AND VISAS

As a U.S. citizen, you need only a passport valid for at least six months to enter Argentina for visits of up to 90 days. Argentina operates a reciprocal entry fee scheme for citizens of countries that charge Argentineans for visas, which includes U.S. citizens. At this writing, the fee (valid for multiple entries over 10 years) is $160. You pay in cash or by credit card at booths near immigration, after which you receive a tourist visa stamp on your passport. You can also pay the fee online before you travel, through the website for the Dirección Nacional de Migraciones.

If you need to stay in the country longer, you can apply for a 90-day extension (*prórroga*) to your tourist visa at the Dirección Nacional de Migraciones. The process takes a morning and costs about 300 pesos. Alternatively, you can exit the country (by taking a boat trip to Uruguay from Buenos Aires, or crossing into Brazil near Iguazú, for example); upon reentering Argentina, your passport will be stamped allowing an additional 90 days. Overstaying your tourist visa is illegal, and incurs a fine of 300 pesos, which you must pay at the Dirección Nacional de Migraciones. Once you have done so, you must leave the country within 10 days.

Officially, children visiting Argentina with only one parent do not need a signed and notarized permission-to-travel letter from the other parent. However, as Argentinean citizens *are* required to have such documentation, it's worth carrying a letter just in case laws change or border officials get confused. Single Parent Travel is a useful online resource that provides advice and downloadable sample permission letters.

While in Argentina you should carry a copy of your passport or other photo ID with you at all times: you need it to make credit-card purchases, change money, and send parcels, as well as in the unlikely event that the police stop you.

Contacts **Dirección Nacional de Migraciones** ✉ *Av. Antártida Argentina 1355, Retiro* ☎ *11/4317-0234* ⊕ *www.migraciones.gov.ar* Ⓜ *C to Retiro.* **Embassy of Argentina** ⊕ *www.embassyofargentina.us.* **Single Parent Travel** ⊕ *www.singleparenttravel.net.*

U.S. **Passport Information** U.S. **Department of State** ☎ *877/487-2778* ⊕ *www.travel.state.gov.*

▮ RESTROOMS

Argentine restrooms have regular Western-style toilets, but cleanliness standards in public facilities vary hugely. You can find public restrooms in shopping centers, gas stations, bus stations, and some subway stations. Restaurant proprietors often don't complain if you ask to use the facilities without patronizing the establishment, but buying a coffee or a drink is a nice gesture.

There's no guarantee of toilet paper, so carry tissues in your day pack. Alcohol gel and antibacterial hand wipes are also useful for sanitizing you or the facilities.

Restrooms are usually labeled *baño* or *toilette.* Men's toilets are typically labeled *hombres,* often shortened to "H" (men), *caballeros* (gentlemen), or *ellos.* Don't get caught out by an "M" on a door: it's short for *mujeres* (women), not "men." *Damas* (ladies) and *ellas* are other labels for female facilities.

▮ SAFETY

Argentina is safer than many Latin American countries. However, there has been an increase in street crime—mainly pickpocketing, bag-snatching, and occasionally mugging—especially in Buenos Aires. Taking a few precautions when traveling in the region is usually enough to avoid being a target.

Attitude is essential: strive to look aware and purposeful at all times. Don't wear any jewelry you're not willing to lose. Even imitation jewelry and small items can attract attention and are best left behind. Keep a very firm hold on purses and cameras when out and about, and keep them on your lap in restaurants, not dangling off the back of your chair.

The most important advice we can give you is that you should not put up a struggle in the unlikely event that you are mugged. Nearly all physical attacks on tourists are the direct result of their resisting, so comply with demands, hand over your stuff, and try to get the situation over with as quickly as possible—then let your travel insurance take care of it.

CRIME
Always remain alert for pickpockets. Try to keep your cash and credit cards in different places, so that if one gets stolen you can fall back on the other. Tickets and other valuables are best left in hotel

safes. Avoid carrying large sums of money around, but always keep enough to have something to hand over if you do get mugged. Another time-honored tactic is to keep a dummy wallet (an old one containing an expired credit card and a small amount of cash) in your pocket, with your real cash in an inside or vest pocket.

Women can expect pointed looks, the occasional *piropo* (a flirtatious remark, usually alluding to some physical aspect), and some advances. These catcalls rarely escalate into actual physical harassment—the best reaction is to ignore it as local women do. Going to a bar alone will be seen as an open invitation for attention. If you're heading out for the night, it's wise to take a taxi.

There's a notable police presence in barrios popular with visitors, such as San Telmo and Palermo, and this seems to deter potential pickpockets and hustlers. However, *porteños* (residents of Buenos Aires) have little faith in the police—at best they're well-meaning but underrequipped, so don't count on them to come to your rescue in a difficult situation. Reporting crimes is usually ineffectual, and is worth the time it takes only if you need the report for insurance.

PROTESTS AND RALLIES

Argentineans like to speak their minds, and there has been a huge increase in strikes and street protests since the economic crisis of 2001–02. Protesters frequently block streets and squares in downtown Buenos Aires, causing major traffic jams. Some are protesting government policies; others may be showing support for these. Either way, trigger-happy local police have historically proved themselves more of a worry than the demonstrators. Although protests are usually peaceful, exercise caution if you happen across one.

SCAMS

Beware scams such as the offer by a seemingly kindly passerby to help you clean the mustard/ketchup/cream that has somehow appeared on your clothes: while your attention is occupied, an accomplice picks your pocket or snatches your bag.

Taxi drivers in Buenos Aires are usually honest, but occasionally they decide to take people for a ride. All official cabs have meters, so make sure this is turned on. Some scam artists have hidden switches that make the meter tick over more quickly, but simply driving a circuitous route is a more common ploy. It helps to have an idea where you're going and how long it will take. Locals say that if you're hailing taxis on the street you are safer opting for ones with lights on top (usually labeled "Radio Taxi"). Late at night, try to call for a cab—all hotels and restaurants, no matter how cheap, have a number and will usually call for you.

When asking for price quotes in touristy areas, always confirm whether the amount is in dollars or pesos. Some salespeople, especially street vendors, have found that they can take advantage of confused tourists by charging dollars for goods that are actually priced in pesos.

Advisories and Other Information Transportation Security Administration (*TSA*). ⊕ *www.tsa.gov.* **U.S. Department of State** ⊕ *www.travel.state.gov.*

▌TAXES

Argentina has an international departure tax of $29 and an $8 domestic departure tax, both of which are included in ticket prices. Hotel rooms carry a 21% tax. Cheaper hotels and hostels tend to include this in their quoted rates; more expensive hotels add it to your bill.

Argentina has 21% VAT (known as IVA) on most consumer goods and services. The tax is usually included in the price of goods and noted on your receipt. You can get nearly all the IVA back on locally manufactured items if you spend more than 70 pesos at stores displaying a Global Blue duty-free sign. You'll be given a Global Blue check for the amount you're entitled to; then, after getting it stamped by a customs official at the airport, you can cash it at the clearly signed tax refund booths. Allow an extra hour to complete the process.

Tax refunds Global Blue ☎ *11/5238–1970* ⊕ *www.globalblue.com.*

▌TIME

Argentina is three hours behind GMT, or three hours ahead of U.S. Central Standard Time.

Time-Zone Information Timeanddate.com ⊕ *www.timeanddate.com/worldclock.*

▌TIPPING

TIPPING GUIDELINES FOR BUENOS AIRES	
Bellhop at top-end hotels	$1 to $5 per bag, depending on the level of the hotel
Hotel Maid at top-end hotels	$1–$3 a day (either daily or at the end of your stay)
Hotel Room-Service Waiter	$1 to $2 per delivery, even if a service charge has been added
Taxi Driver	Round up the fare to the next full peso amount
Tour Guide	10% of the cost of the tour if service was good
Waiter	10%–15%, depending on service
Restroom Attendants	Small change, such as 1 or 2 pesos

Propinas (tips) are a question of rewarding good service rather than an obligation. Restaurant bills—even those that have a *cubierto* (bread and service charge)— don't include gratuities; locals usually add 10%–15%. Bellhops and maids expect tips only in the very expensive hotels, where a tip in dollars is appreciated. You can also give a small tip (10% or less) to tour guides. Porteños round off taxi fares, though some cabbies who frequent hotels popular with tourists seem

to expect more. Tipping is a nice gesture with beauty and barbershop personnel—5% to 10% is fine.

▌TOURS

Ghosts, crimes, and spooky legends are the basis for the Buenos Aires Misteriosa tours run by Ayres Viajes; it's just one of the offbeat options on the company's extensive menu.

Known for superlative customer service, Buenos Aires Tours arranges everything from city walking tours to multiweek Argentine vacations aimed at different budgets.

Informed young historians from the University of Buenos Aires lead private tours that highlight the city's art and architecture as well as its intriguing past at Eternautas.

Academics also serve as guides at Cultour: the highbrow history- and culture-oriented excursions are complemented by general city tours and Tigre boat trips.

For serious insight into the city's Jewish community, sign on for one of the full- or half-day outings organized by Deb Miller's company, Travel Jewish.

B.A.'s new and growing network of bicycle lanes has led to a sudden surge in two-wheel travel. La Bicicleta Naranja has scheduled tours led by bilingual guides; it will also supply do-it-yourselfers with excellent route maps and deliver rental equipment to your hotel.

Graffiti and street art are the focus of one unusual tour run by Biking Buenos Aires; another includes live performances by actors recreating key moments in civic history.

Urban Biking lets you combine cycling with kayaking in Tigre and the Paraná River delta area; the outfit also offers half- and full-day pedaling tours of the city proper.

Large onboard screens make the posh minibuses used by Opción Sur part transport and part cinema. Each stop on the city itinerary is introduced by relevant historical footage (picture Evita rallying the masses at Plaza de Mayo); trips to outlying areas are available, too.

If you would rather rely on public transit and foot power, try Buenos Aires Local Tours, a popular pay-what-you-like service (advance online registration is required).

For a different take on local life, contact the Cicerones de Buenos Aires. Its resident volunteers take groups of up to six visitors on informal outings, providing a true porteño perspective along the way. The experience is free, but donations are welcome.

Tour Companies Ayres Viajes ☎ 11/4383-9188 ⊕ www.ayresviajes.com.ar. **Biking Buenos Aires** ☎ 11/4040-8989 ⊕ www.bikingbuenosaires.com. **Buenos Aires Local Tours** ☎ 11/5984-2681 ⊕ www.buenosaireslocaltours.com. **Buenos Aires Tours** ☎ 11/4785-2753 ⊕ www.buenosaires-tours.com.ar. **Cicerones de Buenos Aires** ☎ 11/4431-9892 ⊕ www.cicerones.org.ar. **Cultour** ☎ 11/5624-7368 ⊕ www.cultour.com.ar. **Eternautas** ☎ 11/5031-9916 ⊕ www.eternautas.com. **La Bicicleta Naranja** ☎ 11/4362-1104 ⊕ www.labicicletanaranja.com.ar. **Opción Sur** ☎ 11/4777-9029 ⊕ www.opcionsur.com.ar. **Travel Jewish** ☎ 877/826-4674 in the U.S. only ⊕ www.traveljewish.com. **Urban Biking** ☎ 11/4314-2325 ⊕ www.urbanbiking.com.

▌ VISITOR INFORMATION

The civic tourism board—Turismo Buenos Aires—operates information outlets with English-speaking staff at both airports and seven other locations around the city, including Centro, Recoleta, and Puerto Madero. Hours can be erratic, but the booth at the intersection of Florida and Marcelo T. de Alvear (near Plaza San Martín) is usually open weekdays from 10 to 5 and weekends from 9 to 6. The board's website includes downloadable maps, free MP3 walking tours, hundreds of listings, plus insightful articles on

porteño culture, though at this writing, all information is available in Spanish only.

Each Argentine province operates a tourist office in Buenos Aires. The government umbrella organization for all regional and city-based tourist offices is the Secretaría de Turismo (Secretariat of Tourism). Limited tourist information is also available at Argentina's embassy and consulates in the United States.

Contacts Argentine Secretariat of Tourism ☎ 800/555-0016 ⊕ www.turismo.gob.ar. **Embassy of Argentina** ⊕ www.embassyofargentina.us. **Turismo Buenos Aires** ⊕ www.turismo.buenosaires.gob.ar.

ONLINE RESOURCES
ALL ABOUT BUENOS AIRES
Mapa Interactivo de Buenos Aires is an interactive online map run by the city government. It allows you to search for specific addresses, as well as facilities and services such as ATMs, hospitals, and bicycle lanes.

CULTURE AND ENTERTAINMENT
The Arts & Media section of the daily *Buenos Aires Herald* (an English-language newspaper) has up-to-date entertainment listings. Run by American expats, *What's Up Buenos Aires* is a slick bilingual guide to contemporary culture and partying in the city.

All About Buenos Aires Fodors.com ⊕ www.fodors.com/community. **Mapa Interactivo de Buenos Aires** ⊕ www.mapa.buenosaires.gob.ar.

Culture and Entertainment Buenos Aires Herald ⊕ www.buenosairesherald.com. **What's Up Buenos Aires** ⊕ www.whatsupbuenosaires.com.

Food and Drink Guía Óleo ⊕ www.guiaoleo.com.ar. **Pick Up the Fork** ⊕ www.pickupthefork.com. **Saltshaker** ⊕ www.saltshaker.net.

INDEX

PHOTO CREDITS

Front cover: Yadid Levy/Alamy [Description: Musician playing the bandeon at Caminito area in La Boca]. 1, Silvia Boratti/iStockphoto. 2, Kobby_dagan | Dreamstime.com. 5, Michel Friang/Alamy. Chapter 1: Experience Buenos Aires: 8-9, HUGHES Hervé/age fotostock. 10, Christopher Pillitz/Alamy. 11 (left), Juanderlust, Fodors.com member. 11 (right), jd_miller, Fodors.com member. 12, Jason Friend/Alamy. 13, Thomas Cockrem/Alamy. 16 (left), Giulio Andreini/age fotostock. 16 (top center), Jon Hicks/Alamy. 16 (top right), P Sinclair, Fodors.com member. 16 (bottom right), Wim Wiskerke/Alamy. 17 (top left), Frank Nowikowski/South American Pictures. 17 (bottom left), Enrique Shore-Woodfin Camp/Aurora Photos. 17 (top right), APEIRON-PHOTO/Alamy. 17 (bottom right), Pictorial Press Ltd/Alamy. 18, edithbruck/Flickr. 19 (left), RH_Miller, Fodors.com member. 19 (right), puroticorico/Flickr. 20, M. Scanel, Fodors.com member. 21 (left), Seamus, Fodors.com member. 21 (right), Rcidte/wikipedia.org. 22, Alvaro Leiva/age fotostock. 23, Peter M. Wilson/Alamy. 24, VinoFamily/Flickr. 25 (left), Rivard/Flickr. 25 (right), feserc/Flickr. 26, TravelStockCollection - Homer Sykes/Alamy. 27 (left), Image Asset Management/age fotostock. 27 (right), José Francisco Ruiz/age fotostock. 28 (left), Eduardo M. Rivero/age fotostock. 28 (top right), Public domain. 28 (bottom right), Jordi Camí/age fotostock. 29 (left), Public domain. 29 (right), Apeiron-Photo/Alamy. 30 (left and top right), A.H.C./age fotostock. 30 (bottom right), Pictorial Press Ltd/Alamy. 31 (left), Archivo Gráfi code Clarín (Argentina)/Wikimedia Commons/Public domain. 31 (top right), Tramonto/age fotostock. 31 (bottom right), Griffiths911/wikipedia.org. 32 (left), Christopher Pillitz/Alamy. 32 (top right), Nikada/iStockphoto. 32 (bottom right), DYN/Getty Images/Newscom. 33 (top), Roberto Fiadone/wikipedia.org. 33 (bottom left), wikipedia.org. 34, fortes/Flickr. Chapter 2: Buenos Aires Neighborhoods: 35, caron malecki, Fodors.com member. 36, KE1TH, Fodors.com member. 37, 2litros > raimundoillanes/Flickr. 38, berhbs, Fodors.com member. 41, lilap/Flickr. 42, blmurch/Flickr. 44-45, iStockphoto. 49, Amanda Bullock. 53, Kobi Israel/Alamy. 54, Julian Rotela Rosow/Flickr. 57, James Wong, Fodors.com member. 60, Alfredo Maiquez/age fotostock. 62, Picasa 2.7/Flickr. 63, Frank Nowikowski/South American Pictures. 64, Sara Nixon, Fodors.com member. 67, Dan DeLuca/wikipedia.org. 68, caron malecki, Fodors.com member. 70, Amanda Bullock. 71, giulio andreini/age fotostock. 74, Michele Molinari/Alamy. 75, Martin Byrne, Fodors.com member. 77, wabauer, Fodors.com member. 79, wim wiskerke/Alamy. 80, Beth/Queen/ZUMA Press/Newscom. 83 (top), Network Photographers/Alamy. 83 (bottom), Shinichi Yamada/AFLO SPORT/Icon SMI. 84 (top), Visual Arts Library (London)/Alamy. 84 (bottom), P. Narayan/age fotostock. 85 (top), Tramonto/age fotostock. 85 (bottom), A.H.C./age fotostock. 86 (top), Keystone/Getty Images/Newscom. 86 (bottom), Public domain. 87 (left), Bruno Perousse/age fotostock. 87 (right), Beth/Queen/Zuma Press/Newscom. 88 (top), Christopher Pillitz/Alamy. 89 (top left), Odile Montserrat/Sygma/Corbis. 89 (top right), Universal/Newscom. 90 (top left), Interfoto Pressebildagentur/Alamy. 90 (top right), SuperStock/age fotostock. 90 (bottom), G. Sioen/DEA/age fotostock. 91 (top), Shinichi Yamada/AFLO SPORT/Icon SMI. 91 (bottom), Picture Alliance/DPA/Newscom. Chapter 3: Shopping: 93, NL, Fodors.com member. 94, Susan Seubert / drr.net. 95 (top), Jon Hicks / Alamy. 95 (bottom), Jeremy Hoare / Alamy. 96, Yadid Levy / age fotostock. 97, Jochem Wijnands/age fotostock. 102, Alexander Hafemann/iStockphoto. 105, Flickr. 107, Courtesy of Marcelo Toledo, Silversmith/www.marcelotoledo.net. 108, Joel Mann/Flickr. Chapter 4: After Dark: 127, Jorge Royan/Alamy. 128, AFP PHOTO/Miguel MENDEZ/Newscom. 138, laubenthal, Fodors.com member. 139, Ernesto Ríos Lanz/age fotostock. 140, wikipedia.org. 141, eyalos.com/Shutterstock. 142 (top), Picture Contact/Alamy. 142 (2nd from top), Christina Wilson/Alamy. 142 (3rd from top), Michel Friang/Alamy. 142 (bottom), Jason Howe/South American Pictures. 143 (top), Archivo General de la Nación/wikipedia.org. 143 (bottom), Danita Delimont/Alamy. Chapter 5: Where to Eat: 153, wim wiskerke/Alamy. 154, nick baylis/Alamy. Chapter 6: Where to Stay: 191, jd_miller, Fodors.com member. 192, Panamericano Buenos Aires. Chapter 7: Side Trips: 207, David Lyons/Alamy. 208, Dario Diament/Shutterstock. 209, Carla Antonini/wikipedia.org. 210, Pablodda/Flickr. 220-221, Jeremy Hoare/Alamy. 222, Chris Sharp/South American Pictures. 223, Pablo D. Flores. 224, Jeremy Hoare/Alamy. 225, SuperStock. 226 (top), Hughes/age fotostock. 226 (bottom), Johannes Odland/Shutterstock. 233, Ken Welsh/age fotostock. 234, Gerad Coles/iStockphoto. 235, Sue Cunningham Photographic/Alamy. 236-237, Fritz Poelking/age fotostock. 236 (inset), Albasmalko/wikipedia.org. 237 (inset), flavia bottazzini/iStockphoto. 238, travelstock44/Alamy. 239, vittorio sciosia/age fotostock. 243, Ricardokuhl | Dreamstime.com. 244, kastianz / Shutterstock. 245, Ksenia Ragozina / Shutterstock. 246, Afagundes | Dreamstime.com. 254, Toniflap / Shutterstock. 265, Alberto/Flickr. 273, Demetrio Carrasco / age fotostock.Back cover (from left to right): meunierd/Shutterstock; elnavegante/Shutterstock; Anibal Trejo/Shutterstock. Spine: Mlenny/iStockphoto.

NOTES

NOTES

NOTES

NOTES

NOTES

NOTES

NOTES

ABOUT OUR WRITERS

 Allan Kelin moved to Buenos Aires five years ago after a few months in Miami, a handful of years in Florence, and much of a lifetime in New York City. He works as a freelance writer, editor, translator, and baker. Allan has contributed to DemandMedia and Travora, as well as translating regularly for the Caribbean edition of *BMW Magazine*. He updated the Side Trips from Buenos Aires chapter.

 Karina Martinez-Carter is a freelance journalist who has contributed to BBC Travel, BBC Capital, *Travel + Leisure,* the *Atlantic,* and *Forbes,* among others. She has been living in Buenos Aires since graduating college in 2010. You can follow her on Instagram and Twitter: @KMartinez-Carter. Karina updated the Where to Stay chapter for this edition.

 From scouting around Buenos Aires shantytowns retracing the steps of Pope Francis to following Venezuela's former President Hugo Chávez, freelance journalist **Sorrel Moseley-Williams** also writes about luxury lifestyle and travel and is training to be a sommelier. She's been in a long-term relationship with Argentina since 2006 and writes for *Departures,* the *Independent,* and *Wallpaper**. She updated the Nightlife and Shopping chapters for this edition.

 Victoria Patience first came to Argentina to spend a year studying Latin American literature. She lives in Buenos Aires province with her Argentinean husband, daughter, dogs, and cats. She is a freelance contributor to many Fodor's guidebooks and also runs her own editing and translation company, Nativa Wordcraft. She updated the Experience, Exploring, and Travel Smart chapters of this book.

 Having moved to Buenos Aires almost a decade ago to live with his husband, **Dan Perlman** is a private chef who trained in New York City restaurants, an advanced sommelier from the Court of Master Sommeliers, and a prolific international food, wine, and travel writer. He is a well-known local restaurant critic and writes the highly regarded food, wine, and travel blog SaltShaker. He updated the Where to Eat chapter.

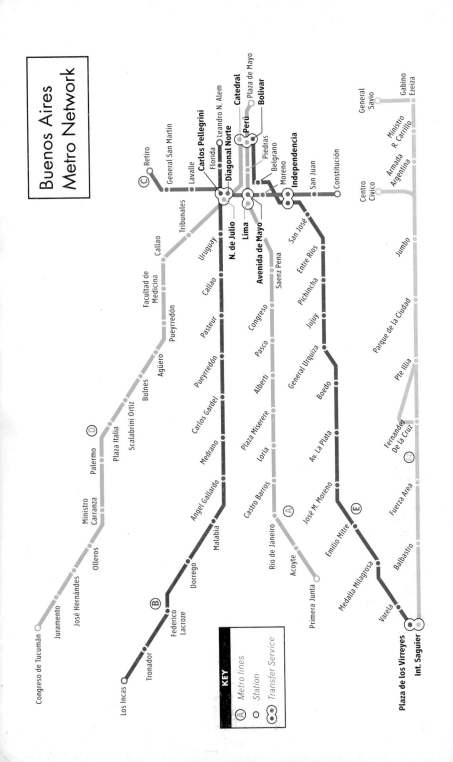

Buenos Aires
Metro Network

KEY

- Ⓐ Metro lines
- ○ Station
- ⊗ Transfer Service